THE CONSTITUTION OF JUDICIAL POWER

THE JOHNS HOPKINS SERIES IN CONSTITUTIONAL THOUGHT
Sotirios A. Barber and Jeffrey K. Tulis, Series Editors

Reflections on Political Identity, by Anne Norton

The Presence of the Past: Essays on the State and the Constitution, by Sheldon S. Wolin

America's Constitutional Soul, by Harvey C. Mansfield, Jr.

The Ennobling of Democracy: The Challenge of the Postmodern Age, by Thomas L. Pangle

The Interpretable Constitution, by William F. Harris II

The Constitution of Judicial Power, by Sotirios A. Barber

Alternative Tracks: The Constitution of American Industrial Order, 1865–1917, by Gerald Berk

THE
CONSTITUTION
OF
JUDICIAL POWER

Sotirios A. Barber

THE JOHNS HOPKINS UNIVERSITY PRESS

BALTIMORE AND LONDON

© 1993 The Johns Hopkins University Press
All rights reserved
Printed in the United States of America on acid-free paper

The Johns Hopkins University Press
2715 North Charles Street
Baltimore, Maryland 21218-4319
The Johns Hopkins Press Ltd., London

Library of Congress Cataloging-in-Publication Data

Barber, Sotirios A.
    The constitution of judicial power / Sotirios A. Barber.
        p.   cm. — (The Johns Hopkins series in constitutional
    thought)
    Includes bibliographical references and index.
    ISBN 0-8018-4587-4 (acid-free paper)
    1. Judicial review—United States.   2. United States—Supreme
Court.   3. Political questions and judicial power—United States.
4. United States—Constitutional law—Interpretation and construction.   I. Title.   II. Series.
KF4575.B37   1993
347.73′12—dc20
[347.30712]   93-20096

A catalog record for this book is available from the British Library.

For Karen

CONTENTS

PREFACE

The United States Supreme Court has been crippled by the combined forces of skillful enemies and incompetent friends, forces united in their inability either to grasp or to tolerate constitutional law as an independent moral voice in American politics. By the Court's enemies I refer to the politicians, jurists, and academic theorists of what I call the New Right. By the Court's would-be friends I refer mainly to the politicians and mainstream academics of a liberal establishment that admires most of the policies of the Warren and Burger Courts in the broad area of human rights.

The New Right claims a conservative function: guardian of the constitutional tradition. This is a fair claim if *conservatism* is taken to signify the economic, racial, and sectarian interests that continue to dominate the Republican party at this writing. The claim also works as part of the New Right's successful strategy of exploiting the public's ignorance of the tradition. But observers who identify the tradition with the constitutionalism of a Madison, a Marshall, or a Lincoln will regard New Right constitutionalism as a modernist teaching, not a traditional teaching. Neither Madison, Marshall, nor Lincoln understood themselves to deny what the New Right (with the establishment left) denies above all else: that popular majorities ought to and can institutionalize a concern for simple justice—justice as something whose meaning is fundamentally different from what popular majorities or anyone else might believe it to be. Judged from this traditional constitutionalist aspiration to reconcile democracy to justice, the New Right will emerge in this book as an anticonstitutionalist force.

In the political climate of the 1980s and early 1990s, New Right constitutional theory might have risen to its present level of popular and institutional influence on its own. But it had help, and from an unlikely source: the liberal politicians and academicians who want to preserve judicial power. These establishment liberals conceive the desegregation, reapportionment, and privacy decisions of the Warren and Burger courts as expressions of a judicially activist style. Although often a useless term (we'll see that all judges are activist at some level and in some contexts), *activism* usually applies to judges who openly make up their own minds about the Constitution and set forth the normative and empirical premises needed to defend their results without pretending to defer to authorities like framers' intentions, judicial precedents, or public opinion. It was thus an activist Court that decided *Brown v. Board of Education.* And it was a majority of ostensibly deferential or conservative justices in *Dred Scott v. Sanford* who claimed a strict fidelity to the framers' conceptions of property, states' rights, and the humanity of African Americans.

Judicial activism is just, says most of the liberal establishment, because the Constitution's continuing legitimacy depends on judges' keeping the document's vague terms in tune with evolving social beliefs. But this theory of a living constitution was hardly an effective argument for liberal ends at a time when the public seemed headed in illiberal directions, and the New Right continued its advance against the judiciary in the Reagan-Bush years, despite isolated setbacks like the Senate's rejection of the Bork nomination.

Nondeferential, publicly responsible judging once had a much better justification than the theory of the living constitution. I refer to the argument that Publius used in *Federalist* 78, an argument I call the classical theory of judicial review. This is the theory that Marshall followed in *Marbury v. Madison;* it is therefore an old theory in some respects. But it is not old in all respects, for it remains the official justification for judicial power to this day. I attempt to show in this book why the classical theory should be the theory of the future, now that it appears that the Court we have known for most of the last two centuries may have a future after all.

The 1992 election hardly guarantees that future, however. Rightists are continuing their struggle against the judiciary, and establishment liberals do not know how to use the classical theory to defend Warren-style judicial activism. In fact, establishment liberals systematically reject the principal presuppositions of the classical theory. They believe (with other modernists, left as well as right) that vague constitutional provisions like *equal protection* and *due process* cannot really guide judges to decisions in controversial cases. They tend also to doubt that judges can rise above partisan commitments. Contrary to the classical presupposition of a continuing people united in political fundamentals, the Court's leftist defenders join its rightist enemies in seeing heterogeneity throughout American political culture, within each generation and between all of them. And central to all arguments against both the classical theory and judicial activism, the Court's establishment liberal defenders agree with its New Right enemies that constitutional words and phrases like *justice, equal protection,* and *due process* refer not to real things (in the nonmaterialist sense of *things* that I use often in this book) but to subjective or conventional beliefs.

Because they reject the classical theory and because they know that activist or nondeferential judging needs defending in America, liberal defenders of the Warren Court have exhausted themselves in a quest of some three decades for a new defense of judicial power. By the early 1980s the failure of this quest was widely evident to observers of all ideological stripes, and the New Right of Reagan-Bush could strengthen its occupation of the federal courts with no need for the public explanations and apologies that an effective opposition could have provoked.

I have written this book from a perspective that accepts the central aspiration of the American constitutionalist tradition: reconciling democracy to justice. From that perspective the New Right and the establishment left (and, as we shall see, the Constitution-based social forces that inadvertently created them) have brought the nation close to disaster. I hope to show that, contrary to the theorists and politicians of the New Right, the classical theory of judicial review supports an activist, nondeferential judiciary and, contrary to the establishment left and right, the classical theory is not merely a good theory but the only good theory.

Yet I must emphasize at the beginning a caveat that I repeat throughout and connect to a philosophic principle at the end: I attempt no proof that the classical theory is true. I try to show only that its presuppositions (about constitutional meaning, judicial duty, and the rest) are, taken as a whole, substantially more difficult to deny than to affirm. I seek not to prove the classical theory but to shift the present burden to its critics and thus provoke the enemies of nondeferential, publicly responsible judging to try to prove, not just assume or assert, that it is unreasonable to expect nonpartisan judges or that when the Constitution refers to things like equal protection and due process it refers either to nothing at all or to someone's version of nothing at all.

We shall see that these are burdens that the Court's critics cannot meet and that the better arguments favor the openly activist mode of judicial power. I am confident of that much.

I do not submit my argument with much confidence that it can actually influence judicial policy, however, for there is no argument that can persuade people who will not listen, and the evidence indicates that the politicians, left and right, who dominate the processes of judicial selection in America—perhaps Americans, generally—are increasingly uninterested in constitutional theory. Worse, some influential Americans are openly hostile to constitutional theory.

Robert Bork is the most visible example. We shall see that constitutional theory is close to activist judging on his list of activities that subvert the American way. The skill of the New Right's campaign against the federal judiciary cautions against confidence that Bork and his allies will ultimately fail in their McCarthyite campaign against constitutional theory. This threat to constitutional theory strikes at something even more important than judicial power, for Publius, Marshall, and Lincoln showed by their examples that a systematic public reasonableness about matters constitutional is essential to the activities of constitution making, maintenance, and reform, and thus integral to the American understanding of the constitutionalist enterprise.

Disaster is therefore a prospect not only for this country but for all who have viewed America as the exemplar of a polity that is both constitutional (reasonably faithful, and faithful with reason, to an old plan for reconciling democracy to justice) and constitutionalist (intellectually and morally capable of new constitutions). The loss of such an example is an evil grave enough to demand every opposing effort, even those efforts with little hope of political success.

ACKNOWLEDGMENTS

I am grateful to the National Endowment for the Humanities for supporting my work on this book with a generous research fellowship. I also thank Princeton's Department of Politics for letting me use its facilities during my NEH fellowship year and my department at Notre Dame for a semester to wrap things up.

Several friends have tried to save me from errors of logic, omission, and excess. Walter F. Murphy commented in detail on all aspects of the manuscript: structure, content, and style. Jeffrey K. Tulis, William F. Harris, and Christopher L. M. Eisgruber reviewed the entire manuscript and offered criticisms of the argument and its manner of presentation. Karen H. Flax, Sue Hemberger, Graham Walker, Gary McDowell, Robert P. George, and James E. Fleming responded generously to my requests for comments on portions of the argument. I am most grateful to these individuals for giving me time they did not have to spare. I expect to regret not following all of their advice.

Part of chapter 1 is taken from an article published in the *George Washington University Law Review*. Most of chapter 2 was originally published in the *University of Chicago Law Review*.

THE CONSTITUTION OF JUDICIAL POWER

1

THE NEW RIGHT'S ASSAULT ON THE COURT

Those who oppose an independent and publicly responsible judiciary in our time, as in times past, include groups who would rather destroy our institutions than live with their policies—such as the Court's recent policies on abortion, school prayer, affirmative action, and school desegregation. But there is an important difference between opposing the Court's decisions and opposing its authority to make those decisions, for some who oppose the former, even very strongly, can still support an openly nondeferential and responsible style of judicial review. People can criticize the Court's results without seeking to emasculate the Court.

It is usually the academic apologists for the Court's popular critics who attack the judiciary as an institution. Partly because academics tend to avoid open statements of political preference—few New Right scholars admit to racism, religious zealotry, greed, a scapegoating resentment of selected forms of welfare, and a desire for vengeance against selected classes of criminals—they make institutional arguments instead. New Right academics thus defend the majority's right to act upon preferences they themselves will not directly and publicly support. And New Right academics typically focus more on the question of judicial authority than on the substance judicial decisions. By avoiding the substantive issues and describing the conflict over judicial power as that between the majority and an elitist minority, these academics become the judiciary's most effective enemies, far more effective than those segments of the public who openly prefer abolishing the judiciary to living with certain of its policies. The latter are a minority speaking as a minority. The judiciary's academic enemies are a minority purporting to speak for a variety of majoritarianism that is easily misrepresented as speaking for democracy itself. We shall see that they do not speak for democracy, unless they can be said to speak for a value that they diminish and degrade.

ROBERT BORK: THE NEW RIGHT'S PUBLIC PHILOSOPHER

The most visible (although not the most thoughtful) New Right constitutional theorist is Robert H. Bork, former Yale law professor, former judge of the U.S. Court of Appeals for the District of Columbia, and unsuccessful Reagan nominee to the Supreme Court. Bork's position on contemporary constitutional issues can be described as a morally relativistic intolerance, for he begins with the premise that all values, preferences, or "forms of gratification" are morally equal, and with religious fundamentalists in the wings, he concludes by asserting that the majority has a right to impose widely contested moral beliefs on minorities. He feels that as long as it avoids overt racial discrimination by law and other clearly unconstitutional acts (such as laws prohibiting miscegenation, parochial schools, and the teaching of foreign languages)[1] the majority has the right to regulate, by nonreviewable standards of reasonableness and morality, private property and privacy in all choices respecting sexual preference, abortion, procreation, marriage, and child rearing.[2] He also believes free speech excludes protection for advocacy of political change through unlawful means (which should mean no judicial protection for mere advocacy by the likes of Communists or the Klan) as well as protection for peaceful criticism of government that does not meet the majority's standards of decorum (which would mean no protection for flag burning or for such language as "_____ the Draft!").[3]

It is not that Bork asserts that homosexuality, abortion, adultery, and foulmouthed and politically subversive speech are wrong, indecent, or ignoble, or that he offers evidence for concluding so, for he recognizes no objective right and wrong except with reference to established ethical systems that have "no objective or intrinsic validity of [their] own and about which men can and do differ."[4] Some practices are wrong because the majority says so, because the Constitution, as Bork reads it, embodies the majority's right to say so, and because there are no standards of what is right or politically true beyond what the established law of a community posits.[5]

Bork does recognize that the Constitution not only authorizes governmental power but also restricts it by enumerating a set of constitutional rights;

hence his reservations in behalf of certain forms of political speech and freedom from overt racial discrimination by government. Yet these concessions may not mean much protection for rights when applied in a manner faithful to Bork's understanding of what constitutional interpretation should be. I say *may* not mean much, because it is not always clear what Bork believes constitutional interpretation should be. We see in chapter 4 that Bork vacillates between a restraintist position and an activist position as needed to approve those decisions—*Brown v. Board of Education,* for example, along with some protection for women, and the application of the Bill of Rights to the states—that he will not oppose publicly. The problem, of course, is that when he shifts to the activist side he shifts to a position he describes as lawless and politically subversive.[6] So if he is to be distinguished from his critics, and assuming (for the moment) that he would prefer consistency to contradiction, he cannot really support the few activist decisions he says he supports.

Inconsistency and the resulting unpredictability are ameliorating qualities in Bork's case, because the position that would distinguish him and to which he returns in the end is completely indefensible. Ronald Dworkin once summed up the dominant practical thrust of Bork's argument as the maxim that courts should give the government the benefit of every doubt in constitutional cases involving individual and minority rights.[7] When Bork sticks to his distinctive approach, he opposes judges' striking down even admittedly "savage" legislation. He will not have them consulting notions of simple justice and decency in cases where constitutional meaning is in doubt, for he rejects the thought that the Constitution reflects or is open to standards beyond the narrowest construction of its terms and what he decides are the more or less immediate preferences of its framers.[8] He believes that where the Constitution is in doubt, judges can only oppose their own personal preferences to the preferences of the government, thereby offending what he believes to be the correct version of democracy.[9]

The word *democracy* does not occur in the Constitution. (And as we see in the next chapter, the term *democracy* does not occur in *The Federalist* as a thing to be praised. To the contrary, *The Federalist* fears unconstrained majoritarianism and prefers terms like *representative republic*.) Nor does Bork give any reasons why anyone should prefer his particular version to other versions of the popular government that the Constitution ordains. He merely assumes that his version is the right one, treating it as something of a historical given. This assumption is consistent with his belief that moral and political principles have no intrinsic value or grounding in reason, being mere products of "sentiment" and "historical experience."[10] He also asserts, still indifferent to evidence, that the "original constitution was devoted primarily to the mechanisms of democratic choice," and he attacks those who emphasize the Constitution's dedication to simple justice for their "fundamental antipathy to democracy."[11]

Although Bork acknowledges as an anthropological fact that a measure of moral unity is necessary to what he refers to as "community," he believes that it is the community (or its representative) that decides the difference between right and wrong. He views the Constitution's primary objective as establishing "mechanisms of democratic choice," and he says "the major freedom of our kind of society is the freedom to choose to have a public morality."[12] By these assertions Bork is trying to justify subordinating individual and minority rights to the rights of the majority. He proposes a normative premise when he says that the majority's right is "the major freedom" that we have. This premise would make other freedoms relatively minor freedoms. When there is a clash between freedoms of different rank, the major defeats the minor. Bork thus implies that in principle there are no rights against the majority.

Constitutional rights constitute no real exception for Bork. He sees rights as originating solely in the will of the majority (or its nominal representative), there being no higher source of value. What is written in the Constitution as an exemption from majority power is itself an expression of majority will, and its normative force lies solely in that fact. This foundational status of majority will gives the current majority the benefit of every doubt in constitutional cases. Where the will of the majority as expressed in the Constitution is in some doubt, majoritarianism apparently favors the will of the majority as expressed by the government. Hence the majority's freedom to impose contested moral views on individuals and minorities in all but nearly universally acknowledged cases of constitutional violation, assuming that such cases are ever likely in a representative system.

Some readers may see a potential for protecting a broad range of constitutional rights in Bork's conception of the Constitution as a mechanism for democratic choice. John Hart Ely's derivation of substantive rights from a process conception of the Constitution is well known. Ely takes the preconditions for a true democracy to include not only such rights as free speech and the right to vote, but also special judicial concern for minorities that are victimized by the kind of prejudice that excludes them from the fluid legislative coalitions envisioned by Madisonian democracy. An ostensibly proceduralist conception of the Constitution could thereby warrant judicial scrutiny of legislation opposed by "insulated" or historically powerless racial and religious minorities, thus characterizing as "process rights" some of the substantive rights of the First and Fourteenth amendments.[13]

But because protection for victims of "prejudice" is nothing more than protection from injury that is imposed without adequate reason,[14] protecting racial and religious minorities supposes a principle that, if the law is to be evenhanded, should prohibit arbitrary treatment of all groups. A fully adequate right to participate in democratic choice might therefore include an across-the-board substantive right to be injured only if the government has a reason that a court can accept as a good-faith effort to serve the public interest.[15] In other words, a proceduralist conception of the Constitution could include a general right against arbitrary treatment that is not directly connected to explicit constitutional guarantees. And if a right against arbitrary treatment were given more than lip service, it could entail judicial protection for privacy in property, in procreation, and in sexual preference, along with other rights that Bork would oppose as "new rights."

A constitution that did no more than protect mechanisms of democratic choice would thus leave judges (and other interpreters) with a great responsibility for determining how a constitutional mandate of democracy would limit the government. Exercising this responsibility would require that judges concern themselves with the philosophic problem of what a proper democracy should be, for a normative conception of democracy would inevitably influence judicial choice among alternative interpretations permitted by constitutional language and history. Pretending to eschew a self-critical and open quest for the best that the Constitution can mean could serve only as a cover for imposing one's undefended preferences on the public. The unavoidable need for interpretation wherever decision serves more than the raw or undefended preference of judges would pose a problem for Bork's attack on moral philosophy if he allowed any distinction among preferences, for moral philosophy would be needed to distinguish better preferences from worse.

But Bork believes gratifications are equal in reason. And as if successfully avoiding either a controversial philosophic choice or an imposition on the public, he repudiates the judicial concern for "immanent ideals of democracy" (or democracy itself, as I would put it) and denies that judges are "warranted in demanding more democracy than either the Constitution requires or the people want."[16] Where the Constitution's practical implications are open to any reasonable debate democracy means what the government says it means. In response to this kind of criticism Bork says the federal judiciary can step in if a state government organizes itself in a manner that crosses the boundaries between democracy and either monarchy or aristocracy.[17] He has also expressed support for the decision in *Baker v. Carr,* although on a different theory from the one used by the Court.[18]

Neither of these moves succeeds. One cannot draw a real line between democracy and other forms of government without some "immanent ideals of democracy." One may think that guidance in drawing the line can come from someone or something else, like the framers or history, but, as I elaborate in subsequent chapters, if there are no accessible entities and relationships like democracy itself and other normative ideas (or better theories thereof) by which to identify, interpret, or test the opinions of the framers and other sources, normative words can signify nothing except that which pleases the powers that be. *Democracy* will join *justice* in the "so-called" category of entities, and the call will be made by those with the power to make their assertions stick.

Bork indicates some protection for participatory rights by a qualified endorsement of *Baker v. Carr.* The *Baker* majority was wrong, he says, to declare the malapportionment of the Tennessee legislature answerable to the equal protection clause. He believes that the equality rationale inevitably led the Court to an arbitrary and unworkable preference for a principle of one person, one vote, which prevents districting that effectively inflates votes to protect geographic, economic, and other interests from statewide majorities. Better to have held Tennessee answerable to Article IV's guarantee to each state of a republican form of government. The Court could have delivered on the promise of a republican form of government by arranging for the electorate of Tennessee to choose between population-based and interest-based schemes of representation (84–86). Bork thus indicates the following doctrine: the guarantee clause guarantees an initial vote by "a majority of the state's voters"—a statewide election or referendum conducted on the principle of one person, one vote—and the popular will thereby collected may authorize anything short of a scheme "in which the majority is systematically prevented from voting."

The difficulties with this doctrine are patent. Notice first that Bork finds republican form to mean majority rule: one person, one vote. That is why he thinks the guarantee clause requires a one person, one vote statewide election at the initial stage of the apportionment decision. But why just the initial stage? Why does the guarantee clause lose its voice after that first vote? By his own understanding of what "republican form" requires, Bork would read the guarantee clause to guarantee not a republican form but a vote in accordance with the republican form on whether to have a republican form. And he can hardly bestow "republican form" on whatever comes out of that vote, for he recognizes that the voters can fail to respect the lines separating democracy, aristocracy, and monarchy.

And how does Bork know that the guarantee clause requires that initial election by the principle of one person, one vote? He indicates at one point the answer we expect from him: he got it from the framers (86). But he indicates in the same discussion that history and the composition of the U.S. Senate prove that the framers did not follow a rule of one person, one vote—in fact, that has to be the main reason for his opposition to a constitutional doctrine of one person, one vote (87). So Bork could not have gotten his meaning of the guarantee clause from the framers, because he reports them issuing conflicting messages. By his denial of "immanent ideals" and his account of what governs when the framers are silent, we are left with Bork's personal preferences; they coexist with his strictures against the imposition of judicial preferences.

Bork's contradiction throws us back upon the harsh implication of "no immanent ideals." Consistency with Bork's proposition would mean protection for only those rights seen as clearly present in the Constitution by judges whose reading of the document and its history assumes that elected officials (however elected) speak for the majority (which the government plays some hand in defining) and that judges should give the majority's view of the Constitution the benefit of every doubt. Few Supreme Court precedents could survive such a rule.

As I elaborate in chapter 4, Bork's approach questions the legitimacy of every case that holds state governments responsible to provisions of the Bill of Rights. We shall also see that, despite Bork's lip service to the *Brown* decision, consistent application of Bork's position would return judicial protection for racial and ethnic minorities to the days of "separate but equal."[19] He scarcely hides the fact that he would permit governmental invasions of personal privacy to range from banning contraception to sterilizing convicts. And a consistent application of his views regarding substantive due process and equal protection would leave legislative majorities a great deal of freedom to discriminate against women, not to mention illegitimate children, the poor, and other non-racial minorities.[20]

Bork's philosophical skepticism also yields a niggardly view of rights that enjoy relatively high textual specificity. By grounding freedom of speech in the Constitution's structure, he can subordinate the freedom to the maintenance of that structure as an end in itself. Freedom of speech thus becomes freedom to express opinions on questions of public policy in a manner that respects the lawful processes for deciding such questions. Bork once acknowledged that his conception of free speech suggests no more freedom for artistic, commercial, or scientific speech. Bork now says that denying protection to nonpolitical speech is "an unworkable rule" because political speech "is assisted by many forms" of nonpolitical speech, and "almost any speech" becomes political "by simply adding a policy proposal at the end" (333).

But this concession on a derivative matter leaves the underlying principle intact. Bork continues to subordinate speech to the political system as an end in itself (335). And he continues his equivocal support for a second implication of that principle. Despite the Constitution's own origin in a proposal to change an established constitution (the Articles of Confederation) by extralegal means, Bork would disallow judicial protection for "speech that advocates violation of the law or civil disobedience"—unless such protection is consistent with "the current state of the [case] law" (333–35). Bork is not unimpressed by the fact that current judicial doctrine rejects his view that there is "no reason for courts to protect any advocacy of law violation." The law currently denies protection only to speech on the wrong side of the line between advocacy and incitement to "imminent lawless action,"[21] and Bork did tell the Senate he would respect that line as a justice. But since the line is not always clear, and since some may draw it in ways that defeat its purpose, a nominee's conception of that purpose is hardly something the Senate could have ignored. In light of Bork's overarching judicial philosophy and his conception of the function of free speech, he should be able to understand how some senators might have questioned the meaningfulness of his promise to respect current doctrine in unpredictable circumstances. We are looking at Bork's constitutional theory, in any event, not speculating on his conduct as a justice, and as constitutional theorist Bork still sees "no reason for courts to protect any advocacy of law violation since that is merely advocacy of a piecemeal overthrow of the democratic system."[22]

In defending this position, Bork surveys the founding's "legacy of suppression" and the tangled politics that produced the Bill of Rights and concludes that constitutional language and history indicate little beyond the fact that "there is something special about speech." So, "we are forced to construct our own theory," he says.[23] To construct that theory, Bork borrows a list of reasons for free speech from Louis Brandeis and finds that only one of those reasons provides a suitable basis for judicial decision. Thus, protecting speech as a safety valve for social frustrations requires prudential decisions that Bork says judges should not make. Protecting speech for the sake of individual fulfillment and happiness arbitrarily disfavors the fulfillment and happiness of those who would repress speech. Protecting speech that quests for political and moral truth beyond the system fallaciously assumes the existence of such truth. That leaves only explicitly political speech that respects established legal processes. The quest for political truth cannot justify advocacy of violence or even nonviolent unlawful acts, because such advocacy offends the legal processes that constitute the sole source of political truth.[24]

Bork claims this view of punishable advocacy is compatible with "a wide range of evaluation, criticism, electioneering, and propaganda" concerning "governmental behavior, policy or personnel, whether the governmental unit involved is executive, legislative, judicial or administrative."[25] But the logic of his position demands that he reject the Holmes-Brandeis test of imminent and grave danger and accept nothing more stringent than Justice Sanford's now discredited dictum in *Gitlow v. New York* that government may move against potentially dangerous speech "in its incipiency." Surely one can reasonably believe that there is much political "criticism" and "propaganda" that could, in Justice Sanford's words, "kindle a fire that, smoldering for a time, may burst into a sweeping and destructive conflagration."[26]

I say Bork can accept no more than Sanford's test. But the logic of Bork's position may demand even less. At the very least, and as reactionary as Sanford's approach seems today, Bork's approach would radicalize *Gitlow*. The *Gitlow* Court could always review a legislative judgment for reasonableness, for *Gitlow* was decided in the heyday of substantive due process. The *Gitlow* Court had a suspicious eye for legislative pretext and was armed with the doctrinal tools to deal with it. Those judges still felt duty bound to strike down admittedly appalling results. By contrast, Bork's skeptical philosophy excludes any suggestion that the Constitution incorporates or reflects independent standards of reasonableness. We must not forget Bork's statement that judges have no business testing legislative judgments for reasonableness and that judges must be prepared to accept admittedly savage results.[27] A court that accepted Bork's statement could do little to protect even political speech before legislators with a paranoic eye for threats to the system. Bork's assurances about protecting peaceful political speech may have been reliable for predicting his conduct as an associate justice; but they are simply incompatible with his conception of judicial duty, and they serve only to highlight the radical nature of his theory.

Bork's antipathy to the American institution of judicial responsibility seems well represented among present-day conservative commentators and jurists, despite its minority position within the academic legal community. But take away Bork's conclusion favoring judicial abdication and leave his skepticism about general normative standards in the law, and one is comfortably within the mainstream of American legal academe. The principal difference between Bork and most of the liberal lawyers who opposed his confirmation is that they attach libertarian results to the skeptical premises they share with Bork. They agree with Bork on the moral equality of preferences; but unlike him, they think that premise supports an expanding area of individual liberty in matters they designate as personal. Oblivious to his own skepticism about the existence of real rights against the community and the state, Bork criticizes libertarians for the "moral relativism" he discerns in their approval of Supreme

Court policy relating to such matters as pornography and privacy in sexual matters. He predicts social turmoil unless government imposes some morality on private activities.[28] And assuming a consensus on the likelihood of turmoil and the need to avoid it regardless of the costs to individual freedoms, Bork would remove all meaningful constitutional restraints on preventing turmoil short of actions that a social consensus would call clearly unconstitutional.

Bork's aversion to turmoil might have led him to recognize an objective standard for the open and responsible exercise of judicial judgment: judges might protect a version of the structure that they believe best for promoting peace and order. But Bork reiterates his moral skepticism by predicting that those who turn to moral and political philosophy in a quest for better versions of contestable standards flirt with a "constitutional nihilism." He believes that this nihilism sets in when judges tire of endless philosophic quests, find no objectively better or worse versions of contestable normative ideas, and conclude that they have license to impose their own values.[29]

Bork refers to the conclusion of some libertarian moral skeptics that all normative constitutional theories are necessarily incoherent,[30] and he criticizes the skeptics for refusing to draw "the apparently necessary conclusion—that judicial review is, in that case, illegitimate."[31] Of course, Bork does draw that conclusion, in effect if not expressly, for to treat judicial review as illegitimate whenever the Constitution leaves room for debate is to treat it as illegitimate for all practical purposes. Bork's observation about the nihilistic consequences of moral skepticism applies to his own position, for nothing—libertarian, repressive, whatever—can follow from the alleged insight that all "gratifications" are equal. If all preferences are equal, why not prefer the excitement of turmoil to the boredom of peace? In identifying a failing of his morally skeptical but libertarian critics, Bork exposes a failing of his own.

WALTER BERNS AND THE
NEW RIGHT'S (RELATIVELY) ESOTERIC TEACHING

This brings us to another of the judiciary's most active contemporary critics, political scientist Walter Berns. Berns's position differs from Bork's in a crucial respect. Bork is a moral skeptic committed to a particular conception of majoritarian democracy as a mere historical given to which he attaches no objective or intrinsic value. If we take him at his philosophic word, Bork's commitments would have to be matters of sheer willfulness; if he genuinely believes that there can be no real reason for choice among preferences, he must include the preferences he expresses in conceiving democracy as he does and in laboring in its service, on and off the bench. Bork's position is therefore indefensible in the sense that, by his own terms, he can offer no reason to accept it. Fear of consequences might motivate testimonials in its behalf or even lead to deeper beliefs and unquestioning habit, and these prospects suggest even more "conservative" methods for defending something—that is, coercion and inculcation.

Berns seems different. He can defend his position in a reasoned way. He believes that his position follows from moral and nonmoral propositions that he can defend in public. He also seems to believe that a reasoned defense is better, for as he once said, "republican government is endangered by the weakness of our attachment to its principles and by our inability to defend it, not so much on the battlegrounds as in the books, so to speak."[32]

Berns disavows moral skepticism. He agrees with skeptics like Bork and Ely that the Constitution is primarily concerned with procedures for arriving at democratically representative decisions. But he claims to take his bearings from the framers, who designed the procedures to protect certain natural rights. He argues that Ely fails to find a principled basis for defining minority rights because Ely is unaware of the framers' conceptions. Principled decision, says Berns, depends on recognizing that "the Constitution was and is designed to secure rights and, in that respect, is informed by moral principle."[33] This rights-based understanding of the Constitution is unusual for present-day opponents of a nondeferential and responsible judiciary, most of whom share Bork's assumption that it is the majority that is the source of rights and other political values, not nature or some other authority higher than the majority.[34] At one point Berns even says that the Constitution provides an "independent judiciary" to secure certain natural rights from hostile majorities, but he goes on to arguments that leave little room for judicial independence.[35]

Berns has what one may call a neo-Hobbesian view of the Constitution, because he finds the Constitution's objectives in the natural rights philosophy of Thomas Hobbes. In Hobbesian fashion, Berns emphasizes the need for strong, coercive government to suppress private threats to life and property. One source of such threats is the common criminal, and Berns has long spoken out against what he perceives as a Warrenite tenderness toward criminals.[36] He believes that a second threat to social peace is criticism of government in the name of high moral principle. Indeed, Berns believes that moralists threaten the peace even more than criminals do.[37] He mentions elements of the religious right, but he is especially hostile to "so-called intellectuals" who speak out and bring lawsuits in behalf of their "private judgments" as to what is just and unjust. He regards these "so-called intellectuals" as a leading obstacle to social peace, and he opposes them as Hobbes opposed the priests and lawyers who agitated against established civil authority (56, 64).

With Hobbes, Berns believes that social peace requires that private individuals agree to "stop disputing the ends of politics" in exchange for "the liberty to pursue private ends . . . liberty understood as privacy: the private economy, private associations, the private family, the private friendship, the private church or no church, and all this with a view to happiness privately defined." The government that results from this agreement will follow a motto of "live and let live," in that it will not represent views regarding religion and the ends of government. Such a government will not deploy its powers to impose religious and ideological views. Instead, it will respond to and respect interests—economic interests, primarily—that can be represented, that admit of compromise (ibid.)

This government will work for ordinary people; by liberating their acquisitiveness it will soften uncompromisable commitments like religion and ideology.[38] This government will have little appeal to the "so-called intellectuals," however. They will become a threat to the American or neo-Hobbesian scheme of government, because they will despise its unprincipled character— its messy, morally unelevating compromises. The "so-called intellectuals" will push for principle in the forums of principle, the courts, because the legislature is the forum only of bargaining and compromise, where principles rarely win. And when principled intellectuals do win in court, Berns maintains, they polarize the community's politics by inducing unelected judges to substitute principled solutions for compromises that have at least the political virtue of enabling peace.[39]

Berns illustrates what he calls the polarizing effects of a politics of principle with an account of *Griswold v. Connecticut.* As we might expect from a writer who believes that a liberal society is one "where men can live private lives" unburdened by moral and sectarian intolerance (59–60), he says that the birth control statute invalidated in *Griswold* "of course, ought never to have been enacted" (64). The statute ought not to have been enacted *because* of its inconsistency with liberal principle. Yet Berns believes the Court erred in invalidating the statute. Responsive to conflicting currents in public opinion, the elected government of Connecticut found itself accommodating both sides of the birth control issue. The statute was on the books, but it was not being enforced. This arrangement was at least partially satisfactory to both sides. It was not altogether coherent, but it preserved the peace. Then along came "those who insist on a purity of principle—in this case Yale professors"— losers in the legislature, appealing to courts, and making "the language of rights . . . the language of our politics." Such was the first great step toward *Roe v. Wade* and the current "battlefield on which single-moral-issue groups face each other like opposing armies." By thus confounding law and morality, our "so-called intellectuals," like Hobbes's priests and lawyers, pose "the greatest threat to representative government" (63–64).

Berns's treatment of *Griswold* suggests that judges should avoid the merits in all constitutional cases that require controversial decisions of political morality or the assertion of political principle. His belief that principled decision subverts the constitutional order explains why he opposes a responsibly nondeferential judiciary. It also explains his attitude toward the Fourteenth Amendment. He views the amendment as the great source of opportunities to confound politics and political morality, opportunities that the Court exploited in protecting property rights, desegregating schools, reforming police practices, and recognizing rights of sexual privacy.[40]

In addition, Berns argues the one person, one vote principle is wrong because majorities should be free to modify the majority principle as necessary to protect private property and insure a politics of give-and-take among a plurality of economic interests.[41] The framers, says Berns, did not want to encourage citizen participation in politics. Following Locke, who continued Hobbes's larger project by proposing an alternative to government through fear of state power, the framers prepared for a politics of compromise by replacing active citizenship with devotion to private acquisition and comfort.[42] But while Berns wants protection for property and privacy, he does not think that courts should provide it. He criticizes judicial activism in the *Lochner* era.[43] He cites Hamilton's argument against a bill of rights in *Federalist* 84 as evidence that the framers originally wanted to protect rights "without mentioning them"—that is, without listing them as exemptions from legislative power to be enforced by courts.[44] "In principle," he says, a Lockean legislature has the constitutional power to be "as oppressive as . . . Leviathan." And he believes that constitutional limitations depend not on courts, but on checks and balances among the other branches and the awareness of politicians that they are subject to their own enactments and the judgment of the electorate (52–54).

It is important to draw out the full implications of Berns's criticism of *Griswold*. By Berns's own principles, the *Griswold* Court invalidated a statute that the Connecticut legislature should not have enacted—a statute that was inconsistent with liberty as privacy. The *Griswold* majority acted on more than mere principle, then; it acted to vindicate *liberal* principle. Berns's opposition to *Griswold* therefore suggests opposition to any judicial assertion of principle—even the assertion of liberal principle. As Berns sees it, the constitutional system would privatize ends and weaken the politics of religious, ideological, and moral principle—even the politics of a liberal or constitutional morality that would defend what is noble or otherwise choiceworthy in the privatization of *other* moral choices.[45]

At this point, Berns begins to set the stage for Bork's moral skepticism. The philosophic decision to privatize ends implies that the overall end of privatization, peace, is superior to all other political ends. Berns joins Hobbes in implying that the bourgeois life is the best life, or that the bourgeois life predominates in the best regime.[46] Now the question is the status of this preference. Is it mere preference, mere assertion of will on the part of those who want peace over those who want, say, the psychological highs of non-peaceful pursuits? Or does Berns believe he has reasons for the bourgeois life—reasons that would persuade everyone in a position to reason aright?

He might argue, for example, that the bourgeois regime is the best practicable regime for human beings in a position to maintain it because it permits private associations of people who despise bourgeois values as long as they do not express themselves in ways that actively subvert the bourgeois regime. And now that judicial Reaganism has demonstrated its political potential, Berns might add a point for the benefit of the "so-called intellectuals": should they be foolish enough to claim power in parts of the bourgeois regime, such as the judiciary and even the university, they will only stimulate the hatching of "principles" that defeat their aspirations to a politics of public reasonableness.[47]

The fact that Berns publishes his opinions for a general public that includes his critics is some indication that he believes he has reasons that should appeal to all who can suspend their preconceptions long enough to give the matters in question careful thought. Bork publishes his views too, of course, and to the extent that publication implies submission to a readership's rational capacities, publication tends to undermine the willful or historicist—that is, the antirationalist—implications of his argument. But aside from the incoherence of any practical argument from moral skepticism, moral skepticism is the content of Bork's argument, and we can take it at face value.

By contrast, Berns attempts a natural rights argument. So we are entitled to add the content of Berns's argument to the implications of its public enunciation and say that he agrees that moral truth supports his preference for the bourgeois regime. Berns has reasons, then, for supporting a liberal regime—not mere private reasons, but reasons that he recommends to all who are in a position to think about how to live, including not only the "so-called intellectuals" but also those who might not initially agree with him that "of course" Connecticut should not have enacted the birth control statute in the first place. Yet, when he rejects a politics of liberal principle and denies the forums of principle—the courts, the universities—their historical if not their rightful place in "our politics," he implies no further concern for the truths that he thinks he possesses. And in calling for an end to the concern for moral truth, he either invites skepticism's denial of moral truth or he registers doubt about the capacity of other people to suspend private preoccupations and prejudices long enough to see the reasons why they should govern themselves by a liberal morality of Live and Let Live.

Whatever the case, Berns cannot deny the distinction between reasons and raw preferences without embracing the moral skepticism he disclaims. So his position must reflect a negative assessment of the demos. It is as if he believes that the limited capacities of ordinary people, and of their sons and daughters in the universities and the professions, force most of us to live as if there were no reasons beyond preferences. And those writers, like Bork, whose social philosophy will either rationalize or reflect the limited moral and intellectual capacities of the demos will espouse some form of moral skepticism. Whatever Bern's private philosophy, the denial of real moral truth will be the public philosophy of the regime he favors. His specific understanding of natural rights leads him to abdicate or withdraw to the background, making way for Bork's appearance as the leading New Right constitutional theorist—the philosophic guardian of the regime, so to speak, despite what Berns once said about the incompetence of skeptics as guardians.[48]

Because Berns's references to electoral accountability and checks and balances do assume some structural limits on the power of elected officials, there would seem to be room in Berns's constitutionalism for some judicial protection for structure-based rights. Thus, he says that "to the judges is assigned the duty, as 'faithful guardians of the Constitution,'" to preserve the integrity of the structure, for it is by the structure, more than by "parchment barriers," that the government is effectively limited (parchment barriers here meaning specified individual and minority rights).[49] Underscoring the importance of protecting the structure of government, he adds that "it would be only a slight exaggeration to say that, in the judgment of the Founders, the Constitution would 'live' as long as the structure was preserved."

One example of what Berns means by protecting the structure is the Supreme Court's decision in *I.N.S. v. Chadha* striking down the so-called legislative veto, a decision he approves.[50] But if there is talk in Berns's writings about institutional integrity and therefore hope for institutional authority like the president's veto, there is not much hope for judicially secured, structurally based individual and minority rights. We have already seen his depreciation of judicial guarantees based on the Bill of Rights and the Fourteenth Amendment, as well as his depreciation of the value of active citizenship. His hostility to judicially secured individual and minority rights is even clearer in his recent analysis of the constitutional freedom of speech.

Berns says that the American constitutional structure "is characterized by speech whose purpose is to gain the consent of others, and the right to speak with a view to gaining consent is given constitutional protection in Article I."[51] Because he opposes publicly voiced "private opinion" concerning the ends of government and the justice or injustice of the laws as "the greatest threat to representative government," it is a matter of some significance that

Berns substitutes Article I for the First Amendment as the source of the constitutional freedom of speech. Speech grounded in Article I is a mere aspect of governmental power, not an exemption from governmental power. This conception of speech would support some rights to communicate directly to one's representatives about public matters, together with some official immunity from prosecutions over statements made in the performance of official duties. These rights and immunities would insure some freedoms to examine and debate issues of public policy. But these freedoms would be derivatives of Article I and its aim, which on Berns's account is consent. They could not logically serve as rights to challenge that means-end system. As derivatives of the system, they could not support a right the framers themselves assumed when they proposed a new constitution to be ratified in a manner that bypassed the procedures of the existing constitution.[52]

Berns thus undermines judicial review of debatable legislative judgments that certain kinds of speech subvert the system, for he contends that establishing checks and balances among the elected branches is the Constitution's way of protecting whatever individual and minority rights there are, and he opposes judicial power to review the reasonableness of legislation generally. He would confine public speech to questions concerning "interests that can be represented"—private economic interests, for the most part, as opposed to "private opinions" about the ends of government (ibid.).

Berns might try to justify his narrow view of free speech by invoking Hobbes. Berns says Hobbes thought he had discovered an indisputable scientific basis for social peace. He contends that Locke and the Founding Fathers improved on aspects of Hobbes's methods without abandoning his findings about human nature, the ends of government, and the essentially unlimited power of government.[53] Berns apparently believes that the tenets of this essentially Hobbesian tradition are indeed indisputable. He seems to agree that the Constitution of 1789 is grounded in moral truths that no reasonable person can deny (52–54), and he uses the Hobbesian tenets as premises for advice about the conduct of judicial power and government generally.

So Berns might draw a narrow view of free speech from indisputable political truths. But there would be an obvious problem with this justification: it would be part of a general philosophic statement about the ends of government, and it would invoke principles of Hobbesian liberalism. Yet from his discussion of the Court's privacy decisions, it is evident that Berns opposes judicial invocations of all political principles, even the liberal principles he considers indisputable. Invoking principles of any kind suggests that people should decide what to believe on the basis of criteria other than "interests that can be represented," and that suggestion subverts what Berns believes is the American system.

Berns is right in suggesting that political appeals to the ends of government subvert any government to some extent. Even statements supporting a government subvert that government to the extent that they implicitly acknowledge the need to say something that supports the government, a need that would not exist without some plausible basis for questioning the premises or the conduct of that government (127). The fact that Berns argues for a politics that excludes a concern for something higher than narrow economic interests is sensible as something he might do precisely because he knows what we all know: there may be something wrong with neo-Hobbesian politics. Berns knows of his neo-Hobbesianism what Hobbes knew of his Hobbesianism—it needs to be defended. It needs to be defended because there are not only sentiments but also arguments against it. So it is false to pretend that it is indisputable. What Berns is actually doing belies the claim to indisputable truth. He also compromises his attack on the "so-called intellectuals," for by defending the principles of his regime he joins its critics to some extent. The logic of Berns's position demands that judges who would serve the neo-Hobbesian politics of interests dismiss any question whose answer requires an argument of principle. His judges could not even rationalize what the elected branches wanted to do.

Berns may not contradict himself in all respects, however. He does contradict himself with the silly suggestion that there is something indisputable about the philosophic teachings that support his proposals for judicial review. He also contradicts himself when indicating support for some meaningful judicial role in debatable constitutional questions, for his judges are not free to defend their decisions in such cases by invoking constitutional principle. To conform to what the system treats as virtue, Berns's judges would have to pretend to be serving nothing more than their own private interests. Yet if Berns's judges confessed that they were serving only their own private interests, they would verify Bork's description of what judges actually do in controversial cases, thus flaunting norms of judicial propriety. That leaves judicial silence, not judicial review, as the only option in constitutional cases, and Berns misrepresents his position by pretending otherwise.

But misrepresentation need not mean contradiction, for Berns can still argue for constitutional principle as a private person addressing a restricted or relatively private audience, not the general public. He can give a principled defense of an unprincipled politics to the academic audience for which he usually writes. He cannot propose to thinking individuals what he proposes for the general public: that reason supports the suspension of their critical faculties. He can only hope to persuade the thoughtful to think of themselves as a "private" community of sorts, apart from the benighted demos. To make his case he might cite the Reaganite reaction against Warrenite judging as evidence that a reformist criticism of the political system cannot be an institutional part of the system—evidence that self-critical striving for improvement is something that individuals can do only as individuals and in a closet, not as citizens in full public view.

This populist reaction against the Court and its allies is evidence for Berns's position. But it does not settle the question against a morally progressive politics. The public cannot lead itself. It needs expert or certified help in rationalizing its unexamined aversions and demands. Since Berns has joined the New Right politicians and theorists who have helped to form the populist reaction against a morally progressive politics, he cannot cite that reaction as proof that an unprincipled politics (or, equivalently, a chauvinistic or reactionary politics) is unavoidable.[54]

THE NEW RIGHT, THE FRAMERS, AND THE FUTURE

Berns's position thus portends results that range from a growing stratification of American society to declining public support for the liberal arts, whose traditional aim is to free the mind from acquisitiveness and prejudice. No elaboration of these prospects is necessary to justify fear that something radical is afoot. The obliteration of the Bill of Rights and the Fourteenth Amendment and the end of judicial review as we have known it for two centuries—these results are radical enough. What I must address here is the New Right's contention that the judicial deference it proposes is in fact consistent with the constitutionalism of the framers. Berns defends this conclusion in a much more thoughtful fashion than writers like Bork, Raoul Berger, and William Rehnquist—but they all suggest that their opposition to Warrenite judicial activism is an attempt to restore an older tradition.

The New Right's contention is wrong. I show in the next three chapters that the constitutional jurisprudence of the Warren Court is consistent with those sources most often cited as exemplars of the framers' constitutionalism. The sources in question are *The Federalist* and the decisions of John Marshall. I show in chapters 4 and 5 that the current right-wing opposition to active judicial vindication of constitutional morality owes much more to certain twentieth-century ethical theories than to either the general political philosophy of the American founding or its specific theory of judicial review.

The Warren Court was not as close to the racial and social injustices of the founding period as are some of the critics of the Warren Court, but the Warren Court was closer to the constitutional jurisprudence of the founding. Most of the critics of Warrenite activism confound the jurisprudence and political morality of the founding with the injustices of the founding period. That is both an insult to the founding and a philosophic mistake. Chapter 5 shows, in addition, that the constitutional thought of establishment liberals in America is but the left-liberal expression of the philosophic mistake that brought us New Right constitutionalism. Chapters 5 and 6 also contend that if judicial review has a future it must return to the legal-moral presuppositions of Publius and John Marshall. The concluding chapter shows how recent moral philosophy has revitalized the classical presuppositions that support the style of judging that the Warren years exemplify for our generation.

Before I begin this larger discussion I should make one more initial observation about the New Right's claim to represent the tradition. In assessing the patrimony of the current assault on judicial independence we have seen that Berns differs with Bork on a crucial matter: the status of rights and general normative ideas like justice. Bork grants no status to such notions beyond convention. Berns believes that the most fundamental of such norms originate in nature. Bork's is the dominant view among opponents of judicial power, at least since the time of Holmes. Bork concurs in premises that unite such critics of judicial power as Learned Hand, Alexander Bickel, Raoul Berger, and William Rehnquist: general norms have no meaning beyond personal or collective preference; and when it comes to preferences in a democracy, those of unelected officials should count for as little as possible.[55]

New Right constitutionalism tries to link this mainstream moral skepticism to the cause of fidelity to the framers. The usual New Right line is that, because norms are inevitably bottomed in arbitrary preference, judges should avoid decisions that can only enact their preferences; and where the preferences of the framers are not clear, judges should defer to the elected branches. The New Right then proposes that judges and constitutional scholars be concerned not with moral philosophy but with describing the framers' intentions. Other writers have set forth the insuperable methodological and conceptual arguments against the New Right's historical approach.[56] I want to add here that it is not possible for moral skeptics faithfully to describe the framers' intentions.

Whoever they were, and however one might collect evidence of their minds, the framers did not publicly admit that their proposals were anything less than their considered opinions about what was in the public interest. They claimed no less for the same reason that politicians generally claim no less. Commands may, but proposals do not, take the form: Do x just because I prefer it. And, as a historical matter, the Constitution originated in a practical proposal and was debated as a practical proposal in the campaign for ratification. If the framers enacted their preferences, they at least pretended to be enacting them as versions of something more. If they enacted their conceptions of free speech, due process, and equal protection, they implicitly enacted

them as the best feasible versions of free speech, due process, and equal protection, not merely their conceptions.[57] To describe their intentions faithfully
one would have to be able to make statements of the following form: *The
framers proposed x as the best feasible version of justice, fairness, or some
other general normative idea.* Because such statements would distinguish versions or conceptions of x from x, they could be rendered as follows: *The
framers believed x to be the best feasible version of x itself, or simple x—justice
or fairness itself, or simple justice or fairness.*

Moral skeptics cannot adopt this last proposition as their own. They
would say: *The framers believed x was the best feasible version of "x."* Or, to
put the skeptics' point less elliptically: *The framers rationalized their preference for x by claiming that it was the best feasible version of a notion that has
no better or worse versions.* The skeptics may be right about the framers as a
matter of ethical theory, though I submit evidence in chapters 2 and 3 that they
are not. But the skeptics cannot function as faithful representatives of the
framers because they cannot say as observers all that the framers said as political actors. Skeptics cannot understand the framers as they understood themselves. Skeptics cannot accept the Constitution as written because their ethical
theory cannot allow the document's claimed connection to ends like justice
and domestic tranquility—that is, *simple* justice and domestic tranquility, not
mere, and therefore possibly erroneous, versions of these ends.

The skeptics' inability to adopt the Constitution's mode of reference
fractures the claim of skeptics like Bork and Rehnquist that their approach to
constitutional interpretation respects the authority of the framers. They reject
the framers' claim to authority when they deny meaning to the heart of that
claim. In addition, the skeptics imply that the framers were either simple-
minded for believing in ideas like simple justice or dishonest for pretending to.
Either implication would deny the framers a virtue that ordinary citizens
associate with persons worthy of authority. So the skepticism of people like
Bork and Rehnquist can only lead to misrepresenting and insulting the framers.

Berns's antiskepticism could enable him to avoid the skeptics' perverse
fidelity to the framers. But in the end Berns insults the framers too. He proposes that judges, academics, and the public generally see America's primary
business as business and adopt the skeptical attitude toward rights—rights as
mere interests that can be compromised in the ordinary give-and-take of legislative politics—that comes from preoccupation with material gain.

Berns's own business, however, is not business. He is an intellectual; since
he distinguishes himself from the "so-called intellectuals," he must be a real
intellectual. And he behaves like one. He does not convey the framers' word to
the flock as if it were written down somewhere in clear, uncontroversial, and

unerring terms. He constructs an amalgam of several teachings whose meanings are themselves controversial, and he defends his construct to readers he
assumes are able to assess it as both a scholarly interpretation and a political
argument. In doing so he appeals to the full range of evidentiary sources—
moral and nonmoral—appropriate to the argument he conducts. He appeals
to the faculties of mind that process evidence and to the belief that evidence is
what counts, even at the level of fundamental political principle.

In other words, Berns sometimes acts the political-moral philosopher; he
sometimes *practices* philosophy as a truth-seeking method. Yet at other times
he asks judges, other officials, and the universities to stop asking questions at
the level of political fundamentals. In attacking Dworkin's call for a fusion of
moral philosophy and constitutional law he indicates by word and by example
that he would substitute for philosophy as a form of truth seeking, philosophy
as ideological doctrine. Instead of recognizing Dworkin's positive contributions to the quality of constitutional debate by engaging Dworkin's interpretive and substantive arguments—something one would expect of any
contemporary constitutional theorist who is interested in testing his or her
views—Berns dismisses Dworkin for not accepting "rights as understood by
the Framers" and "any moral theory that informed the Constitution as written."[58] Coupled with all that he says about "America's business" and the
subversive activities of the "so-called intellectuals," Berns's refusal to engage
the arguments on the other side indicates that what Berns wants taught in the
law schools and the universities is not the problem of rights and the attitudes
and methods of inquiry into such problems, but *what* to think—or say—
about such problems. Philosophy as ideology, then, not process of inquiry.

As I have indicated, one possible explanation for the paradox that Berns
projects—sometimes a truth seeker, sometimes an ideologue—is that he conceives himself as a member of two more or less separate communities: a small,
private community of real intellectuals and a larger community of judges, the
"so-called intellectuals," and the rest of us. To the large community he delivers
a rightist version of the framers' intent as a package of axioms for approaching the problems of American life and law. He and his small communitarians
continually subject that package to the test of philosophy as truth-seeking
method; they defend it here from arguments for change, adjust it there where
those arguments prevail (as in Bork's approval of *Brown*) and where the package admits of change, and market the whole thing for public consumption as a
valid continuation of the same old tradition, not as constitutionally mandated
progress toward truths beyond convention.

Some such hypothesis is worth discussing because Berns doubtlessly respects a distinction between philosophy as truth seeking and philosophy as

doctrine and because Berns cannot expect thinking individuals to walk away from their critical faculties and the live problems of constitutional morality that attract those faculties. He observes at one point that it would be irrational for a people to "exchange its natural freedom for a conventional slavery."[59] Indeed. But how much more rational could it be to abandon that faculty by which we distinguish nature from convention, freedom from slavery, and real freedom from slavery made to seem like freedom?[60] Of course one might also describe Berns's paradoxical use of philosophy to condemn philosophy as the kind of incoherence that results from trying to transform a partisan message into a global principle. He may believe that, if there is no generally attractive theoretical justification for New Right constitutionalism, he should condemn the messengers of that fact as sophistic subversives and hide the truth by denying or isolating the truth-seeking method that can expose New Right constitutionalism for what it is.

Which explanation shall we choose? The two-communities hypothesis may explain more of what Berns has to say. It also respects a thesis that is far from implausible as a matter of constitutional theory. I refer to a proposition of *Federalist* 49. Madison there rejects Jefferson's proposal for putting certain constitutional disputes to popularly elected conventions. I examine the relevant passages at length in chapter 2, but the gist will do for now. Madison points out that frequent constitutional conventions would imply defects in the Constitution and rob the government of that public "veneration" needed by even "the wisest and freest governments." Reason would inculcate "a nation of philosophers" with "reverence for the laws," he says, but "in every other nation, the most rational government will not find it a superfluous advantage, to have the prejudices of the community on its side."[61] One might reason from the truth in this passage to the conclusion that philosophy as truth seeking should have no visible role either in constitutional commentary and judicial decision or in the education of lawyers, political scientists, and others whose beliefs constitute a regular part of the public constitutional debate.[62]

Assume, *arguendo,* that Berns is right about the framers. Because they, like Hobbes, thought "'intellectuals' posed the greatest threat to representative government," they fashioned "arrangements by which [the intellectuals'] influence would be negated or at least minimized."[63] I return several times in the course of this book to the issues of whether legal-moral philosophy as truth seeking is a meaningful and politically worthy activity (I argue that we must believe it so). But our question for now is what Berns's view of the framers does for their authority. Writers who are alarmed by prospects of judges either as philosopher kings or as European revolutionaries betray the weakness of the equipment they bring to the contest. The root issue is whether the Constitution assumes a gap between justice and what people believe about justice and institutionalizes a concern for narrowing the gap. If the framers did believe constitutional government works for justice within the limits of interpretive and political possibilities, there are roles for all of those who strive to substitute knowledge for opinion. That this includes moral philosophers is hardly a revolutionary or otherworldly idea. Our community (as would any real community, I argue later) has long engaged these truth seekers as its functionaries,[64] paying them the regular salary that Athens refused Socrates as an alternative to his execution, an act Madison condemned in *The Federalist* as deserving of "indelible reproach."[65]

What seems clear at this point is that Berns cannot deny the normative gap between truth and mere belief in matters of constitutional morality without surrendering himself to the moral skepticism he condemns in others. Denying the normative gap would implicitly diminish the framers as simple-minded or charge them with duplicity, precisely as Bork inadvertently does. It is equally clear that insults lurk in any attempt to deny a visible public role to the "so-called intellectuals." Denying the intellectuals a role is tantamount to affirming that the framers deliberately degraded their own posterity by establishing a system that actively discourages thought on the highest political and moral level.

To say the framers discouraged philosophy in public affairs implicitly accuses them of fraud, for, as we have seen, Berns himself believes that a people cannot knowingly abandon their faculty for distinguishing slavery from freedom and apparent freedom from the real thing. If the framers are guilty of fraud, the fact that the founding generation fell for it does not do much for its claim to authority. And democracy suffers as a source of authority on any suggestion that the framers' fraud was justified by the public's incurable inability to tolerate reminders of its own potential for fraud—the fraudulent potential in its claim to justice. In sum, if Berns is right, he puts the lie to the claim of *Federalist* 1 that American constitutionalism can vindicate mankind's aspiration to "government from reflection and choice" (3).

But Berns will quickly point out that I misquote *Federalist* 1. It speaks of "establishing" government from reflection and choice, not maintaining government through reflection and choice, at least not choice or even reflection about fundamentals. I may misquote, I say in response, but I do not misinterpret. To appreciate either the Constitution's legitimacy or the validity of Berns's constitutional theory, one must compare both to their alternatives. By discouraging inquiry into those alternatives Berns destroys an essential condition for the full acceptance of what he wants to defend. Or, put another way, he entrusts the defense of his theory and of the Constitution to what he regards as the morally unreflective part of the community—the business part of the community. He can expect this part of the community instinctively (or blindly) to favor that interpretation of the Constitution that flatters business, the interpretation that reduces rights to interests that can figure in legislative compromises. He may think interests sufficient because he thinks his framers were right—"indisputably" right—and because indisputably right, perfectly safe in the hands of guardians who are blind to the arguments that prove they are right.

When Berns speaks about the need to defend constitutional principles "not so much on the battleground as in the books," the books he must have in mind (if we are to save him from contradiction) are books that appeal to the prejudices of those who are prepared to accept "America's business" as justified by no argument beyond its own assertion.[66] (I examine examples in chapter 4.) Berns might call these books good because they would help administer the project of indisputably correct framers. Those of us who need persuading cannot reasonably expect a full examination of Berns's evidence, because his small community of real intellectuals cannot accommodate the need for something—namely, inquiry into fundamentals—it is the point of their position to deny. Perhaps the people with the money will persuade us so-called intellectuals in the officially permissible way—the way that demonstrates the power of money over truth. So when the real intellectuals tell America's business that we so-called intellectuals are the enemy, they are doing the right and constitutional thing.

I would find such an argument an insult not to the so-called intellectuals but to the people and the causes it purports to serve. I would hope to find evidence that America's business wants to believe that its prejudices are true or probably true, true from something other than a business perspective and through something other than force, habit, or bribery. I would expect evidence that exponents of America's business would be insulted to be told that they or their sons and daughters are incapable of seeing the truth from an objective perspective. The reason for my expectations is in the very structure of prejudice. Prejudice presupposes truth and is open to the possibility of truth, because to have a prejudice is to have an inadequately supported belief that something is really true. No one who thinks she has a belief of any sort can believe she is utterly incapable of truth, because to believe something is to believe it *as true* or *probably true*.

Any attempt to escape the paradox of Berns's position thus results in insult aplenty and for everything he purports to serve, from the framers and the Constitution to democracy and America's business. Well, perhaps not everything. For Berns also purports to serve the truth. And perhaps the truth is insulting to everyone beyond the small community of real intellectuals I have hypothesized to save Berns from paradox or to give him his due. In other words, it could well be true that the framers intended to blind us to Berns's version of political truth—namely, the truth that blindness (to political fundamentals) is truth—for that could well be a truth beyond anything most of us could hope to see. And the fact that we might take such a message as incoherent may prove more about us than it does about the message—prove something, that is, to those real intellectuals who can see the truth. So perhaps I can only prove what I do not have to prove: that Berns insults all of his authorities as I happen to see them, and as I hope the reader sees them, not as they may really be.

All of which brings me back to my opening promise, easily kept, to prove nothing. The most I can hope to do is shift the burden to those who say unflattering things about us. And that puts me at risk of an argument that amounts to the most unflattering thing of all, unflattering to author as well as to reader—and that is flattery of both. I think I can do better by myself and by the reader, but the reader must decide. And I must get started. My first argument is that, as it relates to judicial power, Berns's theory of *The Federalist* is wrong, or at least that there is a better (more flattering?) way to read *The Federalist*. In the course of this argument I show how Madison might have reconciled his admiration for Socrates with his insight about the prejudices of the community.

2

JUDICIAL REVIEW
AND
THE FEDERALIST

The New Right's appropriation of *The Federalist* is a triumph of public relations, not scholarship.[1] The general theory of constitutional government in *The Federalist* is simply harder to reconcile with a policy of judicial deference than with a policy of judges deciding constitutional cases on their own and submitting their reasons to the public without deference to legislative or community opinion.[2]

In supporting this conclusion, however, I do not want to repeat errors of New Right theory. So as I turn to *The Federalist* let me assure the reader that I do not justify my understanding of judicial power by appealing solely to the alleged intentions of the framers. I have defended nondeferential, publicly responsible judging elsewhere, and that defense is more of an inference from the relatively uncontroversial meaning of the Constitution's text than from historical authority.[3] Nor do I assume *The Federalist* is either the sole or even the main source for evidence of the framers' intent. Without discussing the difficult metainterpretive issues concerning framers' intent,[4] I proceed here on the safe assumption that *The Federalist* is one of the several prominent sources of framers' intent. I do not assume—though I see no reason to deny—that the authors of *The Federalist* understood or would have accepted the full implications of their argument for judicial review. I aim only at the most plausible and attractive interpretation of what they wrote.

In analyzing *The Federalist* I refer to its authors jointly as Publius, thus adopting their pen name for my purposes. By referring to Publius instead of Hamilton, Madison, or Jay, I acknowledge that my analysis is, as all similar analyses are, an interpretation—a plausible imputation at best, defensible partly on historical but ultimately on moral grounds, since the context of such interpretations is an argument about how the community should conduct an aspect of its affairs.[5] So Publius is not Madison and Hamilton viewed separately or as historically bounded persons. Publius is who *The Federalist* implicitly indicates Publius is: Madison and Hamilton (in the main) standing together and addressing a coherent message to a community comprising both their generation and what the Constitution calls their "Posterity."[6] The main objective of this chapter is to use *The Federalist* to demonstrate something about the framers in general: their position on judicial power may well not be what the judiciary's modern critics say it is. If Publius represents the framers, the New Right is wrong about the framers.

PUBLIUS ON RESPONSIBILITY IN GOVERNMENT

The problem that dominates American constitutional theory in the twentieth century is that of reconciling the power of an electorally unaccountable judiciary with norms of democratic responsibility. But since problems are largely what they are perceived to be, our century's problem with the judiciary may reflect a defect in our own thinking, especially our conception of democratic responsibility. Sanford Levinson points out that John Marshall was comfortable with judicial power because he conceived accountability in terms not only of responsibility *to* someone but also of responsibility *for* a certain set of objectives. The judiciary was supposed to serve the latter, and Marshall thought the latter constitutionally more important.[7] We shall see that the same is true of Publius.

Publius's theory of judicial power is part of his general theory of responsible government. The story starts at a point in *The Federalist* well before Publius focuses on the power of the federal courts. We begin with Publius's reason for wanting a new constitution in the first place: he regards the government under the Articles of Confederation as a bad government. The overall arrangement of confederal and state governments is a failure, he believes, because it is unable to handle social problems like commercial rivalries among the states and paper money and other debtor relief laws that erode the confidence of investors, and because it cannot raise the revenues and troops needed to retire the war debt, inspire foreign respect for treaty obligations, and discourage sedition at home.[8] Not only does "the imbecility of our government" defeat hopes for national security, prosperity, and honor (92), the Confederation's fragmentation of effective institutional power reinforces disintegrative tendencies and territorial rivalries that can eventually lead to war among the states (nos. 6–8, 15).

This practical concern for ameliorating real problems of national security, order, wealth, credit, and honor is basic to Publius's outlook; it influences his treatment of the more legalistic and institutional varieties of constitutional question. His response in *Federalist* 23 to complaints that the proposed government will exercise too many of the most important governmental powers is, essentially, that people should not oppose means that are necessary for ends that they want (146–48). An important passage of *Federalist* 45 condemns "the impious doctrine in the old world that the people were made for kings, not kings for the people" and charges states' rights advocates with reviving this old doctrine in a new shape by suggesting that "the solid happiness of the people is to be sacrificed to the views of political institutions of a different form" (308–9).

In a statement that mitigates Publius's own shortsighted and even disingenuous predictions about the preservation of state prerogatives and "the greater probability of encroachments" by the states upon the central government, *Federalist* 31 acknowledges that such "conjectures . . . must be extremely vague and fallible" (198), and Publius all but leaves the eventual balance between state and nation to popular assessment of which arrangement best serves the people's happiness.[9] Publius's attitude is all the more remarkable because his audience conceives a federal division of power as essential to a legitimate constitutional system. From the way he translates the concerns of states' righters into questions of means and ends, we are led to ask how else substance overpowers institutional form in Publius's constitutional thought.

In *Federalist* 45 Publius states flatly that "the real welfare of the great body of the people, is the supreme object to be pursued; and no form of government whatever has any other value than as it may be fitted for the attainment of this object. Were the plan of the convention adverse to the public happiness, my voice would be, Reject the plan. Were the Union itself inconsistent with the public happiness, it would be, abolish the Union."[10]

This attitude pervades *The Federalist;* it surfaces in the discussion of each of its major topics, from states' rights to the general principles of representation and the separation of powers. Thus, when Publius defends his proposal for a strong executive he says in *Federalist* 70 that if "a vigorous executive is inconsistent with the genius of republican government," we must condemn not (as we might have expected) a strong executive, but republican government. For a "feeble executive" means "a bad government" in practice, "whatever it may be in theory," and a bad government is indefensible (471–72).

Federalist 10 defines a "faction" as a group whose demands are "adverse to the rights of other citizens, or to the permanent and aggregate interests of the community." Publius declares majority faction the great problem of republican government, and he adds that republican government is not to be recommended unless it can "secure the public good and private rights against . . . [majority] faction" (57, 60-1). *Federalist* 51 says: "Justice is the end of government. It is the end of civil society. It ever has been, and ever will be pursued, until it be obtained, or until liberty be lost in the pursuit. In a society under the forms of which the stronger faction can readily unite and oppress the weaker, anarchy may truly be said to reign, as in a state of nature" (352).

To secure minority rights and the common good from majority faction in a manner consistent with the forms of popular government, Publius proposes a plan that exhibits two general and complementary aims: (1) preventing the tyranny of any one segment of the community over others, and (2) providing governmental "energy" for effective legal sanctions and identifying and ameliorating social problems. Publius's plan for controlling the effects of faction, and majority faction in particular, is well known to the general reader through his most famous paper, number 10. What is not as well known is Publius's argument for responsible government. It is the latter that I emphasize here, for it houses his theory of the judiciary.

Publius starts by proposing a national government with power to act directly on the large number of diverse individuals and interest groups that are to comprise the society.[11] The legislature of this government, says number 10, is designed to "refine and enlarge the public views, by passing them through the medium of a chosen body of citizens" (62). The legislature is divided into houses whose "different modes of election," tenure, function, and resulting institutional psychology will divide and weaken the legislature as a whole. This legislative structure makes majorities harder to come by and thus makes majority faction less likely (63–64). But, we learn in *Federalist* 51, the structure also insures one of the conditions for the independence of the executive, normally a weaker branch in popular governments (350). Later papers indicate that the executive power is to exercise the initiatives of government. Its constitution features a unitary organization conducive to decision and dispatch, an independent electoral base, independent constitutional powers, and independent means of support and defense against legislative encroachment, like the presidential veto and a constitutional prohibition against diminution of salary.[12]

It is important to note that the executive is designed to act independently of Congress and even of public opinion for limited periods of time. In a remarkable passage of number 71, Publius asserts that "the republican principle demands" only that the "deliberative sense of the community should govern the conduct" of government. The republican principle "does not require . . . complaisance to every sudden breeze of passion, or . . . transient impulse" of public opinion (482). Publius believes the people agree with this conception of republican government; "the people commonly *intend* the PUBLIC GOOD," realize their capacity for error, and "despise the adulator who should pretend that they always *reason right* about the *means* of promoting it." Thus, when "the interests of the people are at variance with their inclinations," "persons . . . appointed . . . the guardians of those interests" have a "duty" to stand up to the people and "give them time and opportunity for more cool and sedate reflection." Such conduct has on occasion "saved the people from . . . their own mistakes and has procured lasting monuments of their gratitude to the men, who had courage and magnanimity enough to serve them at the peril of their displeasures" (482–83).

Here, then, is a government that is prepared to be less responsive to both public and legislative opinion in the short run so that it can be more responsible in the long run—that is, so that it can achieve objectives that the public ought to approve and can eventually approve. Publius outlines a more explicit conception of responsible government in a section of *Federalist* 63 that compares the Senate with the House of Representatives. "Responsibility in order to be reasonable," he says, "must be limited to the objects within the power of the responsible party; and in order to be effectual, must relate to operations of that power, of which a ready and proper judgment can be formed by the constituents" (424). Because the size of the House and the tenure of its members fall short of these prerequisites—because, in other words, a body that is too responsive to too many too often cannot be as responsible as a body that is not so responsive—the government needs "an additional body in the legislative department, which, having sufficient permanency to provide for such objects as require a continued attention, and a train of measures, may be justly and effectually answerable for the attainment of those objects" (ibid.).

Then Publius says something about the Senate that prefigures his views about "personal firmness" in the executive: "To a people as little blinded by flattery" as those whom Publius addresses, an institution like the Senate "may be sometimes necessary, as a defence against their own temporary delusions." Though "the cool and deliberate sense of the community . . . will in all free governments ultimately prevail," "there are particular moments in public affairs" when some "irregular passion" grips public opinion and "the people . . . may call for measures which they themselves will afterwards . . . lament and condemn." "In those critical moments" the people need "some temperate and respectable body" to check public opinion "until reason, justice and truth, can regain their authority over the public mind." Had the Athenians "so provided a safeguard against the tyranny of their own passions," the form of popular government might have escaped "the indelible reproach of decreeing to the same citizens, the hemlock on one day, and statues on the next" (425).

In these passages Publius suggests that responsibility in government is conditioned on a certain kind of power and a certain kind of visibility: *power* to perform the tasks for which one is held responsible (responsibility *for* something) and *visibility* sufficient to be held responsible by others (responsibility *to* someone). Most important, the tasks for which a government is to be held responsible include controlling the individual and collective tendencies that make government necessary in the first place. Human beings, says number 6, are "ambitious, vindictive and rapacious"; and, says number 10, they are "much more disposed to vex and oppress each other, than to co-operate for their common good" (28, 59). Because human nature is what it is, says number 51, those who found governments "must first enable the government to controul the governed; and in the next place, oblige it to controul itself" (349).

THE TASK OF RESPONSIBLE GOVERNMENT

The elements of Publius's conception of responsibility in government may appear to conflict. The power that a responsible government must have is power to be exercised on the governed themselves. Yet it is the governed who, at the founding, will judge the propriety of the power to be exercised and, subsequent to the founding, the actual exercises of power. Resolution of this apparent conflict lies in Publius's distinction between the immediate *inclinations* of people and their long-range *interests*. We saw this distinction at work in the passage on the executive's personal firmness: "When . . . the interests of the people are at variance with their inclinations, it is the duty of the persons whom they have appointed to be the guardians of those interests, to withstand the temporary delusion, in order to give them time and opportunity for more cool and sedate reflection" (482). And when Publius defends the organization of the Senate he speaks of "some temperate and respectable body of citizens" standing up to public opinion "until reason, justice, and truth can regain their authority over the public mind" (425).

Publius's idea is that, in the long run, the public will come to see the virtue of policies whose value may not have been evident at first. He is not saying that whatever the public approves in the long range will for that reason be in the public interest, for throughout he assumes an objective view of justice, human rights, and the common good. His commitment to democracy causes him to believe that a government of the people can make the people aware of their objective interest. Publius believes the case for popular government depends on its reconciliation to objective values.

Thus, he cannot recommend democracy unless he believes it likely that the mass of the people will eventually support a government whose policies will satisfy the demands of justice, human rights, and the common good. Eventually, his approach calls for inquiry into the substance of these demands, and elsewhere I have defended a conception of the ideal state of affairs implicit in the Constitution's arrangement of offices, powers, and rights.[13] In general, I view this constitutional ideal as a commercial society whose people enjoy those amounts of personal and collective security as are compatible with a strong commitment to individual and minority rights, a commitment that reflects a ruling desire to be and be recognized as a community of reasoning and reasonable beings.

Yet this is not the place to elaborate any particular version of constitutional ends. My object here is simply to note the role of objective values in Publius's thought, whatever the correct interpretation of those ends should be. Objective values of some description are integral to his purposes and enter into his general view of government's fundamental problems and methods. His aim, abstractly stated, is a state of affairs in which a government initially rooted in consent can pursue the common good while honoring individual and minority rights, and his basic method is a government that is insulated from popular reaction for a period of time sufficient to change public opinion for the better without denying the public's ultimate right to judge.

I shall return to Publius's view of responsible government. But first let us see how the judiciary enters Publius's exposition of the principles of the Constitution. The first extended reference to the judiciary occurs in *Federalist* 22, the last of a series of papers devoted to a criticism of the Articles of Confederation. A principal theme of the series is the Confederation's lack of energy, energy for enforcing sanctions for violations of law and energy for identifying and solving society's problems. *Federalist* 15 begins the series; it focuses on the provisions of the Articles that require Congress to raise revenues and troops by directing requisitions to the legislatures of the several states, requisitions as distinguished from laws directly applicable to individual citizens and enforceable through the courts.

Publius calls the Confederation's method of raising money and troops through requisitions the "principle of LEGISLATION for STATES or GOVERNMENTS, in their CORPORATE or COLLECTIVE CAPACITIES, and as contradistinguished from the INDIVIDUALS of whom they consist." This principle, he says in number 15, is "the great and radical vice in the construction of the existing Confederation."[14] What makes this defect such a serious one is that it transforms what are nominally laws binding on the states into "mere recommendations, which the states observe or disregard at their option" (ibid.). The states are free to obey or not, because Congress is politically and economically incapable of mustering the amount and kind of force needed for effective sanctions upon entire states. Legislation for states, says number 16, is the "parent of anarchy" whose only remedy is civil war (99).

The Confederation's principle proceeds from "an ignorance of the true springs" of human conduct, says number 15, because it assumes that "a sense of common interest" can replace fear of sanctions as the foundation for a general obedience to law. The defenders of the Confederation ignore "the original inducements to the establishment of civil power," that "the passions of men will not conform to the dictates of reason and justice without constraint" (97). They also ignore a natural jealousy of power "that disposes those who are invested with . . . it, to look with an evil eye upon all external attempts to restrain or direct its operations." This jealousy gives an "eccentric tendency" to all political association "formed upon the principle of uniting . . . a number of lesser sovereignties." And this eccentric tendency leaves little prospect that the laws of the union will be executed at all if entrusted to the states (ibid.). The laws of the union should operate directly on individuals, for individuals alone are amenable to coercion by the civil magistracies; coercing whole states requires military force or civil war (96).

In the next several papers (nos. 17–20) Publius shifts his emphasis to the potential danger to the states of a central government continually faced with the choice of disintegration or military force. He offers examples from the histories of ancient confederations to support his point that the principle of legislation for states is at once the parent of anarchy and tyranny. And he concludes with the "important truth" that as "legislation for communities" is a "solecism in theory, so in practice it is subversive of the order and ends of civil polity, by substituting *violence* . . . in place of the mild and salutary *coertion* of the *magistracy*" (128–29).

Such is the background for Publius's comment in number 22 on a "circumstance, which crowns the defects of the confederation . . . —the want of a judiciary power." "Without courts to expound and define their true meaning and operation," says Publius, "laws are a dead letter." To courts belong the duty to ascertain the "true import" of treaties and "all other laws" "as far as respects individuals." And since "there are endless diversities" of opinion among judges regarding the meaning of laws—"we often see not only different courts, but the Judges of the same court differing from each other"—"all nations have found it necessary to establish one court paramount to the rest." This one court possesses "a general superintendence . . . and . . . settle[s] and declare[s] in the last resort, an uniform rule of civil justice" (143–44).

Publius finds one paramount court especially necessary in a federal system because he believes it generally true that "men in office naturally look up to that authority to which they owe their official existence." Without a supreme national tribunal, conflict between systems would compound the inevitable "contradictions . . . from difference of opinion" between judges of the same system; "there would be much to fear from the bias of local views and prejudices and from the interference of local regulations" with "the general laws." Such a situation obtains with respect to the construction of treaties "under the present constitution" (the Articles), and "the faith, the reputation, the peace of the whole union, are thus continually at the mercy of the prejudices, the passions, and the interests of every member of which it is composed." In exasperation Publius asks: "Is it possible that the People of America will longer consent to trust their honor, their happiness, their safety on so precarious a foundation?" (144).

From the perspective of the debates in the twentieth century over the nature, scope, and legitimacy of judicial power, one of the remarkable things about these statements from *Federalist* 22 is the ease with which Publius expresses his view that independent judges should ascertain the "true import" of the law at the same time that he takes for granted inevitable controversies concerning the meaning of the law. Publius says these controversies originate in the "endless diversities in the opinions of men" and the tendency of individual judges to favor "that authority to which they owe their official existence." This tendency is particularly significant in a federal republic, for, if we granted the proposition that explains Publius's prediction that state judges will, if permitted, tend to favor state authority, we would expect a nationalist bias among federal judges. Publius thus sees no contradiction between a willingness to entrust the nation's judges with the quest of the law's true meaning and an expectation of both the inevitable controversies over meaning and a nationalist bias among federal judges.

Further evidence that Publius admits the possibility of true meaning in the face of controversy is available wherever he himself takes a position on a matter of legal-moral controversy. *Federalist* 1 affords as telling an instance as any. In it he says Americans may be in a position to decide for the whole of mankind the possibility of establishing "good government from reflection and choice." He exhorts them to "choices . . . directed by a judicious estimate of our true interests, unperplexed and unbiased by considerations not connected with the public good." And he says these things notwithstanding his belief that an objective decision with regard to ratification "is more ardently to be wished, than seriously to be expected," since the proposed constitution "affects too many particular interests, innovates upon too many local institutions, not to involve in its discussion a variety of objects foreign to its merits, and of views, passions, and prejudices little favorable to the discovery of truth" (4).

In this statement Publius presupposes an objective view of the merits of the constitutional proposal despite his recognition of the obstacles to achieving such a view. He therefore proceeds to offer his arguments to all "in a spirit which will not disgrace the cause of truth" (6). He urges his readers to moderation, toleration, and reflection by observing that "the causes which serve to give a false bias to the judgment" are "so powerful" that we find many "wise and good men" on both sides of many important questions (4–5). He proceeds, in other words, on the assumption that a process of open-minded and self-critical striving can raise an individual and a community of individuals above parochialism and prejudice toward truth and a true understanding of the common good. Since this assumption is in the background of every other argument of *The Federalist,* every significant thought of that work evinces Publius's belief that controversy does not preclude truth.

As for Publius's reliance on a nationalist bias among federal officials, consider his theory of checks and balances, the heart of his plan for maintaining the Constitution. That theory turns on the proposition that the personal ambition of officials can coincide with their official duty, as defined by a true understanding of the common good. Publius proposes that regardless of what might motivate the performance of an official's functions, behaving as the Constitution prescribes is acting as one would act if one were moved by a devotion to the common good.

Publius can reconcile a somewhat pessimistic view of human motivation with a belief that constitutional duties serve the public interest if he can somehow harness self-serving ambition to duty. He claims to have linked ambition to duty when he says in *Federalist* 51 that "the great security against a gradual concentration of the several powers in the same department, consists in giving to those who administer each department, the necessary constitutional means and personal motives to resist encroachments of the others. . . . Ambition must be made to counteract ambition. The interest of the man must be connected with the constitutional rights of the place" (349).

Although Publius's theory of checks and balances can explain how he might rely on a nationalist bias among federal judges and others, it provides at the same time some of the institutional conditions for a leadership that is more than simply biased. The theory of checks and balances is Publius's answer to a question that appears initially in *Federalist* 47: on what are we to rely "for maintaining in practice the separation [of powers] delineated on paper?" (331). In numbers 48 through 50 he rejects several alternative answers for reasons that have important implications for the argument he will eventually make for judicial review. I review these reasons briefly.

Federalist 48 dismisses what is perhaps the most commonsensical strategy for maintaining the separation of powers: "mark with precision the boundaries of these departments in the Constitution of government." Publius's well-known response to this proposal is that "parchment barriers" will not work "against the encroaching spirit of power." Means more effective than mere words are needed to defend "the more feeble, against the more powerful members of the government." And in "our republics" it is the legislature that is "everywhere extending the sphere of its activity, and drawing all power into its impetuous vortex" (332–33).

To corroborate his fear of legislative encroachments Publius invokes the testimony of Jefferson and the Pennsylvania Council of Censors. Both criticize legislative acts that, in Jefferson's words, "should have been left to *judiciary controversy*" (335–36). Publius feels that the legislature is particularly dangerous because a legislature of the people's representatives is better at getting what it wants than an assembly of the people themselves. Unlike the latter, the former is "sufficiently numerous to feel all the passions which actuate a multitude; yet not so numerous as to be incapable of pursuing the objects of its passions" (334). Number 48 thus suggests that the nation cannot hope to maintain the constitutional arrangement of offices and powers by relying on that inadequate measure of devotion to law that is typical of representative legislatures.

From Publius's account it would appear that the legislature's responsiveness to public opinion is the cause of the legislature's tendency to disregard constitutional limitations. Publius makes his distrust of public opinion explicit in the next number of *The Federalist,* where the subject is Jefferson's proposal for a constitution for Virginia in which two branches of government could call a convention of the people to correct constitutional violations of a third branch. Although Publius criticizes this proposal, he begins by conceding that "the people are the only legitimate fountain of power" and that "the several departments being perfectly co-ordinate . . . neither of them . . . can pretend to an exclusive or superior right of settling the boundaries between their respective powers." From this it follows that some "constitutional road to the decision of the people ought to be marked out and kept open for certain great and extraordinary occasions" (339).

But Publius then offers objections to Jefferson's specific proposal that bear unflattering implications for public opinion. Frequent appeals to the people would undermine the veneration for the Constitution upon which the stability even of the "wisest and freest governments" depends. Frequent referrals of constitutional questions to the people will disturb "the public tranquility by interesting too strongly the public passions" (340). He says the people, because of their close connection with it, will usually favor the legislature over other branches. They will rarely favor a judiciary whose appointment, tenure, and functions render it "too far removed from the people to share much in their prepossessions" (341–42). And though a popular executive might cause temporary reversals of the normal pattern, the people's decision

> could never be expected to turn on the true merits of the question. It would inevitably be connected with the spirit of pre-existing parties, or of parties springing out of the question itself. It would be connected with persons of distinguished character and extensive influence in the community. It would be pronounced by the very men who had been agents in, or opponents of, the measures to which the decision would relate. The *passions* therefore not the *reason,* of the public, would sit in judgment. But it is the reason of the public alone that ought to controul and regulate the government. The passions ought to be controuled and regulated by the government. (342–43)

Of the institutions mentioned in *Federalist* 49—the electorate, the legislature, the executive, the judiciary, and the Constitution—Publius associates the judiciary and the Constitution with "the reason . . . of the public." In his thinking, public opinion more often expresses the "passions" of the public, passions that "ought to be controuled and regulated by the government." And public opinion is normally closer to legislative opinion than to executive and judicial opinion.

Open distrust of public opinion cannot be a comfortable position for a republican statesman conducting a ratification campaign for the public's approval. Publius must explain the anomaly of trusting the public with the more basic and demanding task of ratification but not the relatively routine tasks of constitutional maintenance. His explanation is that there is something special about the founding generation. Unlike the subsequent generations to whom would fall the responsibility of constitutional maintenance, the ratifying or founding generation is the generation of the Revolution. Revolutionary pressures on the founding generation bring dangers and opportunities that inspire popular confidence in patriotic leaders and repress "the passions most unfriendly to order and concord" (341). When normalcy returns, says Publius, partisan passions will reoccupy their usual position of influence with most people. In normal times, the institution least susceptible to partisan passions will be the judiciary.

What about appeals to the people not just during times of crisis, but at regular intervals? *Federalist* 50 rejects this modification of Jefferson's proposal, arguing that partisanship is likely to affect popular deliberations at any time that does not produce "either a universal alarm for the public safety, or an absolute extinction of liberty" (346). Publius then advances the familiar

proposal of *Federalist* 51: Instead of relying on the virtue of citizens and officials, the country should rely on checks and balances for maintaining the
separation of powers.

Because the defense of each branch of the government "must . . . be
made commensurate to the danger" of encroachment from the others, and
because Publius believes that in our political culture there is more to fear from
the legislature than from other branches, *Federalist* 51 deliberately weakens
the legislative branch. This is accomplished by dividing the legislature into
two houses, "render[ing] them by different modes of election and different
principles of action, as little connected with each other as their common functions and their common dependence on the society, will admit." Publius adds
that as the strength of the legislature requires that it should be weakened, "the
weakness of the executive may require . . . that it should be fortified" (350).
He mentions the veto as one of the executive's methods of defense along with
"some qualified connection between this weaker department, and the weaker
branch of the stronger department" (ibid.). *Federalist* 67 through 77 elaborate
additional ways for strengthening the executive branch.

A most revealing part of Publius's discussion of the executive is the argument in number 71 that links a four-year term of office and the executive's
"personal firmness." Publius considers such firmness essential to a plan that
would enhance the triumph of the public's real "interests" over its temporary
"inclinations" (482–83). Four paragraphs later he raises the question "whether a
duration of four years would answer the end proposed." He admits that neither four years nor "any other limited duration" will serve the purpose completely, though he seems prepared to accept the four-year term as a concession
to democratic fears of executive power (484–85).

THE CONSTITUTION OF JUDICIAL POWER

Publius's views on the presidential office and its complex relationship to public opinion are important for understanding his views on the judiciary, which
follow the papers on the presidency. As with the presidency, Publius's proposals for the judiciary aim at strengthening what would otherwise be a weak
institution. His first major move on turning to the judiciary in *Federalist* 78 is
to defend a life tenure for federal judges, and the principle he employs is the
same as his defense of the tenure for senators and presidents: duration in office
enhances an institution's independence and firmness (522, 526–29).

This principle reflects his pessimism about the deliberative and moral
qualities of public opinion. It also reflects a conception of governmental responsibility that involves the power to stand up to public opinion in the service
of ends—the common good and the protection of individual and minority

rights—whose worthiness and content are independent of public opinion. Thus Publius notes the "natural feebleness of the judiciary" and its "continual jeopardy of being overpowered, awed, or influenced by its coordinate branches." And since "nothing can contribute so much to its firmness and independence as permanence in office," permanency is an "indispensable ingredient" in the judiciary's constitution—"in great measure . . . the citadel of the public justice and the public security" (523–24).

Publius then elaborates the extent and objectives of judicial power. He recognizes a judicial "duty . . . to declare all acts contrary to the manifest tenor of the constitution void." This function is "peculiarly essential in a limited constitution" because it is the only practical way to enforce "specified exceptions to the legislative authority" (524). In an argument to which I return below, Publius conceives the judicial duty to stand up to the legislature to be an aspect of the judicial obligation to enforce the Constitution as supreme law. In a statement that closely parallels his arguments on the firmness of the Senate and the executive, Publius construes the power of judicial review as power to oppose public as well as legislative opinion.

As with the Senate and the executive, Publius seems to regard a strong and independent judiciary partly as an instrument for educating the public. An educational function for the Court seems implicit in his statement that judicial independence is "requisite to guard the constitution and the rights of individuals from the . . . ill humors [of] the people themselves . . . which, though they speedily give place to better information, and more deliberate reflection, have a tendency, in the meantime, to occasion dangerous innovations in the government, and serious oppressions of the minor party" (527).

Although Publius reassures his readers of his commitment to republican principles, including "the right of the people to alter or abolish the established constitution whenever they find it inconsistent with their happiness," he denies that there is a right to violate the Constitution "whenever a momentary inclination happens to lay hold of a majority." He denies that courts should "connive at infractions" supported by public opinion any more than infractions proceeding "wholly from the cabals of the representative body." "Until . . . some solemn and authoritative act," like amendment or revolution, has "annulled or changed the established form, it is binding upon" the people as on their representatives. "But it is easy to see that it would require an uncommon . . . fortitude in the judges to do their duty as faithful guardians of the constitution, where legislative invasions of it had been instigated by the major voice of the community" (527–28). So Publius sets out to provide the conditions for the fortitude needed for judicial fidelity to the Constitution.

"But," says Publius, "it is not with a view to infractions of the constitution only that the independence of the judges may be an essential safeguard against . . . occasional ill humors in the society." Governments will occasionally enact "unjust and impartial laws" that courts have little choice but to live with. On these occasions, "the firmness of the judicial magistracy is of vast importance in mitigating the severity, and confining the operation of such laws" (528). Publius thus defends a power of therapeutic construction—a duty to select interpretive options closest not to legislative intent but to what simple justice would require. He goes on to recognize that the very existence of this power in the courts "operates as a check upon" legislative injustice—"a circumstance calculated to have more influence upon the character of our governments, than but few may be aware of" (ibid.).

Publius concludes this part of his discussion of judicial tenure with a clear statement of approval for the way independence can help transform a weak institution into one strong enough to maintain uncompromising opposition to unconstitutional preferences of both the public and its elected representatives. Thus he holds "inflexible and uniform adherence to the rights of the constitution, and of individuals" to be "indispensable in the courts of justice." And he says that such firmness "can certainly not be expected from judges who hold their offices by a temporary commission" from the other branches. Foreclosing any suggestion of judicial deference to others, Publius says that "periodical [judicial] appointments" would mean "an improper complaisance" to the legislature, or the executive, or both, or to the people—and thus "too great a disposition to consult popularity" rather than "the constitution and the laws" (529).

A JUDICIAL MONOPOLY OF CONSTITUTIONAL INTERPRETATION?

Publius's argument for judicial review is open to a construction we may have good reason to reject, namely, that judges apply the Constitution not only for concrete controversies before the courts but also for the future decisions of other parts of the government.[15] In other words, Publius may imply that the judiciary will ultimately monopolize the general function of determining what the Constitution means. Several considerations favor such a construction of Publius's argument.

To begin with, we have seen him suggest that responsiveness to public opinion is inversely related to firmness in behalf of minority rights and those public objectives that require a long succession of measures.[16] He also says that judges must have more learning than other officials, because of the volume of precedents judges must master, and more integrity, because of their expected firmness in support of principle (348, 529–30, 543–44). He is pessimistic about the states' fidelity to "the articles of union," and he conceives judicial review as a substitute for congressional power to veto state acts (535). This last function for judicial review implies that judicial precedents can function as rules for legislative conduct and that courts can interpret the Constitution for at least some other institutions.

In *Federalist* 80 Publius treats as virtually self-evident the propriety of the grant in Article III of federal jurisdiction over federal questions: "The mere necessity of uniformity in the interpretation of the national laws decides the question. Thirteen independent courts of final jurisdiction . . . is a hydra . . . from which nothing but contradiction and confusion can proceed" (535). Since contradiction and confusion might also proceed from a plurality of interpretations among the branches of the national government, this passage adds to the case for judicial monopoly at the national level. Finally, number 81 defends the decision not to give Congress power to review judicial decisions, arguing that judicial encroachments will be rare and relatively inconsequential and that Congress's power to impeach "is alone a complete security" (545–46).

Despite Publius's arguments from judicial competence, relative fidelity to the Constitution, and the value of uniformity, other considerations suggest the wisdom of concessions to a pluralistic view of who should interpret the Constitution. Admittedly, Publius insists on judicial independence and firmness in cases before the courts (545), and this independence alone should give the judiciary's interpretations of the Constitution great strategic advantage over other interpretations as long as the courts remain within a range of alternatives others can tolerate.[17] The question, therefore, is not so much whether others can ignore judicial interpretations, but whether others have constitutional warrant to use their powers deliberately to undermine the precedential value of judicial decisions. The power to impeach cannot preclude a pluralist approach, for by referring to impeachment as a remedy for "deliberate usurpations," not mere legislative disapproval (545–46), Publius implies that the legislature has some independent power to decide what the Constitution means. Thus the advantages of national supremacy and uniformity in interpretation may not imply a judicial monopoly.

The strongest argument for a judicial monopoly of constitutional interpretation proceeds from the premise of special judicial competence. I have discussed Publius's pessimism about the public's commitment to constitutional principle in normal times. In setting the stage for his theory of checks and balances, Publius observes that the judges' tenure and method of appointment will render them less responsive to popular prejudices than the elected branches will be (341). His conception of governmental responsibility leads him to emphasize that some insulation from electoral pressure is essential to

good government, and he doubts that four years or "any other limited duration" will suffice for executives to educate the public to its true interests—a
result on which he expressly conditions his support of popular government
(425, 482, 471–72). Checks and balances, responsibility in government, and
the rest of his central themes are expressions of his basic desire to reconcile
popular government to minority rights and the common good (51, 61, 352).
And because responsiveness to the public's more immediate inclinations obscures the practical meaning of these values, Publius cannot expect the elected
branches to be as competent as the courts in discerning them.

As we have also seen, Publius does recognize that judges can usurp.
Impeachment is the remedy he proposes. He considers impeachment "the only
provision . . . which is consistent with the necessary independence of the
judicial character" (532–33; see also 545–46). Furthermore, he either ignores
or, in view of his emphasis on judicial independence, implicitly excludes the
potential check against judicial usurpation in Congress's powers to establish
the lower federal courts and regulate the appellate jurisdiction of the Supreme
Court (541, 551–52). We can therefore read him to suggest that, when the
elected branches disapprove what the judges say, their recourse is replacing
irresponsible judges with responsible ones. Such a check would still leave
constitutional interpretation largely in the hands of the courts.

On the other hand, number 78 insists that judicial independence is not the
same thing as judicial superiority over the other branches (525; see also 339).
Publius also seems to assume that judges should remain sensible of the independence of the other branches—in particular, their freedom to refuse cooperation with judicial decisions, at least in extraordinary circumstances. Thus
Publius acknowledges more than once the judiciary's dependence on the executive (523, 545). Finally, we must not forget that Publius's support for a strong
judiciary flows from his central objective of reconciling popular government
to higher standards. His famous statement in number 78 that the judiciary's
power is "neither Force nor Will, but merely judgment" (523) implies that those
standards are not of the judges' own making.

These acknowledgments of objective standards and the judiciary's partial
dependence on others opens Publius's theory to a construction that permits
others some power to decide the constitutionality of their own acts. The mere
possibility of such a construction is of course far from an argument for it, and
because I have attempted that argument elsewhere, I do not dwell on the
matter here.[18] My point is that one can read Publius to acknowledge the
possibility of judicial error and to leave room for other parts of the government to oppose judicial constructions without displacing judicial power to
interpret the Constitution in concrete cases and controversies. The broader

political influence of a judiciary thus confined might depend to a greater extent than is currently the case on the persuasiveness of the Supreme Court's arguments.[19]

PUBLIUS'S DEFENSE OF JUDICIAL REVIEW

The defense of judicial review in *Federalist* 78 consists of three propositions: (1) judicial review does not amount to judicial supremacy, (2) judicial review is rather an expression of constitutional supremacy, and (3) constitutional supremacy insures the supremacy of the people over their government.[20]

The first thing to notice about Publius's argument is the defensive character it derives from the fact that it is addressed to an audience with a democratic outlook. Publius to some extent accepts the leading assumption of his critics over the years: judicial review would be illegitimate if in fact it did lead to the supremacy of electorally unaccountable judges. He also seems to concede his opposition's view of the appearances: a power to declare the legislature's acts unconstitutional does suggest judicial supremacy. So it falls on defenders of judicial review to show that, despite the appearances, judicial review does not amount to judicial supremacy. If defenders of judicial review cannot make that showing, the appearances stand and undermine the legitimacy of judicial review.

According to Publius, then, judicial review does not amount to judicial supremacy; it is an instrument of *constitutional* supremacy that insures the people's supremacy over government. The mediating concept of this argument, the term that connects the judges and the people, is the Constitution. Judicial review implies constitutional supremacy, and constitutional supremacy implies popular supremacy.

The key presuppositions of this argument concern (1) the psychology of judges in constitutional cases, (2) the semantic qualities of constitutional language, (3) the transmission of fundamental constitutional values from one generation to the next, (4) the ontological status of those values, and (5) the Constitution's embodiment of those values. I explicate Publius's defense of judicial review by discussing each of its presuppositions. This discussion begins in this chapter and concludes in chapter 7. This chapter proposes that the classical presuppositions are at least arguable, while chapter 7 defends them as more plausible than their contraries.

The Possibility of Dutiful Judicial Decision

The leading psychological presupposition of Publius's argument is simply that it is possible for judges to decide cases in a manner that is faithful to the law. This presupposition has, of course, long been controverted by theories of judicial reasoning and psychology associated with early- to mid-twentieth-century American legal realists like Oliver Wendell Holmes, Jerome Frank, and Thurman Arnold.[21] It is controverted today by philosophical pragmatists like Stanley Fish and Richard Posner. Yet prominent modern theorists like Ronald Dworkin and Michael Moore affirm the possibility of dutiful judicial performance, even in hard cases.[22] I argue for the Dworkin-Moore position in chapter 7. There I contend that any defensible skepticism about judicial duty presupposes scientific truth and scholarly responsibility; that the latter possibilities sustain the possibility of legal-moral truth; and that striving for legal-moral truth is the most that judicial duty can require. Of immediate relevance here is a problem internal to Publius's argument: How can he assume the possibility of judicial duty in view of his skepticism about the likelihood of law-abidingness among officials generally and his awareness that judging constitutional questions is not a mechanical process free of controversy?

Publius's argument for judicial power may rely on an understanding of duty under law that much of his earlier skepticism directly undermines. Yet it would be a mistake to accuse Publius of a simple view of human psychology. He does not hold that political decision of all varieties is always governed by self-aggrandizing or parochial as opposed to public-spirited considerations.

From the beginning of his argument in *Federalist* 1, he expressly appeals to and therefore presupposes the influence both of self-interest and public spiritedness or virtue.[23] When Publius defines *faction* as either a minority or a majority adverse to the rights of others and the common good, and when he goes on to elaborate a plan for reconciling democracy to higher standards of political morality, Publius supposes that his democratic audience is sufficiently virtuous to respond appropriately to such distinctions and prospects. In *Federalist* 49, as we have seen, he does observe that normalcy diminishes virtue's influence and that it is a lingering revolutionary mindset that explains the relative virtue of his generation. But he also believes that even in normal times the method of appointing judges, their tenure, and other factors will diminish the judges' share in the people's prepossessions (341). And throughout his discussion of judicial appointment and tenure, he wants to elevate and insulate "the few then in society" who can "unite the requisite integrity with the requisite knowledge" to be federal judges (529–30).

Publius may go so far—too far, perhaps—as defending judicial review even on the assumption that, despite all constitutional precautions, some judges may still "substitute their own pleasure to the constitutional intentions of the legislature" (526). We have seen that his general approach to constitutional maintenance involves linking the personal ambitions of officials to the duties of their offices. He expects that self-interested individuals will seek to aggrandize their offices, ambition will check ambition, and in some sufficient respects, all will act not strictly from duty but to dutiful effect (349). On the premise that "men in office naturally look up to that authority to which they owe their official existence," Publius opposes leaving federal questions to state judges, who typically act "from the bias of local views and prejudices" at the expense "of the general laws" (144). And, as I argue above, he can defend a nationalist bias in federal judges if he believes, as he does, that the national government is the best of our governments for realizing the ends of government. Publius thus suggests both that judges can be motivated by duty and that ambition can maintain patterns of decision that the dutiful would favor.

The Possibility of Constitutional Meaning

When Publius contends that judicial review implies constitutional supremacy, not judicial supremacy, he also presupposes that the language of the Constitution has communicative power that is sufficient, even in hard cases, to point judges toward the law and away from those of their predilections that conflict with the law. He assumes that the Constitution has meaning independent of any particular preference and that persons of particular biases can grasp that meaning sufficiently to be guided by it. These assumptions regarding constitutional meaning are of course linked to his belief regarding the possibility of judges' doing their duty. Assumptions regarding constitutional meaning are manifest in the statements of number 78 that a "constitution is, in fact, and must be regarded by the judges as, a fundamental law," that "interpretation of the laws is the proper and peculiar province of the courts," and that in declaring "the sense of the law" judges should be disposed to exercise judgment, not will (524–28).

It may surprise us to see Publius's optimism about judicial fidelity to law coexist with his appreciation of the controversial character of constitutional meaning. But in Publius's thought, adequacy of constitutional communication does not imply the elimination of controversy in the quest for the Constitution's practical implications. Although *Federalist* 78 refers to the judicial function in terms of judgment as opposed to will, Publius does not imply that judgment is mechanical. Construed with the bulk of other things that he says on the subject, he sees judicial judgment as manifesting an attitude of thoughtful concern for principled choice among debatable alternatives—decision that is not willful in the sense of "connected with the spirit of pre-existing parties, or of parties springing out of the question itself" (342).

Thus, Publius has proposed final appellate power over federal questions in "one SUPREME TRIBUNAL" as a way of compensating for what he acknowledges to be "endless diversities" over the meaning of the law; one, final authority makes sense *because* of the endless controversy (143). Yet he refers in the same place to the "true meaning and operation" of the law as something judges must "expound and define" (ibid.), and these terms do not describe the mere conveyance of self-evident meaning. In a passage already quoted above, he uses the term *discretion* to describe judicial duty in the presence of conflicting laws, even though maxims of interpretation provide some guidance in specific kinds of conflict.[24] Publius thus distinguishes *judgment* from *will* without pretending that judicial decision can be something mechanical or free of controversy.

How should we react to this fact? Rather than attempting a theory of decision under law that accommodates the reality of discretion to a principle of constraint, many commentators assume that with no consensus on how to settle interpretive controversies, judicial decisions in hard cases can register only personal preference. Where controversy remains reasonable, they say, preference decides. Publius seems to have a different view. While he acknowledges that controversies over the meaning of laws are unavoidable, he argues that judges must exercise judgment, not will.

We need not conclude that these elements of Publius's view are incompatible and that to render Publius coherent we must embrace theories of *The Federalist* that exclude either discretion or judgment, for modern jurisprudence has produced theories of judicial decision that claim to reconcile the realities of judicial discretion with the value of decision under law.

Dworkin was the first contemporary legal theorist to propose a formidable theory for reconciling judicial discretion and the rule of law. That theory interprets normal judicial controversy over the practical meaning of abstract normative ideas as controversy over concrete "conceptions," not general "concepts." When judges proceed in good faith, the discretion involved in such controversies is a "weak discretion" that is unobjectionable for judges, not the "strong discretion" that a legislature exercises and that conflicts with our traditional sense of judgment under law. When judges exercise weak discretion, they quest in a responsible and self-critical way for the best available argument of legal principle; they try to avoid mere rationalizations of partisan preferences.[25] Thus judicial discretion need not amount to judicial willfulness.

In mentioning Dworkin's theory as a way of rationalizing part of Publius's theory, I am not trying to impose an external order on Publius's beliefs, for Dworkin claims to account for the way ordinary lawyers, judges, and citizens generally think about legal-moral controversies and decisions. Michael Moore makes a similar claim. He maintains that ordinary men and women (and academics too, despite their disclaimers) take seriously the real existence of values like justice. Moore argues that we cannot avoid concluding that the true nature of these values is important to us and that we pursue their nature not through stipulating or reporting conventional definitions or examples (which are always defeasible in light of what we take to be the real standards themselves), but through what we hope will be progressively better theories of the real ideas.[26]

Moore's "moral realist" (as opposed to "moral conventionalist") account both fits and justifies the absence in *The Federalist* of clear definitions and examples of general normative ideas. To mention two well-discussed instances,[27] *Federalist* 10 leaves undefined such notions as "the permanent and aggregate interests of the community," and *Federalist* 84 cautions against any attempt to specify a finite number of constitutional rights. Such lack of definition and specification hardly inhibits Publius's use of normative terms; he takes it perfectly for granted that his readers have an idea of what he is talking about. And his moral realist assumptions are evident throughout his work. Perhaps the clearest instance is his statement in *Federalist* 51 that "Justice is the end of government. It is the end of civil society. It ever has been and will be pursued, until it be obtained, or until liberty be lost in the pursuit."[28]

Publius's philosophic realism is evident also in the account he gives in *Federalist* 37 of one of the difficulties faced by the Constitutional Convention: the "arduous . . . task of marking the proper line" between the powers of the national and state governments. Publius treats this task as akin to the attempts by "metaphysical Philosophers" to "distinguish[ ] and define[ ], with precision" such objects as "the faculties of the mind" (e.g., "perception, judgment, desire") and the "great kingdoms of nature" ("vegetative life," "unorganized matter," "the animal empire"). Although these distinctions have eluded the "most sagacious and laborious" efforts, they remain "pregnant source[s] of ingenious disquisition and controversy" (234). And the fact that Publius accepts the value of continuing controversy and experiment in both the natural and social spheres is enough to suggest that he entertains the philosophically realist assumptions of everyday life.

Further evidence of Publius's realist assumptions appears in the immediate sequel of the passage just discussed. He says that although nature's own "delimitations are perfectly accurate" in themselves, they "appear to be otherwise only from the imperfections of the eye which surveys them." When it comes to "the institutions of man," on the other hand, "obscurity arises as well from the object itself, as from the organ by which it is contemplated." Hence, "no skill in the science of Government has yet been able to discriminate and define, with sufficient clarity, its three great provinces, the Legislative, Executive and Judiciary." Nor have the "continual and combined labors of the most enlightened Legislators and jurists" been successful "in delineating the several

objects and limits of different codes of laws and different tribunals of justice."
Although Britain has pursued these matters "more industriously" than other
nations, the "jurisdiction of her several courts . . . is not less a source of
frequent and intricate discussion" (235–36).

Compounding "the complexity of objects, and the imperfection of the
human faculties" is the "cloudy medium" of language through which "ideas"
are communicated (236–37). Yet Publius assumes the ideas themselves exist
independently of the words that we use to pick them out when he says "no
language is so copious as to supply words and phrases for every complex idea,
or so correct as not to include many equivocally denoting different ideas . . .
however accurately objects may be discriminated in themselves" (236). And
when he praises such things as recent improvements in "the science of politics"
and "most other sciences" (51), the American love of political innovation and
experiment in general (88–89), and the Convention's intellectual and moral
virtues (238–39), he takes for granted the possibility and the value of improv-
ing our knowledge of a complex reality in the face of human imperfections
and inevitable controversy.

WAS PUBLIUS A LEGAL FORMALIST?

I have more to say about Publius's philosophic assumptions in chapter 7. I
mention them here in connection with Moore and Dworkin only to show that
contemporary jurisprudence supplies us with theories that purport to account
for the everyday assumptions of ordinary men and women regarding legal and
moral phenomena. Among these assumptions is the belief that judges can
resolve constitutional controversies without imposing their preferences on the
rest of us.[29] Until we defeat these assumptions by closing philosophic options
of the kind that Moore and Dworkin make available to constitutional thought,
nothing compels us to construe Publius's distinction between judgment and
will as an unworkable legal formalism. Not only are we not compelled to
label Publius a legal formalist, doing so would require us to ignore the bulk of
what he says about language, human cognition, and judicial decision.

Nevertheless, Publius makes several statements that may suggest a formalist's opposition to judicial discretion, or a formalist's equation of discretion with willfulness. There may be three such parts of *The Federalist*. They
discuss (1) the principle of stare decisis, (2) the distinction between the letter
and the spirit of the law, and (3) the adoption of a bill of rights. I discuss them
here briefly.

Toward the conclusion of *Federalist* 78 Publius adds "a further and weighty
reason" in behalf of his proposal for judicial tenure during good behavior: life
tenure enhances judicial expertise in ever-swelling bodies of statutes and case

law. And since "strict rules and precedents" should govern judicial decision, life tenure helps to avoid "an arbitrary discretion in the courts."[30]

Commentators who would consider taking *The Federalist* seriously might have been spared the statement that judges "should be bound down by strict rules and precedents which serve to define and point out their duty in every particular case." For the unconstraining qualities of precedent and the question of where to locate the *ratio decidendi* of a case are major preoccupations of jurisprudence.[31] Friends of Publius might therefore be moved to therapeutic construction of his remarks. They might begin by noting that in the passage just quoted Publius speaks of avoiding "an arbitrary discretion." "Arbitrary" here could signify an attribute of some, not all, acts of discretion, for as we have just seen, in the same number of *The Federalist* Publius refers to "judicial discretion" approvingly and as describing the general process of deciding between conflicting laws.[32]

So while some discretion can be arbitrary and improper, some discretion is an aspect of what judges are supposed to do;[33] and we might see Publius in need of a theory of precedent that could reconcile discretion and the rule of precedent. Such theories are available, and we might look for the one that fits Publius best.[34]

But I need not attempt a saving construction. Taking Publius's statement about stare decisis in a manner most unfavorable to my position, I can simply conclude that the statement conflicts with the larger thrust of Publius's views on the human propensity to disagreement and error and the discretionary element in legal interpretation. It also conflicts with Publius's assurances of the Constitution's supremacy over the judges. Precedent may constrain individual judges and courts; it cannot constrain the judiciary as an institution. Far from reinforcing the belief in the supremacy of a constitutional document and its power to control events, a strict regime of precedent suggests that constitutional meaning is a product of the interpretive power of courts, perhaps of changing historical usage generally.[35]

Publius's friends may want to avoid imputing an unreasonable ignorance to him and to account for what he says as calculated to achieve some recognizable good—ratification of the Constitution, for example. But they cannot accept his contradictions as part of an authoritative interpretation of the Constitution. Although there are important reasons for distinguishing interpretations of the law from the law itself, as Publius does when he acknowledges that judges can err, interpretations of the law typically function as prescriptions of conduct. These interpretations must be internally consistent with respect to their implications for specific actions, since statements that indicate contradictory actions fail as prescriptions.

Accepting Publius's inconsistencies forces a quest for other normative authority (or movement from normative thought to condescending antiquarianism, descriptive history, or explanatory sociology), for it defeats the initial decision to treat *The Federalist* as a normative interpretation of the Constitution. What Publius says about conflicts among laws applies to conflicting interpretations of the law: "So far as they can by any fair construction be reconciled to each other, reason and law conspire to dictate that this should be done. Where this is impracticable, it becomes a matter of necessity to give effect to one, in exclusion of the other."[36]

As fidelity to the law requires excluding parts that are inconsistent with the dominant thrust, fidelity to Publius as framer or authoritative interpreter of the law requires a theory of his principal thrust and a willingness to exclude or to cabin irreconcilable parts. So one must exclude Publius's statement about stare decisis if one is to accept his implicit claim that he is the authoritative interpreter of the Constitution. Accepting his statement about the binding character of precedent entails rejecting his more fundamental contention that judicial review does not imply judicial supremacy and all that he says about discretion, the controversial qualities of legal interpretation, and the judicial obligation to mitigate the injustices of positive law. Fidelity to Publius as a framer is fidelity to the most praiseworthy account of what he stands for generally; it cannot mean fidelity to everything he might say.

In a second statement that suggests a mechanical approach to judicial decision, Publius responds to a charge that distinguishes the letter of the law from the spirit of the law.[37] Number 81 paraphrases the charge as follows:

> The power of construing the laws, according to the *spirit* of the constitution, will enable that [the Supreme] court to mold them into whatever shape it may think proper; especially as its decisions will not be in any manner subject to the revision or correction of the legislative body. This is as unprecedented as it is dangerous. In Britain the judicial power, in the last resort, resides in the House of Lords, which is a branch of the legislature; and this part of the British government has been imitated in the State constitutions in general.[38]

To this objection Publius replies, "there is not a syllable in the plan under consideration, which *directly* empowers the national courts to construe the laws according to the spirit of the constitution, or which gives them any greater latitude in this respect than may be claimed by the courts of every state" (543, original emphasis).

The evasive character of this response is plain, for Publius avoids explicit comment on the indirect or implied power of courts at the same time that he invites a question about such power by underscoring the courts' lack of direct power. And in the sequel he implicitly concedes that judicial decision may be guided by the spirit of the law. After his initial response to the charge in question Publius admits "the constitution ought to be the standard of construction for the laws, and that whenever there is an evident opposition, the laws ought to give place to the constitution." He adds immediately that "this doctrine [of judicial review] is not deducible from any circumstance peculiar to the plan of the convention; but from the general theory of a limited constitution; and as far as it is true, is equally applicable to most, if not to all the state governments" (ibid.). Thus does Publius himself decide a question— the propriety of judicial review—from the spirit of the law in the sense of "the general theory of a limited constitution."

Three paragraphs later Publius denies that either Parliament or the state legislatures "can rectify the exceptionable decisions of their respective courts, in any other sense than might be done by a future legislature of the United States." Notwithstanding final judicial authority in a committee of the Lords, "the theory of neither the British nor the state constitutions, authorizes the revisal of a judicial sentence by a legislative act." And the "impropriety of the thing" in all these constitutions results from "the general principles of law and reason," not from "anything in the proposed constitution, more than in either of them, by which it is forbidden" (545). Here, then, is inference from spirit in a sense similar to the first: inference from general principles of law and reason. Publius's pointed statement that the Constitution does not "*directly*" authorize construction according to the spirit should be read in this context of reiterated inference from considerations beyond the letter. The letter does not anywhere authorize inference from the spirit; it is the spirit that does so.

A third possible basis for contending that Publius holds a mechanistic view of judicial decision is one of his comments in opposition to the adoption of a bill of rights. Like the preceding attempts to quiet fears of judicial discretion, Publius's opposition to a bill of rights is at least in part a tactic for securing the Constitution's ratification. The Federalists came to realize that a bill of rights could be made consistent with their constitutional philosophy, and they promised to introduce a bill of rights after ratification.[39] But during the ratification campaign the Anti-Federalists demanded a bill of rights as a condition for ratification. The Anti-Federalists would thus have required a new constitutional convention or some other way to reopen the proposal of the Philadelphia Convention. And if some of the people most vocally demanding a bill of rights had had their way, reopening the proposed constitution would have proved its undoing (ibid.). Opposing the idea of bills of rights was one way to forestall this result.

Publius argues in *Federalist* 84 that bills of rights are both unnecessary and dangerous. They are unnecessary as limitations on government where government cannot lawfully act without affirmative grants of authority. They are dangerous because prohibiting moves that are not authorized in the first place affords "a colorable pretext to claim more than were granted. For why declare that things shall not be done which there is no power to do?"[40] Publius may even call into question the propriety of any general normative ideas as judicially enforceable limitations on governmental power. He says bills of rights are more appropriate in monarchies than in democratic republics, where electoral accountability "is a better recognition of popular rights than volumes of those aphorisms" found in several state bills of rights "and which would sound much better in a treatise of ethics than in a constitution of government" (578–79). He says no one can define "liberty of the press" in a way that "would not leave the utmost latitude for evasion; and from this, I infer, that its security, whatever fine [constitutional] declarations . . . must altogether depend on public opinion, and on the general spirit of the people and of the government" (580). He says that "the constitution is itself in every rational sense, and to every useful purpose, A BILL OF RIGHTS" (581).

Modern critics of judicial power have invoked these statements to argue for a judiciary concerned not primarily with substantive rights—especially substantive Fourteenth Amendment rights like property and privacy—but with those individual and minority rights that seem essential for the successful operation of the Constitution's system of representative democracy.[41] Reading Publius to support such a process approach to rights may be one way of reconciling *Federalist* 84 with the definition in *Federalist* 78 of a "limited constitution" in terms of judicially enforced exemptions from governmental power.[42] Another way would be to acknowledge the importance of structure but to recognize a full-fledged judicial power as an essential part of a structure whose purposes include preserving democracy and reconciling it to justice— or preserving it by reconciling it to justice.

In this connection one can observe that *Federalist* 84 need not be read as opposed to a judicially enforced bill of rights as part of a broader structure. Publius may only oppose proposals for a separate bill of rights, perhaps as a condition for ratification. He may oppose preoccupation with a bill of rights as a substitute for the other structural means for protecting rights. When he says the Constitution is itself a bill of rights he can hardly mean that the Constitution would be adequate to its purposes without a practice of judicially enforced rights, for he immediately proceeds to describe in a general way the judicially enforceable rights that the unamended constitution already recognizes. Thus, the Constitution already secures "one object of a bill of rights" when it "declare[s] and specif[ies] the political privileges of the citizens in the structure and administration of the government" (581).

The unamended constitution serves "another object of a bill of rights" by protecting "certain immunities and modes of proceeding which are relative to personal and private concerns" (ibid.). These things have "been attended to, in a variety of cases," in the unamended plan, says Publius. And as we read the unamended plan, we find support for his claim in the document's listing of such exemptions as the prohibition against titles of nobility and religious tests for office; a guarantee of the Confederation's debts; a provision for trial by jury; a narrow definition of treason; prohibitions against bills of attainder, ex post facto laws, and state impairments of contractual obligations; and a guarantee of habeas corpus. These existing provisions entitle Publius to say: "Adverting therefore to the substantial meaning of a bill of rights, it is absurd to allege that it is not to be found in the work of the convention. It may be said that it does not go far enough, though it will not be easy to make this appear; but it can with no propriety be contended that there is no such thing" (ibid.). He adds that "it certainly must be immaterial" whether the rights that a constitution contain be listed as a separate bill of rights or incorporated in the document some other way (ibid.).

When modern critics of judicial power invoke *Federalist* 84 against judicially declared substantive rights under open-ended constitutional provisions, they ignore Publius's concession that the rights of the unamended constitution "may . . . not go far enough" (ibid.). This statement further attests Publius's appreciation of the Convention's "fallibility" and the resulting need "to provide a convenient mode of rectifying their own errors, as future experience may unfold them" (232–33). Whether Publius and his generation went far enough in their declaration of rights—whether, if the reader prefers, they gave enough power to judges—must depend in part on how we answer the question whether the structure they provided proves adequate to the ends they sought. It is hard to see how Publius could reject this approach to the question consistent with his understanding of structures as means, his belief that a permanent judiciary is consistent with republicanism, his realistic view of the nature of judicial decision, and above all, his rejection of democracy unreconciled to higher standards.

Yet this conclusion may beg the question whether Publius could have approved the kind of judicial discretion that the Fourteenth and Ninth amendments require. Critics of judicial power are entitled to ask what we are to make of Publius's statement that provisions of bills of rights are typically more appropriate in treatises on ethics than in constitutions. Does Publius not imply the exclusion of moral considerations from constitutional questions? Does he not imply that constitutional decision should proceed from nonmoral judgments about the meaning of positive legal provisions or the concrete intentions, no matter how corrupt, of those whose authority the Constitution asserts? Propositions about law and intentions may be controverted, as any propositions, nonmoral as well as moral, may be. But does not Publius's belittling reference to treatises of ethics suggest that the facts in question are noncontroversial in principle and that the task of judges is essentially one of historical research and conceptual inference unmixed with normative inquiry into the best understanding of the ends of government? I have contended here that Publius's strong support of judicial independence does not presuppose that the application of constitutional provisions and other laws are matters free of controversy. But are the controversies whose propriety Publius acknowledges essentially controversies about nonmoral facts and matters of inference that do not turn on normative reflection and judgment about the ends of government?

Our question at this point is whether one can weigh all that Publius says and impute to him a theory of judicial decision that excludes moral judgments from decisions in constitutional cases. I think the answer is no. To show that the answer is no I put aside all that Publius says about judges' protecting constitutional rights and "mitigating the severity" of "unjust and partial laws" when there is no question of constitutional infraction (528). I limit the present part of my argument to issues involving not the rights of individuals and minorities but the scope of governmental powers. I can inquire into the judicial interpretation of governmental powers, because Publius's argument against a bill of rights includes the claim that the enumeration of powers renders a bill of rights unnecessary (579–80). Because he says nothing about a bill of rights to suggest that he abandons his earlier argument for judicial review, one can infer that Publius would at least support adjudication of claims involving the enumeration of powers, like the scope of the commerce power and the powers to tax and spend.

We seen that for Publius power implies governmental duty in behalf of ends that the grants of power envision. A court cannot address questions of power, therefore, without forming judgments about the ends that specific powers envision. "Not to confer in each case a degree of power, commensurate to the end, would be to violate the most obvious rules of prudence and propriety," says Publius, "and improvidently to trust the great interests of the nation to hands, which are disabled from managing them with vigour and success" (149). In addition, his own description of the ends of power goes considerably beyond what is explicit in the enumeration of powers of Article I, section 8. Number 23 says, for example, that one of the "principal purposes to be answered by union" is "the common defense of the members," and that the national government "ought to be cloathed with all the powers requisite to complete execution of its trust," presumably no matter what inherently unpredictable circumstances might require and regardless of conflicting claims of states' rights (146–47; see also 210–12).

The few separate provisions of Article I, section 8, that mention power over the armed forces, taxing and spending for national defense, and other relevant powers hardly add up to all that it would take to defend the nation in all circumstances.[43] Nor must the supremacy clause of Article VI be read to say that the national government is free to serve its conceptions of national defense without regard for the values arguably served, and served exclusively, by the states, like those jealously guarded aspects of community autonomy and aspiration that often figure in decisions of how properly to educate a community's youth. The states could, of course, exercise such powers in ways that defeat what Congress might believe to be skills and attitudes essential to the national defense, a national market, the nation's prosperity, or what Publius calls "the public peace" of the nation as a whole.[44]

When the Supreme Court sides with the national interests in conflict with the states it invokes the supremacy of "this Constitution, and the laws of the United States which shall be made in Pursuance thereof." This language invites interpreters to form a general conception of the ends envisioned by the Constitution's grant of national powers. Questions of constitutional power always proceed from such conceptions of constitutional ends, all such conceptions are controversial, and no conception can be defended in a manner free of controversy over better and worse substantive results.[45]

Thus in commentary on John Marshall's famous exposition of the general principles of federal power in *McCulloch v. Maryland*, Berns acknowledges that the issue between a strict and liberal construction of national power requires nothing less than a judicial choice between Hamiltonian and Jeffersonian conceptions of "the purpose of the Constitution or, in short, the kind of country the United States was intended to be." Berns says the options facing Marshall embraced different ways of government and even "way[s] of life," with the Hamiltonian vision requiring an industrial society and a powerful, executive-centered national government at the expense of the older, agrarian-based republicanism valued by Jefferson.[46]

Little argument remains among contemporary constitutional theorists on the proposition that controversial philosophic considerations are also present in interesting structural questions, like the bases for legislative apportionment and the extension of the franchise.[47] At the heart of his general theory of constitutional structures Publius himself says that the system of checks and balances is designed to supply "the defects of better motives,"[48] which suggests that a grasp of these better motives, even a theory of the virtues, is essential to a full understanding of his theory of checks and balances.

As Publius explains the structural differences among the branches of the national government and between the national government and the state governments, he consistently refers to the ends such differences are likely to effect. Thus the structure of the national government will, he says, mitigate the effects of majority faction on minority rights and the community's long-term interests (57). And the structure of the Senate will compensate for the House's insensitivity to world opinion and what would otherwise be the absence in the government "of a due sense of national character" (422–23).

The substantive moral dimension of structural considerations appears also when Publius interprets the executive as placed in a strategic position to act, perhaps beyond expressly granted powers, in ways that educate the public to the difference between its objective interests and its immediate inclinations (482–83). More generally, as we have seen, Publius says "Justice is the end of government," and whatever the institutional arrangement, "in a society under the forms of which the stronger . . . oppress the weaker, anarchy may as truly be said to reign as in a state of nature" (352). When the American Revolution rejected "the impious doctrine . . . that the people were made for kings," it rejected all forms of the doctrine "that the solid happiness of the people is to be sacrificed to the views of political institutions" (309).

Statements like these and the general tenor of Publius's defense of the Constitution leave little doubt that he understands institutions as means to ends. In accordance with general principles of legal construction, which he recognizes in several places, questions concerning means are resolved by considering the ends envisioned (259–60). And because Publius's formulation of the ends ("the common defense," "the public happiness," the "public peace") is as general as the language of the Preamble, judges who have a duty to decide structural questions face unavoidable philosophic choices among such competing versions of those ends as the different versions favored by Hamilton and Jefferson. If we grant that Publius's judiciary would have taken up questions involving the scope of granted powers, we are left with no principled and consistent understanding of judicial power upon which Publius might have opposed judicial consideration of questions arising under the Ninth and Fourteenth amendments.

Publius can support an independent judicial power and still agree that, ultimately, the effective enjoyment of constitutional rights will depend on public opinion. His statement that federal judges will share less in the public's prepossessions than will elected officials (341) need not mean that judges will be completely insulated. When *Federalist* 84 predicts the influence of public opinion on the judiciary, Publius implicitly recognizes that all parts of the system are vulnerable to a sustained public sentiment.[49] That the public will inevitably influence judges says nothing about the proper interpretation of constitutional standards, however. Nor does it preclude a judicial role in educating public opinion to better conceptions of constitutional meaning.

Consider the parallel cases of senatorial and executive responsibility. Publius is clear that sooner or later presidents and senators will have to answer to the electorate. Yet part of his case for the presidency and the Senate involves their capacity to transform public opinion. There is no compelling argument that Publius's constitutional philosophy excludes a leadership role for the judiciary in behalf of constitutional values. And I emphasize again that he treats those values as conceptually distinct from what the public believes them to be. These independent values are essential ingredients of his general theory of responsible government. If the effective enjoyment of constitutional rights depends on public opinion, and if the true meaning of rights is conceptually independent of public opinion, it follows that a responsible government will have to educate the public to honor those values. As Publius conceives government's responsibilities, the ultimate influence of public opinion in a constitutional democracy argues for turning public opinion around, not following wherever it might lead.

CONSTITUTIONAL SUPREMACY AS POPULAR SUPREMACY: DO AMERICANS SHARE SOME FUNDAMENTAL VALUES?

We come now to the final proposition of Publius's argument for judicial review: constitutional supremacy means the supremacy of the people. This proposition presupposes that (1) Americans share and will continue to share the same fundamental political values, (2) the specific fundamental values that Americans share are, objectively, the right values, and (3) the Constitution embodies those values.

An obvious objection to Publius's claim in *Federalist* 78 that the Constitution expresses the supremacy of the people is the statement's failure to acknowledge a distinction between the founding generation and subsequent generations—between the people who established the Constitution and those who are to live under it without enjoying the option of debating and ratifying it as a whole.[50] The founding generation itself recorded this difference in the Preamble's paternalistic reference to "our Posterity." And Publius draws a more telling distinction in *Federalist* 49 when he indicates that the patriotic atmosphere of the founding period will separate that generation from the generations of self-serving individuals who will follow when things return to business as usual (340–41). The Preamble and *Federalist* 49 make it appear that the Constitution is the will of the people of 1789 only, not the people of later generations. And the unhappy facts of American history challenge the implicit claim of *Federalist* 78 that the founding generation was unified and would be unified with subsequent generations in one set of fundamental political values. How might Publius and his modern defenders respond to this objection?

To see how Publius might impute a unity of values in the face of apparent disunity, we might consider his distinction between a people's objective interests and its factional inclinations. We have seen this distinction at work in Publius's understanding of responsible government: "When . . . the interests of the people are at variance with their inclinations," responsible "guardians of those interests" (the president, in this case) will stand up to public opinion in order to give the public "time and opportunity for more cool and sedate reflection" (482–83). How much time that might take is difficult to tell, for despite inevitable concessions to time in an electoral democracy, the real test of duty is a certain result: the convergence of inclination and objective interest or the reconciliation of majoritarianism to the real interests of the community and minority rights, both conceived independently of majority will. Shortly after defending a presidential tenure that will give the public time to reflect, Publius says: "It cannot be affirmed, that a duration of four years or any other limited duration would completely answer to the end proposed."[51] As a general principle of constitutional duty, therefore, officials should try to change public opinion for the better no matter how long it might take and even if success is never fully realized.

This principle of constitutional duty is part of the intention that Publius imputes to the people as a whole. He describes elected officials as persons whom the people have appointed the guardians of their objective interests. He says the people commonly intend the public good, acknowledge their capacity for error, and despise adulators who pretend that they always reason right about the means of promoting their common interests (482–83). One can express Publius's distinction between inclinations and interests as that between what one initially thinks one wants and what one really wants, the latter being what remains desirable after a process of deliberation and reflection. The distinction may be useful today, even as an imputation to contemporary public opinion, for one can doubt that many people would agree that elected officials should act on their raw perceptions of their constituents' immediate wishes without deliberating medium- to long-range consequences and consulting further with the public in light of those consequences.

If we grant Publius's distinction between interests and inclinations, it becomes arguable that there is a distinction between real wants and immediate or apparent wants and that what the public really wants is what will survive the transient moment. If the people really want what is in their interest, and if the test of their interest is an objective standard of some sort, then the people really want nothing less than what is objectively in their interest. Sensing this difference between what they think they want and what they really want, the people, it can be said, approve a system whose officials will tend to "withstand the temporary delusion, in order to give them time and opportunity for more cool and sedate reflection" (482). Such is Publius's view of how it is possible for popular will to take the form of constitutional government.

In light of Publius's distinction between the public's interests and inclinations, determining the public's wants turns out to be no simple matter. An observer would first try to discover just what objectively serves minority rights and the "permanent and aggregate interests of the community." This knowledge would proceed not from simple introspection or research into current public opinion but from a philosophic-scientific quest for the ends of government and their effective pursuit. That objectively better and worse grasps of such matters are possible is of course a presupposition of the distinction between interests and inclinations and its corollaries, like Publius's conception of responsible government and his definition of faction.

Because Publius calls for reconciling inclinations to interests, our observer would have to form defensible judgments concerning the public's psychological and material capacity to appreciate and act consistently with economic and social arrangements conducive to the public good. From hypotheses concerning the ends of government and the public's capacities, our observer would propose a theory of the best in us, and that theory would be a hypothesis regarding our fundamental values. Fashioning such a theory would be an exercise in political philosophy as a practical science of human affairs, knowledge of the kind Publius proudly claims when referring in *Federalist* 9 to the new "science of politics" (51).

Assuming, then, that our fundamental values would be given by a persuasive theory of the best in us, not by unreflective expressions of public sentiment, it is conceivable that one basic set of values could lie behind the conflicts that mark American history. Thus some writers argue that the republic has always been committed to the secular pursuits and democratic social relationships of an urban, industrial society devoted primarily to individual and collective economic growth—and they hypothesize such a commitment notwithstanding the continuing presence of constitutionally dysfunctional conditions like racism, religious bigotry, sexism, and economic hopelessness.[52] The persuasiveness of any such theory is not immediately relevant. The question here is how Publius might assume a single set of fundamental values in the face of historical conflicts, and the answer lies in what kind of thing fundamental values might be and how one discovers and attributes them.

Because fundamental values are given only by political theories of the best in us, the existence of fundamental values depends on the possibility of a successful theory, a possibility whose meaning is itself a theoretical matter. Although in a democracy the success of a theory would depend in part (and only in part, for objective values would be at stake) on the public's eventual recognition, Publius, as we have seen, would not demand immediate public recognition. A successful theory would depend, therefore, on its accessibility to the public, or on the capacity of the public to be brought by political leadership to accept an account of its real values or to accept the governance of those who do. The facts of historical conflict alone would not foreclose any of these possibilities.

Publius does seem to recognize that it is impossible as a practical matter to delay indefinitely government's accountability to the electorate. If government does not succeed in turning public opinion around, officials of all sorts, including judges, pay the price. Nothing guarantees success; government can fail—does fail—to make the public sensible of its true interests and its higher aspirations. But government's failure is not enough to settle questions of what the public's true interests and constitutional aspirations are. If these values exist, and Publius assumes that they do, their content is a scientific-philosophic question. Democratic opinion cannot determine the content of fundamental values because the case for popular government turns on the people's capacity to live up to fundamental values, or so Publius holds throughout. Historical conflict may therefore catch up with and defeat constitutional government without invalidating a theory of what our constitutional values are.

I emphasize that disagreement about fundamental values is hardly a sufficient basis for rejecting the proposition that a people holds a set of fundamental values, for disagreement, actual or potential, is an essential condition for that proposition. Clearly, persons who actively debate normative questions presuppose answers that are objectively correct, either by nature or at least with reference to some conventional foundation. In addition, "norms" that are unquestionable or unquestioned are behavioral regularities, not legal-moral or even prudential norms, since any form of words that would guide conduct presupposes the possibility of deliberate deviation, and awareness of that possibility is sufficient to render the form of words debatable.[53]

People knowingly hold a legal norm as such not through unquestioning adherence, but because they believe it can survive a process of reaffirmation as morally or prudentially functional, and this process presupposes the possibility of disagreement.[54] A fully rational pledge of allegiance to the Constitution therefore entails the commitment to reaffirm the Constitution for what it claims to be—an instrument of justice; and an honest commitment to reaffirm entails a willingness to reject whatever fails the test. True fidelity to the Constitution is an *aspirational* state of mind, because fidelity necessitates a multipronged striving—for better theories of justice, better interpretations of the law, and the requisite social policies—for those conditions in which reasonable persons can claim that the Constitution seems to be what it says it is. The Constitution needs those conditions because if it does not appear to be what it says it is, it loses the coherence requisite of conduct-guiding statements.[55]

That an observer of a people can sometimes interpret its conflicts as forms of reaffirmation and striving is familiar enough, both from the rhetoric of our politicians and the commentaries of scholars. The Gettysburg Address is a clear example of interpreting conflict as striving to realize fundamental national aspirations. To cite the best-known recent scholarly example, John Hart Ely has interpreted American history from the Declaration of Independence as the progressive fulfillment of an "original commitment to control by a majority of the governed."[56] Ely imputes this majoritarian aspiration to all generations of Americans despite the continuing and sometimes violent controversy over its validity and despite the constitutional text's rejection of the notion. Without debating the merits of any imputations here, I note only that scholars and politicians do make them; it is possible, and perhaps fairly so, to impute underlying values to a people despite their conflicts and in the face of historical change.

ARE OUR VALUES WORTH HOLDING?

The next presupposition of Publius's argument that constitutional supremacy insures popular supremacy concerns the normative status of the fundamental values involved. The presupposition just discussed raises a different kind of question. Although hardly unmixed with normative judgments, it can be separated from those judgments and presented as an interpretive presupposition in the sense that it imputes something to a body of people; it would identify the political aspirations of a historical community. Its dominant thrust is descriptive of a cultural fact; it is not immediately hortatory. Nor need it indicate the philosophic status of the moral beliefs that ground exhortation. *Such and so is what this people stands for,* says the first presupposition. *And that is good,* says the presupposition to which we now turn—*that is what they ought to stand for.*

That Publius's thought contains this second proposition is evident from two considerations. First, his argument for judicial review is part of a broader argument in behalf of ratification. He is not just commenting on a people and its institutions. He is proposing a course of action and thereby assuming a good to be achieved by all to whom his proposal is addressed—that is, the founding generation and its posterity. Second, Publius recognizes a right of the people to alter any form of government that proves oppressive or inadequate to their happiness. An aspect of this right of revolution is a right of one part of a single people to separate itself from other parts.

In *Federalist* 14, Publius argues that adoption of the proposed constitution is essential to the union's survival and entreats his audience to "hearken not to the unnatural voice which tells you that the people of America, knit together as they are by so many cords of affection, can no longer live together as members of the same family."[57] This passage presupposes a right to do what it prays not be done, as does *The Federalist* as a whole in submitting a proposal for the public's adoption or rejection. By proposing something based on beliefs that can, but need not, unite all generations of Americans, Publius recommends these beliefs to all.

But if Publius did affirm one set of fundamental values, was it reasonable to have done so, and what might those values have been? Although the fundamental values of a people are given by a theory of the best they are capable of—that is, the closest their collective capacities and material conditions can bring them to an ideal state of affairs—the prospect of technological, attitudinal, environmental, and other changes undermines any fixed version of a people's ultimate capacities. And as a people's capacities change, so might theories of their fundamental values. How, then, can Publius reasonably assume that one set of values ought to unite all generations of Americans? I address this question here not so much to defend any particular conception of America's fundamental values as to defend the proposition that Publius presupposes a set of fundamental values. The reasonableness of Publius's presupposition depends on whether any of his values can claim transhistorical status.

Our question recalls Publius's belief in the right of a people to revolt against their traditional political authorities and to dissolve their social relationships. Is there a value or a set of values that, whatever its precise social and institutional manifestations, plausibly characterizes the collective aspirations of Americans, yet remains open to reexamining established institutional and other commitments, including itself? If there is such a value or set of values, perhaps it has to do with *reason* in public affairs, the value to which Publius appeals in *Federalist* 1 as the object of this country's aspirations, the source of the nation's claim to international stature, and this people's greatest contribution to humankind (3–5).

The practice of reasoning in public affairs is the value that Publius invokes throughout his justification for a strong national government. He defends that government as an expression of the proposition that "it is the reason of the public alone that ought to controul and regulate the government," while "the passions ought to be controuled and regulated by the government" (343). And the connection between reason and the national character that one finds in *Federalist* 1 is echoed from Publius's praise of the nation's experimental attitude toward competing forms of government (88–89), to his call for a Senate capable of assessing policy against "the presumed or known opinion of the impartial world" (423).

Passages like these enable one to propose that the fundamental values of Publius's regime would center on the aspiration *to be and to appear reasonable* to all who might be affected by or take an interest in the regime—potentially, to all of humankind. An aspiration to be and appear reasonable is certainly a commonplace of Enlightenment liberalism and one way to label the common ground of moral realists as diverse as Plato and Locke. It is a commonplace, in other words, that would paper over mountains of philosophic and institutional problems, for it is one thing to identify a value and quite another to explicate its practical implications. Yet, in this case, there may be more to a name than merely a name, for debates over the nature and manifestations of reason in public affairs proceed through exchanges of what are called reasons, and perhaps they must proceed in this way, for it is difficult to see how one can have a reasoned rejection of reason's authority.[58]

Our philosophic quests for the nature of reason may thus throw us back upon our commonsense assumptions about reason, reasoning, and reasonable people. The empirical fact seems to be that we do start out with a general idea of what reason imports—its opposition to religious bigotry and its indifference to personalities, or so Publius suggests[59] —and of what, in principle, a reasonable resolution would be—one in which reasonable persons can concur. The circularity of thought about reason may of course indicate the limits of thought and provide thereby a reason of sorts for tolerating the existence of irrational and even antirational private associations that are free to advocate institutions and policies that would abandon the aspiration to public reasonableness. But this circularity may also suggest the irreducible, and therefore imperfectly describable, capacity that we all typically possess in some measure—our nature, so to speak. In any case, for all the unresolved problems, the value of reason can at least claim transhistorical status, it does seem to exclude some political and social possibilities, and it is certainly plausible that the authors of *The Federalist* fancied themselves committed to it.

IS THE CONSTITUTION A GOOD CONSTITUTION?

Publius's treatment of the Articles of Confederation raises one final problem for consideration in this chapter: the relationship between fundamental values and the constitutional document. Would it be reasonable for Publius to assume that the Constitution successfully embodies a commitment to reason in public affairs? In saying that the Constitution is the most authoritative voice of the people, can Publius reasonably suppose that the Constitution's institutional arrangement will continue to manifest the commitment to reason that makes his generation and the generations that follow one people, to the extent that they are and will remain one people?

If by *the Constitution* we refer to the original document and its amendments, the answer to our question must be no, for at least two obvious reasons. First, Publius acknowledges that political exigencies forced the Philadelphia Convention to depart from standards of just and even civilized conduct in several respects, like the provisions for slavery[60] and equal representation of large and small states in the Senate (416). Second, as the subject of a mere political proposal, the constitutional document is to be tested against the requirements of reason and therefore cannot itself be a simple manifestation of those requirements. Thus, it will always make sense to ask whether the document is as good as it can be. Publius submits the written constitution to the electorate as a means to the ends of government. Though ratification will make the document "supreme Law," Publius's treatment of the Articles supplies a precedent, if one is needed, applicable to all instrumental institutions. Answering criticism of the Philadelphia Convention's disregard of the original charge merely to amend the Articles of Confederation, Publius insists that "the happiness of the people of America" is simply more important than preserving that old constitution (260).

Publius also believes the "successors" of those "leaders" who first "accomplished a revolution" and subsequently "formed the design of a great Confederacy" are obligated to "improve and perpetuate" it (89). This obligation—higher in authority, it should be emphasized, than the positive law it disregards—seems connected to Publius's status as an agent of a tradition that is praiseworthy for surmounting conventional barriers to what reason recognizes in changing circumstances as arrangements conducive to "private rights and public happiness." As a proposal originally submitted to the reasoned deliberation of the public there is a sense in which the Constitution originates in an act of deliberate public choice and remains subordinate to that authority. So, as a document, the Constitution cannot fully embody reason in public affairs.

How, then, if reason remains the highest authority, can Publius believe that the Constitution is the people's most authoritative voice? If there is an answer to this question it may be that the amendable, defeasible document is not the real constitution for Publius, or at least not the heart of it. Perhaps, as I have argued, the constitutional document remains coherent and therefore authoritative only to the extent that one can fairly reaffirm its claim to be an effective instrument of justice. The essential dimension of the complex totality we call *the Constitution* would in that case be the abstract idea of popular self-government in which the reason of the public rules the passions. This general idea would entail no particular arrangement of offices and powers. And it would be unconstitutional to deny its influence on the construction of the subordinate arrangements that are the written document. Publius's thought and Publius's example lead in this direction.

In any event, this chapter has taken *The Federalist* as an important source of evidence for the framers' intent. Acknowledging that the general import of *The Federalist* is a subject of controversy, I have outlined what I believe to be a plausible interpretation. I think there is much evidence that Publius does not regard majoritarian democracy as the primary political value. He rejects government by majority faction in the clearest terms. He claims that it is his great objective to reconcile popular government *to* higher standards of political morality. He considers democracy worth saving only if he can replace unrestrained majoritarianism with self-restrained or *constitutional* democracy.

Publius's plan for achieving this objective depends in part on a strong and independent judiciary charged with the duties of judicial review and the mitigation of majoritarian injustices. Although he leaves some room for other entities to oppose judicial interpretations of the Constitution, he seems willing to err on the side of judicial power, because he connects the judiciary with the value of reason and the function of maintaining governmental responsibility to higher standards. He hardly seems willing to sacrifice or subordinate this higher constitutional responsibility to democratic responsiveness. The presuppositions of Publius's plan are still worth debating, for although they are controversial, they enjoy formidable modern support. I return to this debate in the concluding chapter.

3

THE
CONSTITUTIONAL JURISPRUDENCE
OF MARSHALL
AND
SOME OF HIS ADMIRERS

With Bork as their public philosopher, New Right constitutionalists are trapped in a position they cannot defend. Their professed legal-moral conventionalism compels them to pretend that their constitutional judgments flow from mere historical facts, like the few facts of American history that the New Right (somehow) picks out from all the rest and (somehow) elevates to the normative status of "tradition," or the "intent" of "framers" or "ratifiers," or the "understanding of the people at the time of ratification." Yet the facts in question can easily bear constructions that the New Right opposes. My treatment of *The Federalist* is a case in point; I trust it shows that not every fair-minded observer has to believe that the Warren Court offended Publius's constitutionalism.

New Right constitutionalism flows not from brute historical facts but from a populist conception or theory of democracy that is but one among several competing versions of democracy. All sides in the current debate over judicial power should have acknowledged this deeper issue—the nature of democracy—when Dworkin pointed it out in the 1970s.[1] We can get to the bottom of our questions about judicial power only by deciding whether the nation can flourish through institutions that continue to rely on "reflection and choice" about the demands of justice, or whether it is best to accept some kind of "accident and force," either violent and sudden, or relatively quiet and incremental, like the subrational forces behind "peaceful social evolution." Because writers who prescribe for the future are implicitly unwilling to accept all that the future might bring, New Right theorists who want to advise the nation should accept Dworkin's long-standing call for a fusion of moral philosophy and constitutional law.[2] They should accept, that is, the burdens of defending their position for what it is, a philosophic position[3] —one that implicitly claims to have discovered something that all who can reason aright should recognize as the best argument, at least on the current state of the evidence.[4]

Some theorists on the right have in fact accepted this responsibility. I discuss Berns above, and I comment below on Charles Fried. But, to summarize part of my quarrel with Berns, to the extent that one accepts the burdens of argument one submits reasons and thereby submits to criticism from the other side. One cannot advance an argument without implicitly stepping into a context of presupposition that elevates reason over other forms of authority. And this context is different from that which condemns philosophic activity and supposes authority to be rooted in tradition or concrete historical intentions.

The very demands of responsible argumentation thus place New Right theorists at a disadvantage. They face a Hobson's choice between paradoxical options. New Right theorists can either choose to argue for conventional authority and undermine convention in the process by implicitly subordinating convention to nature and reason, as Berns does when connecting convention to peace; or they can try to avoid that difficulty by asserting their position in an arbitrary manner, one closed to responsible argumentation. This last option cannot exist in a pure form; a modicum of reasonableness would have to attend any move recognizable as a response to the problem in question.[5] Nevertheless, a deliberate rejection of reasonableness seems implicit in a number of New Right positions, including Berns's neo-Hobbesian ridicule of the "so-called intellectuals," the postmodernist exclusion of philosophers and philosophy from public affairs,[6] a Burkean hostility toward ethical abstractions and constitutional planning,[7] and a so-called "communitarian" insistence that justice is local, particular, and therefore fundamentally arbitrary.[8]

One would think that conventionalists should be willing to embrace mere assertion (force, ultimately)[9] as an acceptable mode of persuasion, since they affect a belief that all persuasion is bottomed in premises whose authority rests entirely in the fact of their establishment. If assertion works, it works, for true conventionalists would have to believe that nothing succeeds like success.

Yet mere assertion remains more than a practical problem, even for conventionalists. For what in fact *has* succeeded with us, at least in the unselfconscious moments of our everyday lives, is a refusal to grant that mere assertion can establish legitimacy. We do not have to dwell on what the natural lawyer sees as the opposition between reason and mere assertion. Natural justice and moral reality aside, *our conventions* have it that neither ancient fact nor current might makes right. And the restraining influence of these conventions could account for the historiographic form of most New Right constitutional theory. Instead of undermining their substantive message by deploying fresh philosophic attempts to persuade others to their conceptions of democracy and judicial power—and inhibited by convention itself from open and arbitrary self-assertion and other forms of violence—New Right scholars tend to package their message as the lesson of the nation's tradition.

New Right scholarship therefore inclines toward the study and writing of history. New Right scholarship assumes and seeks to promote a context in which ancestral authority is treated as rational authority, and New Right theorists proceed within that context to repeat their version of the ancestors' story. Forced to deny that normatively relevant history can be nothing more than the handmaiden of moral philosophy, New Right scholarship tends for the most part to assume that its version of the tradition is the only plausible one. It is this assumption that I continue to oppose in this chapter.

I attempt in the preceding chapter to show that Publius is aligned against the constitutionalism of those who have most successfully appropriated his name. Chapter 3 does the same for three leading constitutionalists of the nineteenth century—John Marshall, Joseph Story, and James Bradley Thayer— figures whom the New Right has tried hardest to impress against the nondeferential style that produced decisions like *Lochner, Brown, Griswold,* and *Roe.* As before, my larger point here is that the historian's art cannot replace moral philosophy in the field of normative constitutional theory, for historians have to select and render the events and practices they offer as models for conduct. Other writers, Dworkin especially, have made the argument for moral philosophy so effectively that all sides should have accepted it as a commonplace by now.[10] But New Right theorists continue to pretend that history speaks univocally for itself and for their side. So I supplement the arguments for the primacy of moral philosophy with analyses of Marshall, Story, and Thayer that reveal a set of constitutional philosophies quite different from what the New Right has described. I show in this way that the data do not support the New Right's contention that there is something fundamentally new about the judicial activism of our era.

CHRISTOPHER WOLFE AND THE SEPARATION OF "MODERN" FROM "TRADITIONAL" JUDICIAL REVIEW

Christopher Wolfe argues that "judicial review has fundamentally changed its nature in the course of American history."[11] That history exhibits three stages to Wolfe: an early period, when judges were faithful to the Constitution; a transitional period, in which judges believed themselves faithful to the Constitution while actually making law in the form of economic due process; and finally, the present stage of judicial lawmaking, in which judges knowingly circumvent the law while pretending fidelity to it. Wolfe does not contend "that modern Supreme Court judges typically speak explicitly in their opinions about their legislative power." Such candor "is rather rare," he says, "and the typical formulation of judicial power in Supreme Court opinions tends to be in the traditional terms of *Marbury v. Madison:* the judges' power to strike down laws is rooted in their duty to enforce the Constitution." Yet Wolfe insists that judicial rhetoric notwithstanding, "If one presses a little deeper . . . into Supreme Court opinions," one finds "the clearly modern conception of judicial review as legislative power that is altogether dominant in the literature of the legal profession" (120, 242).

Wolfe is far from clear about what enables him to see through the rhetoric that is typical of judges at each of his historical stages. The judges always say they are trying to follow the law. Academic observers like Wolfe deny the judges' claim. How do we know who is right about what the judges are trying to do? Wolfe has no satisfactory answer to this question. He leaves us with no solid way to test his proposition that modern judicial review is fundamentally different from the practice we discern in the opinions of John Marshall and his nineteenth-century admirers.[12]

Wolfe does indicate that his test is not the Constitution's explicit words, for he holds that judges should be concerned for those "principles of natural justice" that are "embodied in the Constitution itself," and he agrees that these principles are embodied implicitly as well as explicitly.[13] Nor does he assume that the Constitution implies these principles in uncontroversial ways; rather, he contends that answers to constitutional questions can be correct without being persuasive to everyone, not even to every "sane person of good faith" (105; see also 38). Nor does he insist that judges confine themselves to the "specific examples that the framers had in mind as they wrote" the Constitution (57). He places greatest importance on "the principles the framers established," and he believes that judges can be faithful to these principles by asking themselves not just whether the framers *would have* applied them in unanticipated ways, but whether "after thorough reflection," the framers "*ought to have* wanted [them] employed" in certain ways (58; his emphasis).

The question for Wolfe is not whether judges must avoid controversial appeals to natural justice, it is whether judges should appeal to "those principles of natural justice" that are "*not embodied in the Constitution* in order to declare an act unconstitutional" (108, his emphasis). John Marshall and most of the tradition up to the late nineteenth century combined their appeals to natural justice "with an argument from the Constitution itself," says Wolfe (ibid.). Modern judges cite the Constitution too, but merely as rhetorical cover-up.

Initially it appears that Wolfe would show that modern judicial review differs from traditional judicial review by showing that modern judges systematically disregard what the true principles of the Constitution import for today's problems. But Wolfe is not saying that traditional judges get the Constitution right and others typically do not. His approval of Marshall depends not on showing that Marshall's interpretation of the Constitution was always right. The difference lies in the approach to constitutional interpretation taken by Marshall and the class of judges Marshall represents. Marshall's "rules of interpretation and his applications of those rules were thoroughly reasonable and cannot be dismissed as an imposition of his own political preferences . . . by those who deny the very possibility of judicial 'objectivity'"(59).

From Marshall's opinions Wolfe gathers a number of interpretive maxims to the effect that judges should look first to the Constitution's words, (usually their ordinary meaning) and with an eye to the context of utterance, the nature of the Constitution, the need to avoid absurdity and conflict, and the public purposes or intentions evident in the words themselves mostly (though not always) without such extrinsic aids as the records of the ratification debate (41–51). Wolfe knows that these "rules" defy precise specification and order of application; he acknowledges that "interpretation will depend on the cumulation of many different factors" (50). He knows interpretation is "not a mechanical process that inevitably churns out the single correct meaning of a constitutional provision" to the exclusion of "some measure of political prudence" (37). Above all, Wolfe cautions against the unreasonable expectation that his rules of interpretation are "capable of banishing conflict" (38).

Wolfe does not want to overemphasize the problem of hard cases in constitutional law, because he agrees (with Dworkin, incidentally) that the existence of "non-absurd, even plausible arguments" on both sides of a question does not preclude the possibility that "the balance of arguments may clearly favor one side." But neither will he deny the existence of hard cases, "especially as time passes and constitutional principles must be applied in circumstances the framers could not have had in mind." Nor need he deny the problem of hard cases, for "even when the rules do not provide what is arguably the single correct meaning," they still serve to limit "the range of possible legitimate interpretations" (ibid.).

From all that Wolfe says, therefore, it appears that the essential difference between traditional and modern judges is an attitude toward the Constitution.

Some judges accept the authority of the Constitution as law; they try to do their duty in an honest effort to discover what the Constitution requires of them. They do their best to avoid using the Constitution as a vehicle for imposing their partisan preferences. But when convinced that the Constitution favors a certain result, they act without deference to the public and its elected representatives. On the other side, modern judges apparently believe that the Constitution itself neither can nor should require anything of them, especially in hard cases. They may pretend an interest in interpretation. But their real interest is the pursuit of extraconstitutional principles and purposes, an interest amply accommodated by vague and general constitutional provisions.

If this is the gist of Wolfe's thesis about a fundamental change in the nature of judicial review, then his is a thesis that is all but impossible to confirm without attributing bad faith to "modern" judges. A case in point is Wolfe's assessment of the opinion for the Court by Chief Justice Hughes in the Blaisdell case, which upheld the Minnesota Mortgage Moratorium Act of 1933.[14] In the face of the contract clause of Article IV, Minnesota sought to aid distressed debtors by providing for limited delays in mortgage foreclosures. Hughes argued that the contract clause had to be construed in a manner compatible with government's obligation to meet emergencies of all kinds, economic as well as natural, and he termed the law a reasonable legislative response to the economic emergency of the Great Depression.

Wolfe notes that Hughes took "the typical modern step of distinguishing between the specific provision," the contract clause in this case, "and a more general, vaguer characterization" of the purpose behind the particular provision, here "economic stability." The effect of this "typical modern step" is to empower government "to pursue whatever economic policy it considers reasonable." And that is enough for Wolfe to conclude that Hughes was intent on lawmaking, not interpretation. "In all honesty," Wolfe appeals to his readers, was Hughes "not saying that . . . the framers embodied a principle in the Constitution that we of later days now know to be defective" and in need of judicial modification "to make it consistent with the public welfare"?[15]

Such appeals to intuition are not always successful, and Wolfe is far from proving that the framers neither would have nor "*ought to have* wanted" the contract clause applied as Hughes applied it. What the framers "*ought to have* wanted" is the interpretive question for Wolfe when he discusses John Marshall (see ibid., 58). Why a different test for Hughes? If it was proper for Marshall to construe the contract clause and other constitutional provisions in light of his controversial views regarding "the nature of a constitution and the requirements of government" (see ibid., 44–45), why was the same conduct not proper for Hughes? And if Marshall, "the greatest judicial representative" of the traditional approach (40), could construe constitutional provisions in light of his view of the ends they envisioned (see ibid., 43–51)—if he could faithfully serve the will of the people through "prudent determinations" about the "means" for securing those ends (88)—it is not easy to see what was peculiarly "modern" about Hughes's construction of the contract clause as merely one part of a greater whole and a means to some broader end like the nation's economic health.

Wolfe is aware that, from Jefferson's time to the present, both friends and critics of Marshall have often regarded his career as attesting the absence of a clear line between interpretation and lawmaking (40, 56–59). Wolfe's affirmative proof that Marshall's method was interpretive, not legislative, comes down to an attempt to shift the burden: "On the whole . . . I do not think that Marshall can be shown to have misinterpreted the Constitution" (59). Although Wolfe knows that many respectable and responsible observers have credited or accused Marshall of judicial lawmaking, he insists that no one has *shown* it.

Assume that Wolfe is correct. The question then becomes: Why not extend a similar presumption to the modern Court? Has anyone demonstrated that the framers either would or ought to have condemned Hughes's opinion in *Blaisdell,* or Peckham's opinion in *Lochner,* or Warren's in *Brown,* or Douglas's in *Griswold,* or Blackmun's in *Roe?* If not, how, on Wolfe's test, can we adjudge any of these cases demonstrable acts of judicial lawmaking? How can we look behind the rhetoric of these cases and discern a willful disregard of constitutional principle? Must the list of constitutional principles exclude commitments to private property and its fruits, including some measure of unequal bargaining power in contract negotiations? Would such a commitment be wholly unconnected with Publius's pronouncement about "the first object of government"—namely, the "protection of different and unequal faculties for acquiring property"? If not, was *Lochner* altogether wrong, and demonstrably so? Is it, moreover, impossible to see *Brown* as a contemporary manifestation of the aspiration to equal opportunity that Lincoln saw as the "leading object" of the American system?[16] And are the results in *Griswold* and *Roe* demonstrably inconsistent with liberalism's commitment to a private sphere, especially as regards matters of salient sectarian disagreement? Until Wolfe answers questions like these, he leaves his readers with a thesis that is hard to test, namely, that the judges who decided cases like *Griswold* and *Roe* did not really accept the Constitution as law that binds judicial decision.

Wolfe's failure to show a fundamental change in the conduct of judicial review reflects an unavoidable conclusion about the question he raises: Whether modern judges typically depart from an authentic American tradition of judging depends heavily on the correct answers to a formidable set of philosophic questions. But this observation has an uneven impact on the currently contending approaches to constitutional meaning. Recognizing a role for controversial philosophic assumption, and therewith philosophic inquiry, in ostensibly historical findings belies New Right constitutionalism because it defeats the possibility of finding the Constitution's meaning through some uncritical openness to historical data.

DID MARSHALL THINK FOR HIMSELF ABOUT THE CONSTITUTION?

Even if different observers could agree on how to describe the approach of a given judge or a given period of judicial practice, justifications of that approach or practice would flow from one of several conflicting theories of what the Constitution requires. Defending any approach or practice would therefore require a philosophic argument, and the very submission of such an argument would concede the appropriateness in constitutional theory of philosophic argumentation generally. What the Constitution means will thus prove inseparable from a controversial theory of what it ought to mean. And that imparts a nondeferential dimension to any and all interpretive approaches and judicial practices. The decision of a New Right jurist to defer to the judgments of the elected branches is itself more than an act of deference because it makes sense only in light of some theory of judicial duty that does not flow from an uncontroversial view of constitutional language, history, or background philosophy. An adequate description of such a jurist would have to report his philosophic decision to let others answer the basic questions about the scope of substantive governmental responsibilities and individual and minority rights.

In other words, our New Right jurist would act on his own best understanding of the Constitution's arrangement of offices—he would not let others decide the institutional question. In fact, it would be accurate to describe him as deciding the most important aspect of the questions upon which he ostensibly defers. To the extent that he lets the elected branches decide specific questions of individual rights and substantive governmental responsibilities he says, in effect, that no enforceable policy standards and rights apply against the elected branches.[17] Deference to other institutions therefore does have controversial implications for questions regarding rights and substantive responsibilities. To describe even the most deferential judge as a mere exponent of restraint would be arbitrarily to disregard an important fact of his position.

Walter Berns shows us how arbitrary such a description can be when he tries to deny the consensus view of John Marshall as perhaps the most independent and nondeferential, some say creative, judge in American constitutional history. C. Herman Pritchett characterized Marshall for a generation of American political scientists when he said Marshall had defended the notion that constitutional meaning may legitimately change over time and that, within limits, each generation may adapt the Constitution to its own needs.[18] Pritchett cited Marshall's statement that the Constitution should not be interpreted as a legal code but rather as a document "intended to endure for ages to come, and consequently, to be adopted to the various crises of human affairs."[19]

Berns correctly notes that when Marshall made this statement in *McCulloch* he was referring to Congress's power under the necessary and proper clause and therefore to flexibility in the choice of legislative means.[20] Berns adds that in *Marbury v. Madison* Marshall said that the Constitution's principles were fundamental and changeable only by constitutional amendment. Berns takes this last statement to indicate Marshall's belief that the times must be kept in tune with the Constitution, not the Constitution with the times (53). I think Berns correctly interprets Marshall's views about unchanging constitutional principles.[21] But Berns is hardly entitled to conclude that "Marshall cannot be counted among the friends of judicial power as that term is currently understood."[22]

Berns errs first in assuming that there is only one current argument for judicial power. Berns gives two friends of judicial power special mention: C. Herman Pritchett and Ronald Dworkin. Pritchett understands himself to be a modern social scientist whose view of the judicial process is strongly influenced by twentieth-century American Legal Realism.[23] Dworkin, on the other hand, is an analytic moral philosopher principally occupied in criticizing and proposing alternatives to the tenets of American Legal Realism and certain post-Realist legal-moral philosophies, some of which support judicial power on arguments that differ from Dworkin's and Pritchett's.[24] Marshall's position therefore must differ from some of the current arguments for judicial power. Yet these differences hardly mean that Marshall's jurisprudence is inconsistent with all justifications of judicial activism or that Marshall would necessarily have opposed such examples of judicial activism as *Lochner, Brown,* or *Griswold.* What Marshall might have done, or what his position admits, turns on Marshall's understanding of constitutional interpretation and the role of the federal judiciary.

Berns's account of that understanding relies heavily on Marshall's opinion in *McCulloch.* Here the Court rejected a states' rights challenge to the second national bank, holding that Congress had the power to charter the bank as a necessary and proper means to authorized national ends.[25] Marshall referred to the history of the earlier bank chartered by Congress in 1791.

Congress established the first national bank after a major constitutional debate between two members of Washington's cabinet—Alexander Hamilton, who favored a liberal construction of national powers, and Thomas Jefferson, who opposed the bank on a strict constructionist, states' rights argument. Jefferson's party later declined to renew the charter of the first bank, but economic difficulties forced the Jeffersonians to charter the second bank in 1816.[26] Marshall referred to this history in *McCulloch* and suggested that in doubtful cases of national power vis-à-vis the states the judiciary should respect the "practice of the government" and the "proceedings of the nation."[27]

Marshall, however, did not decide the question on the basis of some maxim of deference to elected officials.[28] He was not suggesting that the bank would have been found unconstitutional "were the question entirely new."[29] After his observations about the practice of the government he justified Congress's action in terms of a theory of national power. The theory Marshall elaborated was originally Hamilton's.[30] But Marshall did not merely invoke and apply this theory; he argued for it. He supplied reasons for concluding that it was better than its strict constructionist alternative.[31]

Berns himself once recognized this nondeferential character of Marshall's opinion in *McCulloch*. He wrote that Marshall's decision flowed less from the language of the necessary and proper clause—which was amenable to a Jeffersonian as well as a Hamiltonian construction—than from Marshall's choice between Hamilton's and Jefferson's visions of what the nation should become.[32] Marshall pictured what Berns called "a busy commercial society, based on trade and manufacturing, and requiring an active, aggressive, powerful government"[33] when, in a celebrated passage, he summarized his approach to questions of national power vis-à-vis the states: "Let the end be legitimate, let it be within the scope of the constitution, and all means which are appropriate, which are plainly adapted to that end, which are not prohibited, but consist with the letter and spirit of the constitution, are constitutional."[34]

Our question, then, is whether Marshall's ends-oriented approach to constitutional interpretation excludes (1) judicial consultation of first principles and (2) judges' thinking for themselves about the meaning and scope of individual and minority rights. Had Marshall not taken first principles into account, or pretended to, it might be easier to conclude that his choice in *McCulloch* was merely a matter of personal preference. But we hardly find evidence for such a conclusion in the language either of *McCulloch* or any other case. Although Marshall himself was not a political philosopher, he seems to have accepted a Lockean commercialism as a true political teaching.[35] Faulkner says: "What we now see as but one variety of politics appeared to Marshall . . . as the private law, and the public law, dictated by nature itself" (194–95). When Marshall answered questions left open by the positive law, he looked to his understanding of nature (68, 71, 194–95, 209, 217–19).

Marshall agreed with much of Berns's description of the right strategy for moving the nation toward prosperity and liberal toleration: a politics of interests in a commercial society with a strong national government (see ibid., 3–14, 20–23, 33–35, 45–64). Faulkner reports that, although a "subordinate if more noble strain of Marshall's thought" suggested attachment of the older virtues of republican citizenship, Marshall considered the American "way of life as essentially apolitical" (97–98, 134–37, 225–26). Faulkner contrasts Marshall's realism with Lincoln's "more 'idealistic' . . . redefinition of the American union in 'dedication' to the essential proposition . . . that 'all men are created equal.'" For Marshall, says Faulkner, the nation "was merely 'society,' an association of mutual exchange between men acting for their private interests" (97). Marshall would have agreed with Berns that power was indispensable to the protection of rights, and therefore he believed the scope of rights must be influenced by the needs of power. Thus Marshall saw a bill of rights as "merely recommendatory" (79).

Yet for all his agreements with Berns on the ends of liberal government and its need for power in the service of those ends, Marshall exhibited no doubt about the necessity of an independent and powerful judiciary. The essential point here is that Marshall had his own understanding of the principles of the regime, and he acted on that understanding, refusing to defer to the dominant political sentiment of his era. When *McCulloch* rejected the states' rights understanding of the Constitution's original intent, it rejected what Jefferson Powell has described as the "American political orthodoxy," an orthodoxy established with "remarkable speed" almost two decades earlier, after Jefferson's election in 1800.[36]

Marshall's view that rights must be reconciled with the needs of power did not imply the judicial abdication that would follow from Berns's theory of the Fourteenth Amendment. Marshall reserved to the federal judiciary the authority to determine the balance between powers and rights in controversies properly before the courts. As we have seen, *McCulloch* upholds the bank not on the basis of some maxim of judicial deference to the elected branches in cases where the law is not clear, but on the basis of a controversial and unpopular theory of national power. In a line Berns ignores, the *McCulloch* opinion also indicates that even less deference is due elected officials in controversial questions concerning "the great principles of liberty."[37] Marshall acted consistently with this statement, from his subpoena to Jefferson and his narrow definition of the Constitution's requirements for treason in the trial of Aaron Burr,[38] to his expansions of the contract clause to protect the rights of investors.

In what may be the best known of his opinions under the contract clause, Marshall is much closer to Dworkin than to Berns on the subject of judicial power and the alleged creation of "new rights." In *Dartmouth College v. Woodward,* Marshall held a corporate charter to be a contract whose terms the state could not change in a manner that defeated the expectations of investors.[39] Marshall was prepared to concede that corporate charters were not in the minds of the drafters of Article I, section 10. But this fact would not decide the question for Marshall:

> It is not enough to say, that this particular case was not in the mind of the Convention, when the article was framed, nor of the American people, when it was adopted. It is necessary to go farther, and to say that, had this particular case been suggested, the language would have been so varied, as to exclude it, or it would have been made a special exception. The case being within the words of the rule, must be within its operation likewise, unless there be something in the literal construction so obviously absurd, or mischievous, or repugnant to the general spirit of the instrument, as to justify those who expound the constitution in making it an exception. (644–45)

That Marshall may not have shared the substantive constitutional opinions of most modern human rights activists would hardly be surprising; he wrote before the adoption of the Civil War amendments and the political and social-psychological changes wrought by the economic advances and interdependencies of the twentieth century. It is not possible or even important to say what results Marshall would have approved today; it is his approach to constitutional interpretation that is significant.[40] Marshall was clearly active in pursuing a vision he formed independently of, and maintained in opposition to, the politically dominant opinion of his day. That vision included a judiciary dedicated to defending constitutional rights. As Faulkner describes it:

> To be more than weak pretensions the Constitution's claims to permanence obviously had to be enforced. Just as obviously, Marshall thought, the task was principally the Supreme Court's. With the nation's highest judicial authority rested the chief responsibility for preserving a republican fundamental law in a country strongly tending towards democracy. No doubt "the maintenance of the principles established in the constitution" was the duty of all departments. Still, the judiciary's role was first in dignity and authority, for it was to determine the principles to be guarded. While the Americans were to be ruled by a fundamental law, the courts alone, according to Marshall, authoritatively expounded the law's meaning and application. In effect the judiciary ruled the political departments by defining the outlines of their duties.[41]

Robert Bork once indicated some agreement with this assessment of Marshall. In a rather remarkable sketch of constitutional history published in 1984, Bork quietly pushed Marshall off the list of exemplary jurists and made James Bradley Thayer the nineteenth-century spokesman of a tradition that Bork would begin with Joseph Story and develop to include New Right theorists like himself.[42] Bork's 1990 book introduces a Marshall who is somewhat reconstructed. This new Marshall straddles a line between activism and restraint. His activist side is a constitutionally correct pursuit of a nationalist vision of state-federal relations. Bork believes Marshall was correct because he was "faithful to the document," although instead of showing how the Jeffersonian reading that Marshall opposed was unfaithful to the document, Bork merely declares that Jefferson's reading "would have made the national government unworkable."[43]

Bork finds Marshall's restraintist side in *Marbury*'s emphasis on a written constitution (24). He believes Marshall strayed from legal positivism only once, in *Fletcher v. Peck*'s reference to natural justice.[44] In reaching these conclusions Bork ignores Faulkner's research. He also ignores Marshall's opinion in *Dartmouth College* and his dissent in *Ogden v. Saunders,*[45] which made a Lockean argument for recognizing what the Court two generations hence was to call the liberty to contract, an idea Bork condemns as a leading expression of judicial lawlessness.[46]

Bork also fails to state a principled difference between a Marshallean activism in behalf of a structural aim like nationalism and a Warrenite activism in behalf of human rights. And, as we shall see, Bork cannot show that reliance on the Constitution's writtenness precludes a concern for the written aims of the Preamble and the possibility that written provisions can refer to real things whose nature can be approached only through progressively better theories.

In the end, Bork equivocates on Marshall: Even though the nation has accepted Marshall's structural objectives, "it would be a mistake for us to take Marshall's performance, in all its aspects, as a model for judges."[47] Bork thus concedes something to the characterization of Marshall that Wolfe, Berns, and a few other New Right constitutionalists have tried to deny: Marshall as a modern judge.

THAYER ON THAYER'S RULE
AND ON MARSHALL AS MODEL JURIST

A possible factor in Bork's disagreement with Wolfe and Berns about Marshall is that Wolfe and Berns see themselves as moral realists while Bork affects a moral skepticism. From the moral realist perspective of Wolfe and Berns,

Marshall's reliance on principles of Lockean or neo-Hobbesian natural right signals neither extraconstitutional lawmaking nor the imposition of Marshall's personal preferences per se. Wolfe and Berns believe that the positive law of the Constitution embodies certain principles of natural right, principles that have objective meaning and real normative status apart from anyone's personal preferences. Because they see these principles as simultaneously constitutional and valid by nature, Wolfe and Berns oppose left-liberal moral skeptics who, in modernist fashion, deny that the framers could have had a correct political philosophy and who see general constitutional provisions as empty symbols to be filled up with shifting social preferences. So Wolfe and Berns do not oppose all judges who view the law in terms of natural right; they believe that some of these judges, Marshall especially, view the Constitution correctly.

Bork, by contrast, accepts a modernist moral skepticism that locates the content of normative ideas like equal protection and due process solely in individual or collective preferences. He believes that appeals to natural justice are, in reality, appeals from the preferences embodied in the positive law to some extralegal preferences. So he lumps into one category Marshall's occasional "suggestions that courts might apply natural justice," the "defunct doctrine of economic substantive due process," and the postwar arguments "that courts had power to create and enforce against the majority will values that were not in some real sense to be found in the Constitution."[48] They all depart from what Bork calls "the reigning theory" of the constitutional tradition: "that the Constitution is law and is to be interpreted."[49] Bork then takes two or three highly selected passages from Story to the effect that judges should stick to interpreting the law and avoid legislating their abstract philosophic preferences, safely imputes the same to Kent, Cooley, and "other writers" through the first half of the twentieth century, and summarizes the whole tradition with Thayer's rule or dictum that, lest it inadvertently legislate, "a court must not overturn a statute unless . . . convinced not merely that a legislature had probably exceeded its constitutional powers but had made a clear mistake in supposing its act constitutional."[50]

Bork contrasts Thayer's approach to constitutional decision with an approach in which "moral philosophy displaces such traditional sources [of constitutional meaning] as text and history and renders them unimportant."[51] This last approach emphasizes "tendentious," "highly ideological," and "all-encompassing philosophical system[s]" from which judges impose their personal preferences on society in the form of "new rights" that most Americans do not accept. As "abstract moral argument" replaces "history, text, structure, and precedent," constitutional theory discredits "the traditional foundations upon which our constitutional liberties have always rested," thus defeating "our best chance for happiness and safety."[52]

By demoting Marshall's example and elevating Thayer's dictum, Bork proves how opposed different interpretations of the same writer can be. As I read Thayer, he did not approve a version of the tradition that leaves substantial doubt about Marshall as an example for other judges. If we understand Thayer's dictum as Thayer himself understood it, we cannot construe it apart from Thayer's strong admiration for Marshall. In addition, a close look at Thayer's dictum will not reveal a clear and uncompromising fidelity to the Constitution as a law binding the future, a law with which the times must be kept in tune, as Berns puts it. It is also doubtful that Thayer would have used his dictum to achieve the New Right's principal aim of preventing so-called new rights in constitutional cases involving the state governments. Ironically, and I trust instructively, Thayer's dictum will prove useless to the New Right if one interprets his writing as the New Right advises judges to interpret the Constitution's text.

Thayer's dictum is not without its subtleties, and my analysis of it may prove tedious at times. If so, I hope the reader will not fault me exclusively. Part of the responsibility lies with those who seek Thayer's resurrection. By falsely appropriating him, they compel a closer than usual look at his thought.

Given the modern association of Thayer's dictum with the notion that judges should exercise their power in a deferential way, it may surprise the reader to learn that Thayer considered his dictum as something of an antidote to a rigidly formalistic approach to judicial decision. He stressed that the power of the federal judiciary to apply the Constitution against state and federal officials was strictly a judicial power—that is, a power to be exercised only as and when necessary to resolve concrete controversies properly brought before the courts.[53] He understood this limitation to be a means of preventing judicial meddling in "the vast and not definable range of legislative power and choice, . . . that wide margin of considerations which address themselves only to the practical judgment of a legislative body" (9). He acknowledged that many jurists "freely recognized" the restrictive implications of this conception of judicial review. But treating judicial review as strictly judicial was not restrictive enough because it sometimes operated "in a perverted way which really . . . extend[s] the judicial function beyond its just bounds" (12).

Thayer contended it was a mistake to think judges duty bound to answer constitutional questions as if comparing "two contracts or two statutes," "declaring the true meaning of each," and "carrying into effect the Constitution as being of superior obligation." This formalistic model of decision was regrettable because it led judges to disregard the legislature's reasons for enacting a statute. Not only did rigidly formalist judges refuse to adopt the legislature's reasons, they refused even to consider them. "Instead of taking [the legislature's reasons] into account" and making allowances for them as "possible grounds of legislative action," formalist judges turned from all practical considerations toward "a pedantic and academic treatment of the constitution and the laws." Examples of "this petty method" abound, said Thayer. "And so we miss that combination of a lawyer's rigor with a statesman's breadth of view which should be found in dealing with this class of questions in constitutional law" (12–13).

Thayer then stated the basic purpose of his dictum: avoiding "narrow and literal" approaches to constitutional decision and preventing "the courts from forgetting, as Marshall said, 'it is a constitution we are expounding'" (13). To that end, said Thayer, the courts had laid down a "rule of administration," which he formulated several ways, the strongest being as follows: A court can disregard a legislative act not "merely because it is concluded upon a just and true construction the law is unconstitutional," but only "when those who have a right to make laws have not merely made a mistake, but have made a very clear one, —so clear that it is not open to rational question" (21).

In justifying this rule, Thayer reasoned that if judges had "merely and nakedly to ascertain the meaning of the text of the constitution and of the impeached Act" and to determine constitutionality "as an academic question, whether in the court's judgment the two were in conflict," judicial review "would, to be sure, be an elevated and important office, one dealing with great matters, involving large public considerations, but yet a function far simpler than it really is." And what made the function more complicated was that judges

> apply not merely their own judgment as to constitutionality, but their conclusion as to what judgment is permissible to another department which the constitution has charged with the duty of making it. This rule recognizes that, having regard to the great, complex, ever-unfolding exigencies of government, much that will seem unconstitutional to one man, or body of men, may reasonably not seem so to another; that the constitution often admits of different interpretations; that there is often a range of choice and judgement; that in such cases the constitution does not impose upon the legislature any one specific opinion, but leaves open this range of choice; and that whatever choice is rational is constitutional. (21–22)

Thayer conceded that "interpreting a writing merely to ascertain or apply its true meaning" yields "but one meaning," but he insisted that *the ultimate question is not what is the true meaning of the constitution, but whether legislation is sustainable or not"* (30; his emphasis). And whether legislation was sustainable depended on what was reasonable. In reaching their own determination of constitutionality, legislators were not obliged to conform to what the judges thought "prudent or reasonable," because the "judicial function is merely that of fixing the outer border of reasonable legislative action" (27). The reasonableness of which judges should speak, said Thayer, is that within the range of "reasonable doubt which lingers in the mind of a competent and duly instructed person who has carefully applied his faculties to the question" (29).

Before taking up the connection in Thayer's thinking between his dictum and Marshall, let us take one more look at the dictum. One can fairly describe Thayer as having recommended that judges proceed to decision in constitutional questions of a certain kind (I discuss what kind later) through three steps. First, the judge forms a "just and true construction" of what the Constitution imports for a particular statute, say a minimum-wage law covering all of the nation's nonfarm employees. Second, the judge reads the Constitution from the perspective of a legislator who believes the statute serves the nation's needs. And finally, the judge decides whether the legislator's interpretation is beyond some permissible range of options whose center is defined by that construction that is "just and true." Thus, a judge could rightly disapprove our hypothetical statute should the judge believe the Constitution requires some meaningful discrimination between interstate and intrastate commerce. The same judge, however, should approve a statute covering not all employees engaged in intrastate activities but only those with a direct and substantial effect on interstate commerce.

What is interesting about this model of judicial decision is the way in which it requires that a judge take a nonjudicial view of the challenged act. In the second step toward decision the judge abandons that perspective most associated with fidelity to law. The view at the second step considers not just law—which connotes rules that presuppose a disinclination to obey[54]—it focuses primarily on the end or desideratum furthered by the statute in question. It restores the instrumental aspect of the Constitution at the expense of the legal aspect. It compromises means that the Constitution transformed into "supreme Law" by trying to view them once again more as means than as laws.

These provisions were mere means at only one point in time: during the campaign for ratification. Ratification turned them into laws, and Thayer recognizes that, viewed as laws, they yield but one option for the concrete case, not many options. The one option is that indicated by the "just and true construction." Move away from that construction and you move toward an extralegal, purely prudential perspective, where the reasons for action refer to what is intrinsically desirable among ends and what works best among means, not what might be entailed either by our past promises, the promises made by others in our behalf, or the commands of authorities higher than our own preferences and calculations. This is the purely ends-oriented perspective of the constitution maker.

Thayer's second step would place judges in an ambiguous position between the pure practical perspective of the constitution maker and the legal perspective of those who insist on applying the one just and true construction. His second perspective is that of the policymaker who would rather reconcile the Constitution to his preferences than bend over backward to avoid violating the Constitution. This policymaker denies a sharp distinction between what is constitutional and what is not. He insists on a middle category of acts that are, in Thayer's words "not unconstitutional" or "not so clearly unconstitutional . . . as to make it the duty of the judicial department, in view of the vast interests involved in the result, to declare . . . void."[55]

Consider this middle category of acts in connection with what I am calling Thayer's third step, where he also compromised fidelity to the law as law. When speaking of a range of permissible options, Thayer had somehow to connect the just and true construction with those constructions favored by supporters of the challenged law. For if we assume that the true interpretation of the Constitution is our best view of what the Constitution requires, the outer boundaries of interpretation must be tethered to the true interpretation. A restraining connection is necessary if the setting of the outer boundaries is itself to be an interpretive act. If the setting of outer boundaries is not in some way restrained by the true interpretation, it is not restrained by our best view of the Constitution, and the outer boundaries must result from a policy choice. This choice would be one of unelected judges that limited the permissible preferences of elected officials. This policy choice could even mean total defeat for our best view of the meaning and purpose of the Constitution, that is, the meaning and purpose announced by the one true interpretation.

But how is our best view of the Constitution to limit the range of permissible interpretations? Are judges to follow Marshall's method in *McCulloch* and *Dartmouth College* and Hughes's in *Blaisdell* and take what Wolfe terms the "typical modern step" of construing particular provisions and structures in light of "more general, vaguer characterization[s]" of their purposes? In other words, is the connection between *true meaning* and *permissible range of meanings* to be found through judicial judgments of what legislative means are rationally related to the broader purposes indicated by *true meaning*?

This Marshallean approach seems the only alternative to an overtly political process in which judges decide cases primarily through comparing different policy results. Overtly political judges would bend over backward to ignore the just and true construction—and therewith their best opinion of constitutional meaning—if the policy resulting from a true construction compares unfavorably with what the legislature would achieve. Something of this sort could be present in Thayer's suggestion that a judge should permit some degree of unconstitutionality "in view of the vast interests involved in the result." Either approach—Marshall's or the overtly partisan—excludes anything that could be called passive fidelity to the law.

For this reason there is much to recommend in Bickel's view that "the upshot of Thayer's teaching" was that judicial review is "a policy-making process."[56] Bickel reads Thayer to assume with Marshall that "judicial policy choices are to be made with reference to the written Constitution" but that "construction involves hospitality to large purposes, not merely textual exegesis." Bickel comments also that Thayer, "like Marshall, excepting only in *Marbury v. Madison* . . . accepted the consequences of accommodating broad legislative purposes, viz., narrowing the scope of the Court's power to negative legislative and executive power" (ibid.).

Bickel's statement could be more sensitive to matters of importance to Marshall, like the normative differences between the powers and corresponding purposes of the national government and those of the states and the importance of at least some individual and minority rights. *Marbury* was hardly the only occasion upon which Marshall signaled judicial solicitude for individual and minority rights. I have already mentioned *Fletcher, Dartmouth College,* and the Burr case, along with *Ogden v. Saunders,* Marshall's attempt to anticipate federal protection for what the *Lochner* era was to call the "liberty to contract." Deference to elected officials was largely a matter of prudence with Marshall; it was the way of Marshall's constitutionalism when elected officials were furthering his theory of the regime's substantive ends. But prudential deference and principled deference are different things; the former is a tactic within the repertoire of the nondeferential judge.[57] Notwithstanding Thayer's reservations about some of Marshall's greatest opinions, including *Marbury,* it was the activist in Marshall that Thayer admired.

Thayer's criticism of the opinion in *Marbury* and his dictum on the conduct of judicial review are both calculated to alter and amend a practice, not to deny its legitimacy. As Thayer's dictum concedes legitimacy to some measure of judicial activism, his criticism of *Marbury* concedes that "undoubtedly it was reached in the legitimate exercise of the court's power."[58]

An analysis of Thayer on *Marbury* can begin with Thayer's treatment of Marshall's speech to the Philadelphia bar in September 1831. Thayer quotes

Marshall's statement that he and his fellow justices had "never sought to enlarge the judicial power beyond its proper bounds, nor feared to carry it to the fullest extent that duty required" (85). Thayer stressed that Marshall's statement recommends "a twofold rule," with the first part not a "whit less important than the second; nay, more; today it is the part which most requires to be emphasized." For while "great and, indeed, inestimable as are the advantages in a popular government of this conservative influence, —the power of the judiciary to disregard unconstitutional legislation . . . the exercise of it, even when unavoidable, is always attended with a serious evil, namely, that the correction of legislative mistakes comes from the outside, and the people thus lose the political experience, and the moral education and stimulus that comes from fighting the question out in the ordinary way, and correcting their own errors" (85–86).

Connected to this argument from the people's political-moral capacity was Thayer's belief that times had changed. He felt that America at the turn of the century was "a different world from Marshall's" (83). The constitutional business of the Court had increased in volume and variety far out of proportion to the distance in time from Marshall's day, and the nation faced new problems "relating to the regulation of interstate commerce," a "portentous and ever increasing flood" of Fourteenth Amendment litigation, "new problems in business, government, and police which have come in with steam and electricity, and their ten thousand applications," "the growth of corporations and of wealth, the changes of opinion on social questions, such as the relation of capital and labor," and "the recent expansions of our control over great and distant lands" (82–83).

The nation had not responded wisely to "these new circumstances," contended Thayer. While the state constitutions were "adding more and more prohibitions and restraints upon their legislatures," courts were increasingly "enter[ing] into the harvest thus provided for them with a light heart, and too promptly and easily proceed[ing] to set aside legislative acts." The legislatures were "growing accustomed to this distrust" and starting to justify it by shedding moral and constitutional restraints. The people were reacting in kind by sending "unfit persons" who pass "foolish and bad laws," which the courts then proceed to disregard. "The people are glad that these few wiser gentlemen on the bench are so ready to protect them," and judicial interference with legislation grows, contrary to the framers' expectation, and that of Marshall himself, that judicial power would be used in this way only with great delicacy and when indispensably necessary (82–84).

Looking back from the perspective of "these new circumstances," Thayer believed *Marbury* had placed too much emphasis on judicial duty. Thayer felt that experience had shown it would be better both for the nation's immediate interests and even the long-range cause of constitutionalism for the courts to err on the side of deference to elected officials, not on the side of duty to the law. But Thayer was criticizing the shortcomings of the opinion in *Marbury,* not the author's authority to reach that opinion, nor even what Thayer saw as the author's basic approach to the Constitution. For Thayer believed that Marshall himself would have read "these new circumstances" similarly and agreed to amend *Marbury* with Thayer's dictum. The foundations for Thayer's faith in Marshall were the opinions in *McCulloch,* to a lesser extent *Cohens v. Virginia* (77–78, 68–69), and Thayer's own assumption of how Marshall would have responded to better arguments for restraint than those Marshall confronted in *Marbury* (78, 80–81).

Thayer described Marshall's "great service to the country" in purely activist terms: "that of planting the national government on the broadest and strongest foundations" (72). Of the manner in which Marshall performed this service, Thayer thought it "hardly possible . . . to say too much" (46). Yet Thayer proceeded to try, and he did so in terms that highlighted the powers of mind and spirit that enabled Marshall to shape and defend against bitter public criticism that relation between the national and state governments necessary to realize the broad ends of the framers (46–48). In Thayer's praise of Marshall we find all the explanation we could want for Thayer's admiration of *McCulloch* and Bork's attempt to marginalize Marshall. Here are some of Thayer's words:

> Marshall acted on his convictions. He determined to give full effect to all the affirmative contributions of power that went to make up a great and efficient national government; and fully, also, to enforce the national restraints and prohibitions upon the States. In both cases he included not only the powers expressed in the Constitution, but those also which should be found, as time unfolded, to be fairly and clearly implied in the objects for which the federal government was established. In that long judicial life, with which Providence blessed him, and blessed his country, he was able to lay down, in a succession of cases, the fundamental considerations which fix and govern the relative functions of the nation and the States, so plainly, with such fullness, with such simplicity and strength of argument, such a candid allowance for all that was to be said upon the other side, in a tone so removed from controversial bitterness, so natural and fit for a great man addressing the "serene reason" of mankind, as to commend these things to the mind of his countrymen, and firmly to fix them in the jurisprudence of the nation; so that "when the rain descended and the floods came, and the winds blew and beat upon that house, it fell not, because it was founded upon a rock." It was Marshall's strong constitutional doctrine, explained in detail, elaborated, power-

fully argued, over and over again, with unsurpassable earnestness and force, placed permanently in our judicial records, holding its own during the long emergence of a feebler political theory, and showing itself in all its majesty when war and civil dissension came, —it was largely this that saved the country from succumbing, in the great struggle of forty years ago, and kept our political fabric from going to pieces. (47–48)

Thus did Thayer's Marshall combine "a great statesman's sagacity, a great lawyer's lucid exposition and persuasive reasoning, a great man's candor and breadth of view, and that judicial authority on the bench, allowed naturally and as of right, to a large, sweet nature, which all men loved and trusted, capable of harmonizing differences and securing the largest possible amount of cooperation among discordant associates" (48). Thayer's panegyric does not harmonize with that clear separation of judge from framer or legislator, and that perfect subordination to "the morality of the framer or the legislator . . . that continuing and self-conscious renunciation of power," that Bork terms "the morality of the jurist."[59] And one would think that Thayer's admiration of Marshall's judicial statesmanship would make the New Right uncomfortable with Thayer. As Gary McDowell has properly cautioned his New Right colleagues, "judicial statesmanship has . . . been claimed for Justice Blackmun in *Roe,* for Justice Douglas in *Griswold,* and even for Chief Justice Taney in *Dred Scott*—as well as for Chief Justice Marshall in *McCulloch.*" The line between activism of the principled and unprincipled varieties is not especially precise, says McDowell. Orienting judicial review more to the ends envisioned by constitutional provisions than to the meaning of those provisions "is but an invitation for a shrewd judge to step across" the dim line between "'noninterpretive review' and 'loose construction.'"[60]

We should not forget, however, that Thayer's extravagant admiration of Marshall does not translate into approval for all that Marshall tried to accomplish as a judge. I have already mentioned some of Thayer's criticisms of *Marbury.* Thayer also criticized Marshall's doctrines in a few other cases, including *Dartmouth College* and *Ogden v. Saunders.* Thayer classified these two cases as "concerned with the specific restraints and limitations upon the states." He did not regard this class of cases as the area of Marshall's greatest contribution, that concerning "the nature and reach of the Federal Constitution, and the general relation of the federal government to the States."[61] *McCulloch* fell into the latter class, and as much as Thayer admired Marshall's achievements there, he felt that "even so great a man as Marshall erred sometimes, from interpreting too literally and too narrowly the restraints upon the States."

The reason for these errors had partly to do with the magnitude of the task. Upon completing "his great service to the country . . . of planting the national government on the broadest and strongest foundations," Marshall considered "the reach that must also be allowed to the States, and just how the coordination of the two systems should be worked out." But, Thayer believed, this task was too complex for Marshall or anyone else of his era: "Probably no one man, no one court, no human wisdom was adequate, then, to mapping it all out." The solution had to await "time alone, and a long succession of men, after some ages of experience." Time, it seems, completed the "silence, abstinence, generality" of the Constitution, qualities of the document by which "the wisdom of those who made the Constitution . . . was mainly shown."[62]

Yet Thayer could still praise Marshall for his determination "fully . . . to enforce the national restraints and prohibitions upon the States" (47). So, it appears, Thayer could approve Marshall's approach without approving all of Marshall's results. And one reason is plain enough: Thayer employed Marshall's approach in criticizing Marshall's results. Thus, Thayer had a substantive end in view in proposing his dictum as a rule for the conduct of judicial review. That end was the improved moral capacity of the people and their elected representatives.[63]

But making Americans better citizens is hardly an expressed end of the constitutional document. Nor is it an uncontroversial implication either of constitutional history or the Constitution's background philosophy, a fact indicated by Berns's denial that constitutional ends include the improved moral capacity of the people. To prove that it is a constitutional end would therefore require acknowledging that there are in fact different theories of the Constitution's history and philosophy and dealing with those differences in the only responsible way: trying to persuade one's audience to a better theory of the Constitution's history and background, as Marshall did, and Thayer after him. And as Marshall could proceed in this effort with a faith in his own convictions and "little thought" to conventional authority, Thayer could be so confident in his own assessment of the nation's needs under "new circumstances" that he rejected important parts of Marshall's teaching (Marshall's equal or greater emphasis on judicial duty and his restrictions on the states) while remaining convinced that this "great man" would have agreed.[64]

Those who tout Thayer's authority might consider paying Thayer the same compliment he paid Marshall. A "great man" would indeed agree to what no one can successfully deny: Time can improve our knowledge of means, and means should be construed with an eye to ends. Thayer defended his dictum as a means to an end. If he was great enough to be authoritative for us, he cannot have intended by his dictum to close the minds of judges to the very kind of thinking that brought the dictum forth. Under his "new circumstances" the dictum provided a useful amendment to Marshall's greater emphasis on judicial duty. But Thayer's own method and his public praise of Marshall suggest that jurists should be prepared to revise their judgments of what best conduces to constitutional ends in changing circumstances. Thayer becomes unworthy of the authority claimed for him the moment we believe that he would treat fidelity to his dictum as an end in itself under circumstances unfavorable to the end he cited in its defense. A worthy Thayer could not have intended more than a prudential approach to his dictum.

To some extent, Thayer's ends-oriented and prudential approach to constitutional construction renders provisional and speculative any statement of Thayer's view on what the Constitution means or would mean for particular problems. Like any other "great man," as he himself seems to have understood the meaning of that term, Thayer's greater devotion to some ultimate authority (like the public interest or the Constitution) must have left him open to the possibility that his understanding of its requirements was defective. We cannot say with perfect assurance that he would have answered some new question or argument as he did some old question or argument. Nevertheless, and for what it is worth, it is doubtful that Thayer would have approved the New Right's current demand for what amounts to judicial abdication in cases involving *state* encroachments on fundamental rights.

At least two considerations support this conclusion. First, although Thayer had reservations about Marshall's conclusions in *Dartmouth College* and *Ogden v. Saunders,* he praised Marshall's approach to constitutional construction generally, and while Marshall's approach allows prudential deference (deference when and to the extent that it works to achieve constitutional ends), it precludes deference as an end in itself—it precludes a *principled* deference to state officials.

Second, Thayer carefully distinguished situations "where judges pass upon the validity of the acts of a co-ordinate department" from situations "where, as representing a government of paramount authority, they deal with acts of a department which is not co-ordinate."[65] Thayer applied his dictum to cases of conflict between the federal courts and Congress, not between the federal courts and the states. Thayer said that when a federal court considers "whether State action be or be not conformable" to the Constitution, that court "speaks as representing a paramount constitution and government," and though it be a case in which "the judiciary is still debating whether a legislature has transgressed its limit," the court has a duty "to allow to that constitution nothing less than its just and true interpretation" (36–37).

Because Thayer exempted his dictum from application to constitutional questions involving state action, one might expect that it would have no application to the bulk of modern litigation involving individual and minority rights. That expectation is strengthened by Thayer's further statement on one occasion that state action not properly reached by the federal courts under the commerce clause "may yet be controlled by them under other parts of the Constitution, as in such cases as Crandall v. Nevada . . . and Corfield v. Coryell."[66]

This most remarkable statement suggests nothing less than an authority in the federal courts under the privileges and immunities clauses of Article IV and the Fourteenth Amendment to find and apply against the states the full range of what Justice Bushrod Washington refers to in *Coryell* as "privileges and immunities which are, in their nature, fundamental; which belong, of right, to the citizens of all free governments," including many rights nowhere spelled out in the Constitution, like the right to travel, later recognized in *Crandall,* and a right to "protection by the government; the enjoyment of life and liberty, with the right to acquire and possess property of every kind, and to pursue and obtain happiness and safety; subject nevertheless to such restraints as the government may justly prescribe for the good of the whole."[67] Thayer could have cited few sources as pregnant with federal judicial authority over the states as Washington's construction of the privileges and immunities clause.[68] Add Thayer's reference to Washington to his refusal to apply his dictum in constitutional cases involving the states, and you severely compromise Thayer's usefulness to the New Right.

On the other hand, and whether Thayer realized it or not, the end served by Thayer's dictum would seem to make the dictum equally applicable in cases involving the states. For why should the mere involvement of state governments license overreaching courts to retard the people's moral development? In the absence of an obvious answer to this question, critics of the modern Court may be entitled to some of Thayer's arguments. It would depend on whether they could produce a persuasive theory of the Constitution's ends and show that present circumstances make new applications of the dictum effective means to those ends.

I have discussed elsewhere some of the difficulties of formulating and testing such a complex theory.[69] But I need not go into these matters here because, even if the people's capacity for constitutional restraint were part of a successful theory of constitutional ends (and I am convinced, with Thayer and against Berns, that it is)[70] and even if it were shown that judicial insistence on just and true constructions has in fact undermined the requisite popular attitudes (as may well have resulted from the current judicial monopoly of constitutional review [196–98]), Thayer's argument would remain a prudential and factually contingent argument. Our reconstructed Thayer would still be saying that under certain circumstances judicial deference to state officials is a means to shoring up the moral capacities of the people. Such an argument can support no principled pattern of judicial self-restraint. Under the right circumstances it can as easily support a pattern of judicial insistence on just and true constitutional constructions. In fact, it seems arbitrary to deny that a prudential self-restraint is a form of activism.[71] In any event, the New Right has some distance to go before earning the right to invoke Thayer's name.

JOSEPH STORY AND THE ACTIVIST TRADITION

If it takes a close look to expose the doubtful character of Thayer's support for the New Right, a cursory look would seem sufficient to prove the same about Joseph Story, the other nineteenth-century jurist to whom Bork gives prominent mention. Some of the most salient facts of Story's public life and thought seem initially to constitute a checklist of contraries to the tenets and assumptions of New Right constitutionalism. These facts include the consensus interpretation of Story among constitutional historians as an aggressive apologist for centralized national power and judicial supremacy in behalf of a natural right to contract and at the expense of popular democracy. But "facts" often require a second look.

In an impressive challenge to aspects of the consensus interpretation of Story, Jefferson Powell has criticized scholars who fail to give due regard to Story's understanding of himself as a republican.[72] Yet to the extent that Story's republicanism survived his private disappointments with Jacksonian democracy, Story's republicanism seemed premised, at least in his official or public references to the public and its elected agents, on what might be termed a consciously idealized or constructivist view of the public's deliberative and moral capacities. For instance, in his dissent in *Charles River Bridge,* Story said that if the Massachusetts legislature had violated the Constitution "by mistake or inadvertence, I am quite sure that it will be the last to insist on maintaining its own act. It has that stake in the Union, and in the maintenance of the constitutional rights of its own citizens which will, I trust, ever be found paramount to all local interests, feelings and prejudices; to the pride of power, and the pride of opinion."[73] This statement suggests, among other things, that the real identity of the legislature is to be found in its better self, not its transient inclinations, and therefore that judges may occasionally have a better grasp of the true wishes of a popular assembly than the assembly itself.

In light of this suggestion, we should not be surprised by Story's subsequent contention that a decision for the old bridge company would not have signaled a real restriction on the legislature's power (there being no real loss to the legislature in a court's honoring the legislature's own grant to the original franchisee) (846, 847). Nor would such a decision have undermined the public's interest in promoting innovation and progress in internal improvements (since decision for the old bridge company would have enhanced conditions of investor confidence). This kind of thinking should in turn prepare us for the convergence of natural justice and authoritative convention—that is, the convergence of what is simply right with what Americans traditionally and characteristically want. This convergence appears in Story's statement that

> however extensive the prerogatives . . . of sovereignty may theoretically be, in free governments they are universally held to be restrained within some limits. Although the sovereign power in free governments may appropriate . . . property . . . for public purposes, making compensation therefor, yet it has never been understood, at least never in our republic, that the sovereign power can take the property of A and give it to B, by the right of "eminent domain;" or that it can take it at all, except for public purposes; or that it can take it for public purposes, without . . . compensation for the sacrifice of the private property of one for the good of the whole. These limitations have been held to be fundamental axioms in free governments like ours, and have accordingly received the sanction of some of our most eminent judges and jurists.[74]

A more general statement of the same position occurs in Story's famous *Commentaries on the Constitution*. After stating that an independent judiciary is essential if the nation is to secure the administration of justice from "what best suits the opinions of the day" and remind itself that "the precepts of the law rest on eternal foundations," Story argued that the peculiar relationships of public opinion to government make a strong judiciary even more necessary in a republic than in a monarchy.[75]

Story had an argument for those who would have made judges answerable to the will of the people. First, while "the will of the people is, and ought to be, supreme . . . it is the deliberate will of the people, evinced by their solemn acts, and not the momentary ebullitions of those, who act for the majority, for a day, or a month, or a year. The Constitution is the will, the deliberate will, of the people" (473). Second, it is hardly to be assumed that elected officials always express the will of the people "in its true and legitimate sense," for that will is to be gathered from the people's "deliberate judgment, and solemn acts in ratifying the Constitution, or in amending it," not "at every successive election at the polls" (473–74). And finally, "experience" in the states and "general reasoning" both confirm that judges who "sacrifice present ease and public favor" by opposing "the passions, and politics, and prejudices of the day" can realistically hope "to earn the slow rewards of a conscientious discharge of duty; the sure, but distant, gratitude of the people; and the severe, but enlightened, award of posterity" (477–79).

Further indication of Story's uncertain support for the diminished judiciary of New Right ideology is a pattern of opinions that has led even a conservative admirer of Story like James McClellan to call Story not just a nationalist, but an extreme nationalist, and primarily a judicial nationalist.[76] Supporting McClellan's contention are Story's best-known and most controversial opinions, including *Prigg v. Pennsylvania, Swift v. Tyson,* and *Martin v. Hunter's Lessee.*[77]

Prigg is important here for what it reveals about Story's nationalism and his approach to constitutional interpretation. *Prigg* is usually regarded as "highly centralizing in its effect."[78] The case involved a Pennsylvania "personal liberty law" designed ostensibly to further congressional policy under the Fugitive Slave Act of 1793 but actually to assist fugitive slaves by erecting procedural barriers to their recapture and return.[79] Story struck down the Pennsylvania law and declared that Congress had exclusive power to enact fugitive slave legislation.[80] In thus linking Congress's power to the rights of slaveholders and defending both against antislavery sentiment in the North, Story emphasized that "the Union could not have been formed" without adoption of the fugitive slave clause (611). He emphasized also the need for a uniform national policy lest each state approach the problem of fugitives not with an eye to the interest of the nation but rather to a state's "local convenience, and local feelings" (623).

Some observers see ambiguity in *Prigg*'s nationalist thrust because the opinion served the interest of the southern states while denying that Congress could force the states to assist the return of fugitives.[81] But these considerations are hardly decisive. A congressional policy that favored the perceived interests of some of the states would still be an assertion of congressional authority. And a nationalist doctrine could leave dissenting states with some prerogatives without losing its predominantly nationalist thrust. At first blush, therefore, if not in all respects or on closer inspection, McClellan seems justified in finding *Prigg* distrustful of the states.[82] The least one can say is that the facts entitle him to that interpretation. I return to *Prigg* in connection with the question of Story's understanding of the role of moral philosophy in constitutional interpretation.

Martin v. Hunter's Lessee involved certain rights of aliens to inherit property contrary to state policy, in this case a policy of the state of Virginia. *Martin,* decided in 1816, was the second and concluding round of a battle between Virginia and the Supreme Court that began in the 1813 case of *Fairfax's Devisee v. Hunter's Lessee.* In *Fairfax* the Supreme Court reversed a decision of the Virginia Court of Appeals that had denied the right of a British subject to inherit land in Virginia. Marshall did not participate because his brother was involved in the litigation, and Story wrote for the Court. Although McClellan's admiration for Story may be second to none (McClellan ranks Story above Marshall in intellect, learning, as a defender of civil liberties, and "as a statesman and legal and political theorist" [394–312]), McClellan says that Story's opinion in *Fairfax* proceeded "in haughty disregard for Virginia law" to "defend property" by "brazenly imposing the will of the federal judiciary" upon a state (242). When the Virginia court refused the order and challenged Congress's grant of power to the Supreme Court to review state court interpretations of the federal Constitution, treaties, and laws, as Congress had done in the Judiciary Act of 1789, the case came back to the Supreme Court under the later title. Story again wrote for the Court and further infuriated the states' righters by upholding the Act.

In what is generally regarded as Story's most important opinion, *Martin* featured a comprehensive rejection of the basic states' rights argument regarding the nature of the Constitution. The Constitution, said Story, was a charter of government from the people of the entire nation, not a mere contract among sovereign states.[83] In dictum addressed as much to the coordinate branches of the national government as to the states, Story argued that the Constitution imposed an affirmative duty on Congress to establish not only a supreme court, but also "some inferior courts, in which to vest all that jurisdiction which, under the Constitution is *exclusively* vested in the United States, and of which the Supreme Court cannot take original jurisdiction" (328, 331; original emphasis). To suppose a system of federal courts left entirely to Congress's discretion would be to deny that "the object of the Constitution was to establish three great departments of government" and to suppose that Congress "under the sanction of the constitution . . . might defeat the constitution itself" (329–30). Story added that "a construction which would tend to such a result cannot be sound" (330). He believed a system of federal courts essential to the Constitution's objectives because he discerned a constitutional presumption "that state attachments, state prejudice, state jealousies, and state interests, might sometimes obstruct . . . the regular administration of justice" (347).

McClellan sees the same distrust of the states in what may be Story's most creative and ambitious opinion, that in *Swift v. Tyson,* a case of special relevance to Story's bearing on the modern controversy over the role of the judiciary. *Tyson* was overruled in 1938,[84] but had it survived it would have shared several features with a special object of New Right hostility: the application of the Bill of Rights to the states. In commenting on the similarity of the *Tyson* doctrine and the incorporation doctrine, McClellan correctly notes that it was "somewhat inconsistent" for the Court to abandon to the states the common-law property rights for which *Tyson* mandated federal protection while elevating "the liberties imbedded in the Bill of Rights to the federal courts" for application against the states.[85] I leave aside whatever problem of consistency there may be in McClellan's defending *Tyson* while criticizing the doctrine of incorporation (184, 187, 234–37, 260–63, 269–73). Of greater interest here is McClellan's observation that, through an "intense judicial nationalism" and "liberal interpretation of the Constitution," Story "inadvertently prepared the way for the leviathan state" (263, 269–73, 312).

Because he admires Story while nevertheless rejecting the nationalist part of Story's legacy, McClellan treats Story's nationalism as a mistake—a set of doctrines that "destroyed in part the ideals toward which he aimed" (272–73). McClellan believes Story erred in assuming that the judicial nationalism of *Tyson* was essential to what McClellan calls "a noble cause." That cause was "an enlightened system of jurisprudence across the North American continent, so that the free enterprise system might progress in the . . . spirit of honesty and justice," unobstructed by "poorly trained judges in the state courts" whose "parochialism" rendered them "too seldom concerned with the universal truths of ancient and common law and too often inclined to truckle to the will of a people not fully cognizant of their common law rights and duties and their legal heritage" (261).

Treating Story's judicial philosophy as a mistake is to be expected from an observer with McClellan's ideological commitments and the normative nature of the commentary in which McClellan is engaged, a point to which I return. What seems harder to justify is the attempt of Bork and other rightists to use Story's name as an authority for the cause of judicial restraint. In effect, Bork treats as a model something that McClellan treats as a mistake: Story's judicial philosophy. One of them has to be wrong about what Story's judicial philosophy was. *Tyson* indicates that McClellan is right and that a major task of historical revision faces the New Right theorist who would enlist Story to the cause of judicial restraint.

Tyson arose under the Court's appellate power over diversity cases. The case involved a technical question in New York's law of negotiable instruments. Section 34 of the Judiciary Act of 1789 had instructed federal judges to "regard as rules of decision" in diversity cases "the laws of the several states." The rule that was applicable in this case came not from a statute, but from a state court decision decided some two decades earlier by no less a jurist than James Kent, chancellor of New York. Kent had also published the rule in his renowned *Commentaries on American Law*.[86] But because of what Grant

Gilmore called careless dicta and subsequent minor confusion on the part of other New York judges, *Tyson* gave Story an opportunity to take a major step toward circumventing section 34 of the Judiciary Act.

Story could have elected what Gilmore called the "obvious solution to a simple case," namely, rescuing Kent's rule from the minor confusion surrounding it and applying it to the question (32). Instead of doing that, Story declared that section 34 applied only to "the positive statutes of the states, and the construction thereof by local tribunals" regarding matters "strictly local." Thus construed, section 34 excluded "questions of a more general nature, not at all dependent on local statutes or local usages, of a fixed and permanent operation, as, for example . . . the construction of ordinary contracts or other written instruments, and especially . . . questions of general commercial law."[87]

Story then made what amounted to a great claim of power for the federal judiciary. He declared it the duty of the Court "to express our own opinion of the true result of the commercial law upon the question," which law "may be truly declared in the language of Cicero, adopted by Lord Mansfield . . . to be not the law of a single country only, but of the commercial world."[88] Story announced the Court's decision and proceeded to defend it through an argument that discussed "the usual course of trade and business" in English and American cases and Story's own assessment of what would contribute to "the benefit and convenience of the commercial world."[89]

Gilmore called Story's performance a "masterpiece of disingenuousness" that "succeeded in reversing, for all practical purposes, the outcome of the constitutional debate which had allocated control of the substantive law to the states." The implicit message of *Tyson* was that courts could avoid a "narrow view of precedent," consider "the entire range of available scholarly literature," foreign as well as domestic, and also consult "the social and economic consequences of their decisions." In brief, said Gilmore, Story exhibited what we now call "a policy oriented approach to law," an approach that "accurately reflected the creative and innovative spirit" of early American law.[90]

Story's extrajudicial views about constitutional meaning and interpretation can easily be taken to confirm Gilmore's assessment. If Wolfe is right in distinguishing modern from traditional judges and finding a connection between a policy-making judiciary and "the typical modern step" of construing a specific constitutional provision as needed to achieve "a more general, vaguer characterization of its purpose," Story was indeed a modern judge.[91]

Story's *Commentaries* contains a chapter that purports "to ascertain . . . the true rules of interpretation applicable to the constitution."[92] The vagueness and potential contradictions in these rules limit their practical usefulness. We find, for example, that "the first and fundamental rule" is to construe the document "according to the sense of the terms, and the intention of the parties." We also find that "the intention of the law is to be gathered from the words, the context, the subject-matter, the effects and consequence, or the reason and spirit of the law" (ibid.). At one point interpreters should, when plain words fail, attend carefully to "all the circumstances, which had a tendency to produce, or to obstruct" the Constitution's ratification. Yet we are immediately cautioned that such historical materials "must be resorted to with much qualification and reserve," given the incomplete record, the difficulties of ascertaining "the private interpretation of any particular man, or body of men," the great variety of motives behind ratification, and above all, the fact that it was the text alone that was ratified (388–90).

One part of the *Commentaries* says it is a usurpation of sovereign authority to expand federal powers beyond what is enumerated on the strength of "arguments drawn from impolicy or inconvenience" (409–10). Yet other parts extol the constitutional flexibility achieved through general terms (406, 408, 412–13), a liberal approach to the construction of national powers (411–12), and even the merits of interpretations taken from "the practical exposition of the government itself," practices generated by knowledgeable and absorbed elected officials who read and debate the document "with a view to present action, in the midst of jealous interests."[93]

One theme dominates Story's treatment of interpretation, however: specific constitutional provisions as means to broader and more important ends— precisely the approach that liberals like Gilmore have praised and judicial conservatives from Jefferson to Wolfe and his New Right colleagues have excoriated as a favored trick of judges intent on evading constitutional commands. Story's emphasis on the ends of government enables Walter Murphy to conclude that by *intent* Story meant "not the intent of the draftsmen, but rather the spirit of the document as a living thing," something to be found in the document's abstract words and phrases, not in what Story saw as "conjectures" from extralegal writings.[94]

The Constitution is not a surrender of power to a monarch, said Story, it is a document "framed by the *people* for their own benefit and protection," and that means judges should be willing to impute to the people any "intention" "within the letter" of the Constitution that the judges believe advances the people's benefit.[95] For example, the Preamble refers to the common defense, and although this reference "does not enlarge the power of Congress to pass any measures, which they may deem useful for the common defense," said Story, it does help to determine the "extent, and application of the powers actually conferred." So if the "terms of a given power admit of two constructions, the one more restrictive, the other more liberal, and each of them is consistent with the words . . . and one would promote, and the other defeat the common defense, ought not the former, upon the soundest principles of interpretation to be adopted?" (445).

This example is instructive because it occurs in Story's discussion of the Preamble and it refers judges interpreting specific provisions to ends as large as those in the Preamble. By comparison, Wolfe condemns Hughes's describing the larger purpose of the contract clause as "economic stability,"[96] a narrower end than anything found in the Preamble. When discussing Hughes—not Marshall, Story, and other "traditional" judges—Wolfe says this style of interpretation leaves "the government free to pursue whatever economic policy it considers reasonable" (ibid.) Story responded to the same charge when he said that his method of interpretation fell between the impermissible extremes of leaving the Constitution "crippled and inanimate, or, on the other hand, giv[ing] it an extent and elasticity, subversive of all rational boundaries" (135). Yet the great expansion of national power under the Story-Marshall approach excuses observers who see Story's disclaimer as a continuation of the disingenuousness evident in *Tyson*. And Story's words and deeds provide Murphy with sufficient evidence for concluding that Story interpreted the document as a living thing.

STORY AND THE ROLE OF THEORY

With so much going against the New Right's use of Story's name, we need to remind ourselves why Bork attempted it in the first place. The answer lies in the New Right's opposition to a role for moral philosophy in constitutional law. In the early 1970s Ronald Dworkin criticized the leading theorists of the ideological left and right for failing to see a third theory of judicial review—that is, Dworkin's understanding of the classical theory itself. This third theory had judges striving for progressively better conceptions of general constitutional concepts and assuming responsibility for their theories. Dworkin criticized conservatives who pretended to find meaning in the framers' conceptions. He also criticized the established liberal view that judges should look for meaning in evolving community consensus. Dworkin argued that the third theory was the only successful one, both descriptively and morally. He also suggested that the judicial pursuit of better conceptions of general constitutional concepts could be furthered if our universities and law schools would train our future lawyers and judges to deal with the philosophic dimension of legal questions.[97]

Dworkin's critics saw his theory of constitutional decision as a novel and sophistic way to disclaim and to rationalize the partisan political exercise that, they felt, judicial review had become. Some saw Dworkin's call for a fusion of constitutional law and moral philosophy as a ruse for insuring that the nation's judicial elite would be as "liberal" as they believed its academic elite to be. Dworkin's critics on the right then launched a campaign against moral philosophy in constitutional inquiry. They emphasized the study of history and, in some cases, economics.

Story appeared useful in this campaign against moral philosophy because he was a consistent critic of things like "metaphysics" and the "private lucubrations of the closet, or the retired speculations of ingenious minds, intent on theory, or general views, and unused to . . . practical difficulties."[98] Bork fixes on this aspect of Story and ignores all that others have said about Story's active judicial nationalism. Bork locates and lifts from context statements of Story's support for "interpretation . . . according to the sense of the terms and intentions of the parties" and his opposition to "metaphysical refinements" and "trials of logical skill or visionary speculation" in constitutional theory.[99]

In addition, some observers, Dworkin among them, see Story's opinion in *Prigg v. Pennsylvania* as an argument that conceives judicial duty in terms of a positive law whose meaning excludes ideas of natural justice.[100] *Prigg* would thus confirm that Story opposed the fusion of constitutional law and moral philosophy for which Dworkin has called. It would confirm Story's support for what Bork regards as "the morality of the jurist," a morality that requires "abstinence from giving his own desires free play" and finding "the moral content of law" solely in the desires or "morality of the framer or the legislator."[101]

But Story's position on the role of moral-political philosophy is not as clear to all observers as it seems to be to Bork and Dworkin. We confront, to begin with, the hard fact of Story's career as a prolific jurisprude who advanced theories about the nature of the Constitution, the nature of constitutional interpretation, and the nature of a constitutional judiciary. These theories were not effortless readings from the constitutional document. They were politically controversial theories about the document and the political culture the document represented. Identifiable political factions opposed Story's theories, and they did so in a context of published judicial and extrajudicial arguments that appealed to the public's sense of how the law ought to be read.

Story was by all accounts a major participant in an era of grand constitutional theories that began at least as far back as the ratification campaign and ended with the Civil War. As we have seen, McClellan places Story above Marshall in the three categories of judge, thinker, and even judicial statesman.[102] Unlike Marshall, says McClellan, "Story spoke as a philosopher . . . boldly and skillfully . . . engraft[ing] natural law upon the fundamental law of the land . . . using the high bench as a platform to expound upon his constitutional and philosophic principles" (ibid.).

McClellan's assessment of Story's virtues can surely be controverted; and we have seen McClellan's disagreement with some of Story's achievements (309–10). But there is no way to deny the appropriateness of the assessment. Whatever the simple or comparative shortcomings of Story's thought and expression, he was a constitutional theorist of some mettle. The uncontroverted surface of Story's writings entitle McClellan to at least this much, and that is enough for my purposes here. As a constitutional theorist—good, bad, or indifferent—and as a theorist who acted on his theories in his capacity as a judge, Story could have disagreed with other theorists, as he did with Calhoun; but Story could not have intended his criticism of "metaphysics" and "abstract speculation" as critical of all philosophic activity in constitutional thought and adjudication.

Story's opinion in *Prigg v. Pennsylvania* need not confirm a contrary view; no argument compels us to take *Prigg* as a narrowly positivistic exclusion of moral considerations from constitutional interpretation. Christopher Eisgruber's study of *Prigg* starts with Story's own private assessment of the opinion as a "triumph of freedom" and proceeds through an examination of Story's extrajudicial writings to describe the opinion as Story's contribution to a result that was dictated by Story's view of natural justice: the eventual elimination of slavery itself.[103] Eisgruber finds that Story believed preserving the Union was essential to hopes for eliminating slavery, but that the Union could best be preserved through accommodating slavery until such time as the national government could eliminate it. Thus Eisgruber sees reflected in *Prigg* the Constitution's own combination of "a natural law judgment and a pragmatic concession to the exigencies of power and interest."[104]

Eisgruber finds the moral of *Prigg* to be that "any sound interpretation of the Constitution must attend both to its ethical purposes and to its practical compromises" (ibid.). To show that this was in fact Story's view, Eisgruber analyzes an article on natural law that Story authored anonymously.[105] This article outlines a "moral science" that would describe the kind of human conduct needed to bring about various conditions of human happiness. As a practical science of means, this science can be applied only through contingent practical judgments, not through inflexible doctrines. The practical quality of this moral science enables it to justify the political compromises of the Constitution.[106] Judged from such a perspective, the question behind cases like *Prigg* is whether the compromises of the Constitution can be effective means to the eventual achievement of justice.

As a practical science, says Eisgruber, Story's natural law is "not dependent on the sort of metaphysical speculation needed to prove" its own assumptions (312). These assumptions include such beliefs as the essential connection of virtue to happiness, the immortality of the soul, and divine retribution.[107]

Eisgruber insists, however, that it does not follow that Story thought philosophy had no role in constitutional interpretation. He cites Story's "recommendation that the student of law 'should addict himself to the study of philosophy, of rhetoric, of history, and of human nature.'" The philosophy recommended was that "which dwells, not in vain imaginations, and Platonic dreams; but which stoops to life, and enlarges the boundaries of human happiness."[108] Eisgruber says that Story had in mind "political philosophy as practiced by Aristotle, Cicero, and the writers of *The Federalist* rather than that practiced by Plato, Sir Thomas More, and David Hume." The importance of these studies to Story, says Eisgruber, lay not in their theoretical systems or speculative insights, but rather in their power to "sharpen the student's practical faculties for distinguishing good from bad" (313).

One need not accept all of Eisgruber's conclusions to agree he has shown that there is no reason to believe Story would have excluded all forms of moral philosophy from constitutional interpretation. Eisgruber aptly criticizes Bork for overlooking the possibility "that common sense, as Story conceives it, may depend for refinement upon a certain kind of political philosophy" (314 n. 104). He is also right in charging that by ignoring parts of Story's thought, "Bork makes Story appear to be naive about the difficulties of interpreting the Constitution." The parts in question include Story's distinction between different kinds of philosophy and Story's appreciation that the generalities of constitutional language leave much room for debate. Finally, Eisgruber shows that, from Story's perspective at least, Bork poses a false choice between constitutional interpretation and political philosophy, "rather than . . . a choice between forms of philosophy" (ibid.).

STORY AND THE
NATURE OF THEORY IN CONSTITUTIONAL LAW

I conclude this chapter with a comment on Eisgruber's suggestions that philosophic studies have more to do with sharpening the student's faculties for moral inquiry than with imparting moral doctrine and that common sense may need philosophy for "refinement." Eisgruber's imputations to Story seem plausible because they fit much of what Story wrote about the Constitution as a judge and as a scholar. Eisgruber's account certainly explains more of Story's statements and actions than anything Bork or Dworkin have offered. We have also seen some evidence in Story's own discussion of interpretation that he would have approved an interpretation that makes sense of his own writings in light of some public-spirited purpose. As between Eisgruber's interpretation and Bork's, Eisgruber's will be far more useful to those who want reasons for preserving Story's authority.

Eisgruber suggests, then, that the philosophy Story had in mind was more a matter of method than of doctrine and that the method was simply that of refining the beliefs characteristic of common sense—the beliefs, that is, of ordinary men and women who would not admit that they live their lives separated from a concern for things like justice, the general welfare, the blessings of liberty, and so on. I am not talking about interests in institutional things like a more perfect union; a purely formal, nonsubstantive end like that cannot be an end in itself to people interested in the other ends I have enumerated. Recall Publius's statement that he would abandon the Union if it should prove inadequate to the nation's happiness. Nor am I talking about a perfectly unified or coherent set of beliefs about the world, for that is a goal of full-time philosophers, and although the connection, if any, between the wants of full-time philosophers and the philosophic needs of the rest of us may be one of the issues here, my focus is the latter.

If we want a fully responsible approach to constitutional interpretation, an approach that avoids otherworldly doctrines and remains consistent with common sense, we need an approach that can accommodate the undeniable facts of our ordinary experience with general constitutional terms like justice, liberty, equal protection, due process, and the like.

The essential facts of our experience are as follows. On the one hand, all concrete definitions, conceptions, and applications of general ideas like justice seem debatable. On the other hand, in debating the meaning of these ideas, we presuppose that one side can be closer to the truth and therefore that there is a truth to get closer to. If these propositions describe what most of us believe, as seems empirically true for everyday or nonacademic settings, especially in liberal political cultures, then a commonsense or nonmetaphysical approach would have to accommodate them both. A commonsense approach would therefore have to take *justice,* say, to refer to some relationship other than the debatable definitions, conceptions, and examples that try to capture the meaning of justice. A commonsense approach could not accept any academic doctrine that denies the existence of the thing of which the conceptions, definitions, and examples are ordinarily thought to be conceptions, definitions, and examples. Nor could the commonsense approach take any definition, conception, or example as anything other than a defeasible version of the thing in question.

A commonsense concern for justice itself, therefore, would involve a continually self-critical effort to improve one's own views of justice—a continually self-critical concern for becoming more just. A commonsense concern for justice would exclude attitudes like dogmatism and complacency and self-righteousness. For the concern would be for justice itself, not this or that version of justice, and we would know that any given version of justice, including our own, could always prove to be unjust despite our strongest convictions or commitments.

So, if we took the Constitution at its word—it refers to justice, not "justice," or justice so-called, or this or that version of justice, or anything less than justice itself, due process itself, equal protection itself—and if we accepted it as law—that is, as something binding in spite of our disinclinations to obey—then we would accept a role for self-critical striving to improve our understanding of what the Constitution actually says. We would therefore accept a role for philosophy in constitutional interpretation. Not philosophy as a settled body of conclusions to be applied in the doctrinaire manner of ideologues, but philosophy as an attitude and a method—an attitude of self-critical striving for truths that never fully reveal themselves and a method that cannot be much more than the refined give-and-take of ordinary conversation lest it itself become another form of willfulness and dogma. The model for this conception of philosophy is, of course, Socrates, who had the passion, the strength, and the intellect to resist the comforts of dogma and confront the knowing-yet-not-knowing that seems constitutive of the human condition.

The model can hardly be Bork or any other thinker who denies that there can be any truths about justice above and beyond our conventional beliefs. As we began to see in chapter 1 and as I argue in the remainder of this book, Borkean conventionalism proceeds either from a neo-Hobbesian vision that grows progressively blind to itself or from a purely academic denial of the presuppositions of common sense. In either case, Bork's approach seems precisely the kind of "metaphysics" that Story opposed in constitutional thought. I do not know whether Story would have agreed, for Story does criticize Plato and thereby perhaps all Socratics to some extent, and Jefferson Powell claims to have found a strong conventionalist streak in Story.[109] But there is more involved here than a question of intellectual biography. My contention is that Story would have to make some concessions to a Socratic attitude and approach to constitutional meaning in order to save his words and his career from incoherence. I contend further that those who treat Story as some sort of authority assume that he is at least coherent.

Although Socratic attitudes and methods ought not to be confused with what we might believe to have been Socrates's substantive political doctrines, the former inevitably evoke the latter and stoke fears of the kind that motivated Story's hostility to otherworldly speculation. Mention of Socrates may also evoke the moral of his death—a different moral for different people—especially as some erstwhile liberal segments of the university lapse into race- and sex-based forms of antireason not dissimilar to the antireason and ethnocommunitarianism of the New Right.[110]

So resentment of philosopher kings on one side of the current debate and on the other side fears of garrotes made of twisted yellow ribbons may render a Socratic attitude in constitutional inquiry both hateful and dangerous. In the remaining chapters of this book I say more against various forms of metaphysical and epistemological skepticism and in defense of a role for moral philosophy. But the figure of Socrates evokes above all else the ancient distrust of philosophy as an undemocratic force, and I should say something in response to that fear before I move on.

Michael Walzer once rejected Dworkin's call for a fusion of constitutional law and moral philosophy because of the gap between the prejudicial or conventional grounds of democratic deliberation and the truth beyond convention for which the philosopher strives.[111] But Walzer could have understood ordinary prejudice a little better. Ordinary (i.e., nonacademic) men and women assume a difference between truth and convention, and precisely because of this assumption their prejudices are not completely closed to a concern for truth.[112] Prejudice is not altogether closed to truth, because a prejudiced commitment is still a commitment to some proposition's truth. Prejudice is to some extent open to truth because prejudice claims truth, and if tyrannies distinguish themselves by refusing to test such claims, liberal democracies assert a different distinction.

Walzer, speaking as a philosopher and in a democracy, has amended his earlier position and gone on to distinguish two conceptions of philosophy's role—philosophers as kings *versus* philosophers as advisors, roughly—and he advises the rest of us that a reasonable people would reject only the former (ibid.). As it turns out, therefore, Walzer does not really want to separate philosophy from democracy, just democracy and those philosophers who have erroneous views about the relationship between philosophy and democracy. The same holds for Berns. In arguing for excluding philosophic concerns and methods from constitutional law, Berns tries to persuade us to the thought of Hobbes and his philosophic successors. Bork does the same thing when he invokes Alasdair MacIntyre in behalf of the New Right's prescriptions for the Court.[113]

So, as Walzer and Berns and Bork leave the matter, the choice remains not one between philosophy and democracy but, in Eisgruber's words, "a choice between forms of philosophy." And if the form you are defending is the form "that stoops to life" and tries within the limitations of its social environment and the institution through which it acts to enlarge "the boundaries of human happiness," the issue is not whether judges in a democracy can be philosophers, it is whether a democracy can institutionalize a serious concern for honoring its claim to moral distinction. Ironically, academics who deny this possibility operate from conceptions of democracy and the world that are not shared by those ordinary folks who believe that democracy is in fact better than other systems—morally better.

4

THEORIES
OF
JUDICIAL REVIEW I:
THE NEW RIGHT

Because a democratic culture gives Bork's exoteric teaching preeminence over Berns's esoteric teaching, New Right constitutionalism turns out to be a modernist teaching, not a traditional one. The modernist character of New Right constitutionalism becomes clearer in this chapter and the next, where I offer an interpretation of the principal arguments with which American writers have attempted to justify judicial review.

My theory of the theories revolves around the classical defense of judicial review, as presented originally in *Federalist* 78. I submit a hypothesis for the decline of the classical theory in our century. I review the principal reactions to the decline of the classical theory: the New Right's call for a deferential judiciary, and the attempt of the judiciary's supporters to find a new defense for judges who openly think for themselves in hard cases. By reviewing the failures of these reactions, these two chapters set a stage for the main points of the final two chapters: There never was a good reason to reject the classical theory, and informed friends of the tradition will prefer the style of the Marshall and Warren courts to the deferential ideal of the New Right.

MODERNISM AND THE DECLINE
OF THE CLASSICAL THEORY

Chapter 2 identifies five of the presuppositions behind Publius's defense of judicial review. Publius claims judicial review insures constitutional supremacy, not judicial supremacy, and, through constitutional supremacy, the supremacy of the people. Publius's claim presupposes: (1) the adequacy of constitutional language, (2) the psychological possibility of judicial fidelity to the Constitution, (3) the transmission of fundamental constitutional values from the founding generation to subsequent generations, (4) the existence of values that are objectively worthy of transmission, and (5) the Constitution's embodiment of those values. We can organize our thinking about the various theories of judicial review in terms of these presuppositions.

For most of this century modernist doctrines of various sorts have greatly weakened support for these presuppositions. The doctrines in question include particularistic semantic theories, a conception of human choice as incorrigibly self-serving, and above all, a moral and metaphysical skepticism that reduces goods like justice to subjective or merely conventional, and therefore fundamentally arbitrary, preferences.

With regard to the old assumption that constitutional provisions could guide judicial decision contrary to judicial predilections, Edward Purcell has told the story of how referent linguistics, a radically empiricist theory of language meaning, combined with the logical positivism of the Vienna Circle to reduce first-order ethical propositions to highly particularistic and cognitively meaningless expressions of emotion.[1] Referent linguistics held that ethical words like *good* and *bad* stand for nothing beyond the speaker's like or dislike for some particular *this* (48). Abstract expressions like *justice, due process,* and *equal protection* were not only irrational or subrational, they also had no meaning beyond particular historical applications.

To American Legal Realists of the 1920s and beyond (and their successors among contemporary pragmatists and the critical legal studies movement), theories like referent linguistics meant that constitutional provisions could have little or no effect on judicial decisions in hard cases. Because words were meaningful only as applied, constitutional provisions had no necessary meaning in hard cases prior to the moment of application. Added to what the Legal Realists and others regarded as the problematic and largely illusory restraint of precedent, skeptical theories of meaning indicated that in hard cases judges were on their own. Judicial opinions in hard cases were mere rationalizations for results motivated by the judges' extralegal preferences and hunches (82–84).

Less particularistic, though still conceiving meaning to be fundamentally arbitrary, are current conventionalist theories of meaning. The paradigm case theory locates the meaning of a term in what a society's conventions treat as a standard example or set of standard examples. This theory holds that, for example, a particular car and a particular bus somehow become the exemplars of *vehicle* for some community, and the term is then held applicable to things sufficiently similar to the standard examples.[2] By contrast, the criterial theory finds meaning not in established exemplars, but in established definitions. Should convention define *vehicle* as "a piece of machinery used for carrying something," we should find the meaning of *vehicle* in the conventional definition, and we should apply the term to things in the world that are held to bear the two properties "piece of machinery" and "used for carrying something" (see ibid. 296).

Because conventions, by their nature, change, and because conventionalists must hold that there is no real reason for conventions not to change or change in any particular direction, conventionalists cannot believe there is a real reason for constitutional meaning not to change. These facts, added to what once was a modernist prejudice favoring the historical present and future over the past,[3] found many constitutional theorists arguing that the judicial administration of inherently meaningless and flexible symbols was a way to keep constitutional meaning in tune with evolving social conceptions.[4] The Constitution therefore was less law than empty vessel into which new meaning was poured, as new wine into an old bottle, and the nation was better off for it.

In the field of constitutional thought, these modernist theories of language overlap with modernist theories regarding judicial choice, the substance of historical change and collective identity, and central to all the rest, the subjective or purely conventional and therefore fundamentally arbitrary status of normative relationships and entities like duties, rights, and goods. The Legal Realists stressed that, independent of facts relating to the nature of language and precedent, judges were human and, as a psychological matter, could not decide cases in the mechanical manner imagined by the legal formalists who, by the turn of the century, had falsely appropriated the classical theory.[5]

A few extreme Legal Realists insisted that decisions in hard cases flowed from the personal predilections of judges; others held that the way judges were recruited and socialized insured that the personal predilections of individual judges reflected the values of prominent segments of the community (89). In apparent disagreement, the early Alexander Bickel contended that experience had proved judges capable of surrendering deeply held convictions "by introspection, by reflection, by reason, of which logic is a tool and which debate can induce."[6] But Bickel himself considered constitutional meaning an "illusion," and upon further reflection he saw judicial deliberation and debate as means to the uncovering of personal presuppositions—the judges' "deepest selves"—that were "in fact . . . the evolving morality of our tradition" (236).

Bickel's submersion of the self in the beliefs constitutive of tradition reflected the widely entrenched modernist dogma that there are no permanent and accessible moral truths—no accessible moral reality—beyond beliefs that are essentially the products of more or less time-bound and discrete cultures or communities.[7] This dogma has interpretive and metaphysical dimensions.

On the interpretive side, a modern intellectual tradition shaped by historicism has little impetus to look for unifying and transhistorical purposes and identities behind either the cultural differences that have divided all generations of Americans or the dramatic changes from one generation to the next, like the change from the agrarianism of early America to the industrial, nuclear, and postindustrial ages. Even if the current generation were not as divided as it appears to be, times have surely changed and changed dramatically, and it is easy for us to believe that we have changed with them and as profoundly. To say, as I suggest in chapter 2, that Americans from the founding to the present continue to be basically the same people is to say that we are defined less by our economic and social differences than by our common aspirations *and* that our many, often violent, conflicts are to be construed as conflicting versions of some truly common good to which we all aspire, whether we know it or not. That is not an easy proposition to swallow, at least not for us, mainly because the central dogma of our age is that there are no transcultural or objective norms in whose light we can distinguish real goods and wants from apparent ones.

A corollary to this dogma is the modernist conclusion that values are the products either of some positive divine revelation, for which there can be no scientific evidence, or some posited ethical axioms or commitments, usually in the form of cultural pressures operating on individuals. Values so conceived can be studied from the outside by observers who seek to describe their effects on conduct, their cultural causes, and their conventional implications (*democracy implies pluralism,* for example). But there are no arguments that can prove that value judgments are simply, as opposed to relatively, true or false, valid or invalid. At bottom, values are either irrational or subrational expressions of commitment, taste, pressure, or faith.[8]

MODERNIST THOUGHT AS A MISTAKE OF THE FOUNDING

Such was the intellectual atmosphere that choked off the classical presuppositions. Yet this atmosphere did not destroy everything that was originally there and ready to hatch out, for it helped to feed the unnatural growth of what was at best a secondary element of Publius's constitutionalism: the notion that the Constitution was not primarily an instrument for achieving good things, but a set of legal restrictions on those charged with its administration.

Publius, Marshall, and the Constitution as Charter

We see in chapter 2 that Publius's defense and exposition of the Constitution develops to a point that places a greater emphasis on the desiderata that he expected from power properly organized than on the way the Constitution would prevent various forms of governmental wrongdoing.[9] The same is true of Marshall's approach to constitutional interpretation. When *McCulloch* construes the enumeration of powers as means to desirable ends, it renders Article I, section 8, more of an enabling act than a positive corollary of an intention to restrict the government. The alleged conflict between Marshall's deference to Congress in *McCulloch* and his lack of deference in *Marbury*[10] disappears when one views both decisions as Marshall's contribution to the arrangement that he believed most conducive to the Constitution's ends, an arrangement that included power for Congress vis-à-vis the states *(McCulloch)* and power for the Court vis-à-vis Congress *(Marbury)*.[11]

With Publius as with Marshall, the Constitution's restrictions on government made sense primarily in light of ends achievable only through government. The major point of the political effort that produced the Constitution consisted in those ends. The restrictions were derivative and secondary, not fundamental; they were the conduits or channel markers of a dedicated or focused program. These channel markers helped to define the program by setting it apart from others, and in this way they negated the others. But the system's sense depended primarily on the ends toward which it directed social energy. The Constitution was more of a charter or an enabling act than a set of restrictions.

In a manner consistent with the Constitution as charter, both Publius and Marshall acted as if the governing consideration in constitutional interpretation was a general understanding of the substantive ends to which the Constitution stood related as means, if not mere means. They interpreted the provisions of the constitutional text in light of some prior and intrinsically valid or attractive state of affairs that the Constitution was taken to promise or adumbrate. Thus Faulkner can plausibly describe Marshall's approach to constitutional meaning as governed by the conviction that a Lockean commercialism was "the private law, and the public law, dictated by nature itself" (194–95; see also 68, 71, 209, 217–19).

This account of the interpretive process also fits Publius's decision to expound the Constitution primarily in terms of desirable substantive prospects, as distinguished from conventional institutional commitments and the political bargaining that occurred in the closed sessions of the Philadelphia Convention. A focus on the latter would have favored conceiving the Constitution as a mere contractual agreement among institutional actors, in this case the "sovereign states"—precisely the conception that Marshall and Story found rejected in *The Federalist* and to whose defeat they dedicated much of their careers.

Finally, constitutional interpretation in light of prior, though incorporated, desiderata is itself an interpretation that fits not only the writings of authorities like Publius and Marshall, but also the language of the Constitution. To sketch here what I have defended in more detail elsewhere: Taken together, the Preamble and the supremacy clause characterize the law of the Constitution as means to antecedently valid and meaningful ends, including justice, domestic tranquility, the common defense, and the general welfare. The coherence of this declaration, and therewith the coherence of the Constitution itself, depends in part on whether the Constitution's provisions can be fairly construed as more or less effective means to justice and the other ends. And because our understanding of justice and the other ends can always be improved—for the document expressly refers to justice, not this or that conception of justice—the Constitution's coherence depends partly on its capacity to be reinterpreted, if need be, in light of better conceptions of justice; hence the long-standing depreciation of judicial precedent as a controlling source of authority in constitutional litigation.[12]

Publius and Marshall acted as if the way to honor the Constitution's legal dimension as well as its more important instrumental dimension was to seek the most attractive construction that constitutional language and history could plausibly bear. Stopped by stubborn historical facts from denying the Constitution's injustices regarding slavery and the equal representation of large and small states in the Senate, Publius described the relevant provisions not as expressions of injustice or moral indifference, but as regrettable but politically necessary compromises with the true principles of political morality.[13] Pulius's assessment later proved a step toward Lincoln's argument that the Constitution had put slavery "in the course of ultimate extinction."[14] The historical record may also have stopped Marshall from applying the Fifth Amendment to the states in *Barron v. Baltimore*.[15] But the facts did not define a pale that excluded Marshall's view of the contract clause, and Marshall's Lockean persuasion indicated the clause could be useful for protecting vested rights and what later judges would call a "liberty to contract."[16]

Whatever the full implications of the ends orientation one finds in *The Federalist* and in Marshall's opinions, the aging nineteenth century brought at least a rhetorical shift from ends to judicial precedent in constitutional decision. Gilmore described the post–Civil War period as a time dominated by the view of law as a closed body of rules that judges were faithfully to apply, not adapt to changing circumstances. It was a time when judges and scholars "rarely, if ever, bothered with the facts of the cases they decided or with the reasons why the cases had been decided as they had been. . . . It was enough to say: The rule which we apply has long been settled. . . . Indeed, it was . . . unjudicial to say more. Stare decisis reigned supreme."[17]

Gilmore suggested an explanation for this shift in terms of factors like the resolution of some of the old constitutional questions, the accumulated body of precedents, the need for "repose" following the war, and the influence of big business on the thinking of jurists (64–66). I want to propose a supplementary account that highlights the significance of the shift for constitutional theory.

Publius's Mistake?

Publius promises in *Federalist* 78 that a strict rule of precedent will restrain judicial discretion in a meaningful way.[18] He also suggests in *Federalist* 49 that there is something special about the founding generation and that it is better to entrust judges rather than the public with some of the responsibilities of constitutional maintenance after the public-spirited rationality of the Revolution and the founding yields to the self-serving ways of normalcy (340–41). I argue in chapter 2 that Publius's statement about precedent should be treated as a mistake. No one can fully reconcile that statement with Publius's other statements, about constitutional supremacy, for example, and the inevitable controversies over the meaning of legal rules. Nor can anyone reconcile it with our putative desire to accept Publius's views as informed and truthful enough to be worthy of respect, then or now. But I must now say more about Publius's statement on precedent. Without retreating from my view that the statement is a mistake, I want to show how it might make some sense when viewed from the argument in *Federalist* 49.

Federalist 49 takes up Jefferson's proposal for putting some constitutional questions before special conventions of the electorate. Publius rejects this proposal essentially because he distrusts the public's capacity to rise above the influence of its "passions" and because he insists "it is the reason of the public alone that ought to controul and regulate the government" (338–39). In explaining how he can trust the public to ratify but not maintain the Constitution, Publius claims that the exigencies of the founding period make public opinion more informed and public-spirited than human nature ordinarily allows, and that normalcy will inevitably bring a relapse into selfishness and partisanship. At that future point, "the most rational government will not find it a superfluous advantage, to have the prejudices of the community on its side." This argues against frequent public appeals that would imply "some defect in the government" and "deprive the government of that veneration, which time bestows on everything, and without which perhaps the wisest and freest governments would not possess the requisite stability" (340).

Publius thus holds that reason has a greater influence on the founding than on future generations. The greater influence of passion and prejudice may not apply or apply equally to all elements of future generations, however. *Federalist* 49 says that members of the judiciary "are too far removed from the people to share much in their preposessions" (341). And *Federalist* 78 aligns the judges on the side of reason and the Constitution by defending judicial review, referring to the judges as "faithful guardians of the constitution," and praising the "integrity and moderation of the judiciary" as a check upon legislative and popular excess (524–25, 528–29).

If judges are the faithful guardians of the Constitution, perhaps they must be able to see the Constitution for what it is. And since seeing the Constitution for what it is may require viewing the Constitution from the perspective of the framers, perhaps the judges should view the Constitution from that perspective. This conclusion is not a strict deduction from what Publius says, but it is within the limits of plausible imputation, and I ask the reader to assume it for the moment.

If we do assume it, however, we have a problem. Whatever the judges' perspective on the Constitution, they have to communicate their findings to a public whose prejudices and perceived interests differ from the beliefs of the founding. We can assume, moreover, that in communicating their opinions the judges have to be mindful of the role popular prejudices play in maintaining the Constitution. So the channel that, *ex hypothesi,* connects the judges with the founding could not be the same channel that connects the judges to the public. The judges would have to convey decisions reached on rational grounds as if they flowed from the kinds of considerations the public could appreciate, and what the public could appreciate would shape and therefore to some extent restrict what the judges could convey.

I will not pause to ask how restrictions on what the judges communicate might eventually affect the judges' capacity to receive—their capacity, that is, to see the Constitution for what it is. For present purposes I point out that if public support for the Constitution continues, the public's prejudices will include a belief that the Constitution has established institutions that are not prone to frequent injustices and mistakes. Because courts make up a part of those institutions, judges have an incentive to pretend that courts seldom err. Judges should therefore honor old cases when they can, and when they cannot they should prefer reinterpreting old cases to overruling them outright.[19]

Further and more solid reinforcement for stare decisis will come from likely changes in beliefs regarding the nature of authority. The postfounding decline in public-spiritedness will enhance the apathy in some segments of the public and the self-servingness in others that together feed the skeptical reduction of justification to mere rationalization. Demands will tend to become substitutes for claims of the sort that both presuppose and require public justification, and because increasingly skeptical parts of the community will view true justification as a fiction, they will increasingly see authority to consist in successful assertions of power. Ends-oriented arguments give way to arguments bottomed on the opaque or arbitrary preference of some powerful or established authority, like some deity, the framers, the judges, or the current majority. Ends-oriented arguments will decline because arguments are by nature both public and evocative of shared ends, and real ends will be seen as necessarily private. In that atmosphere ends that are defended on grounds other than the electoral or even physical power behind them will be seen as elitist conceits and impositions.

The tandem beliefs that ends are essentially private and that authority is essentially physical and therefore arbitrary will favor various forms of conventional authority—precedent, for example, along with the framers' conceptions and the raw will of the majority—partly because such authority is itself arbitrary, and partly because a public of privatized, self-serving, and therefore morally diminished individuals and groups will be encouraged and flattered by teachings that deny there are moral differences between life choices and stations in society.[20] By this account Publius himself would share some of the responsibility for the decline of his own theory of judicial review. He and his generation would either have resigned themselves to, or actively encouraged, the decline of their own concern for public purposes. Berns would thus have an argument for identifying New Right constitutionalism as a child of the founding.

One large issue would remain, however: whether it was good for the framers to have planned for the closing of the American mind to the perspective of the framers themselves, and therewith to the truth about the Constitution. Berns would either have to deflect this question or answer that the framers erred. At least he would have to give this answer to the public. He could not say to the public that the framers were right to degrade the public unless he could defend the framers in a way that would open the public's mind to precisely the kind of inquiry the framers, on Berns's view, would have foreclosed. Yet if Berns would answer that the framers erred, he would concede the need either to reject this part of Publius's plan or to give that plan a different construction.

Showing that Publius will bear a different interpretation is of course the burden I accept in chapter 2. I should say in fairness to Berns that while I claim to have construed Publius, as distinguished from rejecting him, my construction has it that Publius sometimes falls short of his own purposes.[21] I have tried to support my interpretation with arguments drawn both from Publius's text and from reflections on what considerations should govern the kind of interpretation afoot. But I leave the success of my construction to the reader.

I contend, in any case, that the classical approach to constitutional interpretation and judicial review emphasizes the ends of government and construes constitutional provisions as instrumental to those ends. The classical approach yielded to a legalistic approach after the Civil War. Cut off from the ends to which the Constitution was originally related as means, the legalistic approach of the postwar period reflected attitudinal changes toward public purposes. These attitudinal changes were accompanied by modernist teachings that conflicted with the classical presuppositions regarding constitutional meaning, judicial duty, collective identity, and the status of values.

MODERNISM AND THE SEPARATION OF DEMOCRACY FROM CONSTITUTIONALISM

In the final chapter I return to the manner in which recent ethical theory has revitalized the classical presuppositions. To set the stage for that discussion I examine what the rejection of Publius's presuppositions has meant for modern attempts to justify judicial review. To see that, we must appreciate the part constitutional supremacy plays in the classical theory of judicial review.

We have seen the classical theory come to light in *Federalist* 78 as a defensive maneuver on Publius's part. By defending judicial review against the charge of judicial supremacy, Publius seems to concede that if judicial review means the supremacy of judges, judicial review is illegitimate. He implies, in other words, that unless his defense of judicial power succeeds, some principle of authority that he shares with his audience excludes judicial review.

It is not clear from *Federalist* 78 alone whether this invalidating principle is the separation of powers or the privileged position that popular government accords elected officials.[22] We cannot simply assume that Publius intends the latter. We cannot assume he would say that any practice that offends a principle of electoral accountability is vitiated by that fact alone. Nor can we assume that offense to electoral accountability and offense to the separation of powers are either the same or equivalent offenses. The first assumption would contradict too many of Publius's beliefs, principally that consent of the governed is not a sufficient condition of legitimacy; that justice is to be equated neither with the form nor the substance of popular will; that the people are not always sure of what is in their best interest, or even what they really want; and that there is no way to fix the amount of time it would take for responsible officials to make the public sensible of its true interests. Nor, as regards the second assumption, does Publius's concern for the separation of powers flow from a simple attachment to majoritarian institutions, for he argues that a proper separation helps the government to educate the public to its true interests by insuring some of the conditions for the power to oppose the public's inclinations.

In light of these views it is no surprise that in the end Publius proposes nothing stronger than impeachment as a safeguard against judicial usurpation. Although he speaks to the fear of judicial supremacy at one point, he risks judicial supremacy for the same reason that he is ready to abandon popular government should it prove incompetent to the ends of government: the superiority of those ends to government of any form.

Yet Publius repeatedly acknowledges his audience's commitment to majoritarianism and its institutions.[23] And for this reason Berns has an argument for concluding that Publius would have avoided government by an antimajoritarian institution.[24] Granting that majoritarianism is part of Publius's commitments, majoritarianism is nevertheless only a secondary part and, therefore, a qualified or conditional part. For Publius prefers justice to any form of government, and there is no question about his belief that the future of popular government depends and ought to depend on democracy's reconciliation to justice. If he honors majoritarianism, therefore, he honors it only insofar as majoritarianism can contribute to or help constitute good government.

It thus appears that persons who profess fidelity to Publius's thought would distinguish constitutional majorities—those that pursue constitutional ends in constitutional ways—from unconstitutional majorities and a majoritarianism separated from a proper commitment to constitutional objectives.[25] If Publius is committed to majorities and majoritarianism, it must be to constitutional majorities and a constitutional majoritarianism. We must therefore read Publius's brief for judicial review as an argument primarily for constitutional supremacy, not raw popular supremacy. By his account, the judges are to enforce the Constitution, not the will of the people in any way separable from the language of the Constitution. For, as we have seen Publius indicate, it is only as manifested in the Constitution that the popular will can vindicate itself by rising to the demands of ends that are more worthy than popular government itself or any other form of government.[26]

Although there is a big difference between the argument from constitutional supremacy and the argument that grounds legitimacy solely in popular will, the difference narrows if textual and historical conditions make a third argument plausible. In making this third argument we should first have to construe Publius's distinction between the public's interests and inclinations as a distinction between the public's real wants and its apparent wants. We should then hold that the public's real wants are embodied in constitutional principles and majoritarian expression pursuant thereto, not in mere majoritarian expression. This argument would conflate "what the people really want" with "what the Constitution requires" and locate evidence for the people's real wants in what the Constitution means, as explicated through a competent quest. The reader must decide whether this argument would be a bona fide argument from popular supremacy.

In any event, Publius can find no obligation in any expression of popular will separable from constitutional principle. Paradoxically, perhaps, the sovereign people cannot create the Constitution; the Constitution is rather a first step toward the people creating themselves as a sovereign. Through ratification the people couch a plan of government in a claim—that their power is a means to justice—typical of all who would have their sovereignty voluntarily recognized by others. Fully and completely to be recognized for what it claims to be, our would-be sovereign must do more than organize itself to pursue the ends of government. It must go on to strive for what all whom it addresses— the whole of humankind, as I read *Federalist* 1—can appreciate as progress toward those ends.[27] Because the extent of this progress will always be incomplete and a subject of controversy, the posture of this sovereign must be one of self-critical striving, not willful self-assertion (see 111–15, 140–44, 165, 176, 214). Separated from the Constitution, popular will would take the form of majoritarian willfulness, something fundamentally different from the form implicit in constitutional logic.

I dwell on the Constitution's role in Publius's argument in order to highlight a feature common to all alternative defenses of judicial review. In one way or another, each of the other theories either drops or diminishes the claim that judicial review is an instrument of constitutional supremacy. Each of the other theories is a version of one generic argument: Judicial review in hard cases should be an instrument of popular supremacy—not popular supremacy through constitutional supremacy, but popular supremacy in the sense of popular willfulness.

My contention is not self-evident. Most readers will readily agree that it can apply to theories that defend a nondeferential judiciary as a way of keeping constitutional meaning abreast of changing social values. A decade ago, prominent academic supporters of the Warren Court were candid in their belief that its reforms were extraconstitutional. As these liberals conducted their "quest" for a defense of extraconstitutional or "noninterpretive" judicial review, there was little to debate in William Rehnquist's contention that the

Constitution does not control judges who believe the judiciary should exploit indeterminate constitutional language "to make the Constitution relevant and useful in solving the problems of modern society," as they themselves assess those problems.[28]

That situation has changed somewhat as establishment liberals have found ways to claim that keeping the Constitution up-to-date need not mean extra-constitutional or noninterpretive decisions after all. I review this development in chapter 5, but here it is enough to note that the New Right continues to charge the Warren and Burger courts with extraconstitutional decision and that the new defenses of Warrenite activism remain debatable. In light of this debate it is surely arguable that Rehnquist is right about the false constitutionalism of establishment liberals. I submit arguments to that effect at any rate, even as I contend that Rehnquist and his New Right colleagues do more harm to the Constitution than the liberals they condemn.

While perhaps more debatable, it is also arguable that constitutional restraints are not the controlling consideration in process theories of judicial review. These theories treat democratic processes as ends in themselves and assign judges a special function in maintaining those electoral and governmental processes that are deemed essential for democracy. Process theorists like John Hart Ely have argued that the Constitution has a place in their understanding of the judicial function in hard cases because their theory is a theory of what the Constitution means.[29] But critics of process theory (especially critics on the Right) say that, knowingly or not, process theory rejects constitutional restraints because, in Bork's words, "there is neither a constitutional nor an extra-constitutional basis for making the Constitution more democratic than the Constitution is."[30] And if I am right in arguing that the Constitution would have institutionalized a concern for considerations of greater dignity than public opinion, then process theorists do abandon the Constitution when they characterize it as a mere means to the efficient administration of a popular willfulness.

I return to these matters in due course. But I should first show how my contention about popular willfulness and theories other than the classical theory applies where many believe it least plausible: the constitutionalism of the New Right. The New Right has succeeded in persuading the public that it is the authentic representative of the constitutional tradition. I have contended here that the New Right's claim is fraudulent. If I am right in this and in the further contention that the classical theory is the only one that accepts constitutional supremacy, it will follow that the New Right rejects constitutional supremacy. The New Right will thus prove to be a strain of noninterpretivism. Yet most readers doubtlessly regard New Right constitutionalism as at least a version of the classical theory, and therewith a theory in which the notion of constitutional restraint plays some meaningful role. So further discussion is necessary if I am to show the extraconstitutional—even anticonstitutional—character of New Right thought.[31]

WHY FRIENDS OF THE CLASSICAL THEORY HAVE MORE TO FEAR FROM THE NEW RIGHT THAN FROM THE ESTABLISHMENT LEFT

New Right theorists argue that the practical meaning of general constitutional ideas like equal protection and due process depends on policy choices that judges should leave either to the Constitution's framers (or, equivalently for present purposes, the ratifiers) or to the people's elected representatives. One way to expose the New Right's anticonstitutionalism is to analyze the New Right's inability to find a defensible conception of framers' (or original) intent. I argue here that in their desire to escape the moral and practical difficulties of Raoul Berger's original conception of framers' intent, recent New Right theorists have moved very close to conceptions of original intent that accommodate the nondeferential approach of the establishment liberals they oppose. New Right theorists thus increasingly face a choice between what they regard as the morally indefensible and the institutionally unacceptable.[32] Such a choice would remove all hope of saving New Right constitutional theory for anything other than demagogic purposes. Intellectually self-respecting rightists would be left with the judicial activism symbolized by *Lochner,* which is similar in its underlying interpretive approach to the liberal activism symbolized by *Brown* and *Roe.*

But first I owe an explanation to readers who ask what need there can be for additional discussion of the New Right's theoretical difficulties. A legion of writers from every position on the ideological spectrum has made New Right constitutionalism all but a dead horse among constitutional specialists other than true believers on the right who act as if they are beyond argument's reach and nihilists on the left who take their metaphysical skepticism seriously enough to declare all positions equally arbitrary.

Even Robert Bork implicitly acknowledges the conceptual (albeit not the political) failure of his approach. This acknowledgement is evident in his response to the wholesale rejection of his approach by mainstream scholars; he expresses contempt for the philosophic debate over the role of the Court and announces that he will read no further in the philosophic literature that undergirds constitutional jurisprudence.[33] Bork thus refuses to defend his own philosophic assumptions or debate the issues at foundational levels.[34] He explains his contempt for the philosophic debate by declaring moral philosophy a fruitless enterprise and his critics a tribe of elitists who seek to subvert the American way (6–8, 130–31, 254–56, 337–43).

But because several considerations argue against taking Bork's explanation at face value, it functions less as a justification than as a diversion from his difficulties as a theorist. First, he has yet to confront those critics whom someone with his views should take most seriously—critics who charge that despite the New Right's talk about tradition and framers' intent, New Right constitutionalism is a strain of modernist thought that rejects the constitutionalism of the framers.[35] Second, Bork suspends his opposition to the field of moral philosophy when he finds it convenient to invoke moral philosophers who, he believes, are on his side.[36] Third, charity demands that we doubt Bork really subscribes to the McCarthyite suggestion that elevated establishmentarians like John Hart Ely, Paul Brest, and Laurence Tribe are out to destroy America in the interests of some heretical, if not alien, "intellectual class" (see ibid., n.3, 8–11, 71, 77, 115–17, 130, 136, 206, 241–44, 337–43).

Finally, there is Bork's letter of resignation from the Court of Appeals, reproduced in his 1990 book, that proclaims his desire "to speak, write, and teach about the law." The book goes on immediately to praise teachers of "true things" in a way that invites the public to regard Bork as a true intellectual (316–21). So Bork's calumny of the intellectual class is aimed not at all intellectuals, just those who deny that he is a teacher of true things. And given his refusal adequately to confront the arguments of his critics, one can legitimately wonder whether calumny is his method for displacing those academic forums that favor reflection and analysis with forums that favor, shall we say, more populist skills.

Whatever Bork's motives, his diatribe against constitutional jurisprudence may yet found a movement to diminish outside support for that field of inquiry until it surrenders its leadership to those who have been unable to earn it through their arguments. Such a surrender would be one way to achieve the appearance of intellectual respectability for New Right constitutionalism.[37] It would be a bad thing for the country, however, because it would both cause and symbolize a further decline of reason in American politics and because the nation's successes depend less on the aims of rhetoric than the aims of reason—less on the uniformity and intensity of its beliefs than on how closely its beliefs correspond to material and moral realities essentially beyond the nation's control.[38]

It is too early to predict that Bork and his allies will ultimately fail to change the forum of theoretical reason as much as they have degraded what Ronald Dworkin calls the "forum of principle," the federal judiciary.[39] Dead or alive in academe, New Right constitutional theory is strong enough in other circles to constitute a continuing threat both to judicial power and to constitutional theory. This fact is especially troubling to those who have good reasons to reaffirm the framers' constitutionalism,[40] for the New Right has skillfully distorted the framers' institutional scheme into a denial of the ends for which it was expressly instituted. So academic critics of the New Right have accomplished much, but not enough.

It is true that New Right politicians and academicians are not the first to urge that Americans abandon a tradition of nondeferential judicial power that originated in the Federalists' belief that the value or worth of democracy depends on reconciling majoritarianism to justice. The same demand occurs in the strain of establishment liberal thought that rejects the specific activism of *Lochner,* and it is present to a lesser extent in writers who would protect only the processes of majoritarian willfulness. Why, then, should supporters of the classical theory mark the New Right for special criticism? Part of the answer is that supporters of Publius's constitutionalism have criticized the constitutionalism of establishment liberals; I resume that criticism later in this book.[41] But the New Right deserves special attention, because the New Right poses a more immediate and uniquely more dangerous threat to the tradition.

The New Right's call for a broad policy of judicial deference differs from the old restraintist refrain of the American Legal Realists in two relevant respects. First, the Legal Realists and their now mainstream liberal progeny did not and do not want deference as a general judicial policy, a fact attested by the well-known double standard in modern judicial doctrine between human rights and property rights.[42] Second, and more important here, the Legal Realists generally understood themselves as liberated from what they saw as the simplistic and harmful illusions of the tradition regarding the public-spiritedness of the framers, the nature of constitutional meaning and decision, and the philosophic status of general normative ideas.[43]

By contrast, New Right constitutionalism insists on judicial deference across the full range of constitutional rights—substantive human rights and participatory rights as well as property rights;[44] this general policy of deference makes New Right constitutionalism more consistently antitraditional than Legal Realism and its mainstream successor. And while New Right constitutionalism, Legal Realism, and establishment liberalism share a large debt to Holmes's Darwinian view of law and society (see ibid., 6), the New Right has camouflaged its opposition to the tradition by claiming to be *the* modern representative of the framers' constitutionalism.

By forthrightly rejecting what we might call the rationalist assumptions and claims of the American founding (concerning the reality of justice and other constitutional ends, the possibility of long-range, hence constitutional, social planning, and the possibility of dutiful judicial choice in hard cases) American Legal Realism and establishment liberalism could not avoid setting the old constitutionalism apart for reconsideration in the event of their own failure. New Right constitutionalism offers no such consolation. Because of its remarkably successful masquerade as the framers' representative, the New Right's fall would further bury the tradition in undeserved charges of either irrelevancy or intellectual and moral bankruptcy—at least among intellectuals, an important constituent of any regime dedicated to what *Federalist* 1 calls "government by reflection and choice." The New Right's wrongful appropriation of the tradition confirms ancient wisdom about the difference between real and apparent friends. It shows why friends of the tradition have more to fear from the New Right than from the establishment left.

WHAT IS ORIGINAL INTENT?
NO CONSENSUS ON THE RIGHT

Bork sums up the New Right's general position when he says: "It is necessary to establish the proposition that the framers' intentions with respect to freedoms are the sole legitimate premise from which constitutional analysis may proceed."[45] But there is more than one view of framers' intent in the current literature, and New Right theorists offer no clear or consistent account of what they mean by framers' intent. Conceptions of framers' intent differ to the point where even supporters of a nondeferential judiciary are free to style themselves intentionalists of a sort. Dworkin, for example, can be seen as a kind of intentionalist because he argues that the framers should be viewed as intending, not their momentary and limited conceptions of abstract notions like due process and equal protection, but the abstract concepts themselves and, therefore, the improvements on original conceptions that should come with the nation's maturing moral thought.[46]

David Richards, Michael Moore, and I have argued to similar effect. Richards contends that an orientation to abstract intent is demanded by the changing needs of government, the problem of justifying popular sovereignty, and Madison's rejection of a purely populist conception of justice.[47] Moore shows that when people use words like *death* or *justice,* they typically refer to what they assume to be the natural or moral kinds of things in the world picked out by *death* and *justice*. People thus intend their words to be applied in "the *right* way," says Moore. And, he argues, the right way is to be sought through the processes of reflection and debate, processes whose highest forms are science and philosophy. He denies that the right way can be found through merely historical inquiries into the concrete exemplars and definitions of given historical figures.[48] I contend that New Right theorists actually deny the moral authority of the framers by imputing to the framers something less than an intention to serve the best feasible versions of the ideas to which their words are generally thought to refer in everyday life.[49]

Writers like Richards, Moore, and Dworkin are critics of New Right constitutionalism. They deploy conceptions of intent that differ from the conceptions of intent in New Right thought. Whatever the precise conception of framers' intent, therefore, New Right theorists must avoid conceptions that would encourage judges to think openly for themselves in hard cases. In particular, the New Right cannot admit that the framers intended to refer to anything more abstract than their own versions (whether paradigm cases, concrete applications, or specific definitions) of general ideas like equal protection and due process. To distinguish their approach from one that accommodates a nondeferential judiciary, New Right theorists must also affirm the methodological corollary of their rejection of abstract intent: the priority of historical research over the dialectical, reflective, and experimental methods of fresh philosophic and scientific inquiry.

The Originalism of Raoul Berger

For these reasons it appears that the clearest example of the New Right's affirmative position remains Raoul Berger's initial call for judges to disregard their own understanding of the Fourteenth Amendment and apply its terms in a manner consistent with the racism of the Reconstruction Congress and its northern constituents. Although he calls racism indecent and says it is too late for the nation to frustrate the heightened expectations of racial minorities and other Americans by reversing decisions in areas like voting rights and school desegregation, Berger insists that racism was and remains a problem to be addressed in the future as the Constitution has required all along: by legislation in the states or federal constitutional amendment. Relying on federal judges for social reform, as in the Warren era, risks abandoning the rule of law for rule by arbitrary judicial preferences similar in principle not only to the Watergate crimes but even to the tyrannies of Stalin and Hitler, says Berger.[50]

Ignoring the framers' abstract intentions is Berger's way of avoiding the allegedly unconstitutional levels of judicial discretion he finds in the innovations of the Warren era.[51] Yet Berger's problems are evident to all sides of the debate. To begin with, he indulges a question-begging assessment of the Warren era. Whether the Warren Court was faithful to the Constitution depends in part on whether constitutional words and phrases refer to more than particular historical definitions and applications, and this question can be answered only by a complex philosophic argument of the sort that Berger does not attempt.[52] Moreover, if Berger's assessment flows from a desire to avoid tyranny, he all but contradicts himself by conceding that segregation was "an evil" and "a blight" and remarking that the Warren Court "aroused in our black citizenry . . . expectations confirmed by every decent instinct."[53]

One would think that rational fear of tyranny would vindicate the Warren Court on the further premise that the Warren Court helped to ameliorate an existing evil (racism) similar in its essence to a remote evil (Nazism)— remote at least for this country, and at least in some small part because of the Warren Court. And because a loathing for racism is confirmed by every decent instinct, Berger's reading of the Fourteenth Amendment should be troubling to everyone with decent instincts, for Berger would have judges (whose nonracism still purports to be guaranteed by the nominating process) read and apply the amendment in a manner faithful to the alleged racism of its drafters. The moral costs of a forced and schizophrenic fidelity to an admitted evil would soon lead decent people to ask why anyone is compelled to find indecency in the Fourteenth Amendment, on its face an expression of decency.

Granting all that Berger contends about the limited purposes of the Fourteenth Amendment—that its drafters intended only limited rights regarding access to the courts, inheritance, freedom to contract, and the security of person and property (purposes that fall short of the Court's use of the amendment to secure voting rights, school desegregation, and the application of the Bill of Rights to the states)—granting all this, the amendment would remain a move toward decency (20–24, 52–58, 69–84, 117–33, 134–56). Construed even with the racist attitudes in its historical background, the amendment would represent a clear compromise of those attitudes, for thoroughgoing racists would want no rights at all for the victims of their prejudice, much less the important if limited rights that Berger is willing to concede.

Taking all aspects of the event as a whole, therefore, the adoption of the Fourteenth Amendment would indicate a mixture of attitudes toward race, decent as well as indecent, with movement from indecent to decent. Why, then, construe the event in what Berger all but acknowledges to be its worse light? Why not construe the event in its own best light? Why does fidelity to the framers demand fidelity to their worse selves? Why not fidelity to their better selves? Why should the rule of law be separated from decency, when decency is clearly an aspect of the law?

"Democracy" is hardly an answer to these questions because, as many have now realized, the debate over the role of the judiciary in America is precisely a debate over what democracy ought to be.[54] Nor can one simply assume that judges should be bound by neither the framers' better nor worse selves but by their *true* selves, which is a mixture of better and worse. This conclusion would suggest a theory of collective identity that, so far as I know, no New Right theorist has defended.

The theory, moreover, would be at odds with the framers' view, implicit in the Preamble and the supremacy clause and embodied in the stringency of the amendment provisions, that a people's most authoritative expression, and therefore in a sense its true identity, occurs at its most rational moment. It would also undermine traditional expectations about the coherence and reasonableness of legal principles, achieved if need be through judicial construction and despite the risks of judicial usurpation.[55] So Berger would have no easy time explaining why the framers' true selves should be a contradictory mixture of their better and worse selves as opposed at least to a compromise of their worse selves in favor of their better selves.

Wolfe, Bork, and the Flight from Berger

For these and other reasons—such as the framers' own choice of abstract language, the contrast between Berger's legal positivism and the natural rights philosophy of the founding and Civil War periods, the framers' fear of majoritarian tyranny, and the benefits of a constitution capable of covering unforeseen developments[56]—several New Right theorists have tried to distance themselves from Berger.

Thus, Christopher Wolfe acknowledges that "if [the Constitution] is to survive the passage of time and adapt to the circumstances of future ages," it "must lay down general principles, not specific rules," and its "intent . . . is to be found in the general principles . . . not in the specific examples that the framers had in mind as they wrote."[57] Moreover, according to Wolfe, finding currently applicable intent in general principles involves not only stating the "embodied" principle but determining how the framers "*ought to have* wanted that principle employed" in the instant case (58, his emphasis; see also 34–35, 87–88).

When Wolfe says we seek not just the framers' principles but how they "*ought to have* wanted" their principles employed, he moves from a set of merely historical concerns to a question that is partly philosophic. Writers like Dworkin and Richards would call it a shift from concrete to abstract intentions. And this raises the question whether Wolfe's procedure differs from one that a supporter of the Warren Court could accept. Wolfe's attempt to move from Berger indicates that one may not be able to achieve a significant distance from Berger without going at least as far as Dworkin. Should Dworkin prove to be their ultimate destination, New Right theorists may reconsider their flight from Berger. But for the moment it appears that Wolfe does not want to be stuck within Berger's interpretive regime. Wolfe does not want to say that the framers would have mandated indecent results regardless of their words or that the Constitution compels indecent results even when constitutional language does not—and all this on the paradoxical argument that the nation will end up in an indecent state of affairs (Watergate, Hitler, etc.) if its judges reach out to combat indecency (historical racism in America).

Bork is another rightist who may not want Berger's regime. Bork suggested in 1985 that Berger's approach constitutes "the crucial problem" for New Right constitutionalism.[58] "A major problem with the idea of original intention," Bork wrote, "is that the Framers articulated their principles" in "a world very different in important respects from . . . today." "A constitutional right . . . was illustrated for them by a set of circumstances or dangers that time has changed." And since a modern judge has to apply "that right . . . to circumstances that did not even exist in contemplation when the Framers acted . . . he cannot confine himself to the specifics they had in mind." "To do so," said Bork, "would make rights dwindle" under changed circumstances.

So, "to protect the freedom the Framers envisage, the judge must discern a principle in the applications the Framers thought of and then apply that principle to circumstances they did not foresee." This must be "what Lincoln meant," said Bork, "when he said, as [Gary] McDowell paraphrases him, that 'The constitutional jurisprudence of judicial statesmanship is not limited to the *meaning* of the principles of the Constitution but extends to the *objects* those principles are, in time, intended to achieve.'" Bork noted that "this maxim is at once true, difficult to apply, and susceptible to manipulation in disingenuous hands." "The question is always the level of generality the judge chooses when he states the idea or object of the Framers." The "lowest level of generality" makes provisions for both "individual freedoms, as well as . . . governmental power . . . in time almost worthless." Yet a "higher level" threatens to produce "concept[s] without limits" and "result[s] far beyond anything the Framers intended." All of which leaves us with "no safeguards . . . except the intellectual honesty" of judges and legal scholars "who accept the premises of interpretivism" (x–xi).

Such was Bork's initial attempt to escape Berger. It was unsuccessful in several ways. First, there was a problem of circularity. Bork indicated that judges should look beyond historical meanings to the broader "principles" and "objects" of the framers while avoiding going too far by following the principles of interpretivism; but he seemed to conceive interpretivism as looking beyond historical meanings without going too far. Second, he betrayed a shifting conception of meaning from concrete to abstract. Thus, he indicated (on the concrete side of meaning) that the framers' meaning lay in historical applications and examples; yet he also indicated that judges should go beyond historical meanings in order to protect the freedoms, power, and objects that (on an abstract conception of meaning) the framers themselves envisioned.

To mention one more difficulty, the attempted flight from Berger found Bork agreeing with some of the New Right's critics in at least one key respect: responsible judges must formulate the principles and purposes of some part or parts of our constitutional experience in terms that are broader than that experience. If Bork and someone like Dworkin disagreed, it was over how to select among the different formulations of principle and purpose that seem plausible continuations of that experience—how to select among formulations that fit that experience. Dworkin makes his selections in accordance with what he believes to be a fresh moral argument that puts experience in its best feasible light.[59] Bork has yet to give a clear indication of how he would make his selections. He apparently accepts McDowell's remark that in Dworkin's "academic musings" Rawls replaces Locke and Madison.[60] And Bork cannot be disappointed when neo-Hobbesian writers like Berns and McDowell set a philosophic stage for his attack on philosophy.

But, more often than not, Bork affects a skeptic's contempt for moral and political philosophy of all stripes.[61] By claiming a freedom from philosophic influences, he affects a method far removed from the method of a writer like Berns (252, 256–57). Perhaps Bork senses that Berns's partial reliance on particular philosophic teachings entails submissions to the test of fresh philosophical argumentation as a method—precisely the method Bork would exclude from the process for discovering the major premises of constitutional decision. He might well want to avoid lapsing into the hollow paradox of Berns's philosophically laden constitutional argument for excluding philosophic inquiry from constitutional interpretation—a result that would silence Berns's critics and thereby remove chances for an informed appreciation of Berns's own views.[62] But if avoiding paradox explains why Bork pretends freedom from philosophy we still know nothing about how he would advise judges to choose among different versions of the framers' principles and purposes.

One might have hoped that Bork's long-awaited 1990 book would have contained a more adequate statement of his position. But, if anything, matters seem worse. Before the publication of *Tempting of America* one could have said that Bork was searching, as yet without success, for a theory of original intent at some safe distance between what he regarded as the Scylla of writers like Dworkin and Richards and the Charybdis of Berger. But now one cannot be sure, because *Tempting of America* omits Bork's earlier reference to Berger as a problem for the New Right and even praises him as a theorist who takes "the traditional position."[63] So Bork may no longer be trying to escape Berger.

The conceptual confusion and the vacillation between interpretive positions are still present in Bork's thinking, as we shall soon see. But he may no longer be as uncomfortable with that fact as he was when he identified Berger as a problem. I say this because Bork himself says that our institutions not only "embody . . . wholesome inconsistencies," they also "produce" them, and that it is "appropriate that our laws reflect" America's moral divisions (352–53). He may therefore feel that it is appropriate for our normative theories about the law to reflect these inconsistencies and moral divisions.

So we cannot be sure Bork values theoretical coherence, but if he does, he is a long way from it. Consider his treatment of the *Brown* decision and contrast it with his approach to other Fourteenth Amendment problems. He does more than acknowledge the moral authority of *Brown;* he assigns the decision a rank sufficient to invalidate any constitutional theory with which it is not compatible (77). He therefore claims that his approach to constitutional interpretation can accommodate *Brown.* Bork treats the segregationist intent of the relevant ratifiers not as the content or meaning of the equal protection clause but rather as an erroneous and nonbinding belief.

The framers, he says, erred in their belief that "segregation was consistent with equality" (82). Bork still finds the meaning of the equal protection clause in original intent, but now he treats intent as abstract, not concrete. He finds the evidence for the meaning of the clause, and therefore the controlling intent, neither in historically intended (i.e., segregationist) applications nor historical interpretations (like "separate but equal") but rather in the constitutional text itself considered apart from historically intended applications and conceptions. Bork says: "The text itself demonstrates that . . . equality under law was the primary goal." By 1954, he goes on to say, it was "apparent that . . . segregation rarely . . . produced equality." So, he concludes, the Court had to reject some aspect of the original understanding, and the Court properly elected to support the "purpose" of the Fourteenth Amendment, the purpose being "equality, not separation." Had the Court argued thus, says Bork, the *Brown* result "would have clearly been rooted in the original understanding" (ibid.). Well, perhaps—but only if "original understanding" ought to mean what Bork supposes when discussing *Brown.*

Bork's approach to *Brown* is similar to Dworkin's, and it differs from Berger's. Berger insists that intention be construed as intended application and that, in cases of perceived conflict between text and intended application, "Framers' intention rather than the text is the law."[64] He holds that textual meaning separated from intended application is merely a cover for imposing one's own preferences, especially when textual meaning is used to reverse an intended application (352–53, 357, 369–71). Berger thus concludes that in *Brown* the justices sacrificed the Constitution to their personal moral preferences.[65]

Contrary to Berger, Dworkin holds that the text of the equal protection clause describes an abstract commitment to equality and that the *Brown* Court correctly treated that abstract "conviction" as dominant—dominant over the framers' "concrete conviction that racial segregation did not violate" the commitment to equality. When the Court realized that segregation in fact defeated the equality demanded by the constitutional text, they faced a situation of conflict between the framers' abstract and concrete intentions. Fidelity to the framers demanded a decision consistent with their dominant intention, even if it meant outlawing a practice the framers had intended to permit.[66] If Bork's approach to *Brown* is a fair example of what he means by decision in accord with the framers' principles, he has strayed into Scylla's territory.

But not for long. The memory of *Bolling v. Sharpe* jolts Bork back toward Charybdis.[67] He says that, though morally "unthinkable that the states should be forbidden to segregate and the federal government allowed to," *Bolling* was a "lawless" rewriting of the Constitution that "rested on no precedent or history." "However much one likes the result," says Bork, *Bolling* was "a substantive due process decision in the same vein as *Dred Scott* and *Lochner*."[68]

Bork stays this course most of the time. In addition to permitting the unthinkable in the District of Columbia, Bork would also have permitted admittedly "pernicious" laws against economic liberties struck down by the pre-1937 Court and apparently even what he himself calls the "savage" statute voided in *Skinner v. Oklahoma* (46–47, 62–63).[69] Better, it would seem, to suffer the "unthinkable," the "pernicious," and the "savage" at the hands of our elected officials than permit judges to legislate civilized results, for "the Constitution is a legal document," says Bork, "not an expression of a mood or a general injunction to be 'civilized'" (62).

What drives Bork to these tough-minded conclusions is his antipathy to substantive due process and substantive equal protection, formulas for "social engineering from the bench" (85), and the emblems and tools of the regime against which he now leads the New Right's jihad (ibid., 31–32, 61–64, 83–84, 93). Bork's hostility to this regime is so intense that he seems to reject the due process and equal protection clauses as guarantees even of minimally rational legislation (45–47, 63–67). What is reasonable is "always a matter of perspective," he maintains, a reflection of "moral views about which reasonable men and women may differ," a choice "subjectively" made, often reflecting "trade-offs between desires" (65–66).

If this theme dominates Bork's thought, however, it does not do so consistently. Despite his opposition to substantive equal protection and his view that the framers of the equal protection clause intended to protect only racial minorities, he allows in the end that the Court can legitimately employ the equal protection clause to protect women from unreasonable legislation (65–66, 330–31). He also indicates, albeit ambivalently, that he can live with Justice Hugo Black's argument for incorporating the first eight amendments into the due process clause of the Fourteenth Amendment (ibid., 27, 48, 53, 60, 93–95). His reason for accepting Black's brand of substantive due process is that, unlike the objectionable kind of substantive due process in cases like *Bolling*, Black's theory of incorporation (and the substantive due process embedded therein) "has at least the merit of confining the courts to the enforcement of principles actually in the Constitution" (60).

Yet Bork should be able to see that the same argument applies to *Bolling*. *Bolling* incorporated into the due process clause of the Fifth Amendment a principle of "equality, not separation" that Bork himself finds "written into the text" of the equal protection clause (82). If, as Bork allows, the due process clause of the Fourteenth Amendment can incorporate, say, a freedom of speech found in the First Amendment, it is hard to see why the due process clause of the Fifth Amendment cannot incorporate the equal protection guarantee of the Fourteenth Amendment. Confusing matters even more, Bork's willingness to sanction Black's theory of incorporation—a theory deriving rights against the states from rights originally applicable only against the national government—does not prevent him from criticizing the *Griswold* Court for failing to see that "there is no basis for extrapolating from the rights they [the ratifiers] did create to produce rights they did not" (198).

MICHAEL McCONNELL AND THE FRAMERS' MIND-SET

Further elaboration of Bork's difficulties would serve no purpose here. I have shown enough to support my point: Whether or not he continues to be troubled by Berger's historicism, Bork follows a zigzag course between the approaches of Berger and Dworkin. If the New Right has a single conception of framers' intent, we shall have to find it elsewhere. Where to look next is indicated by Bork's approving references to a relatively recent arrival to the ranks of New Right jurisprudence, University of Chicago law professor Michael McConnell (217, 395, n. 124). Because McConnell has been moved to much thought on the New Right's current dilemma, his could be (but probably will not be) the last of the New Right's attempts for a safe passage between what they regard as unacceptable alternatives.

McConnell develops his position in the course of an attack on the approach to constitutional interpretation in Michael Perry's *Morality, Politics, and Law*.[70] In that book Perry proposes that constitutional theorists recognize the futility of the "liberal political-philosophic project" and find their legal-moral grounding in "tradition." Perry describes the "liberal project" as the search for some basic standard of political morality that is "neutral or impartial among the competing conceptions of human good," conceptions that one finds among the often clashing racial, religious, economic, and ethnic groups of American society.[71]

As I construe the liberal project that Perry criticizes, it is the quest for an argument or a set of reasons about how to live that would in principle appeal to all rational persons as such, without regard to such attributes as race, religious inheritance, and economic class. This project exhibits what I here call rationalist and in some respects secular and individualist assumptions. The liberal project is rationalist in the sense that I intend because it seeks reasons that are simply valid, not merely valid to this group or that. It is secular because it would transcend sectarian attachments with arguments that do not have to invoke divine revelation. And it is individualist in a sense because its quest for true moral and scientific premises implies a socially responsible skepticism toward received or conventional wisdom—because it depreciates conformity and values criticism as the way to improve community beliefs.

So when Perry rejects the liberal project, he proceeds in conventionalist fashion to affirm the priority of particular historical traditions over speculative reason and reason's quest for simple truth about justice and other matters; he also affirms the priority of community over the individual (29–41, 59–63, 133–51, 172–76). McConnell applauds this part of Perry's argument and aptly describes it as having "more in common with the conservativism of an Edmund Burke or the Bible Belt than with the various strains of individualism, rationalism, and secularism that make up modern American liberalism."[72] "If Burke could be summoned from the grave, he would surely agree with Perry that '[t]he ambition of liberal political philosophy notwithstanding, moral discourse must rely on relatively particular moral beliefs that, for the present at least, have withstood the test of experience, especially the experience of a moral community (or communities) over time'" (1504).

McConnell's comment on Burke comes during an attempt to depreciate the role of "self-critical rationality" in law and ethics, rationality as associated with "individualistic or utopian analysis" and as opposed to "defer[ence] to tradition and historical experience when making moral judgments" (ibid.). Too much rationality "is death to tradition," says McConnell, and the question, "Is it rational?" may make little sense "for a belief system in which faith, piety, charisma, love, esthetics, mystery, or wonder play the central role" (1506). McConnell's hostility to quests for reasons beyond his sources of authority may explain his unmediated leap from the observation that there are no mechanical rules or formulas for eliminating controversy to the conclusion that the only way for judges to get the Constitution right is to "steep themselves" in what he assumes to be some canonical version of "the history and philosophy of the Constitution" (1525).

Yet McConnell fails to maintain consistency with both his antirationalism and his call for empathic participation in the thought of the framers. He suspends his opposition to reason long enough to attempt real reasons for that opposition, and he does so without inquiring into the framers' attitude toward reason and traditional authority. Individual intelligence and experience are "necessarily limited," he says, while tradition cumulates the "thoughts and experiences of thousands," much in the manner of a market, which is superior to "seemingly more 'rational' modes of decisionmaking," like central economic planning and the "totalitarian horrors" of "a system predicated on an abstract and unreal vision of the nature of humankind" (1504).

McConnell seems perfectly confident about his arguments for relying on tradition and distrusting reason. He anticipates no objections from what experience has shown about the need to regulate markets, for example. Nor does he hint at an answer to those who might challenge him to explain how a defender of Perry's conventionalism can know that one political system comports more than another with "the nature of humankind"[73] or how a supporter of Bork can know that the "gratifications" of one regime are superior to another.[74] McConnell does not even acknowledge challenges like these, and so one can assume he thinks he has reasons for his conclusions that no sensible person can deny. If so, McConnell would seem to rely on two different sorts of arguments. One would proceed from an empathic unity with traditional authorities like the framers; the other would suppose reason's capacity to progress beyond tradition toward transcultural truths about human nature and experience.

An orientation to framers' intent need not exclude a role for reasoned moral and scientific inquiry. Different approaches to the interpretation of the framers flow from different estimates of the framers' reasonableness and different estimates of reason's authority. If you believe that the framers could have acted unreasonably without diminishing their authority for future generations and that they remain the best authority for their intentions when acting unreasonably, then empathic immersion in their thinking can yield no reason to avoid admittedly unreasonable results. Such is the purely empathic approach to framers' intent.

There would be less conflict between reason and a concern for the framers if we operated from the rationalist assumption that as worthy authorities the framers would want to do the reasonable thing—or that an interpreter who would save their authority would construe their words as if they wanted to do the reasonable thing. The rationalist and empathic approaches to the framers mark conflicting strains in McConnell's thought. Each represents an unsuccessful attempt to break away from Berger. The rationalist approach, the one that assumes the framers as framers wanted to do the right thing, succeeds in breaking away but occupies a position that the New Right associates with Dworkin. McConnell takes the rationalist approach at one point but eventually abandons it. In the end he succumbs to the call for total immersion in the framers' thought. This purely empathic approach turns out to be a radical form of Berger's initial position.

Although McConnell treats Berger with all the deference due the grand old warrior of the New Right's crusade against the Court, he tries to reject Berger's approach to constitutional meaning.[75] In fact, McConnell's criticism of Berger is more emphatic and fundamental than Bork's criticism of Berger. While Bork once saw Berger's approach as a "problem" for the New Right, McConnell classifies Berger's approach as a repudiation not only of the classical theory of judicial review but also of the very notion of the Constitution as law. "We read the Constitution," says McConnell, "to determine what consistent, coherent rules of law our forefathers laid down for the governance of those elected to rule over us."[76]

McConnell holds this quest for contemporary coherence to be the "classical conception of constitutional interpretation," and he finds that the classical conception is threatened not only by "those who claim that it is impossible for us to comprehend what the Constitution was intended to mean," but also by "those who interpret the Constitution as if it froze into place the conclusions reached at the time of the framing about the application of constitutional principles to concrete situations" (361–62). What the framers did cannot help us unless we know why they did it: "Unless we can articulate some *principle* that explains *why* . . . and demonstrate that that principle continues to be applicable today," we cannot successfully perform "the function of interpretation as enforcing the Constitution as law" (362–63, his emphasis).

"If the Constitution is law," says McConnell, "it must embody *principles* so that we can insure that like cases are treated alike, and that those governed by the Constitution can understand what is required of them" (363, his emphasis). Interpretations of constitutional provisions must therefore proceed through principles or theories of what the framers sought to accomplish. A judicial decision that cites the mere facts of past applications "casts no light on the meaning of the constitutional provision" in question; "indeed, it . . . does not interpret the Constitution at all . . . [it rather] suggests that the Constitution does not embody any set of coherent and consistent principles; in short, it suggests that the Constitution is not 'law' in any recognizable sense" (363).

To illustrate how judges ought not to proceed, McConnell singles out the Supreme Court's opinion in *Marsh v. Chambers,* an opinion that Berger has praised.[77] In *Marsh* the Court held that a state legislative body did not violate the establishment clause when it hired a chaplain to say prayers for the assembly. The decision, says McConnell, was "based squarely and exclusively on the historical fact that" the first Congress authorized paid chaplains at the time it drafted the First Amendment. But this evidence of what the framers believed tells us nothing about why they believed it or whether their reasoning "is applicable today."[78] McConnell takes up "four conceivable explanations," rejecting three as "unconvincing" and accepting the fourth (accommodating members far from their home churches) as a plausible account of the framers' purpose. But McConnell sees this purpose as "outdated," and he concludes that "unless I can be persuaded that there is some coherent understanding of the establishment clause, which can be applied consistently in the circumstances of today, I am forced to disagree with the holding in *Marsh*" (ibid.).

McConnell thus suggests that constitutional meaning is given, not by historical facts alone, but by theories of the facts—theories that are coherent, that render the Constitution recognizable as law, and that persuade present-day interpreters. McConnell also seems to hold that a successful theory must exhibit additional properties. Remarkably enough for a New Right theorist, McConnell thinks it a function of a good theory to make the framers look good. The correct approach to the framers will exhibit a certain piety toward them, says McConnell.

> The virtue of piety will incline us to regard our forebears in the tradition as good, wise, and just (probably better, wiser, and more just than they were in fact). This will incline us, in seeking to understand the tradition, to emphasize those elements in the tradition that are most worthy of praise. We like to contemplate the American founders' heroic sacrifices for liberty; we deem the institution of slavery, with its still-lingering shadows, to be out of keeping with the tradition. Piety is therefore the engine of reform, as faithful participants in the tradition ever strive to make it more worthy of an idealized past.[79]

For the "great example" of this approach McConnell cites Lincoln's belief that the nation's fundamental principles were incompatible with the perpetuation of slavery. He contrasts Lincoln's reforming piety toward the Constitution with the abolitionists' destructive criticism of the Constitution as a compact with the devil (1507–8). And he cites Martin Luther King, Jr., as "perhaps the greatest recent example" of one who "drew faithfully upon the (unfulfilled) tradition of the American political community." King's "'dream' of a more just America," says McConnell, "was less a condemnation of the nation than a call for its 'return' to the principles announced, but never fully followed, by the Founders" (1508).

I do not have to belabor the difference between Berger's view and McConnell's conception of "principles announced . . . by the Founders." The idea that a crusading moralist like King—who urged civil disobedience from agreement with Augustine that an unjust law is not a law[80]—was a better interpreter of slaveholding and "Negrophobic" framers than were his racist and states' rights critics concedes most if not all that friends of judicial power could ever want, including much that Dworkin says about the difference between concrete and abstract intentions and a role for moral philosophy in constitutional interpretation. If King's dream was a call to principles announced by the framers, then the framers were not talking about principles whose meaning was to be found through historical research into the specific practices and concrete conceptions of the eighteenth century. The same applies to Lincoln who, as Harry Jaffa shows, gave the abstract doctrine of human equality a rendition that was different from the specific construction of Locke and Jefferson.[81]

If King and Lincoln exemplify fidelity to the principles of the framers, or the framers insofar as they were worthy of being treated as framers, then the framers used the words and phrases of their constitutional documents to refer to real things and relationships, as opposed to parochial and therefore possibly erroneous versions of those things and relationships. These framers— these "idealized" framers, if you prefer McConnell's term—associated the authentic American tradition not simply with historical practices and prejudices, however long-standing or entrenched, for Lincoln and King each wanted to overthrow different traditions in that sense of the term that looks uncritically to historical practices.

Framers of the sort who would have authorized interpreters like Lincoln and King would have associated the authentic American tradition with an aspiration to improve our knowledge of abstract norms like equality and to strive for a national life in accord with the improved understandings and the continuing quest for still further improvements. That judges were to play their part in this striving, opposing public opinion as justice demanded, is indicated by McConnell's own approval of a number of what he expressly calls "activist" decisions. These decisions, he says, exhibit "faithful enforcement of constitutional provisions as originally understood, even under adverse political circumstances."[82]

McConnell's list is hardly what one would expect from a New Right theorist. It includes *Brown,* notwithstanding the racism of the post–Civil War period in the North, and *Brandenburg v. Ohio* and the school prayer cases, notwithstanding, among other things, Marshall's opinion in *Barron v. Baltimore*.[83] He would even include the reapportionment cases, had they been decided, McConnell insists, under the guarantee clause of Article IV, notwithstanding such considerations as language in Article I, section 2, that has long been construed to leave suffrage qualifications to the states, the expressly non-population-based apportionment of the United States Senate, in Article I, section 3, a lengthy history (apparently not an authentic part of the "tradition") of malapportionment in America at all levels of government, and a lengthy history (again, apparently not tradition) of federal judicial abstention under the guarantee clause.[84] Were this all that McConnell had to say on the subject, whatever differences remained between him and Dworkin would lie in their substantive theories of constitutional objectives, not in their approach to constitutional meaning or their view of judicial duty.

But this is not all that McConnell has to say on the subject, and as he continues it becomes evident that he holds at least two theories of constitutional interpretation, one contradictory to the other. I have just reviewed what I call McConnell's first theory, a rationalist approach to the framers. As we have seen, it begins with a conception of principles linked to communicable and still persuasive reasons behind the framers' practices, reasons that sanction applications beyond and even against practices that the framers were willing to permit in their day. McConnell's first theory insists that the Constitution cannot function as law unless it is understood in terms of such reasons. His first theory approves what Wolfe derides as "the typical modern step" of appealing to the general purpose of a provision for its meaning;[85] it exhibits Lincoln and King as model interpreters; it sanctions much of what the Warren Court accomplished; and it seems indistinguishable from the operational aspects of Dworkin's approach to constitutional meaning.

McConnell's second theory is very different. Having entered Scylla's cave, McConnell swings back sharply toward Berger and away from any theory that could display Lincoln or King as figures for judicial emulation. His second theory represents the purely empathic approach. It begins by effectively denying that the Constitution's words and phrases can refer to real things and relationships, meanings that are independent of what particular persons and groups might want or believe them to be. Behind all the academic disputation about how courts should interpret the Constitution, "there are only three answers," says McConnell: the meaning of words (1) "as they were understood by those with the authority to adopt them as law," (2) "as . . . now understood, or as they have been understood, by the American political community," and (3) as "the words should be interpreted to produce the best results, as understood by the person doing the interpreting."[86] McConnell then combines his notion of meaning as particular meaning with the usual assertions (not arguments) to the effect that our system is a democratic system, that the only meaning that can "attain democratic warrant" is meaning consented to "as constitutive . . . by the American people," that that meaning can only be what was "the product of the people's 'reflection and choice,'" and that can only be "original" or "intended" meaning (1527–28).

McConnell all but completes the move back to Berger by distinguishing original or intended meaning from (1) "linguistic" meaning ("any meaning that might be teased out of the language of the text"), (2) "historical" meaning ("meanings that have been perceived by the American political community over time"), (3) "present-day" meaning ("meanings that are currently perceived by the American political community"), (4) "philosophical" meaning ("any meaning that appears normative"), and (5) "some combination" of the above ("any meaning that can both be teased out of the text and also passes one of the other tests") (1526). All meanings not linked to linguistic meanings would overtly reject the authority of the constitutional text—they would be overtly "noninterpretive"—and linguistic meaning severed from original meaning is covertly noninterpretive because it is "functionally . . . no different from . . . no textual basis whatever" (1528). By thus limiting what can be meant by the framers' "principles," McConnell all but announces that the meaning of constitutional provisions is exhausted by concrete historical conceptions (like "separate but equal") or applications closely analogous to the concrete applications of the framers, precisely the position he and most other New Right theorists now want to disclaim.

McConnell resists this result for all of the reasons connected with his initial desire to disassociate himself from Berger's conception of framers' intent, especially the problem of how to apply constitutional principles to changing circumstances. So McConnell needs a way to keep the Constitution useful and sensible without sanctioning what he calls "linguistic," "philosophic," or "historical" approaches to constitutional meaning. And his final answer seems to be empathy with the framers, total immersion in their thought.

McConnell's thinking seems to be that if we were on the same wavelength with the framers we would think as they would today, and our applications of their words would be both up-to-date and faithful to their intent. His call for judges to "steep" themselves in the thought of the framers seems connected with his rejection of "modern rationalism" and his embrace of the notion that "moral principles are rooted in the experience of actual moral communities over time (religious communities among them)" (1502, 1503–07). "Principles" so rooted could have little or no communicative power beyond the outer reaches of their own cultural canopy, where overlap with other systems ceases. So at some point "the question ('Is it rational . . . ?') makes [doubtful] sense." "Is it *rational,*" McConnell asks rhetorically, "for Jewish boys and men to wear little black caps on their heads or for Amish to dress like 17th Century German peasants?" And he gives his answer by approvingly citing "Tertullian's famous remark, 'credo quia absurdam' ('I believe because it is absurd')" (1506, his emphasis). Given the limited communicative power of McConnell's "principles," it is no surprise that he fails to disclose the reasons for his controversial assertions about what the framers would have approved today.

McConnell is far from consistent in his culturally particularistic antirationalism. He takes at least two contradictory approaches to the framers, as we have seen, and he occasionally lapses into the first as he elaborates the second. At one point, for example, he insists that "the Constitution *has* an intelligible philosophy" and is neither "a mishmash of political compromises nor a congeries of inscrutable phrases." He indicates further that he would offer argumentation in support of this assertion if space permitted. But pending such argumentation, he simply reports that "it is my experience and conviction that the Constitution is an elegant and profound statement of a highly attractive conception of government."[87]

This disclosure is little more than an autobiographical statement. In context it amounts to: *Trust me to have seen what I cannot (yet?) show you.* It would enjoy normative force nowhere and apparent normative force only where the speaker would be thought inherently and unerringly competent. It would bring us from Berger's location of meaning in the subjective intent of the framers to a purer form of subjectivism, that of persons who are totally immersed in the framers' subjectivity.

Whatever Berger's problems, he can at least claim an objective view of constitutional meaning. Because his findings of constitutional meaning purport to be objective observations *about* the mind-set and actions of the framers, he can claim that constitutional meaning does not depend on what interpreters want it to be. McConnell is different. He affects total immersion in the framers' mind-set, and total immersion precludes the distance between subject and object that is presupposed in statements *about* something. When totally immersed one can perhaps repeat or announce what purports to be the framers' views. But one cannot reflect upon, explain, justify, describe, or interpret those views, for these operations require the subsumption of particulars under appropriate categories, and one cannot subsume that in which one is totally submerged.

THE NEW RIGHT'S CURRENT OPTIONS

The New Right's end in subjectivism was and remains predictable. The flight from truly common or public—and therefore transcultural—meanings, can only spiral downward toward some form of subjectivism. As we turn from justice and the self-critical rationality through which we try to understand its nature and demands, we can only descend to "justice"—that is, justice so-called—and so-called first by some particular historical community, then by third parties, like the framers, and finally by whoever has the power to make his interpretations of the community and the third parties stick. For if the meaning of constitutional words and phrases is necessarily meaning to some-one, as McConnell contends, the same must in principle be true of all other controversial words and phrases, including those that would describe commu-nity opinions, the framers' applications, the framers' definitions, the framers' philosophy, and the framers' mind-set.

I need not pause to examine the presumed exemption for *trust me* and the communications that would follow that appeal or (eventually) that command. It is enough to observe what seems in store by way of a change in regime. We start with a constitutional culture that befits the reason-giving and reason-exchanging quest for real meanings—a regime, ideally, of public-spirited dis-putation and tolerable if not always friendly diversity among more or less self-directing and self-respecting souls. We end in a place where spokespersons for the inscrutable rely on what McConnell approvingly calls some antirationalist "faith, piety, charisma, love, esthetics, mystery, or wonder" (1506). Whether one gets there by ascending or descending, McConnell's regime bears no re-semblance to the rule of coherent and sensible legal principle. If, as McCon-nell appears to agree, Berger's location of constitutional meaning in the partic-ular applications of the framers leads to a semantic and moral opacity that is irreconcilable with the rule of law, no less can be true of McConnell's implicit location of constitutional meaning in the unexplained and inexplicable pro-nouncements of those who claim immersion in the framers' mind-set.

I do not assume McConnell will persist in his current views. Indeed, I assume that it will be difficult for him to do so, given his contradictions and his desire to reconcile New Right constitutionalism with the rule of commu-nicable and sensible legal principle. No further comment on McConnell's problems are necessary here.[88] I have shown enough to support my point: Although New Right constitutionalists are easy enough to identify in the field—they are the rightists who demand judicial deference while yoking jus-tice with quotation marks from which they exempt (their particular notions of) democracy—they have no coherent conception of framers' intent. Inco-herence has not hurt them politically, of course, and I cannot assume coher-ence is what they want. But if they do want it, they will have to abandon the New Right and join some position, like the Old Right of *Lochner,* that sup-ports judicial power and other instruments for reconciling democracy to jus-tice—justice without quotation marks.

The prospects for such a transformation are not clear. A recent decision illustrates one of the ways in which New Right jurists would turn the Court's methodology in human rights cases in the direction of Berger's original emphasis on concrete intent. In *Michael H. v. Gerald D.*, Justice Antonin Scalia argued for himself and Chief Justice Rehnquist that the Court should protect substantive rights under the due process clause only if they are defined as rights by some specific, as opposed to general, tradition. Justice Scalia explained that judges who move beyond "the most specific level at which a relevant tradition . . . can be identified" do not discover "the society's views," they "dictate" them.[89]

Berger would probably concur with this proposition, perhaps making the most of Scalia's choice of words with a reminder of the comparison that Berger made years ago between the Warren Court and this century's worst dictators. Yet two moderately conservative justices declined to join that part of Scalia's opinion. For herself and Justice Anthony Kennedy, Justice Sandra O'Connor wondered what a methodology of "most specific level" of tradition would do to precedents like *Griswold* and *Loving v. Virginia* and the judiciary's capacity to address unanticipated problems.[90] These, of course, are among the concerns that have motivated the New Right's quest for an alternative to Berger's approach.

That effort got a more recent boost when Justices Souter, Kennedy, and O'Connor attempted to define a middle ground on the abortion question. The O'Connor-Kennedy-Souter joint opinion in *Planned Parenthood v. Casey* refused to overrule "the essential holding" of *Roe v. Wade* while rejecting *Roe's* trimester framework and approving several new restrictions on the abortion right that were held not to constitute an "undue burden."[91]

Rejecting any suggestion that unenumerated rights either could not offend or had to be rooted in specific traditions, the joint opinion argued that substantive due process claims "may call upon the Court . . . to exercise the same capacity which by tradition courts have always exercised: reasoned judgment."[92] Scalia, in a separate dissent joined by the Chief Justice and Justices Byron White and Clarence Thomas, denounced the joint opinion's reliance on "reasoned judgment" as an invitation to judicial inquiry at "a level of philosophical abstraction, in . . . isolation from the traditions of American society."[93] A method of reasoned judgment could only substitute the justices' "personal predilection[s]" for the value judgments of the community. These value judgments "should be voted on, not dictated," Scalia suggested, because "the people" are "free and intelligent" and because they "know that their value judgments are quite as good as those taught in any law school—maybe better."[94]

A week earlier Kennedy, O'Connor, and Souter had joined the Court's decision in *Lee v. Weisman* that prayer at a high school graduation ceremony violated the establishment clause of the First Amendment.[95] A 5:4 majority in *Lee* rejected Scalia's insistence that "a . . . specific tradition of invocations and benedictions at public-school graduation exercises" was sufficient to establish the constitutionality of these practices.[96] A pivotal factor in Kennedy's opinion for the Court was the "subtle coercive pressure" on students who did not want to pray that resulted from a combination of peer pressure and their own desire to graduate with their classmates. That pressure offended what Kennedy called "our own tradition" of governmental protection for a personal "sphere of inviolable conscience and belief which is the mark of a free people" (2656–58). By this appeal to tradition Kennedy implicitly questioned the assumpion that tradition can speak univocally and without the assistance of what Scalia derided as "the changeable philosophical predilections of the Justices of this Court" (2679).

At this writing one cannot conclude that a stable group of moderate conservatives has emerged on the Court or what that would mean for the future. But a Kennedy-O'Connor-Souter block could indicate that some Reagan-Bush appointees are turning away from New Right constitutionalism and toward the older conservativism of John Marshall, as represented in the postwar era by conservative jurists like John Marshall Harlan and in the nineties by libertarian theorists like Bernard Siegan and Stephen Macedo.[97]

Writers of this group can differ about what rights to protect and how strenuously to protect them; in particular, some would return to *Lochner*, while others would not. But they all accept the principal of unenumerated liberties, including some unenumerated privacy rights, and they believe the Constitution demands some meaningful levels of substantive and instrumental reasonableness before statutes and other governmental acts can rise to the dignity of law. Bork terms this group "conservative constitutional revisionists" because they sometimes favor conservative results while departing from the method he attributes to himself, Berger, and McConnell.

Bork assures us that he is "more in sympathy" with the policy objectives of some conservative revisionists than with the objectives of such "ultraliberals" as Dworkin and Justice William Brennan. Regarding the question of constitutional approach, however, Bork says revisionists of the right are as bad as revisionists of the left; they all defend forms of "judicial lawlessness."[98] The task facing these theorists amounts to an "impossible" philosophic achievement, he contends, because the only substitute for his originalism is a constitutional theory so detailed, complete, and demonstrable as to eliminate all disagreement about all aspects of every future case, from the largest question of principle to the smallest question of fact (226).

By thus assuming that his originalism can somehow function as a sub-stitute for an impossible philosophic achievement, Bork implicitly reinstates the formalist model of mechanical judging that he is at pains to disclaim elsewhere in his argument, as when declaring his approval of *Brown.* Macedo characterizes the judges' task more modestly (and in Dworkinian fashion) as answering the "need for a constitutional vision with a robust conception of rights grounded in the text of the Constitution, in sound moral thinking, and in our political tradition."[99]

A conception much closer to Macedo's and Dworkin's than to Bork's is that of Charles Fried, Harvard law professor and Ronald Reagan's solicitor general from 1985 to 1989. Fried clerked for Justice Harlan in the early 1960s, and in his recent book Fried supports Justice Harlan's approach to the Con-stitution in preference to what he calls "a kind of anti-intellectual, textual fundamentalism" championed by Justice Black.[100] Harlan, says Fried, be-lieved "in the possibility—indeed, inevitability—of reasoning and judgment in applying the Constitution." As evinced in his concurrence in *Griswold* and his approach to the question of the Fourteenth Amendment's incorporation of the Bill of Rights, Harlan accepted the idea of substantive due process because he saw the Fourteenth Amendment as "a warrant for protecting 'life, liberty, and property' against extreme and unfair impositions." Harlan "saw no escape from the method of reason" to Black's ostensible literalism, and Fried sees no future in the "disappointed yearning for a mechanical rule of judging that gave us originalism" (ibid.).

So Fried rejects the New Right's brand of originalism (62–65, 72–74, 85). Reminding his fellow Reaganites ("the party of liberty") of the framers' fear of majority tyranny, the lessons of the French Revolution (a "calamity for justice, for tranquility, for prosperity, for liberty"), and "the authority, powers, and methods of John Marshall's judiciary," Fried also rejects "majority will as the presumed default source of law, from which one may only depart on the clearest textual warrant . . . underwritten by the intent of the framers" (67–68). As he sees it, only some responsible conception of "the Constitution as a whole" can guide judges to the meaning of broadly worded constitutional provisions like due process. In Dworkinian fashion, Fried likens the process to treating the specifics of the Bill of Rights as "points on a graph, which the judge joins by a line to describe a coherent and rationally compelling func-tion" (74).

Such were Harlan's extrapolations in *Griswold* and in *NAACP v. Ala-bama,* which had upheld an unenumerated freedom of association.[101] Such also, according to Fried, had been the Court's extrapolations in *Pierce v. Society of Sisters* and *Meyer v. Nebraska,* which had announced rights of parents to educate their children in parochial schools and have them taught foreign languages.[102]

Such, however, was not Justice Scalia's approach in *Michael H. v. Gerald D.*, an approach that Fried criticizes as holding out a false promise of liberation from the burdens of reasoned judgment.[103] Nor was it Justice White's approach for the Court in *Bowers v. Hardwick* (1986), which upheld a Georgia sodomy law as applied against a homosexual act.[104] Fried criticizes White for a "stunningly harsh and dismissive opinion" that invokes community morality and legislative patterns "to preclude reasoning, not assist it." "Unless one takes the implausible line that people generally choose their sexual orientation," says Fried, "then to criminalize any enjoyment of their sexual powers by whole classes of persons is either an imposition of very great cruelty or an exercise in hypocrisy inviting arbitrary and abusive applications of the criminal law."[105]

This kind of thinking removes Fried far from the interpretive position of New Right theorists like Bork, Berger, and McConnell. Just how far is indicated further by his analysis of *Roe*, his reinterpretation of the Reagan administration's judicial philosophy, and his assessment of the Warren years. Fried accepts the standard New Right charge that the postwar federal judiciary prior to Reagan had become an instrument for "reorder[ing] whole institutions and chang[ing] the fundamental nature of society" in the manner desired by "progressive-minded lawyers," "the legal professoriate, the liberal press," and other communicants of "the left-liberal orthodoxies." To this end, Warrenite judges "creat[ed] new constitutional rights" and "manipulat[ed] rules and remedies at every level" (16–18).

Yet Fried has harsh words for any suggestion that everything about the Warren years was wrong. Although Reaganism called for judges who are "more disciplined, less adventurous and political in interpreting . . . the Constitution," Fried reports that throughout his years in the Reagan Justice Department he felt that

> any approach to the role of law and the courts had to take account of the Himalayan fact that it was the Supreme Court in *Brown v. Board*—not the ordinary political system—that had taken the largest step since Reconstruction in dismantling legalized racism and apartheid in this country. It was the courts and the Supreme Court that had moved to civilize the way local police departments dealt with criminal suspects—particularly the poor and the ignorant. And it was the courts and the Supreme Court that had made our system of individual liberty a model for the whole world. It would have been not just Quixotic but anticonstitutional and thus lawless to seek a wholesale reversal of that tradition. (18)

Thus does Fried invite his readers to conclude that Bork's approach is "anticonstitutional and thus lawless." Apparently unimpressed with Bork's lip service to *Brown,* Fried says that Bork's method would "probably" mean reversing *Brown* (65). And the prospect of an anticonstitutionalist theory hypocritically indulging great moral achievements—or the unnecessary, self-defeating, and pointless opposition to great moral imperatives—together with what he calls the "devastating" objections to Bork's brand of originalism (61–65)—these considerations compel Fried to attempt a saving construction of the Reagan project for the courts.

In a move that exemplifies Dworkin's method of interpreting sources of normative authority, Fried tries to make judicial Reaganism look good. Fried proposes that, properly understood, and "whatever stories we [in the Administration] may have told ourselves, the Reagan administration's project of judicial restraint in the end could be no more than a project to reintroduce a conception of law disciplined by a respect for tradition, professionalism, and careful, candid reasoning" (70). Later he speaks of the administration's "real project" as that of "restoring reasonableness and responsibility to the practice of judging" (88). Although Fried can sympathize with part of the impetus behind Bork's originalism—a desire to reverse the alleged subordination of law to policy among judges and legal intellectuals—Fried implicitly contrasts his emphasis on reasonableness in judging with what he describes as Bork's "inability to find in reason itself any criterion to serve as the anchor for the rule of law" (61).

Perceived deficiencies in reasonableness are the grounds of Fried's hostility to *Roe,* and an inspection of his treatment of *Roe* indicates just how deep his commitment to reasonableness may run. He acknowledges the existence of unenumerated constitutional rights and supports a constitutional right to privacy, including the right announced in *Griswold* (72–76). But abortion does not implicate privacy, Fried says, because many of the legislators who oppose abortion believe that abortion is murder. Fried says he knows of no argument that proves "the nonviable fetus" is or is not a person. "On this question the Constitution is silent," he says, and "it is in this space that the legislators must choose," just as they choose between "war and peace . . . socialism and capitalism," and other matters of the utmost importance. Fried holds it "an utter non sequitur" to conclude from constitutional silence that, for legislative purposes, "the fetus is *not* a person."

Unlike the racism that fueled much of the outrage with *Brown*—"an ugly motivation" that is "fundamentally at war" with constitutional principles and for that reason unworthy of judicial consideration—the desire to protect innocent life deserved the Court's respect. That praiseworthy desire created a "moral urgency" that Justice Blackmun's opinion in *Roe* failed to meet. Moreover, says Fried (presumably because he cannot resolve the issue of personhood) no opinion "that could have been written" could have met the moral urgency created by the desire to protect innocent persons (77–78). Yet a few pages later Fried acknowledges a moral motivation in Blackmun's opinion: the desire to avoid what Fried calls "the truly horrible spectacle of women—especially poor and ignorant women—suffering mutilation and death in desperate attempts to end unwanted pregnancies." But then he adds that "it is exactly this conviction of moral rectitude unmatched by any convincing logic that is infuriating—and that distinguishes *Roe* from *Brown,* whose moral principle, after all, is broad and simple and clear" (81).

This last comment from Fried indicates that, although moral considerations properly figure in constitutional judgments, fidelity to the Constitution justifies anger at judges who reason from the depth of a moral conviction, even one that we share, without troubling to show the reasonableness of that conviction. By suggesting that convictions must be reasonable, perhaps even "convincing," before they can legitimately count in constitutional argument, Fried indicates pride of place for the virtue of trying to be reasonable and appear reasonable to others, this reasonableness above such virtues as sincerity and commitment, if virtues the latter be. This position is one that skeptics like Bork and subjectivists like McConnell could not possibly accept.

Given Fried's emphasis on reasonableness, one wonders what he would require of legislators who confront the demand for reasons from the pro-choice constituencies who feel what he himself describes as the true horrors of back-alley abortions. Must pro-life legislators match their conviction that abortion is murder with some "convincing logic" to that effect? Fried does not come right out and say so, but a meaningful reasonableness test for abortion policy hides between the lines of his argument. I say this because even though he feels that "*Roe* gave legal reasoning a bad name," and as hard as he has continued to work for the overruling of *Roe* after his tenure as solicitor general, he apparently feels that it would be responsible for the Court, after overruling *Roe,* to invalidate laws that prohibit all abortions, punish women who have abortions, and outlaw "safe, simple, self-administered pharmaceuticals to induce early-term abortions." "In fact," he says, "medical discoveries might then make this whole constitutional episode moot" (81, 86).

Dworkin has welcomed Fried's reinterpretation of the Reagan administration's call for judicial restraint because Fried would replace "blind" invocations of framers' intent and "some fetish about majority rule" with the promise of "an interpretive understanding of our constitutional history" that is attractive enough to justify the constitutional course of the Court's conservative majority.[106] But Dworkin finds Fried's attempt to redeem that promise "a complete failure" (28). One of Dworkin's reasons is his understandable inability to see how the Court could say that a state can declare abortion murder yet not punish women who suborn the murder of their fetuses or commit murder through self-administered pharmaceuticals. Problems of this nature indicate to Dworkin that Fried can offer no plausible constitutional principle for excluding abortion from the right to privacy, and that the anti-abortion article of the Reagan program is therefore nothing more than a debt to an important electoral constituency (25).

I am not as interested here in an assessment of Fried's substantive constitutional arguments as I am in the criteria of argumentation that should govern his response to Dworkin and our response to him if his response to Dworkin should fail. Recall in this connection Fried's mixed view of the Warren era. We have seen him indicate that opposing some of the Warren Court's practices and decisions would be "anticonstitutional and thus lawless," while opposing others would represent disapproval of partisan courts and thus support for the rule of law.

Fried suggests a test for separating the honorable from the "infuriating," and that test is the test of "convincing logic" or reasonableness. Evidently, it is fair to see partisanship in an unreasonable opinion and even to meet such an opinion with outrage. So if Fried is unable to clarify his position on abortion, his own treatment of the Warren era justifies the conclusion that he is rationalizing the partisan preferences of the religious right, which Fried himself lists as a Reagan constituency.[107] Dworkin also finds Fried unable to give a reasonable defense of Reaganism's opposition to racial classifications that may be needed to overcome structures of racial injustice. Dworkin wants to know what sense it makes to oppose benign as well as invidious racial classifications while not opposing benign classifications by "age or income level or formal educational qualification or other categories government and private institutions use instead of more individual assessments."[108]

In what must count either as a failure in candor or as more evidence of Fried's acceptance of Dworkin's interpretive method (as manifest in Fried's attempt to make Reaganism look good), Fried fails to list racial resentment and fear as ingredients of the Reagan-Bush electoral successes. But if Fried cannot manage a reasonable response to Dworkin's question about racial classifications, then, by Fried's own standards of argumentation, it is not unfair to say that Reaganism's theory on that question serves a constituency that refuses to act against the social, psychological, and economic structures that perpetuate infuriating disadvantages for some racial minorities.

I think Fried would agree that to make judicial Reaganism look good in a

political context he must display its capacity for something beyond reasonableness about specific constitutional issues. Political attractiveness must also
exhibit certain passions. Fried thus expresses anger (fury, literally) in the service of reasonableness by declaring *Roe*'s unreasonableness "infuriating." He
is also angry (though not furious) over the New Right's attempt to deny that
reasonableness is an ingredient of constitutionality—an attempt that makes
the New Right the Antireasonableness Right, as is most evident in McConnell. We have seen Fried suggest that the New Right is "anticonstitutional and
therefore lawless," and at one point he says he wants to free Reaganism from
"the albatross of originalist rigorism."[109] But Fried is also prepared to excuse
New Right constitutionalism as an understandable reaction to judicial ex-
cesses that have given reason a bad name, and one wonders why Justice Blackmun's understandable desire to spare poor women the horrors of unsafe abortions is not sufficient to temper Fried's fury with *Roe*. Perhaps Fried's anger
with the New Right will rise should he fail to rescue judicial Reaganism from
its self-degrading strategy of question-begging rhetoric about democracy and
framers' intent deployed with McCarthyite attacks on the partisans of judicial
reasonableness.

Fried cannot rescue judicial Reaganism unless judicial conservatives turn
from Bork and accept Fried's leadership. And they are hardly likely to elevate
someone who makes them look too bad. In fact, Fried has already said enough
to outrage some of his former colleagues in the Justice Department.[110] Whatever the outcome, Fried has undertaken a combination of theoretical and
political tasks of truly herculean—even Himalayan—proportions.

5

THEORIES
OF
JUDICIAL REVIEW II:
MODERNIST LIBERALISM

New Right constitutionalism is but one variety of the modernist position whose relevant nature lies either in its metaphysics or its epistemology, not its political ideology. The metaphysical or epistemological positions in question result in what appears to the ordinary citizen as a morally skeptical approach to values generally and therefore to constitutional questions in hard cases. Modernist writers are found on both sides of the current debate on the role of the judiciary.

Modernists who support a policy of judicial deference in hard cases tend to argue that deference follows either from the absence of objectively better answers in hard cases (simple ontological skepticism), or from the inaccessibility of objectively better answers (epistemological skepticism), or from the power of legislative or public opinion in either the short or the long run to establish legal-moral truth (shallow or deep conventionalism). Modernists who support a nondeferential judiciary usually combine empirical propositions about institutional behavior and philosophically conventionalist beliefs about values to conclude that judges are better situated to discern the likely direction of popular consensus and therewith the proper direction of legal-moral progress. This chapter explores the connections between modernist theories and shows why no modernist theory can defend the American tradition of judicial review.

ALEXANDER BICKEL AND THE
COMMON THEORETICAL GROUND OF
MODERNIST ATTITUDES
TOWARD JUDICIAL POWER

The career of Alexander Bickel illustrates the continuity of modernism of the left and right and shows why it is hard to defend a nondeferential judiciary on modernist grounds. Moved originally by what he believed was a conflict between his commitment to majoritarianism and his respect for the Supreme Court, especially the Court that decided *Brown v. Board of Education,* Bickel's thought evolved through phases that mixed conflicting elements differently without ever reaching a coherent resolution. Thus, in his most judicially conservative phase (made final not by dawning philosophic certitude but by his premature death) Bickel could call for both judicial restraint and judicial assertiveness in behalf of rights needed to "make the political process work,"[1] a category whose potential for across-the-board judicial assertiveness he failed to appreciate.

Whether Bickel's paradoxes propelled him to seminal insights is a matter of disagreement.[2] But there is no disagreement about his influence on the constitutional debate during most of the two decades following his death. Many writers credit Bickel with inaugurating that debate as the specific quest for a way to reconcile a nondeferential judiciary to majoritarianism within a broadly relativist or conventionalist view of morality and consistently with the American Legal Realist critique of legal formalism.[3] Echoes of Bickel are audible in different and diverse answers to his question, including proceduralist and New Right misgivings about a judicial orientation to moral principles[4] and the continuing call for judicial activism in behalf of evolving social values.[5] Here, then, was a complex figure whose work is difficult to summarize.

If one blurs one's vision to exclude nuances and refinements, however, one can say that Bickel accepted the principal inheritances of his intellectual environment regarding the impossibility of mechanical judicial decision and, more important, the conventionalist nature of meaning and values.[6] In moments of theoretical self-consciousness Bickel wrote as if evolving social beliefs were all that could give meaning to general constitutional standards and that, where stubborn public attitudes did not counsel a prudential judicial inaction, it was the unique function of courts to anticipate the course of social change and either rationalize or invalidate current political choices accordingly.[7]

Had Bickel maintained consistency with this outlook, he would have believed, for example, that the post-1937 Court did the right thing in abandoning constitutional protection for racism and the liberty to contract, not

because the Constitution did or should have mandated these progressive results but because public opinion was heading in that direction and because it
was the Court's function to make the public feel that its emerging opinions
were consistent with constitutional principle.[8] Yet Bickel could appear to
compromise his moral relativism with strong statements in behalf of the Court's
policy against segregation.[9] In the 1960s and early 1970s he could even support judicial toleration of benign racial quotas and court-ordered local taxes
for school desegregation.[10]

As political conditions changed, however, so did Bickel's attitude toward
the power and function of the federal judiciary. White flight from the cities
and growing public resistance to the judicial threat against de facto segregation outside the South made him increasingly pessimistic about the judiciary's
real power to effect a fundamental change in race relations. This pessimism,
added to the unsettling effect of the disruptions of the Vietnam era, moved
law and order closer to the top of Bickel's list of political priorities.[11] In 1970
he published a change of heart about the Court's role as harbinger of evolving
principles.[12] He attacked what he saw as the Warren Court's self-defeating
attempt to impose a liberal ideological agenda on an unwilling nation.[13] Purcell seems justified in saying that the Bickel of this period came "to doubt the
utility and even the existence of actual principles."[14] Bickel came to believe, as
does Berns today, that an insistence on a politics of principle from any source,
including the judiciary, can only destroy a system whose stability depends on
a nonideological social structure whose elements are willing to compromise
principle in the pursuit of ends that can be represented in the ordinary give-
and-take of pluralist politics.[15]

Purcell aptly judges the later Bickel's "simplistic and mechanical" faith in
pluralism to be heedless of gross economic and political inequities.[16] On the
other hand, by condemning the judicial concern for principle as such, Bickel
avoided any suggestion that circumstances could warrant some future judicial
attempt to justify racism, bigotry, and greed in constitutional terms. Perhaps
self-respect was more important to him than theoretical consistency, for his
earlier views on the role of the Court would have suggested judicial rationalizations of the nation's recrudescing vices.

It could be, therefore, that Bickel's final counsel of judicial deference
represents nothing more exceptional than an academic's loss of faith in the
general public. Or perhaps Bickel was voicing a historicist's faith that, to
borrow from Dworkin, "as a river forms a bed on its way to the sea," American politics would eventually etch a path to justice without instituting a real
(i.e., self-critical) concern for justice.[17] Nevertheless, Bickel's later writings
entitle Bork to use Bickel's name in the New Right's crusade for a politics of

popular willfulness.[18] And although Bork is hardly one to complain about ignoring the Constitution, he correctly terms Bickel's early theory an attempt to justify judicial activism without appealing to the Constitution (193, 207).

Bickel did look away from the Constitution and toward evolving social consensus. Because he conformed to an academic orthodoxy that denied the reality of justice and other ends to which popular consensus should aspire, it was difficult for him to appreciate the Constitution's point.

MICHAEL J. PERRY AND THE CONSTITUTIONALISM OF VACUOUS ASPIRATIONS

The same is true of Michael Perry, the most visible of the current theorists whose positions are close to Bickel's. Perry's case is complicated by thought that comes in contradictory phases and by dubious claims to honor the constitutional text and rise above moral skepticism. In his first two phases Perry tried to justify the activism of the postwar Court in human rights cases, including freedom of expression and equal protection cases, cases protecting "participational values," and substantive due process cases involving "the individual's interests in sexual, reproductive, and associational autonomy."[19] These cases included the abortion decisions. In his first phase, represented by an early article on abortion rights, Perry supported *Roe* for keeping the Constitution in step with an evolving social consensus. In his second phase, Perry withheld his opinion on the merits of *Roe* and complained that "the Court failed to articulate any kind of rigorous argument" for its conclusion. Yet he supported the Court's authority to decide the case in the manner it did (351–52). Perry labeled that manner "noninterpretive review."

In "virtually all constitutional doctrine regarding human rights fashioned by the Supreme Court in this century," said Perry, the Court engages in "noninterpretive review" because it grounds decisions in value judgments other than those "constitutionalized by the Framers"—"because the Court reaches its decision without really interpreting, in the hermeneutical sense, any provision of the constitutional text (or any aspect of government structure)" (279, 281).

When Perry said "virtually all constitutional doctrine," he included "most constitutional doctrine regarding . . . freedom of expression . . . freedom of religion, [and] the procedural rights of criminal defendants"—cases where decision can be and usually is rationalized as interpretive of specific ideas expressly present in the constitutional text. He rejected these and other interpretivist rationalizations of this century as "rhetoric designed to create the illusion that it [the Court] is merely 'interpreting' or 'applying' some constitutional provision" (279–80). Implicitly, therefore, he conceived "interpretive review" as an attempt to ascertain the exemplars or definitions that the framers had concretely in mind when adopting specific constitutional provisions.[20]

Insisting that neither the intentions of the framers nor the constitutional text supported noninterpretive review, and therewith the authority of the Court to have handed down the human rights decisions of our century, Perry asked whether noninterpretive review might nevertheless serve "a crucial governmental function that no other practice might realistically be expected to serve . . . in a manner that accommodates the principle of electoral accountable democracy."[21] Such was Perry's version of the question Bickel had introduced almost twenty years before.[22]

In Perry's first statement on the abortion decision, he had accepted Bickel's early view that the Court need not wait for the elected branches to catch up with evolving community standards.[23] The second phase of his thought found Perry trying to formulate an approach different from Bickel's. The task proved difficult. He began by denying that either a uniform tradition or a contemporary consensus existed in a manner "sufficiently determinate" to serve as a noncontroversial foundation of judicial decision in modern human rights cases.[24] But despite this statement it did not take him long to invoke a tradition or consensus of a sort, "a fundamental dimension of our collective American self-understanding" that lies beyond "values . . . constitutionalized by the framers" and that "can serve as a reservoir of decisional norms for human rights cases" (288).

Perry described this American self-understanding in terms of a nation trying "to realize, if only 'partially and fragmentally' . . . a 'higher law.'"[25] According to this self-understanding, "'the will of the people is not itself the criterion in terms of which this will can be judged; it is possible that the people may be wrong.'"[26] This self-understanding "has generally involved a commitment, although not necessarily a fully conscious one, to the notion of moral evolution. . . . We have avoided the pretense that our current understanding of the moral universe . . . was perfect and complete. . . . We know that we are fallible and that we must struggle incessantly to achieve a broader and deeper understanding."[27]

And here was where the Court came in. Its insulation from the immediate winds of public opinion gave it a special competence. "The basic function of noninterpretive review," said Perry, was to "deal with those political issues that are also fundamental moral problems in a way that is faithful to the notion of moral evolution" (293–94). "In dealing with those issues," said Perry in a crucial passage, "the Court, when acting at its best, has not relied on established moral conventions. To the contrary, the Court has used such issues as occasions for moral reevaluations of established conventions and for possible moral development, leading, however gradually and painfully, to the establishment of morally sounder conventions" (294).

The problem with Bickel was his suggestion, whether intended or not, that judges should look to emerging moral conventions. This suggestion, said Perry, implicitly reducing moral conventionalism to moral skepticism, was a "morally skeptical" conception of the judicial function in which "tomorrow's values are assumed to be merely different from today's ('change, not growth')." "My point," Perry went on, "is not that noninterpretive review is or should be aimed at what tomorrow's majority might come to credit as progress, but that the dialectical relationship between noninterpretive review and the process of electorally accountable policymaking leads to a far more self-critical morality. . . . It is not a question of 'controlling' this generation by the predicted values of future ones, but of *aspiring* to give, in any generation, right answers to the fundamental political moral problems that confront that generation" (311–12, original emphasis).

To the extent that Perry's second phase related judicial power to the quest for moral truth beyond social convention, he was to change his mind in his third phase. But his position was never clear, for there were several reasons to doubt that his second-phase rejection of moral conventionalism was as firm as it appeared. To begin with, he allowed that to reconcile noninterpretive review to the value of electorally accountable policy-making, the Constitution should be construed to give Congress the power to strip the Court's jurisdiction in cases where the Court had exercised noninterpretive review. Perry disallowed jurisdiction stripping in cases of interpretive review, however, since blocking interpretive review would offend the principle of constitutional supremacy over all institutions, including electorally accountable legislatures. Perry's position on jurisdiction stripping suggested that democracy (represented in the act of jurisdiction stripping) should supersede the commitment to moral growth (institutionalized in the practice of noninterpretive review). Ranking democracy over moral improvement should have troubled anyone who had accepted Perry's earlier claims about the nation's aspiration to moral growth.

Perry's contrast with Publius was plain in any event. Because Publius could not defend popular government separated from substantive ends like justice, he sought to reconcile popular government *to justice*. Perry sought to reconcile the concern for moral growth, and therewith justice, *to democracy*. If we assume that Perry would not deliberately have elevated democracy over justice (for democracy over justice would have implied a preference for democracy even when tyrannical or mere democracy over constitutional democracy), we can see why Perry might have regarded philosophical conventionalism an attractive option. To avoid a statement that could support tyranny—such as an open preference for democracy over justice—he had either to return to the classical attempt to reconcile democracy to justice or accept the conventionalist claim that, at some deep remove, justice is constituted by what particular communities (democratic or otherwise) believe justice to be. With justice thus constituted by opinion that the legislature may represent best, jurisdiction stripping need not elevate democracy over justice.

Conventionalism was the likely explanation for two other elements of Perry's position: his assumption that the Constitution's language refers to concrete historical conceptions, not abstract ideas with real content, and his contention that virtually all modern human rights cases were noninterpretive in character. Had Perry believed that the language of, say, the due process clause and the First Amendment referred to real things beyond concrete historical opinions, he would have had no reason to dismiss modern interpretations of those clauses as the rhetoric of judges who are merely rationalizing their departures from the Constitution. These judges may well have departed from the framers' concrete versions of those clauses, but new versions would not mean the judges had abandoned the framers' principal aims or the Constitution itself. For the true meaning of the framers and the Constitution could have been the abstract moral entities signified by the constitutional text, and knowledge of these values would have been an object of a self-critical process that was prepared, when feasible, to abandon old conceptions in light of better conceptions.

Finally, conventionalism surfaced in several of Perry's explicit remarks. His statement that judicial decision was "inevitably rooted in the . . . moral culture that has been formative for each justice" (319) suggested either that constitutional language refers to nothing real or that our socially conditioned beliefs foreclose all access to what might be real. Elsewhere he enclosed the terms *magical* and *scientific* in quotation marks, lumping science with magic as nothing more than a cultural artifact, and suggested that truth (the "correctness" of answers to legal, moral, and scientific questions) is a question not of some relationship between belief and transcultural reality but of what people believe works in a particular "place and time" (304–5).

These statements were at odds with Perry's portrait of a nation aspiring to moral truth beyond what "a majority of Americans happens to believe, either in the short term or in the long term" (307). They signaled difficulties in his effort to free himself from the Bickelean conventionalism of his first phase. For if truth is a cultural artifact, there either is no reality beyond long-term social consensus (nothing out there for our propositions to correspond to) or the utter inaccessibility of reality precludes correspondence between it and our accounts of it and argues for defining truth independently of reality and in terms of ungrounded belief. The function of noninterpretive review in that case would be as Bickel had seen it: the enforcement of some underlying social consensus from which the elected branches had deviated. Perry's new theory

of constitutional aspiration thus conflicted with the philosophic conventionalism suggested by his view of truth as cultural artifact. If truth were a cultural
artifact, there could be no understanding beyond long-term social belief to
which the nation could aspire.

Perry may have seen the tension between his conventionalism and his
reference to constitutional aspirations, for the hint of a possible resolution
appeared in his belief that Americans shared a commitment to moral growth,
whether they were always fully aware of that commitment, and true to it, or
not (290, 292). Perry thus suggested that the beliefs of a community were
multilayered, with some beliefs running deeper than those that occupied the
plane of open controversy among the community's constituent groups. The
deeper beliefs would be shared by virtually all elements that saw themselves as
parts of a single community. The shallow beliefs would be associated with
conflicting or potentially conflicting parts of the community.

Thus, people understand the American left in contradistinction to the
American right and center, with each position remaining American in some
respect that makes debate among them more sensible than war or indifference. Although Perry seemed of two minds on the usefulness of the distinction
(292), a distinction between a deep and shallow consensus would have made
sense of his view that judges could oppose popular majorities without invoking standards beyond the community's moral culture. A bifurcated convention would also have explained how he could both affirm and deny a consensual basis for the judicial protection of what he saw as extraconstitutional
rights: protection for the deep beliefs, not the shallow ones, no matter how
durable.

Related problems burdened the most complete statement of Perry's second phase, his book *The Constitution, the Courts, and Human Rights,* published in 1982. There Perry elaborated his belief in right answers during an
attack on the moral skepticism of William Rehnquist and Robert Bork. Perry
stressed that his aspirational approach required not just right answers but also
"discoverable right answers."[28] He classified Bork and Rehnquist as moral
skeptics who denied "at least" the demonstrability of right answers, if not their
existence and accessibility to reason. Although it was not clear whether Perry
was distinguishing two or three varieties of skepticism—namely, nondemonstrability, inaccessibility, or nonexistence of moral truth—he treated the least
"radical" form (nondemonstrability) as the practical equivalent of the most
radical (nonexistence of moral truth), and he opposed moral skepticism of all
varieties (103–4).

Yet the reasons for Perry's opposition to moral skepticism were not what
one would have expected from someone who had been talking about right

answers and aspirations beyond what people believe in the short or long term. He offered no affirmative argument for right answers, and he rejected the view that right answers were unavoidable presuppositions of legal-moral debate. He thus rejected Thomas Nagel's contention that moral skepticism was impossible for anyone with an opinion about the judiciary's proper role.

Nagel had argued that any such opinion "must depend on a political philosophy that is taken to be true."[29] Perry's response eventually contradicted his own view of truth as a cultural artifact and betrayed uncertainty on whether to embrace moral conventionalism or condemn it as moral skepticism. He began by citing Bork as a "counterexample" to Nagel's position. In a statement that retained a distinction between truth and social belief or convention, Perry added that Bork relied "not . . . on a political philosophy that is taken to be true," but rather "on a political philosophy that is taken to be a given in—an axiom of—American political-legal culture."[30]

Perry initially saw nothing wrong with Bork's reliance on cultural axioms. "One can treat a particular political philosophy as a given," said Perry, "one can even be committed to a particular political philosophy, without abandoning one's robust moral skepticism—that is, without supposing that the philosophy can be demonstrated to be true, even without supposing that truth can be predicated of political philosophy." But then he quickly turned to attack the "moral skepticism" of Bork and Rehnquist. That skepticism was wrong because it left "no 'principled'—morally nonarbitrary—ground for objecting to laws authorizing torture, establishing slavery, or even instituting another Holocaust" and because moral skepticism would be "a terribly difficult position to take seriously in this post-Holocaustal age. Moreover, it is, happily, a position not widely shared in the United States today, nor has it ever been. We have taken it for granted . . . that the language of justice—the search for justice—is not morally arbitrary." Moral skepticism was thus "a position fundamentally at odds with our understanding of ourselves as a people committed to ongoing moral reevaluation and moral growth" (105–6).

When Perry described Bork's mode of argumentation as moral reasoning from cultural axioms, he described a conventionalist position. Although conventionalism may be distinguished from skepticism for some purposes,[31] Perry was correct in treating conventionalism as skepticism, because Perry's focus was on the constitutional level, not the level of individual conduct. The question at the constitutional level is not whether there exist norms applicable to individuals, but whether the political community as a whole is, through its representatives, acting in conformity to some norm. Because the conventionalist holds that the community is the source of all norms, the conventionalist can admit no norm applicable against the community. For the community as a whole, no external norms exist, and conventionalism thus merges with skepticism at the constitutional level.

Yet there remained a problem in Perry's attack on Bork; Perry's argument was itself a conventionalist argument in line with his earlier view of truth as a cultural artifact. Perry's conventionalist argument against conventionalism was both ironic and imperfectly executed. For "our understanding of ourselves" is not a conventionalist understanding; it is a moral realist understanding. We do not think we oppose the Holocaust merely because we live in a post-Holocaust age. We oppose it because we think it was wrong and would be wrong in any age. And when we say we quest for justice, we assume that justice is not simply a matter of what we believe—not even deeply and in the long run, for it makes sense to believe that our deepest, most durable, and even most considered opinions can be wrong.

In sum, as Perry acknowledges at one point, our ordinary self-understanding supports moral realism.[32] Moral realism is no less in conflict with Perry's conventionalism than with Bork's. If Bork's affront to our self-understanding makes him a skeptic, Perry is also a skeptic. Such was the tension in Perry's thought. Perry indicated in the preface of this first book that he would say more about "the problem of objectivity in ethics" in a later work (x). That later work was Perry's second book, *Morality, Politics, and Law,* published in 1988. In that book Perry entered the third phase of his thought and resolved the paradox of his first phase in favor of a disguised but unmistakable moral skepticism. He has now reinvented Bickel and reconciled himself to the Bickelean conventionalism he once condemned as moral skepticism.

Perry now holds with McConnell that "meaning is always meaning to someone."[33] Because people disagree over meaning, and because meaning is meaning to someone, "one meaning of a text can contradict another meaning of the text" (ibid.). The content that a community attaches to a particular text depends on what individuals in that community agree the text refers to. The meaning of constitutional norms is therefore "indeterminate" in the sense of dependent for content solely on evolving social beliefs (133–34, 138–42, 155–56). Although Perry wants to preserve a distinction between a present social consensus and deeper, more authoritative beliefs (see ibid., 106–113, 148–51), the line between them is not clear, and in the end present consensus seems to be Perry's criterion of substantive correctness. In addition, Perry seems to hold that the rationalization of present consensus is the proper role of courts.

These conclusions emerge from Perry's change of heart regarding *Roe v. Wade.* He argued in 1976 that "the Court, in deciding *Roe* as it did, struck down laws that were contrary to the evolving, maturing conventions of the moral culture." "No doubt," he added, "these evolving conventions would eventually have generated a radical reform of the abortion laws invalidated in *Roe*. In the interim, however, the toll in human suffering would have been immense." Thus, he concluded in early-Bickelean fashion, "there is something to be said for the ethical function of judicial review, for not waiting for the legislative process to catch up with important and fundamental cultural transformations."[34]

Perry's current position is that the Court erred on the merits in *Roe* and that *Roe* represents an illegitimate mode of judicial action. He now holds that because "the value of fetal life" is such a controversial issue in America, it was "plainly imperial" for the Court to declare a broad right to abort. The Court, he says, should have struck down the Texas statute at issue in *Roe*, but only because Texas permitted abortions to save the mother's life without also permitting abortions in cases of incest and rape, serious health risks to the mother, and serious genetic defects in the fetus. The Court should have mandated these exceptions to the statutory ban on abortions "because it is most unlikely that abortion legislation failing to provide even for these relatively narrow exceptions would be enacted and maintained in contemporary American society."[35]

If Perry means what he says about *Roe*, answers to controversial questions about the meaning of constitutional rights are to be located in those restrictions that American legislatures would be most likely to impose on themselves. Perry began by joining the early Bickel's conventionalist defense of judicial activism; now he is moving toward the later Bickel's denial of real rights against popular majorities.

The best refutation of Perry's current direction is to be found in his vain attempts to disclaim moral skepticism and a theory that would license extraconstitutional judicial action. As we have seen, his first book described the Court's modern human rights decisions as extraconstitutional or "noninterpretivist." Because he wanted to defend the modern court, Perry set out to defend "noninterpretivist judicial review." The interpretivism-noninterpretivism distinction in contemporary constitutional theory is generally credited to Thomas Grey, who initially joined many constitutional scholars in viewing most modern human rights decisions as extraconstitutional.[36] The distinction became popular enough to define the current debate for many theorists, with supporters of judicial power, like the early Perry, lining up on the noninterpretivist side, and critics of judicial power, like Bork, demanding what they called an exclusively interpretivist method in constitutional decision.[37]

Ronald Dworkin attacked the interpretivism-noninterpretivism framework in the early 1980s as confusing, question-begging, and descriptively inaccurate. He claimed that supporters of judicial power should be arguing not that judges do and should ignore constitutional text, tradition, and original intention, but that they do and should interpret constitutional text, tradition, and intention as "presuppos[ing] a *prior* commitment to certain principles of political justice which, if we are to act responsibly, must . . . be reflected in the way the Constitution is read and enforced" (472, his emphasis). Allegedly noninterpretivist judges were thus actually interpreting text, tradition, and intention. Interpretivist critics of the Court were also interpreting text, tradition, and intentions, but hardly in a way that isolated these sources of authority from normative assumptions of the kind at work in allegedly noninterpretivist decision. Critics of the Court often asserted or assumed controversial conceptions of democracy, law, and political obligation, for example. The critics brought their controversial conceptions to their interpretations of text, tradition, and intentions. Their conceptions did not come as uncontroversial inferences from text, tradition, and intentions (472–75).

Dworkin did not persuade everyone to abandon the interpretivist-noninterpretivist distinction; New Right theorists continue to use it because it enables them to say that the other side supports judges who ignore the Constitution.[38] But Grey was persuaded, as were Perry and others, and Perry now characterizes the current debate as between different answers to the question of how to interpret the Constitution, not whether to interpret it.[39] Reconceiving the old debate between interpretivism and noninterpretivism as one between "originalism" and "nonoriginalism"—those, roughly, who seek the framers' meanings of constitutional provisions versus those who consult the current meanings of constitutional provisions—Perry now calls himself an interpretivist who embraces the nonoriginalist approach to constitutional meaning.[40]

Perry recognizes that this shift in terminology may be vacuous in view of the "deep disagreement as to what it means to 'interpret' existing law" (285, n. 47). He confesses that he is "not comfortable with the 'originalist/nonoriginalist' terminology" (279, n. 7). He acknowledges that "it can be difficult, even impossible, to distinguish an originalist position with respect to some issue from a nonoriginalist one" (289, n. 59). He recognizes that others use the terms differently (279, n. 7). And, in a manner that parallels the New Right's vacillation between abstract and concrete intentions, Perry leaves the reader guessing whether originalists must find constitutional meaning in the framers' concrete examples and definitions (and in the institutional "supplements" and doctrinal implications of these concrete intentions), or whether originalists may also look to abstract versions of intent that threaten to erase the line between originalism and nonoriginalism.[41]

No clear and consistent thread unites all that Perry says about originalism and its opposite number. But it is clear that his nonoriginalism is not an approach to what the Constitution means. If interpretivists are concerned with what the Constitution means, Perry's nonoriginalism is a disguised form of noninterpretivism, the approach he defended in his first book. Noninterpretivism is evident in Perry's conception of nonoriginalism as concerned with what he calls "aspirational meaning." "To the nonoriginalist, unlike the originalist, what the Constitution means is not merely what it originally meant," says Perry, for "some provisions signify fundamental aspirations of the American political tradition." Examples of such aspirational provisions are those of the First Amendment "signifying the tradition's aspirations to the freedoms of speech, press, and religion," and the Fourteenth Amendment "signifying the aspirations to due process of law and to equal protection of the laws" (133).

By connecting nonoriginalism to constitutional aspirations, Perry leaves his readers to wonder why the framers could not have meant the things signified by the aspirational provisions—things like the freedom of speech *itself,* equal protection *itself,* and so forth. Perry's answer is to be found in a conventionalist theory of meaning that he makes explicit in *Morality, Politics, and Law.* That theory supposes either the nonexistence of things like equal protection itself or the complete separation of these things from the sphere of human awareness and therewith the sphere of things we can aspire to (since we cannot aspire to things of which we are utterly unaware). He holds that a general principle signified by a provision like the equal protection clause can be nothing more than "a memorandum of particulars"—a memorandum, that is, of past agreements on meaning.

Where there is no agreement on meaning there is, for Perry, no meaning. Parties who disagree may think they are disagreeing over what a provision means. But from Perry's perspective as an observer of the debate, the provision means nothing for the issue at hand, and the participants are trying to decide not what it means but what they will agree it means. Where there is no agreement, meaning must await agreement on whether a proposed application is analogous to a past application (155–56). As Perry describes debate over constitutional meaning, we may think we aspire to improve our understanding of a principle like free speech or due process, but we actually aspire to agree on the application of relatively vacuous (i.e., meaningless with regard to the issue at hand) verbal symbols to particular cases. What we want, it seems, is not meaning but rather to diminish conflict over meaning and to believe that current beliefs about the Constitution are consistent with past beliefs about the Constitution.[42]

Perry thus excludes an implication of any approach that seeks guidance from the constitutional text, namely, that the text has meaning independent of any particular beliefs about what it means.[43] Nor can he admit the leading moral implication of a textualist approach, namely, that decision in conformity with the text reconciles the sovereign people *to* justice, a real thing whose meaning does not lie in any particular opinions. Perry is therefore vulnerable to the charge he once made against modern judges: their claim to be interpreting or applying the Constitution is mere "rhetoric designed to create the illusion" of interpretivism.[44]

If Perry means all that he says, he wants to claim interpretivism not because he accepts some argument that connects the constitutional text to simple justice. He simply wants to participate in a certain kind of discourse and he believes normative constitutional theory, the discourse in question, is governed by a set of cultural rules that makes the authority of the constitutional text "axiomatic."[45] On the other hand, justice does seem one of Perry's concerns when he attempts to disclaim the morally skeptical implications of his approach. His first move in this direction is to profess a "neo-Aristotelian" or "naturalist" understanding of morality in which morality is grounded in an empirical fact of human behavior: the general, although not necessarily universal, desire for human "flourishing" (5, 11–12, 15–16).

In the early part of his discussion of ethical naturalism, as on other occasions already mentioned, Perry accepts a distinction between ethical knowledge, which moral skeptics deny, and moral opinions, whose existence moral skeptics admit.[46] He also agrees that one can have categorical moral knowledge in the sense of knowledge of what actually conduces to a person's flourishing, regardless of what that person wants or believes to be true.[47] These passages have clear antiskeptical import because they affirm some form of moral truth. But with further reflection on the fact that different persons and cultures have conflicting views of flourishing, Perry embraces an epistemological skepticism, which he then makes the foundation for a conventionalist view of morality. He also abandons the distinction between knowledge and belief by concluding that there is no truth of any kind, scientific or moral, beyond culturally determined beliefs (28–31, 36, 39–41, 42–43). Because "reality is, through and through, an inaccessible criterion," truth is not a matter of correspondence with reality; "truth . . . is always relative to a web of beliefs." Thus, "if one or more beliefs necessary to support a claim-belief are not a part of the web of beliefs of a community . . . the claim is not true relative to that community, even though it may be true relative to a different community. In that sense, 'truth' and 'falsity' are relative to webs of belief" (40–41).

Having taken this position Perry puts his conventionalism to the test of his own beliefs by asking whether there would be a standard for condemning a totalitarian society that secured a deep and lasting consensus through devices like torture. This "troubling" question arises when he confronts Richard Rorty's denial that a standard exists beyond the practices of such a society.[48] Because Perry accepts Rorty's views regarding the conventionalist nature of truth,[49] and because Perry wants to disclaim moral skepticism without abandoning conventionalism, Rorty's statement should have made Perry conscious of the prospect that his own conventionalism might be no less skeptical than the conventionalism of Bork and Bickel.

But Perry has yet to dispose of this problem. He experiments briefly with a possible way to disassociate himself from Rorty's statement by asking whether there might be a limited set of culturally independent truths about human nature. These truths could serve to identify a range of morally permissible social options that would exclude bad regimes without denying that a regime's goodness was relative to different webs of belief (44, 47–49). But in the end Perry refuses this escape from Rorty. Perry cannot be certain that a limited range of common human interests exists, although he believes it plausible; and if it does exist, he is not confident it is not "so underdeterminative that every actual way of life in the world today, or virtually every actual way of life, must be adjudged as acceptable as (virtually) every other actual way of life" (49).

Perry then says that what matters in any event is not what exists, but what people believe (49–50). Truth, he says, is what our beliefs tell us we are justified in believing; "'truth' [note his quotation marks] . . . is always dependent on, or 'relative to,' the acceptance of some further belief." "Furthermore, there is no privileged standpoint from which to adjudicate among different webs of beliefs. . . . As Richard Rorty has insisted, there are no '"natural starting-points" of thought, starting-points which are prior to and independent of the way some culture speaks or spoke.'"[50] Perry calls his position "*epistemologically* relativist."[51] Although he acknowledges that it is a form of "moral relativism," he insists that it is not "moral skepticism." The latter excludes moral knowledge and criticism of any kind, while the former admits a conventionalist conception of moral knowledge, a conventionalist conception of truth, convention-based criticism of self and others, and convention-based moral growth (10–11, 28–31, 50–51).

Problems with Perry's disclaimer of moral skepticism begin to appear when one notices that he never gets around to rejecting Rorty's denial that standards exist for criticizing a fully successful tyranny. And it is no wonder. If scientific and moral truth and the standards for criticism depend solely on belief, as Perry says, following Rorty, then it would seem that a tyranny could be a good regime to the extent that it could create, by whatever means, a consensus as to its goodness. This objection could hardly be answered by contending that the very success of a fully successful tyranny would lie in its not being seen for what it is (or was), and a regime that appears just would be no tyranny, because to appear just is to be just. For whatever the other problems in such a response, it would suggest that an acknowledged tyranny could reform itself by employing any and every means to create the belief in its goodness, no matter how its subjects and others might assess those means along the way. If Hitler's military and psychological conquest of the world would have been sufficient to change him from a tyrant to a saint, then why not conceive his methods as the methods of moral growth?

Perry's problems deepen when we recall his earlier assessment of Bickel's conventionalism and the epistemological relativism of Bork and Rehnquist as forms of "moral skepticism."[52] Perry was justified in his assessment, as I have argued. Although epistemological skepticism with regard to normative ideas may not imply the skeptical conclusion that they do not exist, epistemological skepticism can be the practical equivalent of ontological skepticism when the issue in question is the scope and legitimacy of judicial power. Perry says, we recall, that reality is an inaccessible criterion "through and through." It should follow for him that if "due process" and "equal protection" pick out real things, they are completely inaccessible. But if we believe them completely inaccessible, then we cannot believe we have evidence *that* they exist. And with no evidence whatever of their existence, we cannot invoke them or better theories of them as reasons for criticizing beliefs about them.

As a logical matter, of course, skeptics can have no coherent argument against judges pretending to have better theories, for the existence of such a skeptical argument would imply moral truths that skepticism rules out—in this case, the moral proposition that it is wrong for judges to pretend they have better theories when there are no better or worse theories. But we are talking here about the behavior of judges in a political culture that tends to put judicial power on the defensive. In cultural context, therefore, the fact of no reason for judicial intervention outweighs the fact of no reason against judicial intervention. Thus, Bork and now Perry (regarding abortion rights) have argued from epistemological skepticism to a level of judicial deference that amounts to the morally skeptical thesis of no rights against the community.

Perry was also right to treat conventionalism in constitutional theory as the practical equivalent of moral skepticism in constitutional theory. Conventionalism holds with skepticism that at some level the community's beliefs are neither valid nor invalid, just given. If the content of moral standards is given by the community's beliefs, there would be a context in which moral standards would not exist as criteria for criticizing the community. On a conventionalist account, the community would be right so long as it or its representation acted in conformity with its beliefs (or what it believed it believed).

MORAL CONVENTIONALISM
AND A CONSTITUTION OF PROCESS

Some conventionalists might think they can preserve a concern for morality in the form of a morality of process. It might be thought that the community ought to restrain itself as required by processes of deliberation that disclose its true wants, that the community's scheme of representation should be structured accordingly, and that the community's representatives should be held to the norms of that true structure. This thought evokes the theories of John Hart Ely and the later Bickel. A process approach, properly understood, can be attractive because self-critical reflection and dialectical striving for moral truth are processes of sorts.[53] But of course a process approach cannot work on conventionalist or skeptical assumptions, for conventionalists and skeptics cannot admit distinctions between true wants and perceived wants or true schemes of representation and what are believed to be such.[54]

Unless it admits a distinction between justice and injustice, a process approach cannot defend the discriminations it makes among competing processes—it cannot explain why (the process of) unreflective historical change should not be permitted to produce whatever it might without intervention from judicial and other deliberative processes.[55] Nor, as we have seen, can a process approach exclude the protection of substantive rights. There is no nonarbitrary way for a commitment to, say, republican processes to exclude the correlative substantive rights (I would say rights to education, jobs, property, and the rights to cultivate differences of ideological, religious, and social outlook, in addition to rights like speech, petition, political association, and access to the courts) that foster and maintain the virtues of republican citizenship—virtues determined by one's theory of the process at its best. Conventionalists cannot escape skepticism through process approaches, because process approaches have not worked and cannot work in conventionalist hands.

Worse than their ineptitude with process, conventionalists cannot attribute normative messages to their leading normative authority, namely, the community. In fact, they cannot even identify the community. References and attributions to some concrete normative community proceed through assumptions about what or whose beliefs ought to count as a part of the community's beliefs, and all such assumptions presuppose a moral reality that conventionalists cannot admit. To see this communitarian reliance on moral realist assumptions, we should remember that, in a constitutional context, what the community believes becomes a subject of controversy when at least one entity in the community (like the plaintiff in a constitutional case) claims that some governmental entity is violating a constitutional provision. On a self-consciously conventionalist account of such a claim, the plaintiff would be saying that he or she has a better view of what the community believes with regard to some constitutional provision than the government has. The government would in turn dispute this claim, and a court would have to decide who is right. The court would decide which party is giving the most accurate description of the community's beliefs since, as the conventionalist sees it, it is that belief that constitutes the meaning of the contested constitutional provision.

The court would probably operate under the assumption (although, for reasons I leave aside, it would not have to) that the community continues to believe the government can be wrong about what the community believes. Evidence for that belief includes the conventions that permit constitutional claims against the government, for constitutional claims are, *ex hypothesi,* claims about what the community believes, and it would make no sense to allow such claims unless the government could be wrong about what the community believes. So the court could not say the government must be right in each and every constitutional case. The court could not say, in other words, that the government always represents what the community believes the Constitution means.

In a constitutional case, therefore, what the community believes would now be a matter of doubt, and the court would have to find some method of ascertaining the community's belief other than simply accepting either the plaintiff's or the government's account. To discover the community's belief, the court might consider polling the community, conducting an imaginary conversation with an imaginary representative of the community, or consulting what are held to be true reports of competent polls and dialogues conducted by scholars and other third parties. In either case, the court would have to decide several difficult and related questions, including what interests and beliefs to admit as part of the community's interests and beliefs, whether individuals or political interest groups are the bearers of those interests and beliefs, whether the community should try to honor every known interest and belief within some geographical area, what that area is, and whether community identity depends on openness to groups and sensitivity to beliefs and interests currently outside that area. To decide these questions the court would have to decide what constitutes the community. And since it is a human community we are talking about, the court would have to decide all the previous questions and many more regarding what ways of life comport with human nature.

The court of our hypothesis could not be trying to discover the community's answers to these questions, for it would have to answer these questions before it could form an opinion about who or what the community is. With no moral and scientific reality to consult, the court would have to rely on its own inventions or commitments. In order for it to find constitutional meaning conceived as the community's beliefs, the court would first have to imagine the community that the court wants, and then create that community through some means. Only then would the court have a community whose beliefs it could consult. Lief Carter has seen this implication of conventionalism. In explicating "an extreme version" of his own conventionalist view of constitutional meaning and decision, Carter says "the rightness or goodness of any constitutional decision conceivable depends on the characteristics of the performance the Court gives when it justifies the decision. A reader should assess the quality of an opinion by asking how effectively the Court has created in its performance a coherent vision of a community. . . . Above all, the nature of the community in question is . . . up for grabs. . . . The only thing not up for grabs in this hypothesized world is that constitutional decisions are about the constituting, the making, of communities."[56]

The authority of such a godlike court could not be supported by what we currently understand as arguments, for arguments as we know them would appeal to things like convention, goodness, right, and nature, and (by our conventionalist hypothesis) these things would have no existence independent of the court's beliefs or prior to the court's construction of the community. Should that act of construction succeed, the court's beliefs would neither require nor admit any defense other than some kind of force against infidels (nonbelievers) who, despite their residence, would be seen as no part of the community, and whose status as fully human would be doubtful in view of the court's constructed truth about humanity.

As we now see such a situation, it would seem a form of the fully successful tyranny I mentioned earlier in connection with Rorty's conventionalist reduction of truth to belief. Viewed from the perspective of us infidels, power alone would ground the authority of such a court, power as contradistinguished from claims regarding goodness, right, and nature. Goodness, right, and nature—and therewith reason or, more specifically, philosophy and the natural sciences, which seek the nature of goodness, right, nature, and natural things—all would be mere derivatives of power.

Conventionalists like Stanley Fish and Richard Posner thus acknowledge (even celebrate) "force" as the "ultima ratio" of all social systems and therewith everything known to the human mind.[57] Moral norms would not exist for the most decisive actors at the most decisive level of action, and the nonexistence of moral norms at the top would project (to outsiders and reflective insiders) a skeptic's message of might makes right. As prefigured in the current conventionalist (or "pragmatist") attack on the traditional aims of meta-physics, legal and moral theory, and the scientific study of judicial behavior,[58] moral skepticism—a self-conscious metaphysical position—might be missing within the community of our court's creation, as would all other forms of theory about the nature of morality. For where there are no generally and genuinely debatable questions about goodness, rightness, nature, and the meaning of institutions that claim to embody these things and their deriva-tives, there is no impetus to legal-moral theory. Persons within the court's thralldom would be blind to the tyranny that the outsiders and reflective insiders, if any remained, might still be able to see.

Perry could hardly accept this result in view of his criticism of Rehnquist and Bork. We recall that the three-part moral of that criticism is (1) conven-tionalism is skepticism at the constitutional level, (2) skepticism does not conform to our beliefs about the world, (3) our beliefs constitute the test for theories about the world. Since the results that I have derived from Perry's own conventionalism hardly conform to our ordinary beliefs about the world, Perry's conventionalism fails its own test. From all that Perry says in *Morality, Politics, and Law,* one can speculate that his most likely rejoinder to my criti-cism would be that I have ignored key parts of his position, especially his claim that it is impossible for us to question all our beliefs at once.[59]

It may be true (Perry or one of his conventionalist defenders would say) that litigants in a constitutional case are raising questions about the commu-nity's beliefs and therewith the community's identity in some limited respect (11, 30–31, 61–62). But the litigants and the court would continue to share assumptions about the community's identity and beliefs with regard to most other matters, else they could not be in court—an institution constituted by the community's beliefs—doing their respective thing. The court relies on this bank of assumptions, or temporarily closed questions, in order to decide the questions being litigated. If judicial choices amount to judges constructing the community, the construction takes the form of small-scale remodeling that borrows from the community's own deposits and respects the community as the ultimate source of moral capital (30–33). Such remodeling is neither tyr-anny nor a situation that suggests that the community is some unknown or nonexistent thing waiting to be created out of nothing or something so plastic that it can be exactly what some community builder might want, as it might want it. Legal-moral differences, legal-moral controversy, legal-moral theory, and all other aspects of our legal-moral practices would continue as they have within the settled conventions that constitute those practices (cf. 39–41, 53–54).

Our conventionalist might add that even if metaphysical and moral skep-ticism flow from the belief that our conventions lack either scientific explanation or moral justification with reference to some extraconventional physical and moral reality, skepticism is of no consequence to what goes on within our conventional activities. Just as it is impossible to hit a single without playing (under the rules of) baseball or even to open a window without agreeing (with others generally) that window opening is causing a window to move from a closed to an open state, the skeptic cannot advise us on the conduct of our affairs without accepting (or pretending to accept) the beliefs that constitute those affairs (cf. 15-16, 37). Within those conventions all will remain as it appears to the ordinary citizen (see ibid., 53-54). The beliefs that constitute right and wrong in any viable community will run too deep and wide to depend on the word of any particular part of the community on particular occasions of surface controversy (cf. 51).

So, our conventionalist might conclude, we can continue to say that the government and the majority can be wrong even though the community is the ultimate source of standards. The community's authentic beliefs will continue to be matters of controversy on many occasions, partly because the community cannot speak for itself. These controversies will continue to insure the need for such well-established social practices as legal-moral theory, constitutional criticism, and constitutional litigation—all of which involve theories of what the community believes.

The last three paragraphs would be the best I could do to reconcile Perry's position and conventionalism generally to the everyday self-understanding that Perry employs to test the conventionalism-skepticism of Bork and Rehnquist. If conventionalists could do no better, however, their best would fail. Let me go through several reasons why.

First, the conventionalist may prove that my point about the conventionalist court is exaggerated—that the court could not, in the manner of a fully successful tyranny, invent the whole community all at once from nothing whatever except its preferences. But I exaggerate to draw out an unacceptable implication of the courts as community builders. Even if a court works with materials provided by the community, the community to which it ultimately submits its innovations can be, and will be if the court is successful, a different community and a community partly of the court's own making. The scope of the court's reconstructions will be less than total, but partial innovations need be neither modest nor cosmetic.

Consider *Brown* from the perspective of racists armed with conventionalist doctrines. These people could contend that *Brown* attempted revolutionary change and that, at bottom, segregated communities are no better or worse than integrated communities; it all depends on what the community believes. They could claim that *Brown* tried to displace local communities with a national community that was based on arbitrary convictions regarding human community at its best.[60]

Consider also the adequacy of the conventionalist defense had the Supreme Court succeeded (longer than it did) in such acts of community building—or community maintenance, which (Lincoln proved) requires equal or greater power—as *Dred Scott, Slaughter House,* and *Plessy.* Think of *Griswold* and *Roe,* or *Pierce v. Society of Sisters* and *Meyer v. Nebraska,* or *Allgeyer* and *Parrish,* or *Hunter's Lessee* and *McCulloch.* These cases display beliefs about matters as fundamental as the nature and scale of human community at its best, the nature of human personhood, the relationship between positive law and natural justice, and the nature of judicial power and the Constitution itself, the Court's own charter of existence. Limited, yes; but no small acts of construction here, if construction is what they are. And if they are only limited acts of construction, their critics will still see them as the tyrannical replacement of some communities with other communities.

As for the no-practical-difference defense, grant that it is self-contradictory for a skeptic to give advice that presupposes realist beliefs—grant that and you still have not established the practical irrelevance of skeptical views. Skepticism's practical incoherence is a fact that impresses philosophers more than others; contemporary constitutional theory proves both that there is no shortage of advice from skeptics and that audiences rarely notice the contradictions.

Consider Perry's own criticism of Bork. Perry criticized Bork for the message Bork's views communicated to persons who accepted the presuppositions of our everyday moral practices. Perry said the message was "the search for justice . . . is . . . morally arbitrary." That message, said Perry, was "fundamentally at odds with our understanding of ourselves as a people committed to ongoing moral reevaluation and moral growth." The message left us with "no 'principled'—morally nonarbitrary—ground for objecting to . . . torture . . . slavery . . . or even . . . another Holocaust."[61]

Perry thus implied that our everyday moral beliefs presuppose moral validity from some perspective external to those beliefs. To say without qualification that (1) *X is wrong* is thus to commit oneself to (2) *X would be adjudged wrong by any rational person possessing all the relevant information and in a position to reason aright.*[62] When the skeptic denies the possibility of (2), the skeptic says something that, if either true or rationally believable, would defeat (1). And even if this consequence depends not on what the skeptic either implies or intends, it can still flow from the way nonskeptics receive skepticism. So the skeptic cannot assert a priori and unconditionally that skepticism is in fact irrelevant to our practices or that it leaves everything as before.

Finally, conventionalists cannot remove the skeptical implications of conventionalism in constitutional theory by positing layers of convention, one shallow, the other deep. From the realist perspective, deep conventions will still project the message that morality is derivative and subordinate to power and arbitrary commitment. Observers who believe that judges borrow from deep conventions, while legislators work at the surface, can have no conventionalist argument for preferring judicial power, because there can be no conventionalist argument for preferring one level of convention to another. This moral equality of conventions to a conventionalist may explain why erstwhile deep conventionalists like Bickel and Perry exhibit a tendency to head for the shallows when the going gets rough, as it did for defenders of the Warren Court in the 1970s and abortion rights in the 1980s. In addition to these problems, it is not clear what a court is doing when relying on deep conventions. Two or three alternatives appear from different things that Perry and other conventionalists have said.

We recall that Perry once denied that there was a tradition or social consensus sufficiently determinate to settle concrete constitutional controversies. He immediately qualified that position by identifying a deep-seated cultural commitment to moral growth.[63] As he described that commitment, it did not settle substantive questions of constitutional rights as much as it contributed to a question of constitutional power. That question was whether courts should have power to overrule legislation on extraconstitutional grounds. So a court relying on the deep convention favoring moral growth would be relying on a theory of its power to participate in the contests that occur at the level of shallow conventions. The court would not be applying a deep convention to the substantive question of the instant case. It would not be showing the majority's representatives that a momentary impulse was wrong (or right) when measured by what all could see, or should be able to see, as a correct application of something they shared in common.

To answer constitutional questions in hard cases the court would deploy what Perry has come to call the "aspirational meanings" of the constitutional provisions in play, not the past applications and definitions of those provisions.[64] His court may appeal to textual provisions, but (if the judges know what Perry knows) the court understands the textual provisions as indeterminate or lacking in meaning relative to the issues at hand. Textual provisions will not acquire meaning relative to the issues until some point after the court tries to give them meaning (155–56). So, again, the court is deploying either nothing at all or some contested conceptions of which it approves; it is not deploying deeper ideas that all share in common.

Perry's relatively vacuous "aspirational meaning" thus serves the same function as his earlier commitment to moral growth: it empowers judges to participate in the contest among shallow conventional views. Perry's suggestion that the new conception must be analogous to old conceptions (ibid.) does nothing to remove us from the shallows of conventional beliefs. It succeeds only in requiring us to decide what theory of precedent we want to believe. Depending on the theory of precedent we choose, we must make arbitrary (because ungrounded) choices among contending beliefs regarding such matters as how to select the relevant precedent cases, whether to seek the meaning of the formal opinions in those cases taken separately, or as a series, or whether to see meaning in the things that the judges in those cases were trying to accomplish.[65]

If there is anything deep in any of this—something like due process itself, for example, as opposed to contending conceptions of due process—the conventionalist cannot see it as a convention. As per our conventional understanding of convention, a practice or a belief does not reveal itself as a convention until we are aware that it might rationally have been otherwise. And to be aware that a convention might have been otherwise is to see that convention as something we might rationally reject, either now or in different circumstances, in favor of some other practice or belief.[66] So it is only the contestable or shallow conventions that we can perceive as conventions, and that leaves judges with no deep conventions to draw upon consciously. This essential shallowness of convention helps to explain why Bickel and Perry seemed to swim for the shallows that favor judicial deference to popular conceptions of constitutional rights.

The prospect that conventionalists can appeal only to shallow conventions poses a new challenge for modernist defenders of judicial power. They can always abandon the attempt to justify judicial power and simply promote its use for favored political objectives. Such is the thrust of the critical legal studies movement and the purer form of the new legal pragmatism, whose members do not bother to submit constitutional arguments for judicial power. But other options face writers who continue to participate in the enterprise of normative constitutional theory. They must either capitulate to the New Right, return to the classical theory, or find a constitutional justification for judges imposing their partisan preferences on popular majorities. This last option might seem impossible at the outset. Ely thought he had refuted all modern theories of judicial review except his own by showing that each of the others amounted to "a 'judge's own values' approach."[67] Ely's critics then dismissed his theory in the same way. Erwin Chemerinsky has recently attempted a judge's-own-values defense of judicial power, and by discussing that attempt we can see further connections between modernist theories and further evidence that no modernist theory can work.

ERWIN CHEMERINSKY AND OPEN-ENDED MODERNISM

In a recent survey of the major theories of judicial review, Chemerinsky classifies those theories in terms of the constraints they would impose upon judges in controversial constitutional cases.[68] He finds six main types of theory: literalism, originalism, conceptualism, cultural values theory, process-based modernism, and open-ended modernism. Excluding open-ended modernism, each of these types of theory is "designed to avoid judges deciding cases based on their personal values" (108).

Chemerinsky's version of literalism has it that "all constitutional interpretation must be based solely on the Constitutional text" without considering any "extraconstitutional material."[69] Originalists, like Raoul Berger, differ from literalists in that they permit the court to look beyond constitutional language but limit meaning to the concrete intentions of either the framers or the ratifiers.[70] Conceptualists (Dworkin is Chemerinsky's example) ask the justices to form their best conceptions of the abstract intent or general concept that they believe should provide the purpose or point of a provision (ibid.). Cultural value theorists read the constitutional text in light of values not necessarily explicit in the text or the historical record of concrete intentions. Cultural value theorists look either to tradition (Danial Conkle is one of Chemerinsky's examples); current or emerging moral consensus (he mentions Larry Simon, Harry Wellington, and others as deep conventionalists, and he could have mentioned Bickel, Perry, and many others); or, says Chemerinsky, natural law (Michael Moore, for example) (109, 114, 179 nn. 17–19). And process-based modernists (Ely, for example) consult either their best conceptions or contemporary social values to insure fairness in representation and adjudication, while deferring either to text, concrete traditions, or concrete intentions in substantive matters (109).

Chemerinsky contends that none of these theories achieves the one objective they all share. That objective is "determinacy: a model of judicial review that unequivocally informs the Court when to become involved, what values to protect, and what result to reach" (ibid.). Literalism provides no significant level of restraint because constitutional provisions in hard cases "have no determinate meaning." Conceptualism cannot find determinacy "because the Court can state the concept behind any constitutional provision at many different levels of generality" and the choice of levels is "arbitrary." Natural law, tradition, and consensus also permit judges to rationalize "virtually any result." Deep conventionalism cannot help the consensus approach because "there is no formula that a court can use to ascertain what the deep consensus is." The same holds for process-based modernism, for there are "no preexisting criteria" that determine "a fair electoral process" or the rights of criminal defendants. And originalism cannot work for several reasons, including the many opportunities for discretion in deciding whose intentions count and which aspect of intention counts, the problems of distinguishing a group's preferences from the preferences of individual members, and the intrusion of the interpreter's values in "any reading of historical records" (111–14).

Since, as Chemerinsky sees it, no theory "provides an alternative to judges deciding cases based on their personal ideologies," he urges constitutional theorists to acknowledge that "judicial discretion" is unavoidable and weigh the arguments for it and against it. The argument for judicial discretion is "open-ended modernism," which Chemerinsky defines as "an approach that permits the Court to give meaning to all constitutional provisions on the basis of [1] contemporary values that [2] the justices regard as worthy of constitutional protection." He says that "the core characteristic of open-ended modernism is its explicit premise that justices have, and should have, discretion in deciding constitutional cases, and that these decisions are inevitably based on their personal values."

Chemerinsky adds that open-ended modernists "could decide" to employ some of the alternative approaches "except to the extent that the alternatives are predicated on the belief that they significantly restrain judicial decision making." But since, by Chemerinsky's own analysis, the alternatives are not real alternatives, his statement will inevitably suggest that open-ended modernists may, perhaps understandably but certainly disingenuously, identify their position either as conceptualism, a variety of cultural values theory, or process-based modernism (109–10).

Later I return to Chemerinsky's suggestion that open-ended modernists may elect to present themselves as something else. But first I take up his thesis that open-ended modernism is the reality behind the appearances in the field of constitutional theory. He reinforces this point with an overview of Supreme Court history from *Calder v. Bull*[71] to the abortion decisions and beyond. This survey concludes (without mentioning his earlier point about the interpretive biases of history writers)[72] that "since the earliest days of U.S. history, open-ended modernism has been the model that best describes constitutional decision making" (133). The Court, he says, is free to take historical intentions and other sources into account when applying "the Constitution's open-textured clauses," but the justices are not to be governed by these sources. Although grounding judgment in the narrowest understanding of framers' intent would "confine judges more than" the other approaches would, discretion would remain unavoidable.[73] And so "the Court has always used [its understanding of] contemporary morality to determine the appropriate constitutional norms." "Properly focused," therefore, "the debate over constitutional interpretation is really about the question of whether open-ended modernism should continue" (129, 133).

I do not know what to make of Chemerinsky's observation that a narrow or strict originalism would result in more restraints on judges. The remark suggests that originalism is not reducible to open-ended modernism, as he says the other theories are, and that originalism is therefore an alternative to open-ended modernism. In this account of strict originalism Chemerinsky ignores his own agreement with the findings of Dworkin, Murphy, and many others that all originalists must make substantive and interpretive choices of the same kind that they condemn in nonoriginalist writers.

Chemerinsky's point may be that self-styled originalists are, at the present historical moment, more likely to make choices that diminish federal judicial power. Perhaps. But open-ended modernists can also choose to diminish judicial power. We see instances of that possibility in the later Bickel and the latest Perry. Other kinds of theorists can make similar choices. Berns is a self-styled natural rights theorist who would diminish judicial power. Compare Chemerinsky's history of the Supreme Court with Wolf's and it becomes evident how self-styled traditionalists could take both sides of the issue on judicial power. So the question is not whether one can choose to limit judicial power; the question is whether that choice is constitutional. And if it is not constitutional, the Court that chooses it is rejecting constitutional constraints.

Apparently the point needs emphasis. The Court-diminishing choices of the most thoroughgoing originalist could hardly be a simple reflection of the constitutional theory of original sources. Chemerinsky knows but seems to forget that Dworkin and others have shown that, before one can know what the framers intended, one must decide such questions as whose intent counts and what counts as intent. Dworkin's questions have to be answered first; and because they cannot be answered by going to historical sources yet to be determined and looking for categories of things yet to be determined, Dworkin's questions can be answered responsibly only by fresh philosophic arguments.

Fresh philosophic arguments result primarily from the activity of dialectical reflection (Dworkin's writing is a good example), not from historical research (like Berns's) into which historical figures (philosophers, politicians, or whoever) said what and to what effect. Nor do philosophic arguments proceed through extrapolations (consider McConnell's method) from undefended premises that are currently in controversy, for that method would confound philosophy with ideology and thereby reject the possibility of a uniquely philosophic approach.

Fresh philosophic activity is precisely what most of today's self-styled originalists and interpretivists of the New Right want to exclude from constitutional thought. Yet the substantive and interpretive choices that enable originalist arguments cannot themselves be choices dictated by original sources. Moreover, as those choices vary, so does one's conception of originalism. A self-styled originalist who would constrain judicial power might therefore seem to other self-styled originalists as quite unconstrained by original intent. My analysis of *The Federalist* in chapter 2 illustrates this possibility. So it is difficult to see how Chemerinsky can propose that originalism constrains judges more.

Chemerinsky makes a better point when he argues that all approaches to constitutional interpretation can be reduced to open-ended modernism. If the point sounds familiar, it should. For it is, as Chemerinsky indicates, an updated version of the old Legal Realist attack on the pretentions of legal formalism—updated to apply to the would-be successors of the old legal formalism.[74] But the point is overdrawn; it works better against legal formalism than it does against what Chemerinsky calls the natural law approach, as I try to show in chapter 6. It is nonetheless a useful point because it exposes anew the corrosive impact of skeptical assumptions in open-ended modernism. These assumptions surface in Chemerinsky's belief that there are no right answers in hard cases and in his confidence that when the pre–Civil War Court appealed to natural justice and the "natural law meanings" of "abstract constitutional provisions" it was crafting a rhetorical facade for the justices' personal convictions (xi, 131–32).

Natural law and natural right would of course be empty if justice were altogether inaccessible or nonexistent. Literalism would indeed be a facade if constitutional language ultimately referred to nothing. Tradition could have no coherent normative message without transcultural standards to support our decisions of what historical events and practices to include within, and exclude from, our traditions. Deep consensus would be an illusion if our agreements were ultimately about nothing at all. And the vitality of originalism is fully dependent on the possibility that the framers intended something both real and common, for otherwise their talk of a common good was either error or fraud.

APPROACHING THE REAL ISSUES

A brief comparison of Chemerinsky's project with my own will enable me to restate the general point of the last two chapters and recall the test of constitution-based argument that Chemerinsky fails to meet.

Chemerinsky and I divide the field of contending theories differently. He has reason to reduce a fairly complex arrangement of theories and subtheories to a choice between open-ended modernism and some kind of originalism.

Because I have concluded that the pivotal issues are those separating moral realism and the several forms of antirealism, I see the crucial contest as between the classical theory of judicial review and its modernist contenders. By *modernist* I mean those theories that reject the metaphysical, psychological, sociological, and semantic presuppositions of the classical theory.

Although Chemerinsky is a modernist in this sense, by *modernism* he refers to his descriptive and normative thesis that the Supreme Court always has kept, and ought to continue to keep, the Constitution up to date. Nevertheless, Chemerinsky talks less about the theory of John Marshall and *The Federalist* than he does about the theoretical efforts of the post–Legal Realist era. Even Chemerinsky's literalism is a modernist theory in my sense, for it is the moral antirealist literalism of Justice Black. So the negative or critical point of Chemerinsky's analysis is a general comment on what I call modernism in constitutional theory. And his point is: modernist theories cannot restrain judicial power.

Chemerinsky's own open-ended modernism is of course no exception. He says it does not restrain judicial power. Yet Chemerinsky defends open-ended modernism partly because it embraces what the other approaches try to deny. They fail because they attempt the impossible. Embracing what he sees as the fact of no significant textual or extratextual restraints on judges is essential if one is to abandon arguments of the kind that do not work and pursue the kinds of argument that he says will work or might work. And Chemerinsky indicates that the kind of argument that will work is an argument from concrete results—an argument that appeals to the audience's approval of what nondeferential courts have accomplished and, despite occasional ups and downs, will probably continue accomplishing in the long run.

Thus, he says, "arguments about judicial legitimacy wrongly assume that the Court's credibility is related to its theory of decision making. In fact, few besides academics pay close attention to the theoretical underpinnings of decision. Instead, the Court's legitimacy is attributable largely to public acceptance of the results of particular decisions and the methods used to reach those results" (136). He then mentions the popularity of the desegregation decisions as if to say: *If you approve of* Brown *and its progeny, let us support the methods and attitudes of the Warren Court.*

From the perspective of the classical theory, Chemerinsky is not altogether wrong in suggesting some connection between the public's acceptance of likely results and the soundness of any theory. To summarize what I have elaborated elsewhere and touched upon in chapter 2: the Constitution is an instrument of justice. More accurately, it is an instrument for reconciling public opinion to justice. It embodies a theory of responsible government in which government strives for public acceptance of results that are as close to our best conception of justice as material circumstances permit.[75] That theory of responsibility applies to the judicial function as it does to all others. Thus, the justices should interpret constitutional provisions in a manner that serves what they consider the best feasible conception of justice within their deliberative powers and the interpretive limits of the relevant provisions.

Brown I and *Brown II* are good examples of a Court trying to reach the right decision and ordering the remedy that the Court considers practicable and within the interpretive limits of the constitutional rights and powers in question. If everything works as planned, public opinion and the Court may still not end up together on the side of justice, but thoughtful people will believe they have evidence that the Court is at least trying, and in this respect, the system remains a plausible instrument of justice.

But the argument of this summary is unavailable to Chemerinsky. It does approach the concrete problems of constitutional meaning with an eye to policy results, precisely in the manner of John Marshall. But with regard to the results sought, it makes several claims that Chemerinsky cannot credit. It claims that the policies in question are both Constitution-based and approximations to justice. And implicit in these two claims is the further claim that the results sought are sought because they are Constitution-based and approximations to justice, not solely because they conform to someone's wants. So this argument accepts all of the presuppositions of the classical theory, and it is in fact a version of the classical theory. (It may be the best version of the classical theory.)[76]

Because he cannot admit the influence of justice and the possibility of Constitution-based answers in hard cases, Chemerinsky would label this argument open-ended modernism in disguise, not an honest substitute for it. And so Chemerinsky would defend a theory of constitutional interpretation as means to ends whose sole property is that they are desired—not justly desired, or constitutionally desired, or intrinsically desirable to human nature as such, or desirable to Americans, or desirable to our best construction of American aspirations, as might be claimed by moral realists, traditionalists, constructivists, and others whose approaches Chemerinsky rejects—merely desired, presumably by (most of?) Chemerinsky's readers.

I will not dwell on the obvious difficulty of linking a given means (like the method of open-ended modernism) to a given set of ends (policies, progressive or conservative) throughout all reasonably conceivable historical changes. Open-ended modernism would not achieve the results Chemerinsky indicates he favors if the Court were captured by apologists for racism or the religious right. He could respond that these sentiments will not prove durable, but he would intend this response as a scientific prediction (not a philosophic proposition) and we would find ourselves in a complex scientific debate in which the evidence that supports my pessimism might be no more convincing than the evidence for his optimism. So let me argue in a way that relies on Chemerinsky's own beliefs.

The Constitution is a law applicable both to government and to the public. Notwithstanding Chemerinsky's doubts about the prescriptive power of the Constitution, he seems unable to avoid referring to the Constitution as some sort of constraint. He devotes his second chapter to the "reasons why a society should be governed by a constitution."[77] His answer: "protecting deeply imbedded values —separation of powers, equality, individual liberties—from the political process, and . . . serving as a powerful symbol unifying the country" (x). These reasons are reasons for controlling the government as well as the people, of course, and that includes charging the courts with protecting fundamental rights (28, 31, 35-36).

If we let our preference for specific results determine our method of constitutional interpretation, we risk weakening, perhaps destroying, any sense of the Constitution as constraint. If we believe that unelected judges tend to favor minority litigants and conclude, merely because we tend to favor minority litigants, that the meaning of the equal protection clause is given by what the justices can agree is the most just and feasible rendition of equal protection, we leave doubts about our respect for the Constitution as a legal constraint upon our wants.

A theory of judicial review is a poor theory to the extent that it has no answer for doubts about its respect for the Constitution as law. What makes such a theory unacceptable are certain facts about our political culture and one of the functions of theories of judicial review. These theories serve as defenses of judicial review. They contain arguments addressed to the public for supporting judicial power. The public cannot understand these theories as defenses of judicial power unless they preserve some prominent notion of constraints upon the theorists advancing them and upon the justices and the public itself.

If these theories do not preserve a meaningful notion of constitutional constraint, it is difficult for them to answer opponents of the proposition that our "supreme Law" is an instrument of justice. Enemies of judicial power will say what Bork said during David Souter's confirmation process. He called open-ended modernism a "new tactic on the left" by those who prudently hide what they really want: a judiciary that "will enact an agenda too liberal to pass the legislature or escape an executive veto, either at the national or state level." These "extreme liberals" tell us "that since the Constitution is an 'open-ended document,' no result the Court chooses to reach is legally unjustifiable, and therefore nominees are to be judged politically." But the tactic will not work, Bork suggested, because "the American people do not want judges, acting without any warrant in the Constitution, settling their social issues for them." They want judges who respect "the distinction between interpreting and legislating." That distinction "expresses a solid truth that must not be obscured." "The Constitution is law," said Bork. "Like all law it is expressed in language. Language has meaning. Judges who depart from any plausible meaning of the language are not interpreting, they are legislating."[78]

In spite of himself, Chemerinsky eventually indicates agreement with Bork's observation of the public mind. One of Chemerinsky's explanations for the Court's survival over two centuries of "highly controversial rulings" is: "It has long been demonstrated that people feel great loyalty to the Constitution. Therefore, Court decisions deciding constitutional claims also are likely to be regarded as legitimate."[79] This explanation makes sense because of a proposition that Chemerinsky leaves to implication: the public believes, or is at least open to the argument that, the Court's answers are based on plausible interpretations of constitutional language. One can readily understand his leaving this proposition unsaid; it destroys the usefulness of open-ended modernism as a defense of judicial power. For open-ended modernism denies that the Constitution can guide judicial choice in hard cases. The weakness of open-ended modernism as a defense of judicial power may explain Chemerinsky's earlier suggestion that it is prudent for open-ended modernists to pretend to be something else (109–10). I trust it also justifies my view that the basic division is between the classical theory and modernist theories, and that the case for the classical theory—if there is one—is the only case for judicial power.

6

CONTEMPORARY
JURISPRUDENCE
AND THE
INTERNAL PERSPECTIVE
ON
CONSTITUTIONAL QUESTIONS

As constitutional thought in America
has sought a modernist defense of judicial power, developments in moral philosophy have made the classical theory of judicial review respectable again. This fact may not be widely acknowledged at present, but it should be, and it will be as soon as constitutional theorists confront all of the challenges now before them.

The developments in question began with H. L. A. Hart's criticism of the more skeptical strains of American Legal Realism in the early 1960s.[1]

H. L. A. HART AND THE INTERNAL POINT OF VIEW

Although Hart accepted much of the Legal Realists' attack on the formalist myth that judging could and should be free of significant degrees of judicial creativity, he could not accept the extreme Legal Realist view that legal norms provide no guidance to judicial choice (132–37). He argued that the finality of judicial decisions for particular lawsuits did not prove that the law means whatever the judges say; he thus defended law-based criticism of judicial mistakes as a strategy against perpetuating those mistakes (138–41). Hart also argued from a conventionalist semantics that, although the necessary generality of laws meant "uncertainty at the border line" of legal words and phrases, members of a given community could usually agree on clear examples of the most general provisions, and even in cases of little agreement, judges were expected to (and typically did) justify their decisions to the public in terms of generally acceptable social principles (123–25, 200).

Hart rejected the extreme view of the law as mere predictions of what judges would do in fact and judicial decisions as the mere effects of judicial predilection because he was convinced that jurisprudence had to account for a community's legal practices from a perspective internal to those practices.[2] The "internal point of view" was one that accepted the possibility that legal rules could constitute reasons for a course of action and serve as standards for criticizing behavior. To declare that judicial citations of legal rules could be nothing more than either deliberate or unconscious rationalizations of decisions that flowed from extralegal factors (like subconscious needs, raw hunches, or ideological commitments) was to deny reality to law as understood by ordinary people, and to do so in the face of evidence that people take legal rules and relationships very much into account in their daily affairs.

Although other parts of Hart's jurisprudence supported American-style judicial activism,[3] his conventionalist view of language led him to conclude that judges often faced novel situations not covered by the conventional meanings of legal provisions and that, on such occasions, judges had no choice but to fashion new law from such extralegal sources as theories of the community's morality and desirable policy results. Hart proposed that the legal status of these acts of judicial creativity depended solely on whether the community eventually accepted them. As he put it: "The truth may be that, when courts settle previously unenvisaged questions concerning the most fundamental constitutional rules, they *get* their authority to decide them accepted after the questions have arisen and the decision has been given. Here all that succeeds is success."[4]

Hart included the American experience with judicial review in this last statement (141–42). We can see the irony of that fact by applying Hart's statement to Marshall's opinion in *Marbury*. Despite Hart's commitment to a jurisprudence that could account for a legal practice as understood by its practitioners, no part of Marshall's argument in *Marbury* could have been squared with Hart's dictum that "all that succeeds is success." Had Marshall admitted such a construction of what he was doing in *Marbury*—virtually proposing that the nation adopt a judicial invention as fundamental law—he could not have defended judicial review as a constitution-based power, a power compelled by the substantive purposes and organizational basics of the Constitution as a whole.

In the late 1960s Dworkin launched a broad criticism of Hart's jurisprudence.[5] Dworkin claimed, in effect, that Hart had not fully entered the perspective of practicing judges, lawyers, and ordinary citizens.[6]

RONALD DWORKIN'S REVIVAL OF THE CLASSICAL THEORY

Dworkin contended that an accurate general account of constitutional decision as understood by practicing judges suggested a model in which judges resolved hard cases in accordance with their most considered theories of the Constitution. Such a theory would have to contain a complex argument (complex because partly historical, partly philosophic) that the judge considered persuasive enough (to herself and to the public) to "justify the constitution as a whole."[7] From the perspective of such a theory, the American constitutional system consists partly of individual and minority rights (written and unwritten) conceived as general principles of political morality ("judgment[s] about what is right or wrong for government to do") whose proper specification, formulation, and weight constitute continuing controversies into which judges must enter to find what the Constitution means for different social problems (82–87, 138–39).

Dworkin interpreted and justified the assertive exercise of judicial power from *Marbury* to *Brown* and later to *Griswold* and *Roe* as an attempt to honor the moral dimension of American law. In a now famous argument he said that general constitutional provisions were to be viewed not as failures of draftsmen whose real aim was to write their concrete conceptions into law but as successful "appeals to moral concepts" that "could not be made more precise by being more detailed" (134, 136). At any given point in time, or so we suppose from the internal point of view, the argument for preferring one general version or theory of the Constitution (and its specific rules, incorporated moral principles, derived institutional practices, and putative substantive purposes), together with the conceptions of specific constitutional concepts favored by that overarching theory, could be expected to be stronger than the argument for alternative theories and conceptions. So, Dworkin proposed, any given question in constitutional law has an answer that best fits most of the community's constitutional provisions, statutes, precedents, and other legal material and most of the community's moral beliefs.[8] The duty to look for this "right answer" is what constrains judicial discretion in hard cases.[9]

Dworkin's Moral Antirealism

Although Dworkin's early talk of right answers in hard cases suggested a moral realist metaphysics to some observers,[10] he made a point of denying that moral beliefs are "clues to the existence and nature of" a moral reality that is independent of what human beings might believe about its requirements. Instead of what he called a "natural model" of morality, he argued for a conventionalist procedure that he and others call the "constructive model."

This procedure takes "as given" those moral beliefs that a community holds "with the requisite sincerity." It constructs a justification that gathers most of the community's moral convictions into a coherent and publicly defensible whole. It then uses that justification for choosing between competing answers to moral questions that are open.[11] Dworkin preferred this constructive model not only on epistemological and ontological grounds but also on moral grounds.

Dworkin's principal epistemological-ontological suggestion was that constructivism avoided the need to postulate the existence of a special faculty of moral intuition for perceiving mysterious moral entities. His moral argument was that because constructivism denied that moral beliefs involved perceptions of a moral reality that was normative for those beliefs—a reality that could condemn the most entrenched of the public's convictions—constructivist judges were deprived of an argument for insisting on personal moral convictions that could not fit smoothly within some publicly persuasive theory. Constructivists could thus avoid a specific moral error to which realists were inclined: "appeals to unique intuitions that might mask prejudice or self-interest in particular cases" (160–63). Dworkin erred in both of these arguments.

Dworkin erred first in supposing that all but an insignificant few contemporary moral realists hold that there is some special moral faculty for perceiving moral entities that occupy some special realm beyond the natural world of ordinary scientific and commonsense concerns and that possess some unique power to motivate actors who can see them clearly. Many, if not most, contemporary moral realists see moral properties and facts as constituted by nonmoral or natural properties and facts, just as, say, biological properties and facts can consist in physical and chemical properties and facts. A theorist who believes that the appropriate moral and nonmoral entities have real existence might thus hold that, on a given occasion, wrongness (a moral entity) is constituted by pointless cruelty (a psychological and therefore nonmoral state) in the same way that a biologist might find growth to consist in change that can be expressed as linear differences between certain physical states.[12]

In addition, some contemporary moral realists reflect on the possibility of amoralism (i.e., recognizing but being unmoved by moral requirements) and hold that the motivating power, as distinguished from the truth, of moral considerations is contingent on things conceptually external to moral considerations, such as the contingent habits and desires of moral agents.[13] Although a realist will hold the truth of a moral proposition to be a matter of its correspondence with reality, I argue below that no realist need ever claim knowledge of any kind and that some realists hold that justifying a moral belief (as distinguished from demonstrating its truth) is a matter of fitting it into a comprehensive system of moral and nonmoral beliefs, not a matter of deduction from indubitable moral or nonmoral truths.[14]

These and related positions lead some moral realists to conclude that their ontological-epistemological commitments are parallel to, and no less defensible than, the ontological-epistemological commitments that best fit commonsense and scientific practice. Dworkin's strategy for dealing with this "naturalist" or this-worldly strain of moral realism is, by and large, to pretend that it does not exist.[15] He thus begs the question whether his philosophic conventionalism is more plausible than the kind of moral realism that he should regard as a serious alternative to his approach.[16] Jeremy Waldron gives a better antirealist response to the parallel-to-science claim of some moral realists, so let us briefly consider whether he can offer Dworkin any help.

Jeremy Waldron's Moral Antirealism

Waldron's central claim against moral realism is that moralists lack a method for resolving their disagreements comparable to the mainstream method for resolving disagreements in science. Waldron's evidence for this claim is the fact that each substantive moral theory includes "its own theory of what counts as a justification: utilitarians have one view, Kantians another, Christian fundamentalists yet another, and so on." Although these moralists regard their disagreements as important, "unlike their counterparts in the scientific community, they share virtually nothing in the way of an epistemology or a method with which these disagreements might in principle be approached."[17]

Waldron's evidence does not support his conclusion. He does have evidence of disagreement among moral philosophers on the substantive question of what constitutes the good: utilitarian answers range from pleasure to knowledge, Kant said the only unqualified good was a good will, modern Kantians speak of equal concern and respect, and so on. To these answers attach different methods for resolving concrete problems. Kantians and utilitarians would not employ each other's ancillary methods for solving concrete moral problems, because these methods reflect the differences in their answers to the basic substantive issue. Waldron therefore has evidence for a diversity of moral theories. But he cannot argue from this diversity that "there is nothing [philosophers] can say to support [their] claims" against rival theories (174). Contending moral philosophers cannot agree with that proposition without contradicting the presuppositions of the very contest in which they engage.

Waldron is no exception. When he goes against realism in the name of antirealism he assumes that there is a truth of the philosophic matters being contested. When he submits evidence for his position (instead of issuing threats or invoking authorities), he employs what is assumed to be a method for discovering or approximating truth that is available to, and normative for, any rational person. And when he summons realists to test their initial opinions against his offerings, he assumes that all of the participants in the debate either are or ought to be more attracted to the truth, the aspiration of his method, than to their own initial positions.

Waldron can thus criticize moral realists for being "disingenuous" in their account of important facts, in this case their refusal to credit the alleged absence of a mainstream method (ibid.). He can prescribe remedies, as he does when saying realists "ought to be very concerned that they have nothing to offer in the way of a method for approaching moral disputes" and "since they are unable to 'demonstrate the truth' of their judgments or show how they correspond to moral reality, they should be the ones in all honesty to qualify them with 'Of course, it's only my opinion' and so on" (175–76).

The method that unites Waldron and his interlocutors resides comfortably within the philosophic mainstream that embraces Socrates's dialectical approach to moral truth and John Rawls's reflective equilibrium.[18] Rawls describes that mainstream method in a general way when he says, "Moral philosophy is Socratic."[19] I need not hazard a precise description of the method to prove my contention that Waldron assumes the existence of some such method, for he takes utterly for granted the appropriateness of his own argumentative moves and expectations, and he could not do that without assuming methodological beliefs and ambitions that unite him and his critics. Whatever the precise account of the method Waldron and his readers assume, it satisfies the requirements Waldron believes exhibited by scientific method. It is a method that is "loosely defined and controversial in places," and although it is mainstream, not everyone accepts it.[20]

Waldron would insist, however, that there is one requirement that the standard method of moral philosophy does not satisfy. He says that "disagreements do get settled by [the scientific] method and when they do not, we can refer to the terms of the method to explain why" (ibid.). Such is not the case in ethics, as Waldron sees it. Later I examine Waldron's dubious assumption that convergence of opinion in ethics is a good thing. I note here that Waldron can hardly assert either that nothing ever gets settled in ethics or that current legal-moral disagreements will not be settled sufficiently to justify talk of a loosely defined and even locally disorganized but nevertheless mainstream method of moral philosophizing. Nor is it clear what he means when he indicates that disagreements in ethics cannot be explained in terms of the mainstream method of moral argumentation.

It is not clear that Waldron requires a method that would explain moral disagreements in the sense of justifying them, for contending scientists do not seem to justify their disagreements by referring to the principles of scientific method; a scientist typically invokes those principles in behalf of her position on some issue and in opposition to the other side. Someone outside the immediate debate might justify the disagreement as instantiating a social practice that advances the aims of scientific method, but one can do the same in ethics; the argument that disagreement is essential to progress toward ethical as well as scientific truth is as old as Socrates. And if Waldron means *explain* in the causal sense, one can easily explain moral disagreement in terms of the failure of moral method.

Waldron himself illustrates this last point when he explains his disagreement with moral realists in terms that reflect a loosely conceived Socratic method. That method contains what has been described as a say-what-you-really-mean requirement.[21] Waldron accepts this requirement implicitly when he charges that moral realists violate it. "Moral realists," he says, "are simply disingenuous" in failing to acknowledge the absence of a mainstream method that does for ethics what scientific method does for science.[22] Waldron, in the metaphysically realist manner of Socrates,[23] thus assumes that an honest interlocutor with complete information would simply accept the truth. And since Waldron believes his antirealism is true and that his realist interlocutors have enough information to see that, he treats their persistence in realism as an act of dishonesty.

Waldron does not explain why similar explanations cannot hold for first-order moral conflicts. Why, for example, can inadequate information, a lack of the moral imagination needed for thought experiments, simple intellectual incapacity, or dishonesty born of zealotry, bigotry, self-indulgence, or the psychological needs that compete with the need for truth—why can factors like these not explain such present-day disagreements as the moral status of the fetus and the fairness of affirmative action?[24] Waldron cites works that account in this way for the allegedly inadequate convergence of opinion in ethics; yet he ignores such accounts. Waldron thus fails to make a compelling argument against the parallel-to-science variety of moral realism.[25]

Dworkin's Moral Argument against Moral Realism

Dworkin's moral argument for the constructive model proceeds from two undefended assumptions. The first is that a constructivist judge has no reason to impose stubborn personal intuitions on the public. The second is that a realist has no reason to resist the imposition of personal prejudices.

Moore has suggested in response to the first of these assumptions that nothing stops a conventionalist judge from insisting on a personal conviction in the hope of constructing some future theory of the legal-moral system that can reconcile that conviction with the bulk of the community's beliefs.[26] Dworkin, it must be remembered, is not a shallow conventionalist like Bork, the later Bickel, and the current Michael Perry; Dworkin does not encourage judicial deference to legislative reflections of popular morality. His judges have a duty to construct theories that justify the bulk of the relevant legal-moral material. Although these justifying theories are theories of the community's beliefs, they are judicial constructs nonetheless, and they are typically controversial.

One reason for the controversial character of these constructs is that judges develop them to decide hard cases—cases left undecided by the community's surface (i.e., untheorized) legal-moral convictions. A second reason is that no judicial construct that can justify the bulk of the community's legal-moral convictions in a plausible way can be expected to justify every relevant part of the community's beliefs. Judges must therefore be prepared to declare some of the community's beliefs mistakes. Dworkin's well-known device for illustrating both the techniques of his constructive model and its requisite intellectual and moral virtues is his fictional judge, Hercules. Hercules, says Dworkin, is "a philosophical judge . . . of superhuman skill, learning, patience and acumen." And, "of course, Hercules' techniques may sometimes require a decision that opposes popular morality on some issue," like a right to abortion, which Hercules's theory of community morality may favor "no matter how strongly popular morality condemns abortion."[27] With Hercules as a figure for judicial emulation, Dworkin will have difficulty answering Moore's question: If a moral realist can hope for discoveries that can explain troubling intuitions, why can a moral conventionalist not hope for constructions that do the same?[28]

Dworkin contends further that, because moral realism "encourages the analogy between moral intuitions and observational data," a realist can regard a troubling moral intuition in the manner of "the astronomer who has clear observational data that he is as yet unable to reconcile in any coherent account . . . of the . . . solar system." A realist may regard a troubling conviction as true even though temporally "outstripped" by "the explanatory powers of those who observe."[29] Dworkin thus assumes that moral and scientific realists, as such, are committed to the truth of their perceptions and beliefs.

Dworkin may be right about self-styled realists who proceed as if they have closed the distance between belief and knowledge; McConnell and Berns could serve as examples of such dogmatic theorists. Dworkin's description fits Berns's hostility to philosophic inquiry in constitutional theory and McConnell's sweeping assertiveness from total immersion in the alleged source of legal-moral truth. But Dworkin's assumption does not apply to those moral realists who believe that their moral beliefs are fallible.[30]

My own inclination is to make the most of the metaphysical realist hypotheses that separate truth from belief, hold truth normative for belief, and find the truth of a proposition to depend on the proposition's correspondence to reality, not on the subjective strength with which it is held.[31] Serious realists must believe that no evidence whatever is strong enough to place any belief beyond falsification and that their firmest convictions and deepest presuppositions can be mistaken.[32] Realists should therefore be uncomfortable with notions like *commitment* and *conviction* insofar as they suggest axioms, postulates, and foundational beliefs that are unconditionally closed to further inquiry. Realism would thus preclude a commitment even to itself in any strong sense of *commitment*.[33]

Moral and scientific realists are realists in my view less from any affirmative case that can be made for realism than from the standard negative case for realism. That case proceeds through four broad propositions: (1) common sense and scientific practice seem to be governed by realist presuppositions, (2) our everyday reliance on realist presuppositions in science and ethics is sufficient to place the burden on antirealism, (3) no one has yet shown how to liberate scientific thought from realist presuppositions,[34] and (4) no one has offered good reasons to conclude that ethics cannot be as objective as science.[35]

Dworkin is thus a long way from proving that realism must license or excuse intolerance and irresponsibility. If the attitude of realist judges and critics is consistent with their hypothesis about the normative gap between belief and truth, they will be interested in truth, not in their beliefs about truth—truth as independent of what they believe it to be. The realist attitude must therefore be one of self-critical striving. This attitude is antithetical to dogmatic imposition. It demands a diversity of beliefs; it expresses itself through attempts to persuade and an openness to persuasion.[36] Moore can therefore say that moral realists "will develop theories about the nature of equality, liberty, liberties of speech and of worship, cruel punishment, and the like, in a never-completed quest to discover the true nature of such things."[37]

Dworkin's characterization of realism is either misinformed or proceeds from an understanding of realism that affects greater authority than that of leading contemporary realists. Perhaps Dworkin's view of realism is conceived in his own conventionalist union of truth and belief and born of his constructivist effort to display realism in some good conventionalist light. Until Dworkin exposes realism's claims to self-critical openness as pretextual or incoherent, his characterization of realism as impositional should appear ironic. For no one should be more disposed to impose her beliefs on others than the theorist who reduces truth to convention and claims that the deeper meaning of convention can lie only in the constructs of individual interpreters.

Dworkin and the Internal Point of View

Dworkin's philosophic conventionalism creates problems for his jurisprudence.[38] Two of these problems are of special concern here. His conventionalism undermines both his claim to theorize about law from a perspective internal to the practice of law and his related thesis about right answers in hard cases. Relative to the first difficulty, Dworkin has long claimed that his constructivism "does not presuppose skepticism or relativism." Constructivism rather assumes that legal-moral reasoning within the constructive model will proceed from convictions held with "sincerity," and that "this sincerity will extend to criticizing as unjust political acts or systems" offensive to "the most profound of these" convictions. The constructive model "does not deny, any more than it affirms, the objective standing of any of these convictions; it is therefore consistent with, though as a model of reasoning it does not require, the moral ontology that the natural [i.e., moral realist] model presupposes."[39]

Dworkin may move toward an official silence about objectivity because he accepts an antirealist metaphysics in the face of his decision to confront the normative questions of law from the internal perspective of the ordinary citizen. When speaking to ordinary citizens in their language Dworkin cannot deny the legal-moral objectivity and right answers that he would deny "in a calm philosophical moment, away from the moral or interpretive wars."[40] But he does accept an antirealist metaphysics, and although he tries to deny it (78–83), his metaphysics does influence the practical advice he gives to his fellow citizens. He tells them, for example, that they cannot resolve disagreements about what some legal or moral virtue like "courtesy" may require by explicating "the nature" of courtesy or questioning what people "by and large agree about the most general and abstract propositions about courtesy."[41] He tells his fellow citizens that if anyone should challenge such a consensus the questioner marks herself "as outside the community of useful or at least ordinary discourse" about courtesy, and that what she is seeking is the replacement of an old institution with a new one, not the improvement of the old one. He tells them that a proposition about the most abstract meaning of any legal or moral virtue, like courtesy, "fails unless people are by and large agreed that courtesy is" what the proposition says it is.[42]

Dworkin's remarks add up to a message of considerable normative significance. One formulation of that message would be: *There is a level at which the community cannot be wrong about virtues like courage, courtesy, or fairness; if the community has concepts of these things, there will come a point where fidelity to the community's aspirations will mean silence on the part of deviant or eccentric individuals.* Dworkin tries to disclaim this implication of his position (71–72). Let us see why he does not succeed.

When Dworkin speaks as a philosopher to his fellow citizens, he responds to their request for the true meaning of a specific legal-moral virtue or other normative idea with what he calls an interpretive theory of that normative idea. And, he says, his interpretive claim about the idea in question "can be challenged at any time" by "challenger[s] [who] will seem eccentric but will be perfectly understood" (ibid.). For Dworkin's fellow citizens to be open to such challenges, they must be persuaded to see the norm under examination as a concept whose meaning is not fixed, either by nature or convention, but whose meaning changes in accordance with the sociological "dynamics of interpretation" (88). As Dworkin interprets this pattern of change, "our legal culture . . . develops" in a certain way: some forces "resist" while other forces "promote [a] convergence" of diverse opinions regarding the source of law and "the justifying purpose . . . of legal practice as a whole" (87). Centripetal forces include "the general intellectual environment, as well as the common language that reflects and protects that environment" along with "the inevitable conservatism of formal legal education" and the process of judicial selection. Centrifugal forces include divisions of opinion "over justice." With conservative forces preserving parts of our legal culture and progressive forces agitating other parts, the law "develops" as its various parts move unevenly toward new agreements from old agreements through intervening stages of disagreement (87–89).

Such is Dworkin's account of legal development. But it is essentially a sociological account; and his conventionalism, consistently applied, would admit no real reason anyone should take the "dynamics of interpretation" as something worth perserving. What reason could there be in the dynamics of interpretation per se for the established power of any community to open itself to what Dworkin calls some "new and even radical interpretation of some important part of legal practice [which might be] developed in someone's chambers or study" (89)?

Dworkin says that the "law gains in power when it is sensitive to the frictions and stresses" of the ideological divisions that provide its "intellectual sources." He also says that the "law would stagnate" if it "collapsed into the runic traditionalism" of unquestioning consensus about its meaning (88–89). But these comments fall short of the reasons needed. They still do not tell the political establishment why it should consider changing practices it might regard as good. Surely there can be no gain in power in changes from better to worse. Why then consider such changes? If maintenance of the better be "stagnation," can stagnation be all bad? Without answers to such questions there can be no reason to accept Dworkin's dynamics of interpretation as good. And since his theory of interpretation is itself an interpretation—sensitive to a "point" grounded only in conviction, not nature (49, 65–68, 87–88)—there can be no reason to accept that theory when it threatens practices that express our firmest convictions.

Dworkin could find a reason for openness to change if he saw the dynamics of interpretation in terms of potential progress away from parochial prejudices toward objective moral and scientific truth and if he conceived our culture in terms of such progress, as many of its supporters have done. He intimates something to this effect when he observes that we cannot be sure about what our convictions really are unless we give radical views a full hearing (92). This argument for hearing radical views suggests that we are authorities for our own views only after periods of self-critical reflection and debate. I would agree, but I would ask Dworkin why a real conviction is any better morally than a seeming conviction. Is the real conviction better because stronger, as Dworkin suggests when he says law gains in power when sensitive to ideological divisions? And if stronger, in what sense? Can stronger mean more durable when some of the most durable convictions express a zeal that condemns rational self-examination as heresy? Stronger, then, in the sense of that which can survive the test of better evidence? If so, then convictions would be answerable to truth or probable truth, not mere convictions, for evidence is evidence of truth. Stronger, in this rational sense, would conform to the ordinary belief that having a favorable conviction regarding some proposition is believing it true or probably true.

So when Dworkin suggests there is something better about convictions that survive examination, he is either buying into or exploiting the ordinary beliefs of his readers that the conviction that survives debate is more likely to be true and that a conviction is not authentic without a belief that there exists independent evidence to regard it true. These ordinary beliefs are realist beliefs, and if Dworkin could maintain consistency with his constructivism or deep conventionalism, he could not admit them into his theory or his political arguments.

Dworkin's antirealist metaphysics also affects his view on the inside when he suggests that all instances of a certain kind of insider statements—those that appeal to a moral reality—are wrong. Dworkin recognizes that ordinary citizens can and do sensibly say that, for example, slavery is wrong and would be wrong even if no one believed it wrong. He also recognizes that an insider can say that "the 'right answer' to the question whether slavery is wrong" is that slavery is wrong and "that the contrary answer is not just different but mistaken." He recognizes that an insider who makes the preceding statements suggests: "I can prove slavery is wrong the way I might prove some claim of physics, by arguments of fact or logic every rational person must accept" (80–81).

Dworkin then says that someone who would assert this last claim "would assert what external skepticism [i.e., any form of moral antirealism] denies:

that moral judgments are descriptions of some special metaphysical moral realm"[43] (81). And because Dworkin rejects such a realm as "bizarre," he urges his readers to construe insider realist statements not as intending to make claims about a moral reality but as intending to do several other things, namely, to put some emotional emphasis behind the first-order or unelaborated part of the belief (the *slavery is wrong* part of *slavery is objectively or really wrong, and I can prove it*); to state the unelaborated part as a moral belief, not as a mere expression of taste; and to apply the unelaborated part to everyone everywhere (81–82).

One problem with this advice is that Dworkin fails to translate all that is said in the original statements. He claims that his translations "in no way" weaken the original statements or make "them claim something less or even different from what they might be thought to claim" (82). He claims fidelity to the translated statements apparently because his constructivism demands reconstructions of positions he finds absurd, and he simply declares realism and therefore the realist aspects of the original statements "absurd." "*We* do not say," he insists, with an emphasis that banishes realists from the community signified by his "we"—"*We* do not say (nor can we understand anyone who does say) that interpretation is like physics or that moral values are 'out there' or can be proved" (83, his emphasis).

But it is difficult to understand Dworkin's claim that his reconstruction of the original beliefs changes them in no way. Aside from the manifest differences in content, there are practical differences between saying *I sincerely believe slavery is always wrong* and *I can prove slavery wrong to anyone in a position to reason aright.* The former statement reports a belief; the latter reports the same belief and, in addition, claims the ability to do something. The second statement anticipates or at least makes sensible a policy of trying to do what it says it can do: show actual and potential slaveholders that no one who is willing and able to reason aright can really want (or ought to want) to enslave anyone.

The second statement also makes sensible several additional policies in support of the first policy. One of these supporting policies is trying to insure that actual and potential slaveholders enjoy the educational benefits, relative economic independence, and other social prerequisites for reasoning aright. Another is urging actual or potential slaveholders to the dialectical methods of science and moral philosophy that constitute the only way to adduce evidence in behalf of slavery's unreasonableness. Another supporting policy is preserving the social and political freedoms necessary to form and represent the diverse beliefs essential to the pursuit of the truth about slavery. Another is fostering the attitude of self-critical striving that characterizes all who acknowledge their presuppositions about right answers and a moral reality, including the gap and the normative tension between their strongest convictions and the truth. Still other supporting policies involve a conception of community membership that welcomes, not banishes or marginalizes, all whose presence contributes to the self-critical effort to replace opinion with knowledge.[44]

Contrast the policies made sensible by: *I oppose slavery emphatically and unconditionally although it is absurd to think that any reasonable person can be shown that slavery is wrong.* These policies would include imposing antislavery beliefs on actual and potential slaveholders. For if slavery is emphatically, unquestionably, and universally wrong, and if there is no hope of demonstrating its wrongness to everyone—not even to every fully rational and informed person—then there is no argument of principle to be made for self-criticism, debate, and other dialectical means and attitudes (and their concomitant legislative program and institutional rights) as prerequisites to a morally permissible antislavery policy.

At some point (and why not sooner than later?), rightness will be determined not by the quality of supporting arguments but solely by results; and if state imposition of one kind or another is what it takes to make people hate slavery, imposition will be right. A successful policy of imposition would result in antislavery's being morally axiomatic for the community—a "given" because held with "the requisite sincerity." No person known to the community as either decent or rational would think of considering a proslavery argument, for the community would regard a proslavery implication as the reductio ad absurdum of any argument. That attitude would affect the character of the community: the community would be fundamentally an antislavery community, not a community of persons who are antislavery from reflection and choice. The community's utter closure to proslavery arguments would preclude the inquiries through which the community adduces evidence that slavery is unworthy of choice. On theories that connect the wrongness of slavery to slavery's denial of the human potential for reflection and choice, we could fairly describe such a community as slavishly antislavery and the preferred choice of no fully rational and informed person.

Realism, Conventionalism, and Community

A professed antirationalist like McConnell might prefer an axiomatically antislavery community, but I doubt that Dworkin does.[45] Dworkin may even be brought to agree that it is not a real community. To see why it may at any rate be less than an ideal community, we need a closer look at the axiomatic community and the tactic of invoking the authority of the community as a way of closing debatable questions. The axiomatically antislavery community would be a special case of a general type of community: that which founds on a set of specific substantive beliefs, like antislavery or proslavery.

A different type of community is that which founds on a capacity for reflection and choice, a capacity for challenging all beliefs, including a belief in itself. With these two kinds of community in mind, we should notice a peculiarity about argumentative appeals to what the community believes and does. When a participant in legal-moral debate invokes what the community says and does, there is reason to presume that his appeal is false. Consider Dworkin's assertion that "*we* do not say . . . that moral values are 'out there' or can be proved." What makes that statement an appropriate argumentative move are two facts in its context that combine to make a prima facie case that the statement is false. The first fact is one that has to obtain for Dworkin's statement to have a point: that some of us do appear to say or want to say what Dworkin says we do not say. The second fact is that Dworkin includes those of us who appear to disagree in the community signified by his *we,* or so we can assume from his apparent decision to include us among the addressees of his argument. So, at first blush, Dworkin's unqualified "we do not say" seems false; some of us do seem to say such things, even on his own view of who we are.

In fact, most of us seem to say what Dworkin says we do not say. David Brink writes that realism is the mode of common sense, that people generally begin as realists about science and about ethics, and that if they become anti-realists they do so generally from exposure to the sophisticated metaphysical and epistemological teachings of the academy.[46] Although it would seem hard to disagree with Brink, Waldron would turn a related observation to anti-realist advantage. "For every stern preacher who talks about the reality of moral obligation," Waldron says, "there is a gum-chewing sophomore who says that all moral views are just matters of opinion and there's no ultimate standard." The presence of these sophomores transforms "ordinary moral discourse" into a "meta-ethical Babel" that is "no longer . . . unambiguously . . . realist-sounding."[47] Not the least problem with Waldron's remark is a distribution of images that puts antirealism on the side of liberalism and realism on the side of illiberalism. (Liberal intellectuals might have wished for more dignified representation than the gum-chewing sophomore, although Socrates fared worse when Thrasymachus likened him to a snot-nosed kid.)

My argument in this book is squarely to the contrary. I put realism on the side of liberalism, and I emphasize the potential tyranny of antirealism. But the immediate problem is figuring out what Waldron is saying about the gum-chewing sophomore, for we have already seen that Waldron effectively acknowledges the realist structure of ordinary moral discourse.[48] Let me return to that point through a view of the sophomore that differs from Waldron's. If, as Waldron indicates, our sophomore is engaged in the same sphere of moral discourse as our preacher, then our sophomore's "relativism" must be relativism in the sense of toleration of much ideological diversity and personal privacy. Our sophomore would be saying, in other words, that it is a good thing to let individuals make up their own minds about some of the matters that the preacher wants under some forms of social control. This kind of relativism proceeds from realist assumptions, of course, and Waldron cannot interpret it otherwise if he is to see it as a position within ordinary moral discourse.

Waldron cannot respond by chalking up my account of the gum-chewing sophomore as another example of realists "not listening to what actually gets said in our culture, or . . . filtering or discounting some of it . . . on the basis of the very theory they take themselves to be supporting with this evidence."[49] For my account is faithful to Waldron's account of his own first-order moral judgments. When he takes an observer's perspective on ordinary moral discourse, Waldron accepts the antirealist view that there is no moral reality that makes people's moral judgments true or false regardless of what anyone believes. There is no moral reality, he says, *"there are only moral judgments and the people who make them"* (159, his emphasis). But the picture changes for Waldron when he steps into the world of ordinary moral discourse.

"When I condemn an action," he now says, "I usually do so in virtue of some feature F that it has (the action's cruelty, for example, or its hurtfulness)" (171). And with this last statement he admits something in addition to the moral judgment and the person who makes it; now there's an F in the picture, an F to which Waldron refers in descriptive terms as a moral property that causes him to condemn the action. He thus approves Dworkin's view that a person who believes that slavery is wrong must also believe that there is a right answer to the question whether slavery is wrong.[50] Waldron also approves Simon Blackburn's view that the philosophical antirealist who believes it is wrong to kick dogs does not take the "absurd moral view" that "the feature which makes it wrong . . . is our reaction" to the act. "Like anyone else," says Blackburn, the antirealist now acting in the ordinary moral sphere "thinks that what makes it wrong to kick dogs is that it causes them pain."[51]

Waldron does not have to interpret ordinary beliefs about right answers and moral facts as self-conscious metaphysical conclusions—people who make ordinary moral judgments do not have to be philosophers. But I do not see how Waldron can deny that ordinary presuppositions about right answers and moral facts are compatible with realism and incompatible with antirealism. Waldron's account of his own moral judgments justifies the following conclusion: ordinary moral discourse is either realist or interpretable as realist; *it is not interpretable as antirealist.* Applying Waldron's own account of the structure of ordinary moral discourse to his sophomore, when making moral judgments she must either be a realist or hold beliefs that are compatible with realism, lest she be adjudged "absurd."

I hope this view of the sophomore acquits me of Waldron's charge that realists interpretating ordinary moral discourse offer "a better account of their own moralizing and that of their chums" than of "what actually gets said in our culture."[52] In any case, I submit Brink's observation about ordinary moral judgments to the reader's experience, and I do not think Dworkin can deny that some if not most of us in the community at large hold or at least say that we hold moral realist beliefs of the type Dworkin opposes. As I have indicated, evidence that Dworkin cannot deny this last proposition lies in the fact that his invocation of what "we say" takes the form of a counterresponse to what some of us either believe or act as if we believe. So if we reformulated Dworkin's statement to allow for its argumentative purpose, it would read: *We do not say what many of us say.*

Dworkin intends no such paradox, of course; and so we should not take his statement as a general description of the surface metaphysical beliefs of everyone whom he would include in the term we. Because we cannot understand him to intend the unqualified statement that we do not profess or display realist beliefs about morality, I think we must interpret him as intending something like the following: *People often believe that they believe something only to discover through reflection and debate that their real beliefs are not as they initially appeared. Because people are generally aware of this pattern of behavior, most would affirm the abstract statement that people do not believe—do not really believe—what they are sure to find absurd. Aside from sophists who will say anything and the eccentric who might actually believe the unbelievable, we are sure to find realism absurd. So it is fair to say we do not say—not really—what the realists say.*[53]

If this reconstruction of Dworkin's statement is, as I contend, the best if not the only way to save it from paradox, and if Dworkin must be construed to mean what he would have to mean in order to make sense, he seems to believe that if we were fully rational and had complete information, we would accept his antirealist metaphysics because it is true or closer to the truth than realism and because, eccentrics and sophists aside, we all want to be closer to the truth.

Dworkin's reconstructed claim would anticipate or make sensible a policy of trying to demonstrate the truth of the antirealist metaphysics it asserts. If there were enough time for reflection and debate, and where other costs contingently associated with reflection and debate were bearable, Dworkin's reconstructed claim could not be used to justify a policy of imposing anti-realist doctrine. If, when Dworkin said *we say such and so,* he implicitly claimed that he could persuade those who initially said otherwise, then he would suppose a *we* whose membership is determined not simply by its beliefs but by its capacity and willingness to examine and form its beliefs in light of the evidence.

Such a reconstructed claim for an antirealist metaphysics would thus suppose a reasoning community, not an axiomatically antirealist community. For when called upon to do so, representatives of the community would try to demonstrate antirealism by considering anew the arguments on both sides, and an honest willingness to test a thesis implies a willingness to reject it if it fails the test. Just as realism must be open to the possibility of antirealism, a reasoning antirealism must be open to the possibility of realism.

If there could be such a thing, a reasoning community that happened tentatively to accept antirealism would be more of a community in several respects than an axiomatically antirealist community. The reasoning community would be more inclusive in principle; it would be open to anyone willing to put her beliefs to the test of argument. If the reasoning community would be founded on anything it would be a capacity for deliberation and choice that it assumed common to humankind; it would aspire to what it supposed to be a common and shareable end, namely, knowledge. This reasoning community could not be characterized as simply antirealist, however, for it would operate from a belief in the possibility of knowledge, and that is a realist belief. To the extent that it continued to believe in this possibility it would remain a reasoning community, for it would continue to assume that there may be something to reason about and some real point in reasoning about it. If most of its members could reach antirealist conclusions, the community would have to hold these conclusions tentatively, with the understanding that its beliefs could be wrong and with a continuing willingness to test its beliefs.

This last requirement for a reasoning community would secure the membership of realist critics of the antirealist majority. Debate would thus continue in the presence of a belief in the possibility of knowledge, and that is all that a realist could want, since the realist separation of truth and therefore knowledge from belief must open realists to the possibility of error in their own realist beliefs. The realist is at home in the reasoning community no matter what the majority happens tentatively to believe, so long as it remains a reasoning majority. The true realist is not at home in a community that either excludes antirealists or treats realism as a body of axioms. The true realist is not at home in the community of Waldron's "stern preacher[s]" and their academic "chums."

In contrast to the reasoning community, the axiomatic community would be a vitiated community. As we have seen, representatives of the axiomatic community could sensibly invoke its authority only on occasions when the invocation would be false on its face. They would be saying, in effect: *we do not do or say what many of us do or say.* And they could not cure the paradox without transforming the community from an axiomatic to a reasoning community, a community whose representatives would submit their issues with deviant members to the test of honest inquiry. If it remained true to form, the axiomatic community would try to remove the conditions for the paradox through policies of banishing or marginalizing eccentrics and imposing its foundational beliefs. These policies would either make the community smaller or divide it horizontally between believers and nonbelievers and hierarchically as required by the instruments of imposition it employed. At the same time that its apologists would extol the values of community they would deny that there are truly common moral truths or aspirations on which to ground community. This denial of true commonalities would eventually transform communities into things that must be held together not by reason and the promise of progress toward truth, but by hard or soft forms of force. The most challenging of contemporary antirealists make no bones about this last implication of their position.[54]

WHOSE OBJECTIVITY?

I trust that I have shown that Dworkin's metaphysics affects his understanding of our legal-moral practices in a manner that could have important political consequences. The same holds for Waldron. He tries to secure the thesis that metaphysics is irrelevant through what we have seen to be a self-contradictory denial that legal-moral discourse has a workable method for distinguishing better from worse answers. Waldron pulls back from the (internal) consequences of his (outsider's) antirealism when he says that the question of judicial power must be settled, not on the basis of a metaphysical dispute, but "on the basis of moral arguments about fairness, justice, and democracy."[55] But because the very structure of these moral arguments presupposes realism—a metaphysical position—the truth of antirealism would, if seen by insiders (to the extent that they could see it), disable moral argument and replace it with either an assertive or a retiring nihilism, depending on the psychology of the individual nihilist.

In the end, Waldron and Dworkin are in the same boat. They cannot just decree the political irrelevance of metaphysics. To establish the irrelevance of metaphysics they would have to make it happen—make it happen politically. In other words, they would have to remove metaphysical debate from public view. This would mean, among other things, disciplining half-smart meta-physicians (or Berns's "so-called intellectuals") who could not appreciate the reasons for maintaining silence in public. For some of us half-smart meta-physicians would surely demand to know what real reasons there can be for such silence. I will not speculate on how Waldron and Dworkin might arrange this isolation of philosophy or why they would want to try. But the question does invite comparisons with the social stratification Berns needs to secure the interests he serves, and it should cause a reconsideration of Bork's attempt to exclude moral philosophy from constitutional law. Perhaps we should even reconsider Bork's tactical fusion of New Right jurisprudence and McCarthy-ism. If philosophy deflates conventional morality, if we can aspire to no higher morality, and if we happen to share Bork's distaste for the turmoil that could easily replace deflated convention, can a McCarthyite assault on moral philos-ophy be all bad?

I have also tried to show that Dworkin's antirealist metaphysics under-mines his claim to speak from a position within our legal-moral practices. With regard to this last point I have both assumed and submitted that the presuppositions of our everyday legal-moral understanding are realist in both form and content. We ordinarily speak about what *is* fair in the same descrip-tive form as we speak about what is red or blue; and we are concerned about *fairness,* not just about fairness so-called.[56] Dworkin can show that his anti-realism is compatible with an insider's understanding only if he can demon-strate that "we [insiders] don't [really want to] say" what the realists say. If I am right in contending that Dworkin commits himself to this proposition, we should assess his prospects for defending it.

A brief reminder may clarify the issue. Dworkin recognizes that "the policy of judicial activism presupposes a certain objectivity of moral princi-ple; in particular it presupposes that citizens do have certain moral rights against the state, like a moral right to equality of education or to fair treat-ment by the police. Only if moral rights exist in some sense can activism be justified as a program based on something beyond the judge's personal prefer-ences."[57] Were it not for Dworkin's equivocal references to "a certain objec-tivity" and the existence of moral rights "in some sense," his statement would indicate the thesis of this book: A successful defense of judicial power is not merely compatible with realist assumptions, it depends on realist assump-tions. Without the equivocations, realism would be the only plausible inter-pretation of the statement that activism "can . . . be justified" "only if moral rights exist."

As Dworkin's statement stands, and in view of his antirealist moral phi-losophy, his defense of a nondeferential judiciary may not depend on realist assumptions, but it does depend on moral objectivity "in some sense" of objectivity and on the existence of moral rights "in some sense" of existence. Dworkin's prospects for defending his claim that "we [insiders] don't [really want to] say" what the realists actually say depends on whether we insiders can admit an antirealist sense of objectivity and rights. Let us therefore consider the available senses of moral .objectivity and the existence of moral rights.

As we saw when examining the constitutional theories of McConnell and Perry, a useful distinction obtains between moral skepticism in a strict sense and two other forms of moral antirealism, namely, subjectivism and conventionalism. Moral skepticism denies moral objectivity because it denies, inter alia, that first-order moral propositions can be true or false. Subjectivists and conventionalists do not deny that first-order moral propositions can be true or false. The subjectivist says that moral truths correspond to the subjective beliefs of individuals—that, for example, *cruelty is wrong,* can be true, but only for someone who believes it true. Conventionalism holds that moral truth is relative to the more or less established and continuing beliefs attributable (in some way) to some community. Conventionalism and subjectivism are the two forms of relativism, and although each may be equivalent to moral skepticism at the constitutional level, as I contend, some relativists disclaim skepticism, as we saw in Perry's case.

These are the metaphysical alternatives to moral realism, and so, in addition to a moral realist sense of moral objectivity and the existence of moral rights, we can have both subjectivist and conventionalist senses of these notions. The question here is which of these senses makes plausible Dworkin's thesis that judicial activism depends on moral objectivity and the existence of moral rights. The only likely candidates are the moral realist and the deep-conventionalist senses. For Dworkin rejects subjectivism when he seeks to justify activism on some basis "beyond the judge's personal preferences" (ibid.). He also rejects shallow conventionalism when he rejects a rule of judicial deference to elected officials (138, 146–47). And his acceptance of a conventionalist metaphysics would not force him to deny (although he does deny) that, as an empirical matter, moral realist presuppositions govern the internal point of view of practicing judges and ordinary citizens.

Our question, then, is whether Dworkin can impute deep-conventionalist presuppositions to ordinary citizens and practitioners who defend judicial activism. As a first step toward showing that he cannot, let me recall a feature of the constructive model of decision in hard cases that sets Dworkin apart from shallow conventionalists like Bork. Dworkin's constructive model excludes judicial deference to legislative and electoral beliefs about what the Constitution means; the model requires judges to form their own best theories of constitutional meaning. But a constructivist believes that the general moral words and phrases of the Constitution can have no meaning beyond what some group believes. So the constitutional theory of a constructivist judge is actually a theory about certain of the legal-moral aspects of the community's beliefs.

What justifies the constructivist model? Dworkin's moral argument for constructivism notwithstanding, the constructivist can hardly support a realist claim that justice justifies the model, for a constructivist can refer only to justice so-called, not *justice*. Nor can he make the realist argument that the nature of interpretation requires a constructivist approach in constitutional cases; hence Dworkin's statement that interpretation is itself an interpretive concept.[58] To be consistent with his constructivism to the extent that he can be, the constructivist must say that, at some level of its beliefs, the community believes that judges ought to fashion their own theories about what the community believes the Constitution means.

This attribution to the community should sound familiar; it is one way to describe Bickel's early suggestion that the public recognizes the utility of a strong judiciary for the purpose of rationalizing the public's preferences in constitutional terms.[59] Although Bickel proved lacking in Dworkin's tenacity when Bickel abandoned deep conventionalism for shallow conventionalism, Bickel began as a deep conventionalist. He originally held that activist judges could derive their values from no source beyond deep convention, and he rejected a rule of judicial deference on occasions when the Court was persuaded that the public was gripped by sentiments it would abandon.[60] True to his conventionalism, Bickel had always assumed that history establishes the difference between right and wrong.

Notwithstanding Dworkin's own conventionalism, he has criticized Bickel's position as equivalent to the skeptical stance of no moral rights against the community.[61] Dworkin has said that "the suggestion that rights can be demonstrated by a process of history rather than an appeal to principle shows either a confusion or no real concern about what rights are. A claim of right presupposes a moral argument and can be established in no other way" (147). When the later Bickel adjusted his position on judicial power in response to what he perceived to be the Court's policy failures and the public's turn against the judicial assertiveness of the Warren era, he provided a case in point for Dworkin's rejection of history as a foundation for rights.

Yet Dworkin's constructivist method also makes rights hostage to history. Hercules's constructions in hard cases remain constructions of the community's legal-moral beliefs. Although Hercules may add something that was not mentioned before—like a new version of the Constitution's meaning as a whole or a new conception of a specific constitutional provision—his creativity is constrained by the bulk of decided cases, statutes, the community's moral principles, and so forth.

Dworkin insists that interpretation differs from invention because the historical beliefs that constitute the legal-moral material of the judges' constructions rule out some constructions.[62] Because, on the conventionalist model, the community's legal-moral beliefs constrain the constitutional constructions of judges, and because no one can deny that the community's beliefs may evolve to a point that rules out the very notion of rights against the community (as Bork's case illustrates), a conventionalist cannot maintain the unconditional existence of rights against the community. And because it is conceivable that, from time to time, the state's claim to represent the community may be a just claim, conventionalists cannot maintain the unconditional existence of rights against the state.

The moral realist stands in a different relationship both to the community and the state. She can say that there will be moral and even constitutional rights against the community and the state even if public opinion is far too antirights to be construed as in any way prorights. A moral realist can hold, for example, that an antirights community is corrupt and that individuals and minorities have rights against that community despite its antirights axioms and practices. The deep conventionalist's logic requires him to say that in such a case it would make no sense to claim the community is wrong, for the community would lack the conventions needed for that assessment to have any meaning. A deep conventionalist would thus be unable to call a fully successful tyranny a tyranny. Deep conventionalism would thus seem useless to defenders of a nondeferential judiciary. If the case for an independent and assertive judicial power depends on the existence of moral rights "in some sense," moral realism must supply that sense. To repeat an observation I made in connection with Chemerinsky's open-ended modernism, deep conventionalists who would defend judicial power must pretend to be something other than what they are.[63]

Dworkin is wrong to suppose that his constructivist sense of moral objectivity and rights can work in the brief for judicial power. Because our metaphysical presuppositions can and do become the subjects of conscious examination and controversy, and because antirealist answers disable the political beliefs of all but schizophrenics, the case for a nondeferential judiciary depends on the possibility of a moral realist metaphysics.

7

DEFENDING
THE
CLASSICAL
THEORY

This concluding chapter takes up the skeptical challenges to the presuppositions of the classical theory. Far short of contending for the truth of these presuppositions, I contend only for their respectability. I show what the return of moral realism to philosophic respectability should mean for the classical presuppositions and why theorists who would defend judicial power need no more—and should seek no more—than to shift the burden where it belongs: on moral conventionalism and the other forms of moral antirationalism.

We shall also see, however, that the relatively narrow theoretical issues of judicial power raised here open eventually on a more urgent question: Is the Constitution really the instrument of justice that it claims to be? Since the classical defense of judicial power is part of the Constitution's larger claim, the case for judicial power depends on the case for the Constitution. Although the latter is still partly a matter of theory, it has always meshed with political problems that demand much more than success among theorists.

THE SEMANTIC POWER OF THE
CONSTITUTIONAL DOCUMENT IN HARD CASES

The first of the classical presuppositions concerns the power of the constitutional document to guide judicial decision in hard cases. Moore and other moral realists have argued systematically and at length that properties of language and language usage like vagueness, generality, ambiguity, and open-endedness need not defeat the Constitution's normative power.[1] Reviewing some of these arguments should indicate the prospects of a realist response to skeptics about the meaningfulness of constitutional language.

Constitutional Vagueness

Consider vagueness. A skeptic believes that the vagueness of constitutional terms like those of section 1 of the Fourteenth Amendment precludes right answers regarding their meaning either in the abstract or as applied in particular cases. The argument for right answers supposes that terms like *equal protection* and *due process* refer or can refer to things that are both real and approachable through better theories of their nature and their requirements in concrete situations. A realist can rescue the possibility of right answers by construing vagueness as a property not of words but of our beliefs or conventions regarding the application of words. Moore puts it thus: "Vagueness is a conventional feature of language use—a word is vague when competent native speakers don't know what to say—greater vagueness means a greater number of items for which there is no governing linguistic convention and, hence, no guidance . . . by such convention" (126). But if the meaning of a term is given by the nature of what it signifies—"tiger" by tiger, "life" and "death" by life and death, "due process" by due process—and if that nature is approximated through better theories, then, as Moore puts it, "the vagueness of the phrase cuts no ice as an argument for indeterminacy in the phrase's correct interpretation" (130). Reflection and debate can bring us closer to what we are looking for; we can have better and worse answers, and the best available answer is the right answer for now.

The prospect of constitutional meaning in hard cases does not mean that each substantive constitutional term successfully refers to something that exists independently of what we believe about it or that exists as separate and distinct from other constitutional ideas. Whether a given term refers to something distinct and real will depend on the right answers to broader questions of legal-moral theory, including the purposes of the Constitution as a whole and its proper arrangement of rights and powers. It may be true, for example, as per the effect of Justice Miller's opinion in the *Slaughter House Cases,* that the most persuasive theory of judicial power combines with the best theory of state-federal relations to imply that the Fourteenth Amendment's privileges and immunities clause refers to nothing not already covered by other constitutional provisions.[2] Miller's theory makes the privileges and immunities clause a case of unsuccessful reference, something that judges can properly ignore.

Walter Murphy has shown that Miller treated the clause as a mistake, an unconstitutional constitutional amendment.[3] The same can be said for Bork's treatment of the Ninth Amendment as an inkblot that obscures rights judges might otherwise have protected.[4]

We will be justified in believing that a term refers to something real if hypothesizing such reference seems the best way to explain other beliefs that survive critical examination. We do not believe the word *centaur* refers to anything real. We can account for that belief by the influence of other beliefs, including what we call our experiences and the laws of biology. Should our experiences change in ways that could be explained best by the existence of centaurs, we would have reason to believe some of our old beliefs were wrong.

The same holds for due process. We could not reasonably deny that *due process* referred to something real if hypothesizing the existence of due process proved the best way to explain a belief that it exists and if we cannot deny its existence without denying other things that we believe. We cannot coherently say, for example, that due process is nothing more than rhetorical dressing for whatever process serves our interest, if we believe increased personal wealth is in our interest, and if we think it is possible for a government unfairly to transfer wealth from one person to another. And if on some occasion someone behaves as if she believes some action unfair (say, by greeting a seemingly unjust transfer of property with appropriate anger or resentment) while stubbornly refusing to call the action unfair, we are entitled to question her honesty, especially if we have independent grounds (like past experience of her eristic nature) for suspecting dishonesty.

Nor can reflective persons say that apparent disagreements over the meaning of due process prove either its nonexistence or its merely conventional existence. That position would preclude affirming the existence of anything in either our moral or nonmoral experience in the face of apparent disagreement over its meaning and existence. An apparent-agreement test of meaning and existence would be sophistic, of course, for it would defeat itself at the mere appearance of some critic.[5]

Little more can be said for deploying a narrowly materialist test of existence against the proposed existence of due process. Such a test would rule out the existence of far too many nonmoral things in addition to moral things like due process.[6] These nonmoral things would include the species frog, as opposed to the touchable things that, for some reason, are called frogs; triangles, as opposed to what we, on a strict materialist account, naively call representations of triangles in books, blueprints, and elsewhere; and thoughts, intentions, motives, pleasures, pains, and other so-called mental states that are naively thought to supervene on (what are naively thought to be) patterns of (what are naively thought to be) neurobiological events. Indeed, a narrowly materialist test of existence would exclude any "thing" (naively thought to be) captured by any communicable symbol beyond ostensive designations of this or that (unnamed) this, in this or that here and now—we could not even say "particular this" or "tangible this," since the notions of particularity and tangibility make sense only in a world that seems to accommodate their opposites.

It should go without saying, although it does not, that we should not profess a strict materialism that our patterns of speech and conduct indicate we do not really hold. But if we did hold it, we would have to do so in some nonverbal way, because we could not communicate a strict materialism even silently to ourselves without the use of general words that referred *ex hypothesi* to absolutely nothing at all.[7] So our experiences in the world give us strong reasons to believe that someone who does dismiss due process and other legal-moral ideas on materialist grounds as well as the other grounds mentioned— an agreement test of existence and the reduction of normative words to instruments for rationalizing selfish interests—is probably guilty of sophistry, that is, professing to believe what the evidence of one's own words and deeds indicates one does not really believe.

These considerations justify doubt that there is a compelling argument for abandoning the presuppositions of ordinary legal-moral practice. One can doubt that reason compels giving up, say, the sense that a trial can be unfair (imagine trials by ordeal) even if some entire community deeply believes it fair. We can also doubt that there is a persuasive reason to describe some tyrant's advance in his country and beyond as a march from indecency to decency through terror. Doubts like these protect beliefs on which we in fact rely, and these beliefs presuppose that things like decency and due process are real, not just a matter of what people believe or can be made to believe.

A judge who sees no reason to abandon these presuppositions can conceive vagueness as a property not of due process but of our conventional understanding of due process. Such a judge can believe that "due process" refers in a perfectly precise fashion to due process itself. She can say, in other words, that our conventions or beliefs about due process leave its application in some particular case or class of cases unclear, but that it either does or does not apply in specific ways to that case or class, and that we can justify an answer through a process of reflection and debate.

At its moral and intellectual best, this process of reflection and debate will be pursued with the concentration, refinement, courage, and tenacity of a Socrates. But even at less than its best, it can be a praiseworthy instance of commonsense moral deliberation. This process tests an optional answer in a given case against the relevant beliefs and experiences of the interlocutors, amending or even abandoning some beliefs as needed to accommodate beliefs that are either not in question or that have survived criticism in a way that demands their place in some overall and workable conception of justice. We might think, for example, that after having considered all of the arguments about relevant consequences and principles we have improved our under-standing of due process to the point that we can call for a relaxation of the right to confrontation in child abuse cases generally or in some particular child abuse case.

Due process will, of course, remain vague as applied in unanticipated future cases, and future reflection may cause us to see a past decision as erroneous. Indeed, we should resist blind confidence in our answer to any particular case. We should continue the process of self-critical striving because we have reason to believe—that is, our everyday presuppositions plus the incoherence of skepticism leave us with an argument that favors—the follow-ing propositions: (1) whether we know the right answer, and whether we are in a political position to assert it, there is a right answer; (2) the right answer is the proposition that corresponds with, or comes closest to, the nature of due process itself and what it requires here and now; (3) the right answer is demon-strable to all who can reason aright; (4) all who would reason aright would have reason to agree with that answer; and (5) a process of self-critical striving for an answer in which honest and competent inquirers can agree will pro-duce evidence—defeasible evidence, but still evidence—for what due process means and requires.

Constitutional Conflict and Constitutional Adequacy

A similar argument can apply to what many observers regard as a further defect of constitutional language, the apparent conflict between different con-stitutional provisions.[8] As in cases involving the application of federal labor laws to state government personnel and the threat that zealous press coverage poses to fair criminal prosecutions, constitutional provisions can appear to conflict—the Tenth Amendment with the commerce clause in the first exam-ple, and the First Amendment with the Fifth and Seventh in the second exam-ple. Yet there is no conflict among the textual provisions themselves. What we sometimes construe as a conflict in the text is actually a conflict among litigat-ing parties who interpret the text in ways favorable to diverse interests.

A judge who is interested in the truth about constitutional meaning is hardly limited to the interpretive options proposed by litigants. The constitu-tional text justifies her assumption that each of the constitutional provisions at issue in a case is a functioning part of a workable instrument for reconciling popular government to justice. The requirements of such an instrument in concrete cases are to be determined with an eye to the best substantive theory of what the Constitution means. That theory will guide the judge to what seems the proper relationship between constitutional rights and powers generally, between different institutions at one level of government, and between different institutional levels of a federal system.[9] That theory will also help her describe what I have elsewhere called a constitutional state of affairs—the social conditions in which it will be politically feasible for judges and others to honor all genuine (i.e., nonmistaken) constitutional provisions without provoking political reactions that will reverse progress toward constitutional ends (55–62, 75–76, 105–8, 169, 174–77).

To clarify this last suggestion, I should add that the recommended approach to constitutional conflicts need not imply that, properly construed, the Constitution is perfectly adequate to its ends or that it should be interpreted in whatever manner its ends might require. Neither the Constitution nor its officers can guarantee the social conditions for their effectiveness. Conditions may make it impossible for a judge to honor each of the constitutional provisions at issue in a particular case. The Constitution cannot govern in every imaginable situation.

Grant that the Constitution presupposes that the ends of the criminal law can be achieved in a manner that honors the right to a fair trial, or that national security can be achieved in a manner that respects Congress's authority to declare war, or that racial justice can be achieved without Congress's exceeding a fair interpretation of its enumerated powers and without the judiciary assuming legislative powers. Grant all these things and we could still imagine conditions under which we had to forgo either a fair trial or the punishment of the guilty. We could also imagine a situation in which the survival of the nation demanded the exclusion of Congress from any role in war making. And we could easily imagine a situation in which no honest version of congressional or judicial boundaries would be adequate to an attractive version of racial justice.

Because the Constitution is a commitment both to certain ends (like national security) and to certain means (like fair trials and a role for Congress), the Constitution becomes incoherent when and to the extent that social conditions preclude plausible versions of constitutional institutions as effective means to constitutional ends (49–52, 187–96). Because an incoherent measure cannot measure, there is no possibility of constitutional action by any actor under conditions of constitutional incoherence. An actor may seek to restore the conditions of constitutional coherence, as Lincoln did in waging civil war and, arguably, as modern judges have done in mandating taxes and fashioning complex codes to remedy problems like segregated schools and inhumane prison systems. But when constitutionally ungovernable conditions obtain, the Constitution has no prescriptive force. It tells judges and others nothing—neither what to do, nor what to avoid doing.

Yet the possibility of constitutionally ungovernable conditions does not preclude right answers. It in fact presupposes right answers to the following questions: (1) What is a constitutionally governable state of affairs? (2) Does a constitutionally governable state of affairs obtain? (3) Is a proposed course of action likely to restore a constitutionally governable state of affairs? Nor does the possibility of constitutionally ungovernable conditions defeat other parts of the classical theory of judicial review. We can see this in connection with the second presupposition of the classical theory: the psychological possibility that judges can be faithful to the Constitution.

THE POSSIBILITY OF JUDICIAL FIDELITY
TO THE CONSTITUTION

This second presupposition involves only the possibility of judges' conforming to their constitutional duties, not the reasonableness of expecting that most judges will be good judges. However we may conceive a bad judge, most of us agree that the proportion of bad to good varies with the political season, and that guarantees disappointments for everyone. Publius's argument for judicial power is part of his case for the Constitution as a whole, and both arguments suppose a supply of fit persons for federal judgeships and other offices, along with a nominating process that recruits such persons.

This dependence on fit judges is merely another respect in which the validity of Publius's thought depends on social contingencies. Publius's case for judicial power and all other constitutional institutions is therefore unpersuasive under some circumstances. I return to this point several times in this chapter. But first I want to ask why someone might have reached a much stronger conclusion, namely, that an honest concern for getting the Constitution right in hard cases is a psychological impossibility no matter what the broader sociopolitical environment.

Perhaps the answer best known among constitutional theorists occurs in the early writing of Jerome Frank. That answer comes in two inconsistent parts. First, Frank classified "the ideas and beliefs of all of us . . . roughly . . . as of two kinds: those . . . based primarily on objective observation of objective data and those that are entirely or almost entirely a product of subjective factors." Frank called beliefs of the second kind "biases." The "deeper roots" or "real foundations" of our biases are "often . . . childish aims which are not relevant to our adult status" and are psychologically painful or impossible for most of us to admit. We thus "delude ourselves by giving 'reasons' for our

attitudes." The reasons we give to ourselves and others are mere "rationalizations" that enable us to believe we act from "'principles' which . . . are conclusions reasoned out by logical processes from actual facts in the actual world."
"Rationalization not only conceals the real foundations of our biased beliefs,"
it conceals the way biases contradict "other beliefs which are related more
directly to clear reasoning from real knowledge of what is going on in the
outside world."[10] Rationalization is more evident in law than in other practical enterprises, because law seeks goals whose contradictory character rationalization conceals: "the re-creation of a child's world" of "certainty, rigidity,
security, [and] uniformity," and "expert practical adjustment" to a real world
of "probability," "novel circumstances, [and] tentativeness" (33).

The first thing to note about Frank's thesis is its limited scope: it denies
objectivity only in some areas of discourse, namely, the first-order propositions of law and fact that constitute the premises that rationalize judicial conclusions in concrete cases. Frank's statement does not deny objectivity in the
natural and social sciences generally, nor does it deny objectivity in scientific
statements about legal phenomena. A theorist who denied scientific objectivity could not claim the psychological knowledge that Frank claimed. What
he claimed to know and his decision to publish it evince his assumption that he
and his readers could desire whatever good accompanies or consists in the
scientific truth about legal reasoning. He also assumed that one might desire
the truth about law more than one might desire the psychological goods connected to the illusions of law.

Yet Frank had more than a detached, scientific aim. He assumed that the
scientific truth about legal reasoning was a matter of great practical significance to the everyday work of lawyers and judges, and he urged judges to own
up to their use of legal principles to conceal their biases. Facing the truth was
an essential step toward a more mature judicial ethic that accepted its political
responsibilities and welcomed discretion and individuation in concrete cases
as demands of justice (139–44). Frank stated flatly and with his own emphasis:
"The fact is, and every lawyer knows it, that *those judges who are most lawless,
or most swayed by the 'perverting influences of their emotional natures,' or
most dishonest, are often the very judges who use most meticulously the language of compelling mechanical logic, who elaborately wrap about themselves
the pretense of merely discovering and carrying out existing rules.*" The "pretense" of these dishonest judges increases "those evils which result from the
abuse of . . . judicial power" (148).

By contrast, "the honest, well-trained judge with the completest possible
knowledge of the character of his powers and of his own prejudices and weak-
nesses is the best guaranty of justice" (ibid.). Such a judge will either take

pleasure in or courageously endure "the pain of suspended judgment" that is essential "to arrive, by reflection, at adequate judgments" (172, 179). Good judges will follow the ways of scientists who refuse first suggestions, retain an open mind, and generally devote themselves to "breaking up tradition" in pursuit of truth (172–73). They will treat rules and principles not "as finalities while unconsciously using them as soporifics to allay the pains of uncertainty" but as "fictions 'intended for the sake of justice'" and therefore to be "molded in furtherance of those equitable objects to promote which they were designed" (179–80).

One must of course agree with Frank that, as I observe above, any given arrangement of offices, powers, and rights can indeed fail to achieve the ends for which it was established. Publius believed that the Constitution's arrangement of offices, powers, and rights could fail. Americans can expect the Constitution to fail at some point, and pretending otherwise sacrifices truth and the cause of constitutionalism to illusion and the cause of a particular constitution whose vitality depends on the principles sacrificed.

A moral realist makes no concession to conventionalism by acknowledging the contingent character of the Constitution's coherence and authority. Moral realists and conventionalists agree that the Constitution's particular arrangement of offices, powers, and rights is a conventional arrangement. Individual constitutional words and phrases like *due process* can refer to real entities and relationships, but governmental institutions are matters of convention. Because realists deny that conventions can constitute or guarantee real values, realists should deny that any constitution can be perfect or meaningful in all circumstances.[11]

When favorable circumstances do obtain, however, it would seem difficult to deny that it is at least possible for judges to exercise "painful suspension" of their personal predilections in quests for interpretations that best serve the ends for which the Constitution says it was established. A moral realist can regard such quests as precisely what the Constitution demands.[12] Part of Frank's thought resonates with this position, as Frank himself came to understand when he later embraced what he called "the fundamental principles of Natural Law, relative to human conduct, as stated by Thomas Aquinas."[13]

Frank's hopes for unbiased and responsible judges were inspired by his confidence in the methods and attitudes of science. A more thoroughgoing skeptic than the early Frank might insist that all beliefs, nonmoral as well as moral, are incorrigibly nonobjective and biased. That thesis would deflate the possibility of unbiased judges, but it would also contradict the truth claim implicit in its own enunciation. And even if it were possible for someone to hold it and assert it in a fully conscious and nonsophistic way, no one can justify believing it. One reason no one can justify such a pervasive skepticism is that realist assumptions are at work in the conventions that constitute the practice of justification. When beliefs are justified, they are justified as true or probably true, and truth and probability are taken to mean correspondence or probable correspondence with realities whose existence does not depend on what people believe about those realities.

Of course, reasons for believing a proposition true cannot guarantee the proposition's truth. But reasons that survive criticism or experimentation can reasonably be understood to constitute evidence for truth, and reasons will cease to be adequate reasons if they fail to appear as good (if defeasible) evidence for truth. A skeptic cannot give reasons if giving reasons is giving evidence for truth (truth being what we have evidence of, if we have evidence at all)[14] and if skepticism denies that there are truths. A skeptic who tries to support skepticism with reasons suggests the following absurdity: *One can infer the truth of the proposition that there is no truth from other propositions that cannot be true.* Skepticism can follow not from reasons, therefore, but from some other source of conclusiveness, like force.

One would have thought this prospect would have silenced the thoroughgoing skeptic. Yet some skeptics display the audacity of Achilles at the Gates. Two such figures among contemporary legal theorists are Stanley Fish and Richard Posner. Instead of pulling back from the conclusion that all moral and nonmoral beliefs are grounded in force, they seize it and brandish it. Fish thus applauds Posner's view that scientific conclusions are at bottom no more grounded in evidence of truth ("the popular picture of 'good' reasoning") than are legal-moral conclusions and that the latter are grounded either in armed force or in what Fish calls "softer versions" of armed force, such as "some sacrosanct first principle," "the pronouncement of someone in a position to make his or her authority stick," or "the taking of a vote."[15] The conclusion that all authority is really force "is of course a shocking one," says Fish. But as one not easily shocked, he says the conclusion follows from the fact that serious disputes between different groups "could be resolved only by rational rather than forceful means only if the content and method of rationality could be stipulated apart from the agenda of any particular group," and that is a possibility he and Posner deny.[16]

This puncturing of popular beliefs about good reasoning in science and morality may excite our admiration for intellectual daring, but lest it strike us dumb, we should notice that neither Fish nor Posner openly assert that force is the ground of their own belief about force grounding all scientific and moral beliefs. Fish comes close to an equivalent assertion when he suggests that there can be no evidence of what epistemological skeptics see as the incorrigible "partiality" of the human perspective,[17] but neither Fish nor Posner say any-thing like: *We are right about the force-grounded status of all moral and non-moral beliefs not because those beliefs are in fact force-grounded, but simply because we took a vote, or because we or some authority we accept can make our pronouncement stick, or because we (with the help of friends) have the muscle to force our critics to say and eventually to believe that we are right.*

Not only do Fish and Posner not say anything like the foregoing, they cannot (coherently) say it because such an assertion would assume, among other things, the truth of its embedded empirical claims about the existence, weight, effectiveness, and availability of the muscle in question, and these assumptions would, of course, be scientific-realist assumptions. To avoid con-ceding that they believe that any of their beliefs correspond to reality and that they advance those beliefs on the assumption that evidence (for their corre-spondence to reality) supports them and justifies criticizing persons who be-lieve otherwise—to avoid, in other words, the concessions to moral and scien-tific realism that even an ostensibly antirealist metaphysics must make, Fish and Posner might follow the example of an embarrassed Thrasymachus and abandon their talk, if not their sense, of force as source.[18]

Skeptics who either remain capable of embarrassment or fear the condi-tion for removing their embarrassment—that is, silencing all systematic reflec-tion and thereby skepticism itself as a self-conscious position—these unheroic, survival-minded skeptics might retreat to a restricted skepticism.[19] They would be moral skeptics but not scientific skeptics. These moderate skeptics would hold that, unlike scientific propositions about judging (which could be backed with more or less objective evidence or by scholarship that aspires thereto), an overpowering element of subjectivity would make legal-moral reasoning in hard cases incorrigibly biased. A self-critical attitude toward first-order legal-moral beliefs could, they would argue, do no more than ex-change one prejudice for another, and that would defeat the second presup-position of the classical theory.

A moral realist response would concentrate on moderate skepticism's concessions to scientific realism. Leading moral realists now argue that their assumptions about morality are as defensible because they are much the same as a scientific realist's assumptions about nonmoral reality and that scientific realists have no good reason to deny the extension of their assumptions to the fields of ethics and law.[20] Thus, moral realists and scientific realists both find it plausible that there are things in the world that do and should influence what we believe about them.[21] They both allow the possibility of right an-swers in cases not covered by established conventions. They both hold truth to be a correspondence with reality, a correspondence to which we should and, in varying degrees, do aspire. Some moral realists agree that neither moral nor scientific realism can proceed from undeniable principles or sensory experiences and that a good reason for the provisional acceptance of a belief is its overall compatibility with other beliefs that are momentarily not in question.[22]

Crucial areas of agreement between some moral realists and some scientific realists involve the existence of nonmaterial as well as material things and the supervenience of nonmaterial facts and properties on material facts and properties.[23] These shared assumptions preclude a scientific realist's rejection of moral realism from a belief that disagreement about truth indicates no possibility of progress toward truth. And a radically materialist ontology would preclude not only the supervenience of moral facts and properties on material events, it would preclude the supervenience on those events of mathematical and all other nonmaterial facts and properties. It would reduce reference to nonverbal, ad hoc, physical gestures, though it would be impossible to say so, since such an account of reference would preclude the meaningfulness of all symbols, including its own.

Most important for the issue at hand, scientific realists also assume they can repress personal predilections that obstruct progress toward truth about the world. If, as leading contemporary moral realists claim, the metaphysical and epistemological hypotheses of scientific and moral realism are the same, scientific realists will have difficulty proving it impossible for judges to strive self-critically for right answers in constitutional cases. It becomes difficult, in other words, to show why judges cannot possibly respect the principles of truth seeking, or why they cannot possibly prefer truth to competing goods, or why they cannot possibly prefer the reputation of good judge while trying hard to earn it. And that would make it difficult to show that judges cannot possibly accept the Constitution's authority, for striving self-critically for right answers to constitutional questions is a general way to describe what accepting the Constitution's authority means.

THE PEOPLE AS A PEOPLE

I move now to the third presupposition of the classical theory. We see in chapter 2 that when Publius defends constitutional supremacy as the supremacy of the people he supposes that the people of his generation are united in one coherent set of fundamental political values. Those who believe that Publius's argument remains a good argument suppose that Americans are still more or less united in those values. No presupposition of the classical defense of judicial power is harder to swallow if one focuses on the sometimes violent cultural, economic, and ideological divisions of American history.

Even today, white and black racism, an unjust and seemingly incurable gap between cultures of wealth and poverty, intensifying hostilities between repressive religious commitment and permissive secular rationalism—these things mock suggestions of meaningful unity in America. But, as I suggest in chapter 2, observers do not have to focus on the appearances of history; observers can try to interpret the conflicts of American life as surface cracks atop bedrock—as conflicting versions of real goods that continue to assert a unifying influence. I concede that optimistic interpretations of history are all too often the staples of demagoguery and wishful thinking. But they may occasionally be something better.

That optimistic interpretations can be respectable is indicated by their status as a familiar feature of scholarly theorizing. Consider how an ostensible moral realist like Berns finds an underlying unity in the values of a neo-Hobbesian outlook. Consider also how conventionalists like Ely and the early Perry construe the divisions of American history in terms of unifying values like representative democracy and moral growth. Even a skeptic like Bork can see something solid beneath surface patterns he does not like, as when he penetrates two centuries of what he calls judicial lawmaking and discerns an "American orthodoxy" that opposes judicial lawmaking as antithetical to "American liberties."[24]

Moral realists can hope to impute unity in the face of division because they can hope to interpret social conflict as a dialectical effort to achieve something whose possibility they allow, namely, knowledge about justice— the common aspiration of all who recognize their versions of justice as mere versions of the truth. A realist's hope for such imputations may of course depend on the historical material to be construed, for it is difficult to render all historical developments, practices, and attitudes—slavery, for example, or the gore and freakishness of the American Civil War, or the continuing grip of racism on America, or the recrudescence of economic despair—as segments of some dialogic ascent.

But if the line between interpretation and invention makes a realist's imputation of a deeper unity contingent, antirealist imputations of deeper unity are conceptually impossible. Neither shallow nor deep conventionalism can interpret political division as dialogic aspiration. When conventional understandings clash, as they do in hard cases, conventionalists cannot hope to interpret the contestants as aspiring to knowledge, because conventionalists insist there is nothing to know beyond the sphere of contested or contestable opinions. Dworkin would say there is typically a deeper convention that organizes the terms of legal-moral debate, as a consensus about courtesy's having to do with respect would both enable and limit a debate over what is worthy of courtesy as respect.[25] But Dworkin allows conflict at the deep as well as the superficial level, and for a conventionalist, conflict at the deeper level would have to be conducted through methods other than debate.[26]

Perry seems to think that a way out of this difficulty is for conventionalists to see debates among competing conceptions of an idea, religious liberty for example, as aspiring not to knowledge but to an agreement that can end the debate—that is, to consensus or peace.[27] But it is hardly plausible that persons who debate the meaning of religious liberty seek consensus or peace as such. They seek either the truth about religious liberty or victory for their initial position. Contestants may well settle for something short of total victory as the conflict grows to threaten more than their conceptions of religious liberty; some contestants will compromise, some will not. But if peace or consensus is all they want, why debate in the first place? And even if there were some point to entering a debate solely for the sake of ending it, peace is a value that attracts competing versions, and Perry's conventionalism cannot allow that there is something for contestable versions to be versions of—something of which we can seek evidence by which to test our beliefs.

Only a scientific and moral realist can hypothesize the existence of moral and nonmoral facts that would explain both why peace is thought to be a value and which conceptions of it are in fact valuable. Aside from those skeptics who avoid absurdity by saying nothing, only a realist can avoid the absurdity of urging that we maintain "the moral discourse of the constitutional community" while insisting that at bottom we have nothing to talk about (158). If realism is respectable, the optimistic interpretations of the antirealists can also be respectable, as can the third presupposition of the classical theory.

CAN THE CONSTITUTION EMBODY REAL VALUES?

We come, finally, to the fourth and fifth presuppositions of the classical theory, which I discuss together. They pose two questions: Is there a value or set of values in whose quest all generations of Americans ought to find unity? If there is such a worthy end, can the Constitution embody a commitment to it? We have seen Publius's answers to these questions in his defense of the Constitution as means to such ends as "the public happiness" and "justice."[28] I have also argued that the substantive content and instrumental implications of the Preamble warrant an abstract description of the Constitution's overall end as that state of affairs that would either achieve or strive to achieve ends like happiness (comprising things like "domestic Tranquility," the general Welfare," and "the Blessings of Liberty") and "Justice."[29]

It falls to philosophic and scientific methods to discover (1) whether the evidence favors the existence of these several ends, (2) whether they can be unified conceptually, (3) whether this set of ends outweighs its competitors in value, and (4) the prospects for progress toward these ends. There is a reasonable possibility of right answers to these questions as long as the briefs for moral and scientific realism are as strong as those of their competitors.

Although I continue the discussion below, I sketch here the main points of my argument for moral realism and the activity of moral philosophy. In sum, moral and scientific antirealists have problems facing the practical implications of their position. And they cannot achieve consistency with their own (realist) assumptions. These problems have helped to make the parallel-to-science argument for moral realism respectable among contemporary philosophers. Add that respectability to the realist presuppositions of moral life and scientific practice, expose the mistake that aligns realism with intolerance, and constitutional theorists have no reason to abandon the realist presuppositions of their tradition.

If this argument is correct, there may be a value or a set of values worthy enough to unify all generations of Americans. This prospect makes the fourth presupposition of the classical theory sufficiently viable to function in the case for judicial power. It also indicates content for the fourth presupposition: justice and the other ends of government and the processes of science, moral philosophy, and political action through which we strive for such ends.

I have followed a similar strategy to support the preceding presuppositions of the classical theory. If, as I have tried to show, moral realism is respectable, constitutional language may have the power to influence judicial decision in hard cases, judges may be capable of dutiful conduct, and Americans may constitute one political community. The fifth presupposition presents special problems, however. For if moral realism works for the other presuppositions, it is not at all clear that it can work for the fifth.

Realism and Constitutional Imperfection

Moral realists can hope to justify findings regarding the existence of ends like justice and the superiority of some conceptions over others. But realists cannot collapse the normative gap between a genuine end and any of the conceptions it attracts, no matter how worthy or entrenched the latter may be, and such a closure of the normative gap seems implicit in the Constitution's claim to supremacy. If, as per the Preamble, the constitutional arrangement of offices and powers is but a complex system of means to some end like justice, declaring the means supreme law is an irrational elevation of means over ends (40–46). A conventionalist can hope to cure this problem by declaring that the Constitution's arrangement of offices and powers constitutes the end. But the conventionalist thus conflates a conception of justice and the real thing, and a moral realist cannot do that.

So realists must reject the fifth presupposition of the classical theory—unless or to the extent that they can find the Constitution's arrangements less of a commitment to some concrete conception of the end of government than an expression of concern for the real thing. I refer of course to much more than a concern for Berns's "interests that can be represented," for that is the concern of an axiomatically bourgeois community in which no fully rational person could prefer to live, except perhaps as a resident alien of some sort, with no better place to go. I refer not to a concern for interests, therefore, but to a concern for things like justice itself, a concern whose clearest expression is the Socratic compulsion to get to the bottom of the moral questions that trouble ordinary citizens, and to do so in that fully responsible way that combines the aspirations of science and friendship. Realists can save the fifth presupposition, I submit, by seeing the Constitution as an embodiment of a continuing desire for reflection and choice regarding the ends of government.

This solution to the problem of the fifth presupposition invites two objections. One objection is that no part of America's self-understanding can plausibly take a Socratic gloss. But this objection is easily handled. A commitment to science over tradition regarding political fundamentals in this "empire of reason" is one of America's founding myths.[30] Publius at least pretends to citizenship in the community that this myth helps define. He credits his audience with a capacity to combine "philanthropy" and "patriotism" in its ambition to "establish good government from reflection and choice." Treating a recently improved "science of politics" as the pride of his generation, he confidently promises arguments that "will not disgrace the cause of truth." And he measures the state and confederal constitutions of his day by a principle he assumes his readers accept: the "real welfare" of the people is the end to which all political establishments, including the one he proposes, must bend.[31]

This founding commitment to giving and exchanging "reasons . . . [that] will be open to all, and may be judged by all" (6) remains a component of the nation's constitutional identity even among theorists who came of age after waves of antirealist doctrine had purged the academic mainstream of Publius's confidence in reason. We see a shadow of the old aspiration to reasonableness in Dworkin's argument that treating people as equals is integral to liberal constitutionalism[32] and that constitutional adjudication should proceed through theories that "fit and justify the most basic arrangement of political power in the community . . . from the most philosophic reaches of political theory."[33]

Ely would honor a vestige of the old commitment by dedicating judicial power to stopping political incumbents from "systematically disadvantaging some minority out of simple hostility or prejudic[e]" and "choking off the channels of political change."[34] Strong reminders of Publius's aspiration appear in Richards's view of the Constitution as responsive "not only or essentially to private rights as such, but to a conception of the public good and basic rights articulated through public argument and debate" and of constitutional interpretation as "the imputation of reasonable purposes to . . . text and history."[35] The old commitment to public reasonableness is a strong element of Murphy's view that a belief in the "equality of human dignity and worth" and the related emphasis on "the necessity of government by consent" and the right to revolution are essential articles of the constitutionalist's creed.[36] And even a skeptic like Perry can (somehow) assign central constitutional importance to moral growth through conversation, and do so unembarrassed by the fact that he would "keep the conversation going" about what he holds to be nothing of any substance at all.

Untenable though it may be, therefore, the suggestion that the Constitution is an embodiment of reason imports no alien doctrine. Establishment liberals like the later Bickel and New Right theorists like Berns, Bork, and McConnell do have important arguments against valuing self-critical political inquiry as foundational—the risk of "turmoil," for example; but a lack of interpretive fit with the nation's historical self-understanding is not one of those arguments.

An Antirationalist Argument

The serious objection to my proposal for curing the problem of the fifth presupposition is an argument against self-critical political reason that can be put as follows:

A commitment to give and exchange reasons about political ends like justice is not a commitment to political truth; it is but a version of political truth. It is a kind of liberalism, and liberalism is but one ism among many. Reason constitutes no escape from axiomatic regimes; it is rather the axiomatic center of its own power. The regime of reason, even at its idealized best, would remain a mere conception of the political good; as such and by its own argument, it could not be the final choice of those who seek political truth.

Experience with liberal regimes confirms the abstract point. These regimes tolerate illiberal private associations (expressions of antirationalism) only when the latter are not too serious about their professed ends or too threatening when they are serious. Tell a Nazi that until he can gain a constitutional majority through constitutional means he can only parade through Skokie, not burn it down, and you are telling him he cannot really be a Nazi. You do the same when you tell white supremacists and black separatists that the state that punishes adults for child abuse and neglect cannot enact the educational, social, and economic policies that would guarantee the racial and cultural purity of their children and grandchildren. Nazis and racists who accept your attempts to justify legal barriers to illiberal ends are not full-blooded Nazis and racists.

Liberal professions of diversity and openness to fundamental change are therefore as phony as the domesticated antiliberals who are the drugstore cowboys of liberal academe. Pointing out the limits of liberal toleration is not to pick on liberalism, of course, for ultimate closure to diversity and change is a quality of political regimes in general. No historical regime has conceived, or perhaps in logic can conceive, its health to include an openness to its own destruction. Because the Constitution is and must be a conventional arrangement that claims the status of law, it cannot avoid commitment to a mere conception of the truth at the expense of the real thing. Socrates can personify no regime, because no regime can embody a concern for simple justice at the expense of the conception it enacts as law. That makes the fifth presupposition of the classical theory false.

I reject this attack on the fifth presupposition partly because, as I suggest at the end of chapter 2 and elsewhere, the Constitution may well be open to its own rejection.[37] But even if we accept the Constitution's closure *arguendo,* closure would be fatal to the fifth presupposition only if toleration had to be unlimited. But I do not see why it has to be. The impossibility of a perfectly tolerant constitution does not imply that some constitutions can be no better or worse within the limitations of legal systems, generally. Nor does the inherent closure of constitutions imply that no constitutions can make progress toward the ends of government.

Describing the American Constitution as a regime of reason may be as jingoistic under any reasonably foreseeable conditions as it is under the nation's present circumstances, and if it is, the classical theory loses the support of the only theorists who can hope to defend it. But the loss of such support might still not rule out the possibility of achieving and maintaining a state of affairs in which honest and informed observers could reaffirm the Constitution as an arrangement through which probably better conceptions of justice are in fact replacing probably worse conceptions. Such a constitution would manifest concerns that would bring it somewhere reasonably near the moral potential of its genus.

Favorable circumstances would enable reasonable persons to argue that, in each of its parts and as a whole and within the limits of the politically possible, the American system displays a real concern for self-improvement. Its elected officials and most of its electorate could fairly be described as reasonably prepared for the sacrifices necessary to achieve and maintain the conditions under which each element of society has good evidence that the system is striving for justice and the other ends of government.[38] And its judges, constitutional scholars, social critics, and other constitutional interpreters could fairly be described as participants in a process that actively seeks that understanding of the Constitution's provisions that can redeem the document's highest claims within the limits permitted by the best understanding of the rule of law.[39] Where one can make a reasonable case that these conditions obtain, one can confirm a reasonable version of the fifth presupposition of the classical theory.

More needs to be said about the practical implications of this conditional defense of the fifth presupposition. But to show that even this much is possible I must return to the argument against the fifth presupposition, for I have not answered the heart of that argument, and I have strong doubts that I can.

Is Reasonableness a Prejudice? Who (Really) Wants to Know?

My contention to this point is that it may sometimes be reasonable to interpret the Constitution as an expression of the desire to live by what reason discloses about how to live. But, even if you grant me this possibility, a life of reason may not be good and living such a life may foreclose an awareness of what is good. It is possible, in other words, that the practice of exchanging reasons is itself both a mere conception and a closed conception of the good—closed because its practitioners cannot break out of a circular course in which one rationalist prejudice is the only thing that can follow another. This possibility jeopardizes the fifth presupposition of the classical theory even under ideal circumstances.

One reaction to this or any attack on reason might be to dismiss it as a waste of time. For what argument can one offer critics who say, in effect, that no argument counts? We might justify ignoring the critics of reason by revisiting the Socratic rule that debaters should say only what they really believe. The full story behind this rule is not clear to me, but one of the reasons for it seems obvious. Where the question in debate is a practical question—a question of how an individual or group ought to live or, in the present case, how a nation ought to conduct its affairs—there is little point in answering arguments that people are not really willing to live by.[40] The cause of reason in public affairs does not demand otherwise. None of us could live by that cause if it insisted that action await inquiry into everything or anything that anyone might conceivably question. The value of reason in public affairs can demand no more than attention to proposals that reasonable people seem willing to live by. The trouble with the critics of the regime of reason is that they do not seem able to put their money where their mouths are, and that fact may cancel our obligation to give them a hearing under a sensible conception of what it means to value reasoning about how to live.

That the critics of reason are not really serious about abandoning it is evident in their habit of supporting the various forms of antirationalism with reasons they consider accessible to the public—a habit or practice that contradicts the antirationalist content of their intended message. When Bork and Berns cite philosophic authority for their attack on philosophy, they submit to the method of philosophy in support of not submitting to the method of philosophy. When McConnell offers an argument for his antirationalism, he submits to moral argumentation an argument against submitting to moral argumentation. And when Fish founds his antifoundationalist criticism of Posner's program for reforming American law on what Fish describes as a fact of the human condition (its heterogeneity) he submits to scientific and philosophic methods his moral judgment against relying on scientific and philosophic methods in moral judgments.[41]

Any form of antirationalism that forgets itself long enough to seek justification in reason is both incoherent and limited by the reasons that justify it. For an example of a limited antirationalism, recall that Berns's specific opposition to philosophy in constitutional thought does not seem to rule out philosophizing by some group of real intellectuals who discuss the most important political questions only in private and confine their public activities to antirationalist, probusiness propaganda.

These problems put the critics of reason in a bind. They cannot participate in a practical debate without explicit or implicit proposals of some kind. Yet if they should refuse reasons for their proposals, we cannot be sure that they are in fact proposing anything, for it is difficult to comprehend a pointless proposal as a proposal. Antirationalists might behave irrationally, of course, but being irrational is not the same thing as being antirational. Besides, it is hard to see how anyone could respect the arguments *of* the irrational as such, or even what could be meant by such arguments. Yet arguments *for* irrationalism have to be rational, which either contradicts or limits the irrationalism argued for. Antirationalism thus seems more of a political threat than a nonsophistic intellectual position.

One cannot leave it at that, however, precisely because antirationalism is a political threat. Its theoretical incoherence has not prevented it from abetting rightist forces that will continue to threaten the politics it has weakened, the politics that would merge patriotism with philanthropy, strive for government by reflection and choice, and reconcile democracy to justice. In the manner of a double agent, antirationalism appears not only in the themes of professed antirationalists like McConnell and anti-intellectuals like Berns and Bork; it is at work in the moral conventionalism of establishment liberalism. The latter is actually a moderate antirationalism, since part of its message is that reason cannot confirm our deepest practical commitments. We have seen its own potential for tyranny in the Perry-Bickel dash for the shallow conventionalism of judicial deference and in the way Dworkin misrepresents, ridicules, and marginalizes those who claim evidence for a moral reality that can support real rights against the community. A position of such pervasive political influence and consequence can and does compel the hearing that it may not deserve.

But how do we conduct the hearing? Operating as we do under norms of reasonableness, how can we persuade interlocutors who seem deaf to their own contradictions? Perhaps we cannot persuade them. Perhaps we partisans of reasonableness should acknowledge that we are trying to persuade no one but ourselves. Admitting this may not license un-Socratic methods against resident aliens, for we may have few if any real resident aliens. The antirationalists in the current debate are, after all, still publishing their reasons for antirationalism, and with no apparent intentions to behave as if they were serious about force, total immersion, other worlds, and all that. In any case, the partisans of reason may be able to persuade at least themselves and the moderate antirationalists (who combine scientific realism with moral conventionalism) that legal-moral reasonableness is not just another prejudice. I try to do that by returning to the antirationalist argument.

The central point of the (now moderated) antirationalist argument is that a life of giving and exchanging reasons, when reasons are called for, would be but a version of the good, and that version may not correspond to the good itself. Someone committed to knowledge of the good would therefore have to be open to a life of unreason. Because reason cannot be open to persuasion by unreason, which unreason may yet prove closer to the good, a constitution bottomed in the value of reasoning cannot be fully open to knowledge of the good. And this closure makes it impossible to cure the problem of the fifth presupposition.

Antirationalists can add that perceptions of their alleged incoherence and potential contributions to tyranny may indicate little more than the power of convention on our self-understanding. Antirationalism could be true despite its clash with a deeply entrenched reliance on reason, and incoherence disables only those academics who cannot face the fact that working political systems cannot reflect the symmetry of some Platonic soul. Even if the aversion to tyranny is far less localized than the yen for coherence, it may reflect no more than the psychology of a self-indulgent culture that would rather rationalize its failings than undertake the discipline of reform. Finally, the antirationalist can say, if acknowledging the limits of reason condemns one as a purveyor of incoherence and an abettor of tyranny, leading contemporary moral realists deserve these epithets no less than antirealists, since many of the former deny with the latter that reason can penetrate beyond mere beliefs to self-justifying truths and infallible perceptions of reality.

Saving the Fifth Presupposition

I concede that the aspiration to be and appear reasonable may betray immersion in the prejudices of a liberal culture. I concede further that an understanding of understanding as discursive may be more evidence of culture's grip. That grip may not be total, for we can at least wonder whether there is some genuinely antirationalist way and whether it might be shown (if that is the word) by some means short of torture, total immersion, and other methods now used for training people who are not supposed to think for themselves. Yet I concede that wondering about antirationalism in this way may be a liberal's way of wondering.

A moral realist can also concede that the potential tyranny in moderate antirationalism proves nothing about the fifth presupposition of the classical theory. That presupposition points beyond mere beliefs to something real, and our aversion to tyranny may reflect nothing more than a cultural axiom. But if these are concessions realists—the alleged partisans of reason—can make, they hardly constitute anything that the partisans of moral convention can assert. A deep cultural aversion to tyranny would constitute a deep convention and therewith a conventional point against any position with a potential for tyranny, including moderate antirationalism, which describes the surviving form of moral conventionalism. Moreover, an entrenched aversion to tyranny should constitute a conventionalist ground for a metaphysics that excludes tyranny, and moral realism is the only metaphysics that might fit that description. The same holds for academic conventions favoring coherence and discursive reason, at least as long as greater political forces support these conventions, as they now do and will continue to do until the New Right and its bedfellows succeed in their opposition to legal-moral theorizing.

One may therefore enlist the arguments from the incoherence and tyrannical potential of moral conventionalism to serve with what should be other conventionalist grounds for moral realism and the presuppositions of the classical theory, including the fourth and fifth. These other grounds include the conventional distinction between nature and convention, the ordinary distinction between knowledge and opinion, the everyday understanding of scientific truth as correspondence with a theory-independent "outside" reality, the descriptive form of moral propositions in live moral discourse, the everyday assumption that moral disagreements can be real disagreements, the conventional assumptions of scientific practice regarding the existence of nonmaterial facts and properties and their supervenience on material facts and properties, and the ordinary assumption that beliefs tested in full and fair debate are more likely to be true than their unexamined alternatives. These and other conventional assumptions and beliefs would support the presuppositions of the classical theory were it not for academic teachings to the effect that these assumptions and beliefs are *merely* conventional.

But the worm has turned: because this convention*alist* teaching rejects convention*al* beliefs, it implicitly summons us to a perspective beyond convention. I have reviewed Dworkin's unsuccessful attempt to deny the relevance to political life of that outside perspective. Dworkin proves unable to escape the practical influence of what he regards as the simple truth about morality—its merely conventional nature—as seen from the outside. And even if Dworkin could talk himself into a schizophrenic ignorance of his view of the simple truth about convention, a realist could not, for realism takes nature to be more important than convention, more important because the best conventions in scientific and moral inquiry strive to organize and maintain quests for knowledge of nature, not for ways to persuade the public to some partisan worldview.

Realists thus describe the good judge as striving for that interpretation of, say, the equal protection clause that comes as close as politically and institutionally feasible to what her best self-critical effort reveals as the best available version of its true meaning. Realists say that good framers can have intended no less. Realists hold that a semantically good, or minimally coherent, constitutional document must be read to mean no less, for that is what the document says when it presents the equal protection clause and Article III as instruments of justice, as distinguished from "justice." So a convention-based argument for the fourth and fifth presuppositions would work as a strategy for silencing conventionalist critics of the classical theory; but, at least among realists, doubts about those presuppositions will remain, and no conventionalist argument can remove them.

The Aspiration to Escape Prejudice

The apparent inadequacy of a conventionalist argument for the classical theory poses the problem of how to reach conclusions about reality in ways that avoid contamination by the unexamined prejudices that constitute our conventional beliefs. Moore formulates the problem as one of "thinking intelligibly about an Archimedean point outside all science by which to judge science itself."[42] He and Dworkin join an imposing list of formidable thinkers who say it cannot be done. As Moore puts their position: "Only if we allow our-selves to rely on *most* of our scientific beliefs can we question *some* of those beliefs at any one time. Even though we can question each of them at some time, we cannot do so all at once" (495).

But from this common ground, Moore and Dworkin derive different lessons for legal-moral inquiry. Dworkin seems to grant a great power to all of us who involve ourselves in legal-moral matters; somehow we collectively de-cide what shall be meant by truth and reality, and there can be no other meaning of these and related notions (like interpretation and right answers) for us in the legal-moral area of our lives.[43] Dworkin thus keeps faith with his contention that there is no reality beyond our legal-moral beliefs that can assist us in criticizing the most fundamental of those beliefs. Moore responds with an observation that should silence Dworkin's conventionalism: Dworkin must be wrong, for if he were right he would allow "Pegasus to fly whenever enough people talk about him enough in a systematic way."[44] And Pegasus could fly any time. For if Dworkin is serious about no external standards, he cannot even say how many people or how much talk or what kind of talk are sufficient to return Pegasus to someone's sky—really return him, mind you, or as really as anyone can possibly want.

Moore would avoid the flight of Pegasus by denying that law, morality, religion, and other nonscientific enterprises can decide for themselves such matters as what exists, the nature of truth, and the nature of meaning. Moore observes that criticism of "suspect enterprises" like "astrology, phrenology, religion . . . or sociobiology" is enough to show that "our normal, science based notions of truth and justification" provide us with a perspective external to other enterprises for assessing the existence of "the entities, states or rela-tions presupposed" by nonscientific enterprises (497–500). Moore is a moral realist because he is a scientific realist and because he believes moral reality, moral truth, moral meaning, and moral justification pass the tests of reality, truth, meaning, and justification employed in our scientific practices and everyday descriptive discourse. Moore is a skeptic about the other enterprises mentioned because he believes their assumptions fail the tests of our normal scientific understanding (497–504).

Moore thus accepts an external test for legal-moral and other nonscien-tific beliefs. But as per his statement about no Archimedean point outside the world of science, he denies that there can be some perspective external to our normal scientific beliefs for testing those beliefs. At one point he says flatly: "We are stuck with our scientific theories about what is true." Parts of those theories with which we are stuck are what he calls "the 'ontologically commit-ting' parts" that "tell us what states, processes, events, qualities or relations exist." And they tell us that something exists if hypothesizing its existence coheres sufficiently with our other beliefs to explain our belief that it exists. Thus, we are justified in believing that there are particular things, from lemons to rights, and kinds of things, from natural kinds of things like lemons to moral kinds of things like rights, if our observations and reflections indicate that hypothesizing the existence of each explains our beliefs about them and does so in a manner that seems compatible with other beliefs about the world, other beliefs that we take to be true.[45]

Moore recognizes that conventionalists about science could agree with much of what he says about the nature of scientific knowledge. For he accepts a nonfoundationalist epistemology that many observers associate with conventionalist metaphysics. This epistemology holds that the justification of either a scientific or a moral belief depends on its coherence with other beliefs not now questioned, not on undeniable first principles or unerring empirical observations.[46] Moore insists, however, that an important difference separates his nonfoundationalism from conventionalism. Conventionalists conflate the justification of a belief with its truth; they hold that the truth of a belief depends on whether it is acceptable and fits other acceptable parts of a coherent system of beliefs. Moore agrees that coherence can determine when we are justified in believing something true. But he separates a theory of justification from a theory of truth. What justifies a belief that a proposition is true is not the same as what truth is. Moore holds truth to be correspondence with reality, not mere coherence of beliefs. He also holds that this gap between justified belief and truth is normative in the direction of truth. Moore thus sees science as committed to pursue better theories of what is true.[47]

Moore has had a problem explaining (at least to readers like me) how a strict coherentist epistemology can support either an obligation or a policy of striving for truth as correspondence with reality. How, for example, can one be obligated to strive for something that is altogether inaccessible? As Graham Walker observes, if truth is altogether inaccessible, how can one have grounds to suppose even its existence, much less the possibility of progress toward it?[48] When Moore says we are "stuck with our scientific theories," he undermines something he clearly wants to preserve: prospects of bringing theories closer to an understanding of reality. It is not clear, however, that he means it when he says we are stuck within our scientific theories, for his belief that there is no Archimedean point can be confirmed only from an Archimedean point.

Fish is persuasive when he cautions that antifoundationalists who assume they can experience the partiality of the human perspective "unwittingly reinstate the objective viewpoint they begin by repudiating."[49] Fish's observation applies to Moore's assumption that spatial metaphors involving Archimedean points and God's-eye views can illustrate the human predicament. Moore can hardly confirm this assumption without some grasp of the human condition or, if not some actual grasp, the belief that he has it. Belief in some actual grasp competes with a coherentist epistemology, yet Moore asserts the latter notwithstanding its conflict with the former and even though the latter itself is only a belief.

More generally troubling is Moore's conclusion that our commonsense intuitions about science and morality require ethics to accept some contact with an outside perspective while science can do without such contact. No outside perspective for science seems false. Pegasus aloft is, after all, an issue for the natural sciences, not ethics. If we mean it when we say *Pegasus cannot fly,* we must be willing to add, *regardless of what anyone, including us, thinks.* When making this last statement we are not just presupposing some contact with reality, we are affirming that something is true even if it should be opposed to all our beliefs. We are thus projecting ourselves into a situation that our self-conscious moments might lead us to believe is inconceivable because we cannot see how we can affirm something contrary to all of our other beliefs. This limitation on our understanding tempts us to conclude that in saying Pegasus cannot fly we are reporting nothing more than one of our beliefs, and that in affirming that belief we are relying solely on other beliefs, including beliefs about what it means to affirm something. Yet we still seem to mean it when we say *Pegasus cannot fly, regardless of what anyone or everyone might believe.* So when we say *Pegasus cannot fly no matter what,* we are effectively denying that we are reporting a mere belief.

Our scientific and commonsense belief that Pegasus (really) cannot fly is thus at odds with the suggestion that we are stuck with our mere scientific beliefs. In science no less than ethics, we make unreflective statements about the world that presuppose some power to rise above and in some way oppose or at least wonder about our beliefs, all of them, even all of them at once. If we are stuck with any of our beliefs, one of them seems to be the belief that we are stuck with none of our beliefs. And this fact suggests either some extratheoretical contact with reality or an outside reality that exercises some constraints on what we believe about it, which in turn suggests *some* extratheoretical contact with reality.

Yet I would not take this observation as far as Walker does. Walker observes that Moore's coherentist epistemology calls into question his realist ontology. "Without . . . at least some real glimpse of truth unmediated by convention," says Walker, Moore's "'realism' must itself be merely conventional, and his . . . perspective on . . . the . . . Constitution must remain, on its own terms, insufficiently persuasive."[50] Walker would link moral realism to an Augustinian epistemology that allows the human mind moral insights predicated on "reliable glimpses of . . . transcendent goodness," which are "somehow a reflection of . . . God." Humanity's fall from grace pulls man away from these insights, however, and this explains to Walker the tension between man's "experience of [moral] indeterminacy and the simultaneous experience of goodness and order" (134–35).

But Moore's external or scientific check on moral beliefs is sufficient for him to deny that he needs a supernatural route out of legal-moral conventionalism. He can escape any moral conventions that contradict his secular scientific and philosophic beliefs. A right to abortion, for instance, would depend not on religious convictions or personal preferences, no matter how widespread and entrenched, but on evidence adduced through philosophic and scientific inquiry into such questions as the nature of life, personhood, and liberty.[51] Similarly, the constitutionality of capital punishment would depend in part on what the sciences of psychology and sociology had to say about the nature of cruelty and its causal role in the demand for the death penalty.

Walker can answer that science cannot check convention if science is itself convention. But, although true, this response would not explain why the theory that science is convention-bound precludes realist assumptions and aspirations in science. We must not forget that realism, not conventionalism, is the only second-order theory compatible with our first-order moral and nonmoral conventions, and an argument that purports to escape convention (as a conventionalist argument does) concedes the realist belief in a reality beyond convention. Moreover, realism does not have to win a total victory (I argue below that it cannot afford such a victory) to justify the realist approach in constitutional law and thought. Realism may need direct contact with reality to establish the truth of realism, but realism as mere contender is strong enough to vindicate the classical theory of judicial review—strong enough when added to the advantages realism gains from the realist structure of moral discourse and the incoherence of antirealism. Realism enjoys these advantages because a conventionalist epistemology vindicates convention-bound arguments in science and ethics, and convention-bound arguments leave standing the realist presuppositions of common sense by showing that there can be no persuasive denial of these presuppositions and that they are best explained by realist hypotheses. Moore and other contemporary realists make both arguments.[52]

Finally, Walker's Augustinian resolution faces problems of its own. One of these problems emanates from what contemporary moral realism would regard as one of Walker's strengths, for Walker's is at bottom a secular philo-sophic argument for a particular religious understanding of reality; it is not a religious appeal. He claims that an Augustinian resolution makes "better sense of human moral experience" and thus works better for realism in con-stitutional theory than Moore's attempted fusion of a realist ontology and a coherentist epistemology. He expressly submits this claim to "the judgment of reason."[53] He also seems to recognize distinctions between reason and faith and between a scientific way of knowing and a religious way of knowing (99–100).

The problem with Walker's proposal for constitutional theory is whether he can submit a religious teaching to a test of experiential reason in a manner that saves the integrity of both. A religious teaching that might pass a test of experiential reasonableness (Walker's own test) would remain a mere hypoth-esis, subject to the continuing challenge of allegedly better theories and there-with open to rejection as new evidence might demand. And it is not clear that a religious teaching as such could acknowledge its fallibility and accept a continuing subordination to secular reason.

These issues aside, Walker's argument against Moore can survive if stated more moderately: Moore cannot have an extreme or unqualified coherentist epistemology. He cannot believe with Perry that moral reality is "inaccessible through and through." If he believed this, as Walker points out, he could not believe that he had evidence for the existence of a moral reality. Moore must be open to some form of foundationalism.

And, in fact, Moore may agree. Recall my argument that one can be certain that there is no Archimedean point only from an Archimedean point. Moore deploys a similar argument when he says that conventionalists who say there is no truth beyond convention pretend to stand outside their everyday belief system "for just a peek at how the universe is—namely, to see that there is no way that it is." So, says Moore, when Nelson Goodman invokes "James's 'buzzing, blooming confusion' . . . as his basic belief . . . against which he is willing to judge all other beliefs," Goodman attempts an "illicit . . . return to foundationalist epistemology."[54] But Moore also pretends to step outside. He could not be confident that we cannot step outside the conventions of science without believing that he knows the limits of human thought, and to know these limits he would have to have some sense of *what* limits human thought— which limit would have to be beyond human thought. If using a belief about the chaos outside as a measure of other beliefs defeats Goodman's claim to antifoundationalism, Moore compromises his antifoundationalism when using his belief about human limitations in criticizing Goodman.

Moore also steps outside when he denies the truth of the commonsense belief that we can step outside the conventions of science, for if we believed we had utterly no glimpse of reality, we could not distinguish nature from convention, as we do, nor aspire to exchange opinion for knowledge, as we also do. All of which suggests that we may be stuck with the belief that we are stuck with none of our beliefs. What we may be stuck with, in other words, is the possibility of genuine knowledge about and within science as well as ethics, law, and all other areas of experience and thought.

On the other hand, moral realists may well want to resolve their problems within the general framework provided by the antifoundationalist epistemology that Moore and some other realists have adopted in recent years. Before I indicate how that framework might admit the foundationalist qualifications that seem necessary to sever the connection between coherentist epistemology and antirealist ontology, we might review the ways in which moral realism can profit from an antifoundationalist epistemology. First, antifoundationalism enables moral realists to argue that scientific beliefs are no less theory-laden than moral beliefs and that if theory-ladenness justifies skepticism about moral entities, it does the same for those parts of nature that are the objects of science. The relative implausibility of the latter aids moral realism by placing an additional burden on those who argue for moral skepticism from theory-ladenness.

Second, although antifoundationalism implicitly purports to step outside, it explicitly denies that anyone can step outside, and it thereby deprives skeptics of the outside platform from which they deny the presuppositions of ordinary scientific and moral beliefs. Finally, antifoundationalism enables realists to rely on a coherentist strategy for justifying realist beliefs. Realists can thus point to humanity's scientific achievements and contend that it is relatively implausible to deny the existence of some independent physical reality that exerts a constraining influence on our theories of it.

With the achievements of science in mind, we can say that the dependence of observation on theory need not be understood as some conceptual iron curtain between reality and the human intellect. Those who assume an impenetrable curtain assume an exclusively materialist ontology that renders its own enunciation meaningless, for materialism itself is a metaphysical position and therefore neither a material thing nor a property of matter. Yet nature may also include nonmaterial essences that separate clusters of matter from each other in recurring and systematic ways. We cannot deny the existence of such essences merely because they may be nonmaterial. The arrangement of elementary particles that constitutes the separate kind of thing we call iron is nonmaterial, as is the genetic "code" that seems partly responsible for a frog's being a frog. So even if our seeing frogs is theory dependent, that does not mean that when we see a frog we are imposing something on nature, for nature may be imposing something on us—that is, frogness or the nature of frogs may be what causes us to see all those individual frogs as frogs and give them all one name, which in English is *frog*. Theory dependence entails no access only if you suppose an exclusively materialist metaphysics, which of course has to be argued for—to the extent that it makes sense to argue for an exclusively materialist metaphysics.

But assume that everything we know about frogs is theory dependent in a conventionalist sense and that what seems to be recent progress in our knowledge of frogs is thoroughly dependent on changing methods of selection, observation, and experimentation, which in turn reflect changes in our theoretical conceptions. The fact remains that we do seem to know a lot more about frogs today than we did a century ago. Some might try to deny that we know more, deploying either a perceived-need-to-know standard or a yet-to-be-learned standard of how much we know. They could say that because (for some reason) our need to know is now greater or because we now know just how much we do not know, we know less than before. But if we now have a greater appreciation of how much we do not know, we do know more than before, and a perceived-need-to-know standard would fall to the reductio that those who could not care less know everything there is to know. So we do seem to know more about frogs and iron and other things in the natural world, notwithstanding the theory dependence of our knowledge. And a not unreasonable account of why we know more is that our theories and associated methodological innovations are closer to the truth about the natural world than they used to be.[55]

If this explanation proves to be the most plausible explanation of our apparent progress in knowledge, we have some evidence that we are getting something right and doing something right in our quest for knowledge of the world. We have evidence, in other words, that at least some part of our current beliefs is right, even if we cannot identify which part. It seems that some generalization, some aspect of our methodology, some inchoate notion, some inarticulate assumption, some aspect of our observations—*something* in or about our system of beliefs is right (cf. 210–12). In addition, the fact (if it is a fact) of continuing progress indicates that the part that is right is in some sense stronger than the parts that are wrong, for that hypothesis would explain the apparent progress. This prospect in turn justifies our belief that, if we continue the dialogue between theory and observation in science, at some theoretical limiting point beyond actual experience perfect coherence will coincide with or otherwise guarantee truth in those minds that are open to nature on whatever the evidence indicates are her terms.[56] It also justifies the belief that, in our everyday world, the investment in science will bring us closer to the truth. And if, as contemporary realists argue, what is plausible of science is plausible of ethics, the possibility of progress in science indicates the possibility of progress in ethics.[57]

Adding the realist presuppositions of common sense to the incoherence of antirealism and the possibility of knowledge about and within science, ethics, and law should supply content for the fourth presupposition and give the fifth presupposition of the classical theory something between a fighting chance and the upper hand. The goods of knowledge about simple justice and other aspects of moral and nonmoral reality and the capacity for action in accordance therewith would justify the desire to be and appear reasonable. That desire could represent a value that, to some extent, rises above its possible parochialism simply by being sensitive to that possibility—at least as sensitive as any of its (sophistic) critics.

Realism, Pluralism, and the Problem of Convergence

In connecting the value of reasonableness to American law and culture and defending it against the charge of potential tyranny, I must remind the reader about the paradox of philosophical realism as I see it. Because realism refuses to count belief as truth it is doubtful that true realists can be firmly committed to their own position. They start out as realists and may be stuck in their position for as long as the balance of the arguments leaves them there, but they must follow the arguments even to a (probably nonassertive) nihilism beyond reason if that is where honest debate directs them. Insofar as they take a position that others recognize as antiskeptical, they simply reflect their best self-critical assessment of who has the better argument for now.

Contemporary moral philosophy has not proved the case for realism in the sense of putting its findings beyond debate. And to a true realist this inconclusiveness may be a good thing, for a realist should be the first to take up the cause of antirealism as soon as the antirealists fall silent. The reason for trying to defend antirealism, aside from its possible truth, would be that the absence of debate over the findings of realism would foreclose the possibility of understanding and reaffirming those findings and obscure the normative gap between belief and truth. Realism properly advances hypotheses, not tenets. Contemporary moral realism begins with the fact that everyday life, scientific practice, and legal-moral practice presuppose a normative gap between belief and truth; it then submits tentative answers to various antirealist claims that no such gap exists.

I have touched upon a few of the realist responses to antirealism, including realist responses to metaphysical materialism and conventionalism based on theory-ladenness. To mention one more, consider the antirealist claim that the lack of convergence in moral beliefs at both the popular and theoretical levels indicates no moral reality for beliefs to converge upon. Some realists answer that the influence of religious commitments on moral opinions at all levels inhibits the kind of debate that moral progress requires, and that moral thought would benefit from shedding this influence just as scientific thought once did.[58]

I have reservations about this response. First, true realism, as I conceive it, must be open and responsive to the possibility that it is mistaken. This openness inclines one toward a willingness to be persuaded either by argument, including claims to theological insight, or, to some extent, by nondiscursive evidence, including some that proceeds from what are thought to be religious experience and works of art, especially art of an unsettling character.

Second, because convergence can be a guarantor of error as well as a sign of truth, it can only be the object of a realist's ambivalence. On the one hand it is something to pursue because truth would compel the agreement of all fully open and rational persons with complete information, and the agreement of competent and honest inquirers can reasonably serve as a defeasible index of truth or a step toward it. But since a realist cannot help believing that there is a normative gap between belief and truth, she should resist convergence, because convergence yields the illusion of knowing, which weakens the incentive to seek truth, the incentive being a Socratic awareness of ignorance.

Finally, with regard to constitutional theory, agreement is not necessarily a good thing, because it is only through a complex interpretive, empirical, and substantively normative debate that we can hope to reaffirm—and therefore fully to see—the Constitution for what it implicitly claims to be: an effective instrument of justice and other ends.

Resolving this and other issues among realists or between realists and antirealists is not necessary here. I have sought to persuade the reader only that there is a debate among respectable positions. This debate indicates substance for the fourth presupposition and a solution to the problem of the fifth: the value of being and appearing reasonable about the requirements of justice and other issues about how to live and what to believe. Self-critical inquiry and debate are the active expressions of that value, and the debate presupposes that there is something genuinely debatable and worth debating. To the extent that the contemporary constitutional debate includes worthy realist opponents of antirealism, there is at least a possibility of right answers in hard cases. And that possibility justifies the quest for right answers, which in turn argues for the fourth and fifth presuppositions.

A fighting chance for objective values, and objective values constitutionally embodied, completes the case for the classical theory as a whole. Now we can at least hope that key constitutional words and phrases refer to real legal-moral entities and relationships. Now we can also hope for judges and indeed a people who, at their best, take pride in their attraction to the truth about those entities and relationships. Lest the mere existence of an argument for the classical presuppositions seem insufficient to restore the classical theory to a position of presumptive superiority, I again remind the reader that the respectability of the classical theory is not the only factor. It stands with two other factors that favor the classical theory in any forum that is sufficiently free of modernist prejudices to give all sides a fair hearing. Those other factors are the durability of the commonsense presuppositions favoring the classical theory and the incoherence of antirealist attempts to deny those presuppositions.

Respectability is enough for still another reason: certitude would be too much. Remember that the philosophic realism that supports both the classical theory and the broader constitutional aspiration to reconcile public opinion to justice must be sensitive to the possibility of its own error. Certitude for the classical theory would close the normative gap between opinion and knowledge that a true philosophic realism must try to keep open. Widespread certitude for the classical theory would destroy parts of the medium, that medium being constitutional debate, in which both the theory and the Constitution live as separate and therefore recognizable things. Certitude for the classical theory would thus guarantee the theory's self-contradiction and silence.

BEYOND THE CONSTITUTION OF JUDICIAL POWER

A brief final comment will recall the contingency that confronts the classical theory along with all other constitutional arguments and constitutional government as a whole: the coherence of the constitutional document and its interpretations depends on conditions that no human institution can guarantee. Because history can change in unpredictable ways, the Constitution will fail sooner or later.

This fact has implications for all who pledge fidelity to the Constitution. They must do their respective parts to achieve and maintain the conditions for constitutional meaningfulness. Judges, for example, must try to interpret constitutional provisions in ways that vindicate the Constitution's claim to be an instrument of justice. They should also look for judicial means to remedy unconstitutional social and political conditions. When they reach the limits of their power they should consider exhorting legislatures and even the public to maintain constitutional conditions, for there is no good reason to deny the judiciary a hortatory function.[59] Eventually, legislative and public opinion will have to support the maintenance of constitutional conditions or (which amounts to the same thing) the pursuit of constitutional aspirations. Chief among these aspirations is a state of affairs in which every competent person has reasons to believe that the Constitution is actually working as a means to justice (211–13). These reasons will have to include evidence of a public wanting to realize its better self through its support for judges who proceed responsibly and self-critically but without apologies in testing some of the public's conceptions of justice.

The fifth presupposition shows that the classical theory of judicial review depends on the case for the Constitution as a whole. The best case against the classical theory may therefore be that the constitutional system is proving inadequate to its own aspirations. I have argued here that skepticism about the meaningfulness of those aspirations, among intellectuals and opinion leaders first of the establishment left and subsequently of the right, has not defeated the classical theory in the sphere of philosophic debate; the theory is still good enough as theory.

Modernist skepticism, however, has weakened the conditions for the classical theory as part of a concrete political proposal by persuading the best credentialed of our young people that constitutional aspirations are illusory. Some of these young people end up as judges and as writers who most influence judges and other thoughtful segments of the population. A crucial stratum of the population is thus brought to believe that a more or less willful assertion of personal preference is all that can lie behind judicial choice in hard cases. The academic popularity of this teaching greatly diminishes the number of people who can perform as good judges. It also reduces the number of people who can recognize good judging or appreciate the point of constitutional government. So the prospects for a constitutional state of affairs has declined, and evidence of that decline includes the present anticonstitutionalist leadership of the federal judiciary.

I do not conceive my argument as an argument against skepticism only, for the Constitution itself is surely partly responsible for the skepticism. The central problem of constitutionalism in America has always been whether an acquisitive society could institutionalize a concern for doing the right thing. This concern expresses itself in a quest for goods that are intrinsically shareable, like knowledge of justice. Acquisitiveness seeks goods that are intrinsically not shareable, like property and praise. Whatever Publius considered the end of government, Berns is right about an essential element of Publius's plan being the liberation of human acquisitiveness. The commitments and patterns of thinking that hatched out with the success of this part of Publius's plan (like reconceiving reasonableness as individualistic economic rationalism) weakened the plausibility of shareable goods to the point that the great bulk of establishmentarian intellectuals of the left and the right were brought to deny the existence of shareable goods. Thus, certified grade-A products of Publius's system like Stanley Fish and Richard Posner can agree—and resonate with large numbers of their well-selected students and professional readers, who are also certified products of the system and thus prepared to believe—that talk of justice is mere rhetorical cover for personal preference, laws cannot really constrain judges, and, in effect, nothing succeeds like success.[60]

Constitutionalism dies as this message takes hold, for constitutionalism supposes a fundamental difference between what is right (or good) and what a nation believes, which is what "succeeds." Yet the anticonstitutionalist message is not simply anticonstitutionalist. It is also both a product of the system—at least partly the result of Publius's decision to accept and foster human acquisitiveness—and even functional to its higher aspirations. We constitutionalists need the Fishes and the Posners because we must continually meet their challenge in order to reaffirm what seems destined never to be certain: the superiority of the constitutionalist thesis that something like justice—not success for this or that version of justice, but simple justice, and therefore self-critical striving toward knowledge of it—is the end of government. Because of the uncertainty of our position, our need for the debate is a continuing one, and therefore we cannot win completely.

But we must prevail in that debate, if only incompletely. We must prevail because we should. So far, ours is the better argument. We have offered better reasons both to those who will listen to reason and to those who think they have reasons not to. We should prevail because, notwithstanding our doubts, no one seems able to articulate a reasoned rejection of living according to reason (i.e., the better arguments). We should prevail because we still cannot help favoring the conclusion that people who live without reflection live without choice and therefore would reject an irrationalist life if they had a choice.[61]

Publius's argument for judicial power is a contingent practical argument in the end—an argument that depends on whether the Constitution is actually working as an instrument of justice and other ends. The success of Publius's argument thus depends on whether the Constitution's (real) supporters can do better against anticonstitutionalist forces that may be stronger in this country today than they have ever been.

NOTES

1. THE NEW RIGHT'S ASSAULT ON THE COURT

1. Robert H. Bork, *The Tempting of America: The Political Seduction of the Law* (New York: Free Press, 1990), 47–49, 113–14.

2. Robert H. Bork, "The Struggle over the Role of the Court," *National Review* (17 September 1982): 1138; Robert H. Bork, "Tradition and Morality in Constitutional Law," Francis Boyer Lecture on Public Policy (Washington, D.C.: American Enterprise Institute, 1984), 3–4; *The Tempting of America*, 44–49, 62–64, 95–100, 113, 116–23, 290–91; at 288 Bork attempts to backslide on his disapproval (62–63) of *Skinner v. Oklahoma*, 316 U.S. 535 (1942).

3. Robert H. Bork, "Neutral Principles and Some First Amendment Problems," *Indiana Law Journal* 47 (1971): 20–35; Bork, "Tradition and Morality," 3–4; Bork, *Tempting of America*, 127–28, 196, 248.

4. Bork, "Some First Amendment Problems," 10.

5. Ibid., 2–3; see also Bork, *Tempting of America*, 49, 61–67, 121–23, 201, 226–29, 252–59.

6. Bork, *Tempting of America*, 6–8, 44, 130–31, 254–56, 337–43.

7. Ronald Dworkin, "Reagan's Justice," *New York Review of Books* (8 November 1984): 29.

8. Bork, *Tempting of America*, 62–65.

9. Bork, "Some First Amendment Problems," 18–19; *Tempting of America*, 2–6, 49, 64, 114–16, 123–24, 130, 342.

10. Bork, "Tradition and Morality," 8.

11. Ibid., 9.

12. Ibid.; see also Bork, *Tempting of America*, 121–26.

13. John Hart Ely, *Democracy and Distrust: A Theory of Judicial Review* (Cambridge: Harvard University Press, 1980), chaps. 3, 5.

14. Laurence Tribe, "The Puzzling Persistence of Process-Based Constitutional Theories," *Yale Law Journal* 89 (1980): 1075–76.

15. See Sotirios Barber, *On What the Constitution Means* (Baltimore: Johns Hopkins University Press, 1984), 123–27; Walter Berns, "Taking Rights Frivolously," in *Liberalism Reconsidered*, ed. Douglas MacLean and Claudia Mills (Totowa, N.J.: Rowman and Allenheld, 1983), 61–62.

16. Bork, "Role of the Court," 1138.

17. Bork, "Some First Amendment Problems," 19; Bork, *Tempting of America*, 87.

18. *Baker v. Carr*, 369 U.S. 182 (1962); Bork, *Tempting of America*, 84–90; the following passages refer to this work.

19. Observers who have seen through Bork's lip service to *Brown* include Paul Brest, "The Fundamental Rights Controversy: The Essential Contradictions of Normative Constitutional Scholarship," *Yale Law Journal* 90 (1981): 1105–9; Dworkin, "Reagan's Justice," 29; and Charles Fried, *Order and Law: Arguing the Reagan Revolution: A Firsthand Account* (New York: Simon and Schuster, 1991), 65.

20. Bork cannot manage a consistent application of his views on substantive due process and equal protection. See *Tempting of America*, 61–66, cf. 150, 330. This work is referred to in the following passages.

21. *Brandenberg v. Ohio*, 395 U.S. 447 (1969).

22. Bork, *Tempting of America*, 335.

23. Bork, "Some First Amendment Problems," 22.

24. Ibid., 25–26, 30–31. Bork's 1990 book reaffirms this position: political truth is generated only by speech that remains functional to the constitutional system; see *Tempting of America*, 333–34.

25. Bork, "Some First Amendment Problems," 27–28.

26. See ibid., 33, where Bork cites 268 U.S. 669.

27. Bork, *Tempting of America*, 62.

28. Bork, "Tradition and Morality," 4; Bork, *Tempting of America*, 121–25.

29. Bork, "Tradition and Morality," 8–9. In *Tempting of America*, 251–57, Bork attempts to deny that he is a moral skeptic. The first part of his strategy is to affirm that he has a personal morality. The second part contends, in effect, that while there may be moral truth, it is not demonstrable to the community at large and therefore cannot be the subject of a general consensus required for democratic legitimacy. Since philosophic error can be innocent, Bork's personal morality is not in question; it is irrelevant in any event. Moral skepticism is a philosophic position about the ontological status of values. Conceivably, one can be concerned with the welfare of others without believing that it is in any sense true (or false) that one ought to be so concerned. This latter belief is moral skepticism.

As for Bork's second argument, it amounts either to an extreme epistemological skepticism (the belief that we cannot have better or worse theories of moral truth) or moral conventionalism (the belief that moral truth is as the community conceives it). I argue in chapters 5 and 6 that these positions amount to moral skepticism at the constitutional level, where the concern is the existence of accessible norms that bind the community or define its strivings. At no point does Bork prove that there is no consensus or that one is needed, nor does he indicate what kind of consensus may be needed. I contend in chapters 5 and 6 that one cannot rest with unexamined assumptions about these matters. In any event, one can deny that Bork is a skeptic and still conclude, as does Richard Posner, that he requires judges to behave as if they were; see Richard Posner, "Pragmatism versus the Rule of Law" (Washington, D.C.: American Enterprise Institute, Bradley Lecture, transcript of 7 January 1991), 11. When I refer to Bork's skepticism I of course refer to his judicial philosophy.

30. See Brest, "Fundamental Rights Controversy," 1105–9.

31. Bork, "Tradition and Morality," 8; Bork, *Tempting of America,* 208.

32. Walter Berns, *The First Amendment and the Future of American Democracy* (New York: Basic, 1976), 182.

33. Walter Berns, "Judicial Review and the Rights and Laws of Nature," *1982 Supreme Court Review* 49 (1983): 55–56.

34. The pull of mainstream Reaganite constitutionalism may have been a factor in Clarence Thomas's confirmation retreat from his well-publicized "natural law" approach to constitutional questions. See Clarence Thomas, "The Higher Law Background of the Privileges and Immunities Clause of the Fourteenth Amendment," *Harvard Journal of Law and Public Policy* 12 (1989): 63; compare Thomas's confirmation testimony, *New York Times,* 12 September 1991.

35. Berns, "Rights and Laws of Nature," 77–80.

36. Walter Berns, *For Capital Punishment: Crime and the Morality of the Death Penalty* (New York: Basic, 1979), 125–27; Berns, "Taking Rights Frivolously," 52–54.

37. Berns, "Taking Rights Frivolously," 63–64. The following passages refer to this work.

38. Berns, *First Amendment,* 26–30.

39. Berns, "Taking Rights Frivolously," 59, 63–64. The following passages refer to this work.

40. Ibid., 63–64, 66, n. 43; Walter Berns, "The Constitution as a Bill of Rights," in *How Does the Constitution Secure Rights?,* ed. Robert A. Goldwin and William A. Schambra (Washington, D.C.: American Enterprise Institute, 1985), 67–71; Berns, *For Capital Punishment,* 125–27.

41. Berns, "Constitution as a Bill of Rights," 69–71.

42. Berns, "Rights and Laws of Nature," 55–56; Berns, "Taking Rights Frivolously," 59–60.

43. Berns, "Rights and Laws of Nature," 51–55.

44. Berns, "Taking Rights Frivolously," 55–56. The following passage refers to this work.

45. Berns, "Constitution as Bill of Rights," 53–54, 63–64, 69–70.

46. Ibid., 63–64; Berns, "Rights and Laws of Nature," 64–65.

47. Compare Berns, "Constitution as Bill of Rights," 71, n. 57.

48. Berns, *First Amendment,* 181–82.

49. Walter Berns, "Do We Have a Living Constitution?" *National Forum* (Fall 1984): 31–32; Berns, "Rights and Laws of Nature," 54–55, 79; Berns, "Constitution as Bill of Rights," 59–61.

50. 462 U.S. 919 (1983); Berns, "Do We Have a Living Constitution?" 31, 33.

51. Berns, "Taking Rights Frivolously," 61–62.

52. See Berns, *First Amendment,* 83, 100–101, 109–12, 117–18, 120–21, 126–27, 151–54, 159, 171–73, 177–79, 182, 186–87.

53. Berns, "Taking Rights Frivolously," 52-56, 62-64. The following passages refer to this work.

54. A concern for some principle cannot manifest itself as a commitment to "our" version of it. A concern for justice, say, must be a concern for justice itself, since any particular version of justice may be unjust. A principled politics—a politics concerned with principles—must therefore find ways to institutionalize a self-critical striving for moral progress. This is why reaction and jingoistic assertiveness cannot be principled.

55. See Learned Hand, *The Bill of Rights* (Cambridge: Harvard University Press, 1958); Alexander M. Bickel, *The Morality of Consent* (New Haven: Yale University Press, 1975); Raoul Berger, *Government by Judiciary: The Transformation of the Fourteenth Amendment* (Cambridge: Harvard University Press, 1977); William H. Rehnquist, "The Notion of a Living Constitution," *Texas Law Review* 54 (1976): 693.

56. For the essential arguments, see Ronald Dworkin, *A Matter of Principle* (Cambridge: Harvard University Press, 1985), chap. 2; Walter Murphy, "Constitutional Interpretation: The Art of the Historian, Magician, or Statesman?" *Yale Law Journal* 87 (1978): 1752; and David Richards, *Toleration and the Constitution* (New York: Oxford University Press, 1985), 33-45.

57. See Ronald Dworkin, *Taking Rights Seriously* (Cambridge: Harvard University Press, 1977), 137-39.

58. Berns, "Taking Rights Frivolously," 56-57.

59. Berns, *First Amendment,* 173.

60. See Barber, *On What the Constitution Means,* 224, n. 43.

61. Jacob E. Cooke, ed. *The Federalist* (Middletown: Wesleyan University Press, 1961), 340.

62. Compare Michael Walzer, "Philosophy and Democracy," *Political Theory* 9 (1981): 393-94.

63. Berns, "Taking Rights Frivolously," 64.

64. For my defense of the proposition that the community thinks it has engaged truth seekers as functionaries, see Sotirios Barber, "Stanley Fish and the Future of Pragmatism in Legal Theory," *University of Chicago Law Review* 85 (1991): 1040-41.

65. Cooke, *Federalist,* 425. The following passage refers to this work.

66. Berns, *Future of American Democracy,* 182.

2. JUDICIAL REVIEW AND *THE FEDERALIST*

1. In addition to Berns, rightists who invoke *The Federalist* include Raoul Berger, "'Original Intention' in Historical Perspective," *George Washington Law Review* 54 (1986): 310-11; Bork, *Tempting of America,* 154; Christopher Wolfe, *The Rise of Modern Judicial Review* (New York: Basic, 1986), 74-77.

2. For a discussion of the concept of judicial activism, see Sotirios Barber, "Epistemological Skepticism, Hobbesian Natural Right, and Judicial Self-Restraint," *Review of Politics* 48 1986: 374. I join the many writers who reject a definition of judicial activism that refers to noninterpretive review or sanctions the judicial creation of new rights, for few judges admit to noninterpretivism or agree that they should, or do, create new rights rather than announce better conceptions or changed practical implications of existing rights. See Ronald Dworkin, "The Forum of Principle," *New York University Law Review* 56 (1981): 471-76; Michael Moore, "Do We Have an Unwritten Constitution," *Southern California Law Review* 63 (1989): 110-14.

3. Barber, *On What the Constitution Means,* 183, 206-20.

4. See Dworkin, "Forum of Principle," 471-500.

5. For a defense of this understanding of interpretation, see Michael Moore, "A Natural Law Theory of Interpretation," *Southern California Law Review* 58 (1985): 286, 388-96.

6. I join a number of writers in rejecting the split personality view of *The Federalist,* but I do so because I read *The Federalist* with an eye to illuminating a normative debate. Assume that a work speaks to a practical question, and you commit yourself to interpreting the work in a manner that would enable it to function in a practical argument. Such an interpretation must find ways to iron out the material's inconsistencies. I try to do that in at least one part of the analysis that follows. For an overview of the historians' debate, see Douglas Adair, "The Authorship of the Disputed Federalist Papers," *William and Mary Quarterly* 1 (1944): 97, 235; Alpheus T. Mason, "Publius—A Split Personality," *American Historical Review* 57 (1952): 625; George Carey, "Publius—A Split Personality?" *Review of Politics* 46 (1984): 5.

7. Sanford Levinson, "Accountability to What? Accountability to Whom?" Paper prepared for Project '87 Conference, Philadelphia, 25 May 1987.

8. See Cooke, *Federalist,* 91-92. The following passages refer to this work.

9. Ibid., 198, 119; David F. Epstein, *Political Theory of* The Federalist (Chicago: University of Chicago Press, 1984), 52-54; see Herbert Storing, "The Problem of Big Government," in *A Nation of States: Essays on the American Federal System,* Rand McNally Public Affairs Series, ed. Robert A. Goldwin (Chicago: Rand McNally, 1963).

10. Cooke, *Federalist,* 309. The following passages refer to this work.

11. See generally ibid., nos. 9, 10, 15, 51.

12. See generally ibid., nos. 69-74.

13. Barber, *On What the Constitution Means,* chaps. 4-5.

14. Cooke, *Federalist,* 93. The following passages refer to this work.

15. For challenges to the presumed judicial monopoly, see John Agresto, *The Supreme Court and Constitutional Democracy* (Ithaca: Cornell University Press, 1984); Sanford Levinson, *Constitutional Faith* (Princeton: Princeton University Press, 1988), 37-53; Walter Murphy, "Who Shall Interpret? The Quest for the Ultimate Constitutional Interpreter," *Review of Politics* 48 (1986): 401.

16. See Cooke, *Federalist,* 341-42, 423-25, 481-84. The following passages refer to this work.

17. See ibid., 532-33, arguing that impeachment is the only method for removing judges that is compatible with judicial independence, and opposing provision for removal "on account of inability," though conceding that "insanity" is a disqualification. The following passages refer to this work.

18. Barber, *On What the Constitution Means,* 197-98, 216-18.

19. See Murphy, "Who Shall Interpret?" 408, 417.

20. Cooke, *Federalist,* 525.

21. See generally Edward A. Purcell, Jr., *The Crisis of Democratic Theory: Scientific Naturalism and the Problem of Value* (Lexington: University Press of Kentucky, 1973), chap. 5.

22. Dworkin, *Taking Rights Seriously,* chaps. 4-5; Michael Moore, "The Semantics of Judging," *Southern California Law Review* 54 (1981): 151; Neil MacCormick, *Legal Reasoning and Legal Theory* (Oxford: Clarendon, 1978), chaps. 3, 5-9.

23. Cooke, *Federalist,* 3-4. The following passages refer to this work.

24. Ibid., 525. These maxims would include the preference for fundamental laws, like the Constitution, over ordinary legislation and the preference for later over earlier legislation. Such rules of interpretation are "not derived from any positive law," says Publius, "but from the nature and reason of the thing" (526). Similarly, "reason and law conspire to dictate" that courts should try to reconcile conflicting statutes "so far as they can, by any fair construction" (ibid.). And he continues to expect disagreement over the meaning of the law when he later returns to his recommendation that federal courts have jurisdiction over federal questions and certain other kinds of controversy (534–35).

25. Dworkin, *Taking Rights Seriously*, 31–39, 136–37.

26. Moore, "Natural Law Theory of Interpretation," 288–337, 371, 379–81, 393–96.

27. Morton G. White, *Philosophy,* The Federalist, *and the Constitution* (Oxford: Oxford University Press, 1987), 194.

28. Cooke, *Federalist,* 352. The following passages refer to this work.

29. For statements of the conflict between Moore's realism and Dworkin's "deep conventionalism," see Moore, "Natural Law Theory of Interpretation," 298–301, 309, 363–66, 373; and see Michael Moore, "Metaphysics, Epistemology and Legal Theory," *Southern California Law Review* 60 (1987): 453. This conflict need not concern us at this point, for both theories purport to account for the sense that legal-moral questions are amenable to reason. See Ronald Dworkin, *Law's Empire* (Cambridge: Belknap, 1986), 135–39. I return to this problem in chapter 6.

30. Cooke, *Federalist,* 529.

31. For an overview, see George Christie, *Jurisprudence* (St. Paul: West, 1973), 919–60. Jefferson Powell shows the limited constraining power of rules of interpretation in the founding period and generally; see "Consensus and Objectivity," 862–89.

32. Cooke, *Federalist,* 525.

33. Dworkin, *Taking Rights Seriously*, 31–39.

34. For a review of the options, see Moore, "Natural Law Theory of Interpretation," 358–76. For an application in constitutional criticism of what Moore calls a "pure natural law theory" (a theory Moore rejects), see Barber, *On What the Constitution Means,* 4–7.

35. Powell, "Original Understanding of Original Intent," 910, 940–41.

36. Cooke, *Federalist,* 525–26.

37. See *The Complete Antifederalist,* ed. Herbert J. Storing (Chicago: University of Chicago Press, 1981), 2:417–19 ("Essays of Brutus").

38. Cooke, *Federalist,* 542. The following passages refer to this work.

39. Storing, "Constitution and the Bill of Rights," 18.

40. Cooke, *Federalist,* 579. The following passages refer to this work.

41. See Ely, *Democracy and Distrust,* 93–94, and Walter Berns, *Taking the Constitution Seriously* (New York: Simon and Schuster, 1987), 124–29, 214–29. The difficulties of these theories beyond their relevance to *The Federalist* do not concern me at this point.

42. Cooke, *Federalist,* 524. The following passages refer to this work.

43. Louis Henkin, *Foreign Affairs and the Constitution* (Mineola, N.Y.: Foundation, 1972), 15–19.

44. Cooke, *Federalist,* 147.

45. This fact may be reflected in Publius's own suggestion of similarities between the convention's task of drawing lines between state and national powers and some of the difficulties confronting "metaphysical philosophers" (ibid., 234).

46. Walter Berns, "The Meaning of the Tenth Amendment," in Robert A. Goldwin, ed., *A Nation of States* (Chicago: Rand McNally, 1961), 141–43.

47. For criticisms of Ely's attempt to separate structural issues from substantive moral questions, see Dworkin, "Forum of Principle," 500–518, and Tribe, "Puzzling Persistence," 1070–71. For the connection between structural questions and more fundamental metaphysical issues, see Epstein, *Political Theory of* The Federalist, 116–17.

48. Cooke, *Federalist*, 349. The following passages refer to this work.

49. Ibid., no. 63, says "the cool and deliberate sense of the community ought in all governments, and actually will in all free governments ultimately prevail over the views of its rulers" (425).

50. Cooke, *Federalist*, 525. The following passages refer to this work.

51. Cooke, *Federalist*, 484. The following passages refer to this work.

52. See, e.g., Martin Diamond, "The Federalist," in *History of Political Philosophy*, ed. Leo Strauss and Joseph Cropsley, Rand McNally Political Science Series, 2d ed. (Chicago: Rand McNally, 1972), 631; Barber, *On What the Constitution Means*, chaps. 4–5; Berns, *Taking the Constitution Seriously*, chap. 4.

53. Richard E. Flathman, *Political Obligation* (New York: Atheneum, 1972), 156–58.

54. Ibid.; see also Barber, *On What the Constitution Means*, 59–61, 84–85, and Michael Perry, "Moral Knowledge, Moral Reasoning, Moral Relativism: A 'Naturalist' Perspective," *Georgia Law Review* 20 (1986): 1030–39.

55. See Barber, *On What the Constitution Means*, 54–62, 75–76, 105–15, 186–96.

56. Ely, *Democracy and Distrust*, 5–7, 223–24.

57. Cooke, *Federalist*, 88. The following passages refer to this work.

58. Barber, *On What the Constitution Means*, 224–25, n. 43.

59. Cooke, *Federalist*, 5–6.

60. Cooke, *Federalist*, 281–82. The following passages refer to this work.

3. THE CONSTITUTIONAL JURISPRUDENCE OF MARSHALL AND SOME OF HIS ADMIRERS

1. Dworkin, *Taking Rights Seriously*, 140–41.

2. Ibid., 149. Stanley Fish has proved the converse: that writers who regard the aims and methods of philosophy as illusory really have no practical advice to give. See his "Almost Pragmatism: The Jurisprudence of Richard Posner," *Chicago Law Review* 57 (1990): 1457–58.

3. See Dworkin, *A Matter of Principle*, 33–57.

4. See Moore, "Metaphysics, Epistemology and Legal Theory," 481–83.

5. See Barber, *On What the Constitution Means*, 224–43.

6. See Bork, *Tempting of America*, 133–38, 253–55.

7. See Michael McConnell, "The Role of Democratic Politics in Transforming Moral Conviction into Law," *Yale Law Journal* 98 (1989): 1504.

8. See William Schambra, "Progressive Liberalism and American 'Community,'" *The Public Interest* 80 (Summer 1985): 31–48. I explain the quotation marks around *communitarian* in chapter 6.

9. See Fish, "Almost Pragmatism," 1452–54.

10. Dworkin, *Matter of Principle*, chap. 2.

11. Wolfe, *Rise of Modern Judicial Review*, 117. The following passage refers to this work.

12. For a similar assessment of Wolfe, see Powell, "Review—Consensus and Objectivity," 869.

13. Wolfe, *Rise of Modern Judicial Review,* 108. The following passages refer to this work.

14. *Home Building and Loan Association v. Blaisdell,* 290 U.S. 398 (1934).

15. Wolfe, *Rise of Modern Judicial Review,* 221. The following passages refer to this work.

16. Speech to Congress, July 4, 1861, in *Abraham Lincoln: His Speeches and Writings,* ed. Roy P. Basler (New York: Grosset and Dunlap, 1962), 607.

17. The elected branches as a whole would thus function in the manner that Publius ascribes to monarchy, albeit an elected monarchy, for while in office elected officials could lawfully enact whatever measures they could get away with. See Cooke, *Federalist,* 578-79.

18. C. Herman Pritchett, *The American Constitution,* 2d ed. (New York: McGraw Hill, 1968), 49-50.

19. Ibid., 50, quoting from 4 Wheat. 316, at 415 (1819).

20. Berns, "Rights and Laws of Nature," 53. The following passage refers to this work.

21. See Barber, *On What the Constitution Means,* 86-94.

22. Berns, "Rights and Laws of Nature," 53.

23. Pritchett, *American Constitution,* 44-58.

24. Dworkin, *Taking Rights Seriously,* vii-xv.

25. 4 Wheat. 424.

26. See *John Marshall's Defense of* McCulloch v. Maryland, ed. Gerald Gunther (Stanford: Stanford University Press, 1969), 4.

27. 4 Wheat. 401.

28. Marshall did suggest that in doubtful cases of national power judges should respect the considered opinions of Congress and the nation. Rather than intimate that judges should simply defer to others in such cases, however, he presented a carefully reasoned defense of what Congress had done. This defense would have been superfluous had Marshall accepted a maxim of simple deference. See Barber, *On What the Constitution Means,* 78-83.

29. 4 Wheat. 402.

30. See Gunther, *Marshall's Defense of* McCulloch, 4-5.

31. 4 Wheat. 401-8, 413-18.

32. Berns, "Meaning of the Tenth Amendment," 126, 141, 144.

33. Ibid., 145; see also Robert Kenneth Faulkner, *The Jurisprudence of John Marshall* (Princeton: Princeton University Press, 1968), 80-83.

34. 4 Wheat. 430.

35. Faulkner, *Jurisprudence of John Marshall,* 3-33. The following passages refer to this work.

36. Powell, "Original Understanding of Original Intent," 934-35.

37. 4 Wheat. 401.

38. *United States v. Burr,* 25 F. Cas. 30, 38 (C.C.D. Va. 1807) (No. 14,692d); *United States v. Burr,* 25 F. Cas. 55, 159-80 (C.C.D. Va. 1807) (No. 14,693).

39. 4 Wheat. 518 (1819). The following passage refers to this case.

40. We have seen Faulkner's comment on the contradictory strains in Marshall's

constitutionalism between republican virtue and the self-serving attitudes wrought by commercialism. It is at least arguable that this tension could eventually have opened Marshall to what Faulkner calls a Lincolnian idealism.

41. Faulkner, *Jurisprudence of John Marshall,* 200.

42. Bork, "Styles in Constitutional Theory," 53-60.

43. Bork, *Tempting of America,* 21. The following passages refer to this work.

44. Ibid., 25-26, citing 6 Cranch, 135, 136 (1810).

45. 12 Wheat. 213 (1827).

46. Bork, *Tempting of America,* 43-44.

47. Bork, *Tempting of America,* 28.

48. Bork, "Styles in Constitutional Theory," 53; see also Bork, *Tempting of America,* 23-24, 43-44.

49. Bork, "Styles in Constitutional Theory," 54.

50. Ibid. Bork's support for Story remains unequivocal; see *Tempting of America,* 5-6, 134, 289.

51. Bork, "Styles in Constitutional Theory," 59; see also Bork, *Tempting of America,* 134-36.

52. Bork, "Styles in Constitutional Theory," 59-60.

53. James Bradley Thayer, "The Origin and Scope of the American Doctrine of Constitutional Law," in Thayer, *Legal Essays* (Boston: Boston Book Co., 1908), 7-12. The following passages refer to this work.

54. Flathman, *Political Obligation,* 156-58.

55. Thayer, "Origin and Scope," 31, quoting Thomas, J., Opinion of the Justices, 8 Gray, 21.

56. Alexander M. Bickel, *The Least Dangerous Branch: The Supreme Court at the Bar of Politics* (Indianapolis: Bobbs Merrill, 1962), 36. The following passage refers to this work.

57. John P. Roche, "Judicial Self-Restraint," *American Political Science Review* 49 (1955): 762-72.

58. James Bradley Thayer, *John Marshall* (Boston: Houghton Mifflin, 1901), 62; see also p. 77. The following passages refer to this work.

59. Bork, "Tradition and Morality," 11.

60. Gary M. McDowell, *The Constitution and Contemporary Constitutional Theory* (Cumberland, Va.: Center for Judicial Studies, 1986), 39-40.

61. Thayer, *John Marshall,* 66-67.

62. Ibid., 72-73; cf. 53, where Thayer says the framers left the nature and scope of judicial review to be decided by the future. The following passage refers to this work.

63. Ibid., 85-86; Thayer, "Origin and Scope," 38-39.

64. Thayer, *John Marshall,* 47, 62-64, 82-86.

65. Thayer, "Origin and Scope," 33. The following passage refers to this work.

66. James Bradley Thayer, *Cases on Constitutional Law,* 2 vols. (Cambridge, Mass.: C. W. Sever, 1895), 2:2190, citing *Crandall v. Nevada,* 6 Wall. 35 (1868) and *Corfield v. Coryell,* 4 Wash. C.C. 371 (6 Fed. Cases 546) (1823).

67. 6 Fed. Cases, 551-52.

68. For an argument that this broad reading of Washington's opinion is faithful to his words and intentions, if not the words and intentions of those who framed Article IV, see Ely, *Democracy and Distrust,* 29, 198 n. 64. Thayer's citation is all the more

remarkable because it occurred after the Supreme Court had rejected applying Washington's theory to the states in a series of post–Civil War decisions that culminated in the *Slaughter House Cases,* 16 Wall. 36 (1873). For the story of this development, see Laurence H. Tribe, *American Constitutional Law,* 2d ed. (Mineola, N.Y.: Foundation, 1988), 529–30.

69. Barber, "Epistemological Skepticism," 386–88.

70. See Barber, *On What the Constitution Means,* 159–65, 172–77. The following passage refers to this work.

71. See Roche, "Judicial Self-Restraint," 770–72.

72. H. Jefferson Powell, "Joseph Story's Commentaries on the Constitution: A Belated Review," *Yale Law Journal* 94 (1985): 1285–1314, esp. 1286–87, 1299–1304, 1310–14.

73. 11 Peters at 839–40. The following passage refers to this case.

74. Ibid., 862. See also Story's statement at 851 that it would violate "the first principles of justice to presume that the Legislature reserved a right to destroy its own grant," citing *Fletcher v. Peck* as "turning upon the same principle of political and constitutional duty and right." Similar statements occur at 852 and 859.

75. Joseph Story, *Commentaries on the Constitution of the United States* (Boston: Hilliard, Gray, 1833), 3:470. The following passages refer to this work.

76. James McClellan, *Joseph Story and the American Constitution: A Study in Political and Legal Thought with Selected Writings* (Norman: University of Oklahoma Press, 1971), 263.

77. 16 Pet. 538 (1842); 16 Pet. 1 (1842); and 1 Wheat. 304 (1816).

78. Alfred H. Kelly, Wilfred A. Harbison, and Herman Belz, *The American Constitution: Its Origins and Development,* 6th ed. (New York: Norton, 1983), 255.

79. 1 Stat 302 (1793).

80. 16 Pet. 616–18. The following passages refer to this case.

81. See Kelly, Harbison, and Belz, *American Constitution,* 255–56.

82. McClellan, *Joseph Story and the American Constitution,* 261. The following passages refer to this work.

83. 1 Wheat. 324–25. The following passages refer to this case.

84. *Erie Railroad v. Tompkins,* 304 U.S. 64.

85. McClellan, *Joseph Story and the American Constitution,* 184, 187. The following passages refer to this work.

86. See Grant Gilmore, *The Ages of American Law* (New Haven: Yale University Press, 1977), 31–33. The following passage refers to this work.

87. 16 Pet. 18–19.

88. Ibid., 19. For the possible significance of Story's reference to Mansfield, consider Gilmore's statement that even after "a quasi-Blackstonian" emphasis on precedent was overcoming Mansfield's influence in Britain, a "pure Mansfieldianism flourished" in pre–Civil War America. Not only were Mansfield's cases often cited, said Gilmore, "but his light-hearted disregard for precedent, his joyous acceptance of the idea that judges are supposed to make law—the more law the better—became a notable feature of our early jurisprudence." And, Gilmore added, "Justice Story in particular, both in his opinions and in his non-judicial writings, never tired of acknowledging his indebtedness to, and his reverence for, Lord Mansfield." Gilmore, *Ages of American Law,* 24.

89. 16 Pet. 19.

90. Gilmore, *Ages of American Law,* 34–35.

91. Wolfe, *Rise of Modern Judicial Review,* 221.

92. Story, *Commentaries,* 1:383. The following passages refer to this work.

93. Ibid., 392. A clear example of this last is Marshall's reference in *McCulloch* to the debates in Washington's cabinet over the constitutionality of the first bank and the government's subsequent experience with the bank.

94. Walter F. Murphy, "Constitutional Interpretation: The Art of the Historian, Magician, or Statesman?" *Yale Law Journal* 87 (1978): 1752, 1762, quoting Story, *Commentaries,* 1:387.

95. Story, *Commentaries,* 1:396–97.The following passage refers to this work.

96. Wolfe, *Rise of Modern Judicial Review,* 221. The following passages refer to this work.

97. See generally, Dworkin, *Taking Rights Seriously,* chap. 5.

98. Story, *Commentaries,* 1:392.

99. Bork, "Styles in Constitutional Theory," 54, quoting Story, *Commentaries,* 1:383, 1:vi.

100. See Ronald Dworkin, "Law of the Slave Catchers," *Times Literary Supplement* (5 December 1975): 1437; Robert M. Cover, *Justice Accused: Antislavery and the Judicial Process* (New Haven: Yale Unversity Press, 1975), 161, 166.

101. Bork, "Tradition and Morality," 11.

102. McClellan, *Joseph Story and the American Constitution,* 308–10. The following passages refer to this work.

103. Christopher Eisgruber, "Justice Story, Slavery, and the Natural Law Foundations of American Constitutionalism," *University of Chicago Law Review* 55 (1988): 273, esp. 296–319. The quotation occurs on 273 and is from *Life and Letters of Joseph Story,* ed. William W. Story, 2 vols. (Boston: C. C. Little and J. Brown, 1851), 2:392.

104. Eisgruber, "Story, Slavery, and Natural Law," 296. The following passage refers to this work.

105. *Encyclopedia Americanae,* ed. Francis Lieber (1832), 9:150–58.

106. Eisgruber, "Story, Slavery, and Natural Law," 308. The following passages refer to this work.

107. Ibid., 302–3. Eisgruber depreciates the role of theology in Story's thought, 308–12.

108. Ibid., 312–13, quoting from *The Miscellaneous Writings of Joseph Story,* ed. William W. Story (Boston, C. C. Little and J. Brown, 1852), 527–28. The following passages refer to Eisgruber, "Story, Slavery, and Natural Law."

109. See Powell, "Joseph Story's Commentaries," 1297–99, 1311–14.

110. For a liberal's reaction to the current assault on academic freedom in the name of minority rights and sensitivities, see C. Vann Woodward, "Freedom and the Universities," *New York Review of Books* (July 18, 1991): 32–37.

111. Michael Walzer, "Philosophy and Democracy," *Political Theory* 9 (1981): 393–94.

112. See Michael Walzer, "Flight from Philosophy," *New York Review of Books* (2 February 1989): 42–44.

113. See Bork, *Tempting of America,* 10, 254. On 154–55 Bork says, "The philosophy of original understanding is . . . a necessary inference from the structure of the government apparent on the face of the Constitution." Because nothing else can prevent

courts "from assuming powers whose exercise alters, perhaps radically, the design of the American Republic," "we would have to invent the approach of original understanding" even if the framers "had never endorsed it."

4. THEORIES OF JUDICIAL REVIEW I: THE NEW RIGHT

1. Purcell, *Crisis of Democratic Theory*, 47–48. The following passages refer to this work.

2. See Moore, "A Natural Law Theory of Interpretation," 295.

3. See Purcell, *Crisis of Democratic Theory*, 151.

4. For an influential statement of this position, see Charles P. Curtis, "The Role of the Constitutional Text," in *Supreme Court and Supreme Law*, ed. Edmond Cahn (Bloomington: Indiana University Press, 1954), 64–70. See also Bickel, *Least Dangerous Branch*, 103–10. The continuing influence of the Curtis-Bickel view is evident in Michael J. Perry, *Morality, Politics, and Law* (Oxford: Oxford University Press, 1989) 122–36, 155–60, 175–78.

5. Purcell, *Crisis of Democratic Theory*, 82–85, 87–89. The following passage refers to this work.

6. Bickel, *Least Dangerous Branch*, 83. The following passage refers to this work.

7. For an updated expression of this dogma, see Perry, *Morality, Politics, and Law*, 29–32, 60–63.

8. See Purcell, *Crisis of Democratic Theory*, 41–45.

9. See Storing, "Problem of Big Government," 79–81, 85–87. Storing's summary of the lessons of *The Federalist* include the following statement: "While a government ought to be so ordered that it will not act badly, it must also and preeminently have the capacity to act well" (86).

10. See Bickel, *Least Dangerous Branch*, 14–15, 36.

11. See Faulkner, *Jurisprudence of John Marshall*, 96–113. The following passage refers to this work.

12. See Barber, *On What the Constitution Means*, chap. 3. I should comment briefly here on an aspect of the New Right's current view of precedent. They must generally oppose fidelity to precedent lest they obstruct hopes of reversing constitutional policies of the Warren era. They must also oppose fidelity to precedent in the name of greater fidelity to what they term the intentions of the framers. Those intentions, they must eventually claim, are binding merely by virtue of their enactment. To claim them valid because right would involve concessions to the sole process by which one tries to determine not only their rightness, but also what they would have to mean in order to support their claim to rightness. That process, of course, is the philosophically informed and motivated quest for the best interpretation the Constitution can bear. Validity by enactment is therefore the only possible theory the New Right could adopt without abandoning its opposition to moral philosophy in constitutional law. Without a philosophic effort of its own, however, the New Right cannot hope to distinguish better from worse, valid from invalid, methods of enactment itself. If there can be a real reason for preferring one form of enactment to another, then concessions must be made to the process of trying to distinguish real reasons from apparent ones, as well as to the ontological and epistemological assumptions on which such a process rests, assumptions that include some access to a perspective or state in which a compelling reason can be seen for what it is by all who are capable of reasoning aright. And if reason can help

us to better conceptions of enactment, it can help us to better conceptions of such notions as justice, due process, and equal protection. So the New Right cannot even allow real moral differences between different methods and kinds of enactment, including those that go by the name of framers' intent and judicial precedent. The New Right's preference for one over the other is purely arbitrary on the New Right's own terms.

13. Cooke, *Federalist,* 416–17, 481–82.

14. Basler, *Abraham Lincoln,* 313–14.

15. 7 Pet. 243 (1833).

16. See *Ogden v. Saunders,* 12 Wheat. 213 (1827); Pritchett, *American Constitution,* 695.

17. Gilmore, *Ages of American Law,* 63. The following passage refers to this work.

18. Cooke, *Federalist,* 529. The following passages refer to this work.

19. Compare *Planned Parenthood v. Casey,* 112 S. Ct. 2791 (1992).

20. I do not claim by this argument that conventionalism cannot be justified; nor do I contend that majoritarianism is necessarily grounded in conventionalism. But a conventionalism that is justified by some argument is not a pure conventionalism, because justifying conventionalism involves subsuming it under some nonconventionalist desiderata or source of authority. To say, for example, that some particular continuity with the past preserves stability is to justify a conventionalist practice in terms of what is thought to be a true conception of a real value. And a justified majoritarianism accepts the limits on majoritarianism that are implicit in the argument that justifies it. If, for example, government by consent flows from a principal of human equality, legitimate consensual government would have to accept some egalitarian limitations and pursue policies that would move the general population to support these limitations.

21. I have proposed in particular that Publius's reliance on checks and balances for constitutional maintenance is either a mistake or in need of supplementary institutions to educate the public in the virtues of republican citizenship. See Barber, *On What the Constitution Means,* 177–85.

22. The language in question is as follows:

> The interpretation of the laws is the proper and peculiar province of the courts. A constitution is in fact, and must be, regarded by the judges as a fundamental law. It therefore belongs to them to ascertain its meaning as well as the meaning of any particular act proceeding from the legislative body. If there should happen to be an irreconcilable variance between the two, that which has the superior obligation and validity ought of course to be preferred; or in other words, the constitution ought to be preferred to the statute, the intention of the people to the intention of their agents.
>
> Nor does this conclusion by any means suppose a superiority of the judicial to the legislative power. It only supposes that the power of the people is superior to both; and that where the will of the legislature declared in its statutes, stands in opposition to that of the people declared in the constitution, the judges ought to be governed by the latter, rather than the former. They ought to regulate their decisions by the fundamental laws, rather than by those which are not fundamental. (525)

I interpret this passage to say that judicial review is not an instrument of judicial supremacy; it is rather an instrument of constitutional supremacy, and constitutional supremacy in turn means the supremacy of the people over their representatives.

23. See Cooke, *Federalist,* 51, 61, 65, 88–89, 308–9, 315, 338–39, 424–25.

24. Berns, "Constitution as Bill of Rights," 64–65.

25. For further discussion of the notion of constitutional majorities in this substantive sense of constitutional, see Barber, *On What the Constitution Means,* 211–214.

26. See Cooke, *Federalist,* 61, 308–9, 341–43, 352–53, 424–25, 482–83. The following passage refers to this work.

27. See Barber, *On What the Constitution Means,* 127–31, 211–13. The following passage refers to this work.

28. William H. Rehnquist, "The Notion of a Living Constitution," *Texas Law Review* 54 (1976): 693.

29. See Ely, *Democracy and Distrust,* 87–88, 88–101; Perry, *Morality, Politics, and Law,* 122–31.

30. Bork, "Styles in Constitutional Theory," 56.

31. For what amounts to a similar application of the term *anticonstitutional* to elements of the Reagan Right, see Fried, *Order and Law,* 18.

32. See Erwin Chemerinsky, "Foreword: The Vanishing Constitution," *Harvard Law Review* 103 (1989): 43, 92–94.

33. See Bork, *Tempting of America,* 10–12, 133–35, 143, 254–56.

34. That Bork needs such a defense is evident enough in the controversial nature of his philosophic assumptions, which include, most notably, the exclusively positivist nature of law (ibid., 6, 60, 67), the purely subjectivist-conventionalist nature of morality (61–67, 79–80, 191, 226–29, 231, 253–59), the subjectivist-conventionalist nature of language meaning (39, 92–95, 103–4, 180, 198, 213–14, 216, 218, 220–21, 242, 352–53), and the fundamentally majoritarian nature of constitutional democracy (49, 201, 252). Instead of defending such assumptions through a quest for some common ground from which he and his critics might exchange evidence and arguments, Bork prefers question-begging counterassertions and disclaimers. For a good example consider Bork's assertion that "at some point, every theory not based on the original understanding (and therefore involving the creation of new constitutional rights or the abandonment of specified rights), requires the judge to make a major moral decision" (251–52). Of the judge who employs Bork's approach, he adds: "The principles of the actual Constitution make the judge's major moral choices for him." This is the typical New Right claim to freedom from philosophic decision and responsibility. Bork confronts (176–77) Dworkin's lengthy criticism of that claim (see Dworkin, *Matter of Principle,* chap. 2) with what amounts to a two-sentence reassertation of the claim. Central to Dworkin's critique is a well-known set of paired distinctions between concepts and abstract intentions on the one hand, and conceptions and concrete intentions on the other. Bork asserts with no supporting argumentation that Dworkin's "distinction between a concept and a conception is merely a way of changing the level of generality at which a constitutional provision may be restated so that it is taken to mean something it obviously did not mean" (213–14).

35. See, e.g., Sotirios A. Barber, "Judicial Review and the Federalist," *University of Chicago Law Review* 55 (1985): 836; Harry V. Jaffa, "What Were the 'Original Intentions' of the Framers of the Constitution of the United States?" *Puget Sound Law Review* 10 (1987): 351; Macedo, *New Right v. the Constitution.*

36. See Bork, *Tempting of America,* 82, 137, 155, 177, 254. The following passages refer to this work.

37. See Jon Wiener, "Dollars for Neocon Scholars," *Nation* 250:12 (Jan. 1, 1990).

38. Bork's moral skepticism would compel him to dismiss this proposition. See Bork, "Neutral Principles and Some First Amendment Problems," 1, 25, 30–31. For additional evidence of Bork's skepticism, see Bork, *Tempting of America*, 219–20, 228, 231, 242, 252–59.

39. Dworkin, *Matter of Principle*, 69–75.

40. I assume here that there is some merit to the originalist's concern for framers' intent. This assumption contrasts with Chemerinsky's view ("Vanishing Constitution," 103–4) that, after decades of powerful scholarly criticism of New Right originalism, critics of the New Right cannot now avail themselves of originalist arguments. Yet Chemerinsky himself resorts to originalist premises when he notes the framers' concern for natural rights and their distrust of populism (65; he says "majoritarianism") *and* when he assumes that these facts about the framers' beliefs warrant two normative conclusions for present-day constitutional choice and criticism: (1) "The Constitution . . . does not support the priority of democracy," and (2) "majority rule cannot claim axiomatic, authoritative status as the starting point for constitutional analysis" (74–75).

An explanation of Chemerinsky's contradiction is his apparent agreement with the New Right on two points: framers' intent must be concrete, not abstract, and the distinction between concrete and abstract intent is merely a matter of different levels of abstraction among which interpreters are free to choose as their personal values dictate (92–93). Without trying to summarize here all that I argue elsewhere about the nature of constitutional interpretation, I contend that whoever the framers are thought to have been, as a practical political matter they had to present their constitutional proposals not as instruments of parochial and therefore potentially unjust conceptions of normative ideas like justice, but as instruments of the ideas themselves. The Constitution records this fact in the only way it can. It must employ abstract language because it refers to equal protection itself, not some racist conception of equal protection, or due process itself, as opposed to some potentially unfair conception of due process. Those who accept the Constitution's claims are therefore left with no choice but an orientation to what Chemerinsky and modernists generally refer to as "abstract intentions" or general "concepts." And since, as I prefer to put it, the (real) meaning of equal protection itself, due process itself, or, generally, justice itself can be pursued only through a philosophic process (proposing and debating the best practicable hypotheses about constitutional meaning), then an appreciation of the role of moral and natural science (in court, in the professional journals, and to the extent feasible, throughout the nation's public life) is a requisite of good citizenship in this regime.

The correct kind of originalism, which one finds in what I call the classical theory of judicial review, is therefore impervious to the usual argument that judges cannot decide the historiographic and conceptual problems of ascertaining framers' intent in what Chemerinsky terms a "value-neutral" way (92). To refute the classical theory one would have to demonstrate either an ontologically skeptical thesis with regard to the reality of justice, or an epistemologically skeptical thesis to the effect that justice is so totally inaccessible to the human understanding that progress toward it is impossible, or the antidemocratic thesis that popular government does not have the capacity to manifest and institutionalize a concern for justice. Although I cannot avoid some sympathy with this last possibility, an aim of this book is to show that the skeptics have not demonstrated their case against the classical theory.

41. See, e.g., Barber, *On What the Constitution Means,* 13–37, 131–33; Macedo, *New Right v. the Constitution;* Jaffa, "What Were the 'Original Intentions,'" 356–58, 394–95.

42. For a recent criticism of the double standard, see Macedo, *New Right v. the Constitution,* 59–67.

43. See generally, Purcell, *Crisis of Democratic Theory,* chap. 5.

44. See Bork, *Tempting of America,* 223–30.

45. Bork, "Tradition and Morality," 10.

46. Dworkin, *Taking Rights Seriously,* 134–36; Dworkin, *Matter of Principle,* 48–50.

47. David A. J. Richards, *Toleration and the Constitution* (New York: Oxford University Press, 1986), 35–45.

48. Moore, " Natural Law Theory of Interpretation," 340–41.

49. Sotirios A. Barber, "The Federalist and the Anomalies of New Right Constitutionalism," *Northern Kentucky Law Review* 15 (1988): 444–46.

50. Berger, *Government by Judiciary,* 91, 105, 113–18, 314–15, 407–12.

51. See Raoul Berger, "A Response to D. A. J. Richards' Defense of Freewheeling Constitutional Adjudication," *Indiana Law Journal* 59 (1984): 340, 352–57, 365–71, where Berger attacks the concern for abstract intentions as a mere cloak for imposing personal predilections. See also Berger, *Government by Judiciary,* 284–85, where Berger claims that his position flows from the Constitution, not from some background theory of democracy.

52. For an overview of the issues, see Moore, "Natural Law Theory of Interpretation."

53. Berger, *Government by Judiciary,* 408–9, 413. The following passage refers to this work.

54. Dworkin, *Taking Rights Seriously,* 140–41. See also Perry, *Morality, Politics, and Law,* 164; Chemerinsky, "Vanishing Constitution," 74–87. Although Dworkin's original observation stands unrefuted, the assumed antagonism between judicial power and democracy continues to exert a strong influence on contemporary constitutional discussion, especially on thought from the Right. Perhaps worse, the alleged antagonism seems capable of reasserting itself in the thinking even of modernist (and postmodernist) liberals who say they have seen through it. I show this with regard to Michael Perry in Barber, "Michael Perry and the Future of Constitutional Theory," *Tulane Law Review* 63 (1989): 1289, 1296.

55. See Richards, *Toleration and the Constitution,* 36–37; Cooke, *The Federalist,* 259–60; Francis Lieber, *Legal and Political Hermeneutics* (St. Louis: F. H. Thomas, 1880), 43–54. On the other hand, some may try to deny that constitutional construction should strive to view the constitutional system as a coherent whole. For a defense of the "wholesome inconsistencies" that American institutions are alleged to "embody and produce," see Bork, *Tempting of America,* 352–53. Yet Bork's very attempt to defend the "inconsistencies" as "wholesome" (in their capacity to "achieve compromise" and "dilute absolutism," for example) suggests that he finds the system coherent at a different level or in light of some larger end. In Bork's case the end in question is probably some conception of domestic peace, a possibility that would explain how a neo-Hobbesian like Berns can support the constitutionalism of a moral skeptic like Bork.

56. For an overview of most of the arguments against Berger's position, see Richards, *Toleration and the Constitution,* 34–45.

57. Wolfe, *Rise of Modern Judicial Review,* 57. The following passage refers to this work.

58. Bork, foreword to McDowell, *Constitution and Contemporary Constitutional Theory*, x. Bork wrote as follows: "But, oddly enough, it is McDowell's treatment of Berger that raises the crucial problem of the interpretivist school." I construe this as indicated in the text because Bork gave no indication that he thought McDowell's account of Berger's position inaccurate. The following passage also refers to this work.

59. Ronald Dworkin, *Law's Empire* (Cambridge: Harvard University Press, 1986), 327-38, 379-99.

60. McDowell, "Constitution and Contemporary Theory," 23, 29.

61. Bork, *Tempting of America*, 253-57. The following passage refers to this work.

62. For an argument that competent reaffirmation depends on the possibility of critical rejection, see Barber, *On What the Constitution Means*, 289-92.

63. Bork, *Tempting of America*, 223. The following passages refer to this work.

64. Berger, "A Response to Richards," 341, 356. The following passage refers to this work.

65. Berger, *Government by Judiciary*, 117-34.

66. Dworkin, *Law's Empire*, 361-63.

67. 347 U.S. 497 (1954). This companion case of *Brown* outlawed segregation in the public schools of the District of Columbia. There being no equal protection clause applicable to the national government, the Court incorporated an equal protection guarantee into the due process clause of the Fifth Amendment.

68. Bork, *Tempting of America*, 83-84. The following passages refer to this work.

69. In *Skinner*, 316 U.S. 535 (1942), the Court voided on equal protection grounds a statute providing for the sterilization of a limited class of felons. The following passages refer to Bork, *Tempting of America*.

70. McConnell, "Role of Democratic Politics," 1501.

71. Perry, *Morality, Politics, and Law*, 55-57. The following passage refers to this work.

72. McConnell, "Role of Democratic Politics," 1504. The following passages refer to this work.

73. Such judgments are not possible for Perry; see *Morality, Politics, and Law*, 47-49.

74. Bork can know no such thing; see Bork, "Neutral Principles and Some First Amendment Problems," 20; Bork, *Tempting of America*, 255-59.

75. Michael W. McConnell, "Federalism: Evaluating the Founders' Design," *University of Chicago Law Review* 54 (1987): 1484. Berger, says McConnell, "stands for the honorable tradition that a scholar must put aside his own social and economic predilections and look only to original sources in seeking the meaning of the United States Constitution."

76. Michael W. McConnell, "On Reading the Constitution," *Cornell Law Review* 73 (1988): 360-61. The following passages refer to this work.

77. 463 U.S. 783 (1983). See Berger, "A Response to Richards," 350.

78. McConnell, "On Reading the Constitution," 363. The following passage refers to this work.

79. McConnell, "Role of Democratic Politics," 1507. The following passages refer to this work.

80. Martin Luther King, Jr., "Letter from a Birmingham Jail," in *What Country Have I? Political Writings by Black Americans*, ed. Herbert J. Storing (New York: St. Martin's, 1970), 121.

81. Harry V. Jaffa, *Crisis of the House Divided: An Interpretation of the Lincoln-Douglas Debate* (Seattle: University of Washington Press, 1959; Chicago: University of Chicago Press, Phoenix Reprints, 1982), 317–29. McConnell either does not know or chooses to ignore Jaffa's celebrated analysis of Lincoln's "creative" construction of the Declaration of Independence.

82. McConnell, "Role of Democratic Politics," 1535.

83. *Brandenburg v. Ohio,* 395 U.S. 444 (1969); *School District of Abington Township v. Schempp,* 347 U.S. 203 (1963); *Engel v. Vitale,* 370 U.S. 421 (1962); *Barron v. Baltimore,* 7 Peters 243 (1833). McConnell says, without elaboration, that a "good case can be made" that the Civil War amendments "were . . . designed to nationalize some issues of individual rights, unrelated to slavery, where the prior system of state autonomy had proven injurious to our ancient liberties" ("The Role of Democratic Politics," 1531).

84. McConnell, "Role of Democratic Politics," 1535–40. The reapportionment cases are *Wesberry v. Sanders,* 376 U.S. 1 (1964); *Reynolds v. Simms,* 377 U.S. 533 (1964). See also Kelly, Harbison, and Belz, *American Constitution,* 637–38, 639–40.

85. Wolfe, *Rise of Modern Judicial Review,* 221.

86. McConnell, "Role of Democratic Politics," 1524. The following passages refer to this work.

87. McConnell, "Role of Democratic Politics," 1525; his emphasis. The following passage refers to this work.

88. For additional discussion, see Sotirios A. Barber, "Whither Moral Realism: A Reply to Professor McConnell," *Chicago-Kent Law Review* 64 (1989): 111.

89. 491 U.S. 110, at 128, n.6.

90. Ibid., at 132, citing, inter alia, *Griswold v. Connecticut,* 405 U.S. 438 (1972), *Loving v. Virginia,* 388 U.S. 1 (1967), and *Eisenstadt v. Baird,* 405 U.S. 438 (1972).

91. *Planned Parenthood of Southeastern Pennsylvania v. Casey,* 112 S. Ct. 2791, 2816–22 (1992).

92. Ibid., 2805–6. I assume here that the joint opinion rejected Scalia's clarification of his specific-tradition rule at 2874.

93. Ibid., 2875.

94. Ibid., 2884–85.

95. 112 S. Ct. 2649 (1992).

96. Ibid., 2678–81. The following passage refers to this case.

97. Macedo, *New Right v. the Constitution,* 49–57, 59–62; Bernard Siegan, *Economic Liberties and the Constitution* (Chicago: University of Chicago Press, 1980).

98. Bork, *Tempting of America,* chaps. 9, 10. The following passage refers to this work.

99. Macedo, *New Right v. The Constitution,* 49.

100. Fried, *Order and Law,* 72–75. The following passages refer to this work.

101. 357 U.S. 449 (1958).

102. 268 U.S. 510 (1925); 262 U.S. 390 (1923).

103. Fried, *Order and Law,* 65.

104. 478 U.S. 186 (1986).

105. Fried, *Order and Law,* 82–83. The following passages refer to this work.

106. Ronald Dworkin, "The Reagan Revolution and the Supreme Court," *New York Review of Books* (July 18, 1991): 24. The following passages refer to this work.

107. See Fried, *Order and Law,* 19.

108. Dworkin, *Reagan Revolution and the Supreme Court,* 27.

109. Fried, *Order and Law,* 85.

110. See reviews by Frederick D. Nelson, "Recanting the Revolution," *National Review* (May 13, 1991): 46–48; and Gary L. McDowell, "Point Man for Reagan's Court Changes Was Pointing the Other Way," *Washington Times,* 29 April 1991.

5. THEORIES OF JUDICIAL REVIEW II: MODERNIST LIBERALISM

1. Bickel, *Morality of Consent,* 62–63. This sketch of Bickel's work is indebted to Edward A. Purcell, Jr., "Alexander M. Bickel and the Post-Realist Constitution," *Harvard Civil Rights–Civil Liberties Law Review* 2 (1976): 521–64.

2. Compare Purcell, "Bickel and the Post-Realist Constitution," 563 ("Bickel was not a seminal figure") with McDowell, *Contemporary Constitutional Theory* ("Bickel's work was at once seminal and paradoxical").

3. See, e.g., Brest, "Fundamental Rights Controversy," 1065–66; Chemerinsky, "Vanishing Constitution," 70–72; Ely, *Democracy and Distrust,* 71–72.

4. Compare Ely, *Democracy and Distrust,* 88–92; Bork, *Tempting of America,* 251–59; and Berns, "Rights and Laws of Nature," 80–81; with Bickel, *Morality of Consent,* 7–8, 12, 95.

5. Compare Erwin Chemerinsky, *Interpreting the Constitution* (New York: Praeger, 1987), 129–30, with Bickel, *Least Dangerous Branch,* 24–26, 236–39.

6. See Purcell, "Bickel and the Post-Realist Constitution," 526–27, 536, 551.

7. Bickel, *Least Dangerous Branch,* 69–72; see also 24–31, 64, 68–69, 236–39.

8. By "principle" Bickel seemed mostly to mean an internally consistent and generally applicable rule of conduct reflecting an existing or emerging moral consensus; for example, a prohibition against legislation containing racial classifications. Yet he seemed to link these rules with ends or policy results, entities that do not possess the logical properties of rules. He could thus hold that the Court could, without offending principle, stay its approving or disapproving hand regarding benign racial quotas until experience should prove quotas either progressive or reactionary. Purcell points out that this made the application of principles depend on prudential calculations regarding favored results, thus appearing to eliminate adequate principles as the validating condition for judicial action. See Purcell, "Bickel and the Post-Realist Constitution," 536–37, 540–41.

9. Such, at any rate, is Purcell's impression; see ibid., 536–37, 539.

10. See Bickel, *Least Dangerous Branch,* 71–72; Alexander M. Bickel, "Beyond Tokenism: The Civil Rights Task that Looms Ahead," *New Republic* 150 (4 January 1964): 11, 14; and Alexander M. Bickel, *Politics and the Warren Court* (New York: Harper and Row, 1965), 42, n. 17.

11. See Purcell, "Bickel and the Post-Realist Constitution," 547–48.

12. Alexander M. Bickel, *The Supreme Court and the Idea of Progress* (New York: Harper and Row, 1970), 99. For a discussion of the continuing ambiguity of Bickel's position, even at this stage of his thought, see Purcell, "Bickel and the Post-Realist Constitution," 550–51.

13. Bickel, *Idea of Progress,* 113.

14. Purcell, "Bickel and the Post-Realist Constitution," 551–53.

15. Bickel, *Idea of Progress,* 83–95.

16. Purcell, "Bickel and the Post-Realist Constitution," 554–55.

17. Dworkin, *Taking Rights Seriously,* 145.

18. Bork, *Tempting of America,* 342. The following passage refers to this work.

19. Michael J. Perry, "Noninterpretive Review in Human Rights Cases: A Functional Justification," *New York University Law Review* 56 (1981): 280, 315–16, 321. The following passages refer to this work.

20. Perry's less precise definition of interpretivism was "the effort . . . to ascertain, as accurately as available historical materials will permit, the character of a value judgment the Framers constitutionalized at some point in the past" (ibid., 279). Had Perry believed the framers "constitutionalized" general ideas rather than concrete conceptions, he would not have denied the interpretive character of successive conceptions of the expressed ideas as specific as those in the First Amendment and most of the provisions of amendments Four through Eight. Contrast Perry with Ely, who saw all modern First Amendment cases as interpretivist because he conceived interpretivists as moving against the "contemporary counterparts" of "the *sorts of evils*" that the framers sought to prevent through specific constitutional rights. See Ely, *Democracy and Distrust,* 13–14.

21. Perry, "Noninterpretive Review," 281–82.

22. Bickel, *Least Dangerous Branch,* 24: "The search must be for a function which might (indeed must) involve the making of policy, yet which differs from the legislative and executive functions; which is peculiarly suited to the capability of the courts; which will not likely be performed elsewhere . . . which can be so exercised as to be acceptable in a society that generally shares Judge Hand's satisfaction in a 'sense of common venture'; which will be effective when needed; and whose discharge by the courts will not lower the quality of the other departments' performance by denuding them of the dignity and burden of their own responsibility."

23. Michael J. Perry, "Abortion, the Public Morals, and the Police Power: The Ethical Function of Substantive Due Process," *UCLA Law Review* 23 (1976): 699, 704, 735–36.

24. Perry, "Noninterpretive Review," 283–85. The following passage refers to this work.

25. Ibid., 289, quoting Robert Bellah, "American Civil Religion in the 1970's," *Anglican Theological Review* 8 (July 1973).

26. Perry, "Noninterpretive Review," 288–89, quoting Robert Bellah, "Civil Religion in America," *Daedalus* 96 (1967): 4.

27. Perry, "Noninterpretive Review," 292. The following passages refer to this work.

28. Michael J. Perry, *The Constitution, the Courts, and Human Rights* (New Haven: Yale University Press, 1982), 102. The following passage refers to this work.

29. Thomas Nagel, "The Supreme Court and Political Philosophy," *New York University Law Review* 56 (1981): 519–20.

30. Perry, *Constitution, the Courts, and Human Rights,* 104–5. The following passage refers to this work.

31. See Michael S. Moore, "The Interpretive Turn in Modern Theory: A Turn for the Worse?" *Stanford Law Review* 41 (1989): 880–90.

32. Perry, *Constitution, Courts, and Human Rights,* 40–41. The following passage refers to this work.

33. Perry, *Morality, Politics, and Law,* 133. The following passages refer to this work.

34. Perry, "Abortion, Public Morals, and Police Power," 735–36. Perry's debt to Bickel is expressly evident on 699, 707, 713–19. Of "the ethical function," Perry said: "in applying the substantive imperative of due process . . . the Court is, in effect, called upon to ascertain the contents of social conventions. In so doing, the Court exercises the ethical function of judicial review: The Court brings culturally shared ideals, sensibilities, and norms to bear on the political process" (735).

35. Perry, *Morality, Politics, and Law,* 174–75.

36. Thomas Grey, "Do We Have an Unwritten Constitution?" *Stanford Law Review* 27 (1975): 703, 710–14. See also Jesse H. Choper, *Judicial Review and the National Political Process: A Functional Reconsideration of the Role of the Supreme Court* (Chicago: University of Chicago Press, 1980), 137; Paul Brest, "The Misconceived Quest for the Original Understanding," *Boston University Law Review* 60 (1980): 234; Terrence Sandalow, "Judicial Protection of Minorities, *Michigan Law Review* 75 (1977): 1183.

37. For this description of the contest and a partial list of the principal contenders, see Dworkin, "Forum of Principle," 471–76. The following passages refer to this work.

38. See, e.g., Robert H. Bork, "At Last, An End to Supreme Court Activism," *New York Times,* 29 August 1990.

39. The shift in the terms of this debate is best described and defended in Moore, "Do We Have an Unwritten Constitution?" 110–14. Perry's change of heart occurs in Michael J. Perry, "The Authority of Text, Tradition, and Reason: A Theory of Constitutional 'Interpretation,'" *Southern California Law Review* 58 (1985): 551. Grey abandoned the interpretivism-noninterpretivism distinction in "The Constitution as Scripture," *Stanford Law Review* 37 (1984): 1.

40. Perry, *Morality, Politics, and Law,* 122–31. The following passages refer to this work.

41. Compare Perry, *Morality, Politics, and Law,* 126 ("The originalist project is not to speculate about what the ratifiers' beliefs would have been in our day, were they still living, and then to decide the case on the basis of their beliefs") with 127 ("The originalist, on the basis of available historical materials, must engage in a hypothetical conversation with 'the framers' . . . in an effort to discern which principle *they* [Perry's emphasis] most likely would have chosen, in the conversation, confronted by the various possibilities, that is, the various candidate principles, from relatively narrow/concrete to relatively broad/abstract, as being the one that best captured the purpose or point or meaning of what they did") and 289, n. 59 ("An opinion written by an originalist judge who thinks that the relevant original belief is so general as to constitute, in effect, an aspiration or 'principle' . . . is likely to look much the same, perhaps even identical to, an opinion written by a nonoriginalist judge. . . . Query, however, whether *disinterested* [Perry's emphasis] historical inquiry will disclose many, or any original beliefs so general as to constitute aspirations or principles. . . . Of course, a judge who professes to be an originalist but has an instinct to do justice . . . may succumb to the temptation to ally her originalism to bad history—that is, she may . . . credit bad history—so as to have the latitude to do justice"). The following passages refer to this work.

42. See ibid., 155. For additional comment on Perry's understanding of meaning, see Barber, "Michael Perry and the Future of Constitutional Theory," 1298–1301.

43. See Barber, *On What the Constitution Means,* chap. 2; Moore, "Do We Have an Unwritten Constitution?" 115–18, 125–30.

44. Perry, *Constitution, the Courts, and Human Rights,* 11.

45. See Perry, *Morality, Politics, and Law,* 131–32. The following passage refers to this work.

46. See his approving citation of Moore's formulation of moral skepticism, ibid., 10, n. 7, citing Michael S. Moore, "Moral Reality," *1982 Wisconsin Law Review,* 1081.

47. Perry, *Morality, Politics, and Law,* 10, 18–20. The following passages refer to this work.

48. Ibid., 45–46, quoting Richard Rorty, *Consequences of Pragmatism* (Minneapolis: University of Minnesota Press, 1982), xlii.

49. Perry, *Morality, Politics, and Law,* 42–43. The following passages refer to this work.

50. Ibid., 40–41, quoting Rorty, *Consequences of Pragmatism,* xx.

51. Perry, *Morality, Politics, and Law,* 40 (his emphasis). The following passage refers to this work.

52. In *Morality, Politics, and Law,* Perry says: "an epistemological skeptic is necessarily a moral skeptic—epistemological skepticism holds that there can be no knowledge of any kind, including, therefore, moral knowledge," 228, n. 5.

53. See Barber, *On What the Constitution Means,* 59–61.

54. See Ely, *Democracy and Distrust,* 54, 57–59, denying the existence of (1) "a discoverable and objectively valid set of moral principles" and (2) one valid "method of moral philosophy" and asserting that reason is "inherently an empty source" and that those who invoke it exhibit "a systematic bias . . . in favor of the values of the upper-middle, professional class from which most lawyers and judges, and for that matter most moral philosophers are drawn."

55. See Dworkin, *Matter of Principle,* 58–59; Tribe, "Puzzling Persistence of Process-Based Theories," 1070–71; Barber *On What the Constitution Means,* 49–50, 56–59.

56. Lief Carter, *Contemporary Constitutional Law Making* (Elmsford, N.Y.: Pergamon, 1985), 58–63, 161, 164. Carter addresses the reader: "You must understand . . . that my argument compels me to avoid the claim that I can 'prove' to you that I am 'correct.' . . . How much you accept depends on your own beliefs and experiences" (12).

57. See Richard A. Posner, *The Problems of Jurisprudence* (Cambridge: Harvard University Press, 1990), 18–19, 83; Stanley Fish, "Almost Pragmatism: Richard Posner's Jurisprudence," *Chicago Law Review* 57 (1990): 1449, 1452–54.

58. See Fish, "Almost Pragmatism," 1447–49. The term *pragmatism* enables Fish, Posner, Rorty and other conventionalists to deny that they in fact occupy a metaphysical position—viz., conventionalism. For what should be accepted as proof that contemporary pragmatism is plain old conventionalism (a form of metaphysical idealism) in disguise; see Moore, "Interpretive Turn in Legal Theory," 892, 901–3. One way to account for pragmatism's interest in denying that it is metaphysics in disguise is the concession all metaphysical positions make to metaphysical realism—the view that one or another form of reality exists independently of what human beings might believe about reality, and that belief is therefore fundamentally different from truth. In saying, for example, that reality is constituted by beliefs or convention, conventionalists propose the belief-independent truth of conventionalism itself, contrary to their thesis that truth is belief. Fish can thus term all metaphysical positions forms of "essentialism," his term for philosophical realism (Fish, "Almost Pragmatism," 1457–58).

For another explanation, let me sketch one that resonates with contemporary pragmatism: A gap between belief and knowledge might be taken as a normative gap that compels as it justifies the attempt to replace belief with knowledge. All waking eyes would then turn to the life of Socrates as model. (Those who think they know, other than that they do not, are asleep.) But Socrates seems socially irresponsible because he could not find real reasons for behavior others considered productive (of apparently good, as opposed to good, things). Socrates as model will not work, therefore; it means disruption. And there is no rational possibility for Socrates as king. (See Alan Bloom, *The Republic of Plato* [New York: Basic, 1968], 387–88, 409–10.) Enter, eventually, Hobbes and the flight from Socrates as model, the flight from the quest for real reasons to an unreflective and therefore blind but not uncomfortable Peace. (See my discussion of Berns in chapter 1.) So, neo-Hobbes, perhaps, as real philosopher king (author of a fully successful tyranny? Consider Tocqueville, *Democracy in America,* vol. II, Bk. 4, 56) with leaders of the "free enterprise system" (and their public philosophers) only apparently in control. Enter, finally, the new pragmatist wave of the flight from philosophic responsibility and real justice or real anything. *Force is truth,* they chime, as expected. *Appearance is reality. Dream your Dreams!*

59. Perry, *Morality, Politics, and Law,* 28. The following passages refer to this work.

60. Compare Schambra, "Progressive Liberalism and American Community," 31–32, 40–48.

61. Perry, *Constitution, the Courts, and Human Rights,* 105–6.

62. See Moore, "Metaphysics, Epistemology and Legal Theory," 482–83.

63. Perry, *Constitution, the Courts, and Human Rights,* 93–95, 98–99.

64. Perry, *Morality, Politics, and Law,* 139–42. The following passages refer to this work.

65. For a recent overview and analysis of the contending theories of precedent, see Moore, "Natural Law Theory of Precedent."

66. Compare Dworkin, *Law's Empire,* 65–67, 88–89, on the transition from preinterpretive to interpretive understanding.

67. Ely, *Democracy and Distrust,* 43–70.

68. Chemerinsky, *Interpreting the Constitution,* 106–10. The following passage refers to this work.

69. Chemerinsky should have found it impossible to identify anyone who fits this description, if for no other reason than that the constitutional text itself refers to what Chemerinsky treats as extraconstitutional material. Nevertheless, Chemerinsky names Justice Black, ignoring, among other things, the originalist approach of Black's famous dissent in *Adamson v. California,* 332 U.S. 46, 68 (1947).

70. Chemerinsky, *Interpreting the Constitution,* 108, 178, n. 11. The following passages refer to this work.

71. 3 Dall. 386 (1790).

72. Chemerinsky, *Interpreting the Constitution,* 112. The following passages refer to this work.

73. Ibid., 115. See also 74–78, where Chemerinsky adopts a distinction between "strict originalism" and "moderate originalism." Because "intent can be stated at many different levels of abstraction, the distinction between [strict] originalism and moderate originalism is not always clear." But strict originalism seems oriented to the framers' concrete intent while moderate originalism is concerned with the framers' general pur-

poses or abstract intentions. Thus "moderate originalism endorses the view that the meaning of the Constitution shifts over time." Moderate originalism takes two principal forms, the "conceptualism" of writers like Dworkin and the model that asks "what the framers would have done had they been confronted with modern circumstances." Both of these forms of moderate originalism are "completely indeterminate." One founders on the "level of generality" problem; the other permits judges to "come to any conclusion . . . and simply argue that because the result is just, that is what the framers would have done."

74. Chemerinsky, *Interpreting the Constitution,* x. The following passages refer to this work.

75. See Barber, *On What the Constitution Means,* 49–61, 72–78, 105–8, 121–22, 159–65, 197–203, 210–20.

76. See ibid., esp. chaps. 3, 4.

77. Chemerinsky, *Interpreting the Constitution,* 26. The following passages refer to this work.

78. Bork, "At Last an End to Supreme Court Activism."

79. Chemerinsky, *Interpreting the Constitution,* 136. The following passage refers to this work.

6. CONTEMPORARY JURISPRUDENCE AND THE INTERNAL PERSPECTIVE ON CONSTITUTIONAL QUESTIONS

1. See H. L. A. Hart, *The Concept of Law* (London: Oxford University Press, 1961), chap. 7. The following passages refer to this work.

2. See ibid., vii, 55–56, 86–88. See also Neil MacCormick, *H. L. A. Hart* (Stanford: Stanford University Press, 1981), 5.

3. These included a conception of practical reasonableness whereby it is good to empower courts to register the greater determinacy of a community's purposes (as expressed in its laws) that comes with the passage of time; a deep-conventionalist view of a community's morality that favors courts over popularly elected legislatures; and social-democratic policy commitments of the kind with which Americans often associate the Warren era. See MacCormick, *H. L. A. Hart,* 8–12.

4. Hart, *Concept of Law,* 149. The following passage refers to this work.

5. Dworkin, *Taking Rights Seriously,* chap. 2.

6. For a similar reading of Dworkin, see Neil MacCormick, "Dworkin as Pre-Benthamite," in *Ronald Dworkin and Contemporary Jurisprudence,* ed. Marshall Cohen (Totowa, N.J.: Roman and Allenheld, 1983), 188.

7. Dworkin, *Taking Rights Seriously,* 106–7. The following passages refer to this work.

8. For the difficulties in pinning down the precise content of Dworkin's right answer thesis, see Moore, "Metaphysics, Epistemology and Legal Theory," 475–83.

9. Dworkin, *Taking Rights Seriously,* 31–39, 82–90, 137–43.

10. See MacCormick, "Dworkin as Pre-Benthamite," 184–85.

11. Dworkin, *Taking Rights Seriously,* 159–68. The following passage refers to this work.

12. See David O. Brink, *Moral Realism and the Foundations of Ethics* (Cambridge: Cambridge University Press, 1989), 175–78.

13. Ibid., 43–50. See also Moore, "Moral Reality," 1122–23. Brink calls this theory

of moral motivation "externalism" because it holds that the motivation to act on moral beliefs is contingent on personal and environmental factors external to those beliefs. Jeremy Waldron is a moral antirealist who thinks that moral realists who adopt the externalist view of moral motivation are unable to say that moral realists take morality more seriously than moral antirealists. Externalism says that it is possible for some people who believe in moral truth to be unmoved by their moral beliefs, and Waldron asserts that the test of moral seriousness is the motivation to act, not the stubbornness with which one holds one's moral beliefs. Waldron concludes from this that an antirealist actor can take her moral beliefs as seriously as a realist actor. See Jeremy Waldron, "The Irrelevance of Moral Objectivity," in *Natural Law Theory,* ed. Robert F. George (New York: Oxford University Press, 1992), 168–69.

Waldron erroneously assumes in this argument that it is possible to be (or be perceived as) an antirealist moral actor. Although Waldron acknowledges some difference between first- and second-order moral theories (166), his comment on externalism and moral realism is insensitive to the fact that moral realism and antirealism are not moral theories in the sense of coherent moral codes or sets of first-order beliefs about the conduct of everyday life. Realism and antirealism are types of academic theory *about* the moral beliefs of everyday life. Moral realism accepts the everyday presupposition that there is a moral reality that is independent of anyone's beliefs about it; moral antirealist theories try to deny that presupposition. But when the antirealist leaves the classroom or other academic forum and enters the sphere of everyday life, his conduct cannot sensibly conform to his academic teaching. When the antirealist assumes the role of moral actor, his words and deeds must evince realist beliefs, lest others not see him as a moral actor. The same holds for the antirealist who would say something of relevance to moral actors, as Waldron tries to do in counseling political actors, especially judges, to disregard the current debate between realists and antirealists as irrelevant (see 159, 164–65, 176–82).

Thus Waldron himself starts an essay on the "irrelevance of moral objectivity" by assuring his readers that he is not calling moral "objectivity in the sense of fairness, impartiality, or even-handedness . . . irrelevant or unimportant in law or anywhere else" (158). At a later point he describes his own everyday moral criticism of actions as justified not by his feelings but by moral properties of the actions themselves. "When I condemn an action," he says, speaking as a momentarily displaced classroom antirealist, "I usually do so in virtue of some feature . . . that it has (the action's cruelty, for example, or its hurtfulness)" (171). And still later he says, "the case for judicial review must be won" not in the contest between moral realism and antirealism (i.e., the contest over the existence and accessibility of things like fairness itself, justice itself, and democracy itself) but "on the basis of moral arguments about fairness, justice, and democracy" (182).

Waldron's problem is that self-conscious antirealists cannot speak normatively of, or justify their conduct with reference to, moral objectivity, justice, democracy, and the like. Nor can they have a normative theory of something like democracy itself, for they say there is nothing like that to have a theory of. Nor can they mean it when they say something like, *It's wrong to kick dogs just for fun.* As self-conscious moral antirealists they have to put all the normative words in quotation marks, and, in everyday life, justice is not the same thing as "justice" or justice so-called. Waldron may have a point when he says realists are not necessarily activists. If externalism is correct (an issue I need not discuss here) and if taking morality seriously necessitates what Waldron calls action (something I doubt but need not discuss), then Waldron can conclude that realists do not have to take morality seriously. Even so, a realist or a person whose presuppositions realism describes would remain the only ones who can take morality seriously if anyone can. And insofar as an antirealist would want to be seen as moved by a concern for goodness or rightness themselves—as distinguished, say, from the chauvinist's concern for his tribe's opinions of goodness or rightness—he must act as if he accepts moral realist presuppositions. The conventionalist activist, a chauvinist by definition, would have to pretend to more than mere chauvinism; he would have to pretend to believe that his tribe's opinions were true or closer to the truth than rival opinions.

14. See Brink, *Moral Realism and the Foundations of Ethics,* 130–43; Moore, "Moral Reality," 1106–17.

15. See Dworkin, "A Reply by Ronald Dworkin," in *Ronald Dworkin and Contemporary Jurisprudence,* ed. Marshall Cohen (Totowa, N.J.: Rowman and Allenheld, 1984), 277. Dworkin indicates here that "almost no one" who says "slavery is really unjust" means that the injustice of slavery is a belief forced upon us by the nonmoral or "physical properties" of slavery. Dworkin would thus relegate to insignificance the naturalist variety of moral realism, which holds, inter alia, that (1) specific moral properties (like injustice) sometimes or always supervene on (or vary systematically with) specific nonmoral properties (like the forced labor of reasoning noncriminals for the net benefit of others), (2) instances of (1) constitute moral facts, and (3) moral facts can explain the moral beliefs of fully rational persons with complete information. Assuming both the truth of a moral theory that holds a particular instance of slavery wrong and a rational and informed actor's belief to that effect, a moral realist who is also a naturalist could say that the actor's belief is caused by the wrongness of the slavery, which wrongness is consequent on a set of nonmoral facts.

David Brink argues that these ultimate nonmoral facts could even be the "materialist or physicalist" facts of a materialist ontology. "A materialist account of moral facts and properties should be no harder to give than is a materialist account of other supervenient facts and properties," says Brink. If materialism is a true philosophic position, Brink adds, then all "higher-order facts and properties, such as chemical, biological, social, psychological, and economic facts and properties must be . . . organized combinations of physical facts and properties." "A materialist version of ethical naturalism will make the same claims about moral facts and properties; moral facts and properties are just one kind of higher-order fact and property" (Brink, *Moral Realism and the Foundations of Ethics,* 178–79).

16. See Moore, "Metaphysics, Epistemology and Legal Theory," 462–63.

17. Waldron, "Irrelevance of Moral Objectivity," 173–74. The following passages refer to this work.

18. See Gregory Vlastos, "The Socratic Elenchus," *Oxford Studies in Ancient Philosophy* 1 (1983): 29–32, 38–39; cf. John Rawls, *A Theory of Justice* (Cambridge: Harvard University Press, 1971), 19–21, 48–51.

19. Rawls, *Theory of Justice,* 49.

20. See Waldron, "Irrelevance of Moral Objectivity," 173–74. The following passage refers to this work.

21. Vlastos, "Socratic Elenchus," 35–36.

22. Waldron, "Irrelevance of Moral Objectivity," 174.

23. See Vlastos, "Socratic Elenchus," 48; cf. Moore, "Metaphysics, Epistemology and Legal Theory," 481–83.

24. See Brink, *Moral Realism and the Foundations of Ethics*, 206–7.

25. Moral antirealists who are also scientific antirealists can say that the parallel-to-science strain of moral realism proves nothing, since science is at bottom as arbitrary as ethics. This radical antifoundationalist or contemporary pragmatist shares important premises with modernist theorists who propose normative alternatives to the classical theory of judicial review. These premises include beliefs in the conventional nature of meaning and value, the impossibility of judicial duty in hard cases, radical cultural heterogeneity, and the ultimate authority of force. I comment on these tenets in this book, insofar as they figure in the prescriptive and explanatory writings of modernists who avoid antifoundationalist extremes. But I cannot have much to say to the radical antifoundationalist or pure pragmatist. Because his position allows him neither a prescriptive nor an explanatory voice, he is not part of the debate to which this book would contribute. No real foundation whatever means no real reason to do or believe anything in particular. So the radical antifoundationalist cannot propose anything controversial or argue with anyone about anything, and if he finds himself doing these things, he contradicts himself. See Barber, "Stanley Fish and the Future of Pragmatism."

26. Moore, "Metaphysics, Epistemology and Legal Theory," 460–61.

27. Dworkin, *Taking Rights Seriously*, 105, 118–19, 126–30.

28. Moore, "Metaphysics, Epistemology and Legal Theory," 460.

29. Dworkin, *Taking Rights Seriously*, 161. Waldron gives the same mistaken account of realism. See Waldron, "Irrelevance of Moral Objectivity," 167–68.

30. For the possibility of toleration and fallibility in moral realism, see Brink, *Moral Realism and the Foundations of Ethics*, 90–95; Moore, "Moral Reality," 1104–5.

31. See Brink, *Moral Realism and the Foundations of Ethics*, 15–22 (distinguishing realism from alternative philosophic positions); Moore, "Interpretive Turn in Modern Theory," 878–81 (same).

32. See Brink, *Moral Realism and the Foundations of Ethics*, 27, 31–36, 90–95, 125–30. Waldron substitutes caricature for analysis when he says "realists seem to crave a foundation for our moral commitments in something more stable than" emotions which can be "strong, steady, and remarkably resistant . . . to . . . change." See Waldron, "Irrelevance of Moral Objectivity," 169.

33. Compare Brink, *Moral Realism and the Foundations of Ethics*, 127–28. (The realist position in ethics may be wrong despite its status as the philosophic position favored by the evidence.)

34. See Moore, "Metaphysics, Epistemology and Legal Theory," 495–501. Moore accepts the view that thought cannot altogether free itself from scientific beliefs and therewith the realist presuppositions of science. He extends no such immunity to ethics. He holds the existence and nature of moral entities answerable to scientific thought. He is a moral realist because he believes that the most persuasive beliefs about nonmoral facts, properties, and relationships support a naturalist version of moral realism.

35. Compare Brink, *Moral Realism and the Foundations of Ethics*, 11–13. Although Brink announces his plan to defend moral realism by an affirmative as well as a negative argument, he concedes that few if any of his specific arguments will silence the antirealists. "But I assume," he says, "that the argumentative standards here are those of systematic comparative plausibility. Even if none of my arguments is unanswerable,

they pose problems and puzzles for the moral antirealist and display the various virtues of realism. Taken collectively, my arguments should make the case for moral realism . . . plausible and worthy of serious consideration. Those who wish to reject these claims not only will have to respond to particular arguments but also will have to articulate an alternative set of views with comparable resources." I am struck by two features of Brink's statement. If, to begin with, "the argumentative standards . . . are those of systematic comparative plausibility," the case for realism is a case to be made within the confines of what we find plausible, which, on realist premises, precludes any claim that the case for realism is simply true. Second, Brink refuses to claim that all who can reason aright will accept his arguments, even such as might appear unanswerable. Once he has made his play, he will simply await the return from the other court.

36. Waldron indicates that realists claim "to take their moral commitments more seriously than" antirealists because realists regard their beliefs as response[s] to . . . matter[s] of objective fact," not "contingent feeling." See Waldron, "Irrelevance of Moral Objectivity," 167. I argue here that realists should take moral truth far more seriously than their opinions about its requirements. See also Barber, *On What the Constitution Means,* 111–15, 140–44.

37. Moore, "Do We Have an Unwritten Constitution?" 135.

38. For a challenging treatment of these problems, see Moore, "Metaphysics, Epistemology and Legal Theory."

39. Dworkin, *Taking Rights Seriously,* 162.

40. Dworkin, *Law's Empire,* 82. The following passage refers to this work.

41. Walter Murphy has pointed out to me that Dworkin's example of "courtesy" loads the dice in favor of moral conventionalism because it is more plausible to say that courtesy is exclusively conventional than it is to say the same about other virtues, like courage, temperance, and perhaps even justice. I show in the concluding chapter that moral realists can believe that some legal-moral terms in current usage may have only conventional content without holding the same for all legal-moral terms. Because Dworkin uses "courtesy" to exemplify all legal-moral terms, my analysis of his argument speaks to his metaethics, not to his specific views on courtesy.

42. Dworkin, *Law's Empire,* 68–72. The following passages refer to this work.

43. Dworkin continues to assume that nonnaturalism is the only realist position worth discussing.

44. Compare the constitution-based policies sketched in Barber, *On What the Constitution Means,* 59–61, 75–76, 126–31, 159–63, 211–13.

45. Although Dworkin supports a model of community whose typical citizen would respect "the principles of fairness and justice instinct in the standing political arrangement of his particular community, whether or not he thinks these the best principles from a utopian standpoint," he describes the politics of that community as "a theater of debate about which principles the community should adopt . . . which view it should take of justice, fairness, and due process" (Dworkin, *Law's Empire,* 211–13).

46. Brink, *Moral Realism and the Foundations of Ethics,* 23–24.

47. Waldron, "Irrelevance of Moral Objectivity," 166.

48. See n. 13, this chapter.

49. Waldron, "Irrelevance of Moral Objectivity," 166. The following passages refer to this work.

50. Ibid., 164–65, citing Dworkin, *Law's Empire,* 82–83.

51. Waldron, "Irrelevance of Moral Objectivity," 171, quoting Simon Blackburn, "Rule-Following and Moral Realism," in *Wittgenstein: To Follow a Rule,* ed. Stephan H. Holtzman and Christopher M. Leich (London: Routledge and Kegan Paul, 1981), 179.

52. Waldron, "Irrelevance of Moral Objectivity," 166.

53. Compare Vlastos's distinction between "overt" and "covert" beliefs, "Socratic Elenchus," 50–52.

54. See Fish, "Almost Pragmatism," 1451–53.

55. Waldron, "Irrelevance of Moral Objectivity," 182.

56. See Brink, *Moral Realism and the Foundations of Ethics,* 25–29.

57. Dworkin, *Taking Rights Seriously,* 138. The following passages refer to this work.

58. Dworkin, *Law's Empire,* 49.

59. Compare Bickel, *Least Dangerous Branch,* 24–26, 30–32, 42–43, 90–91, 109, 188, 199, 239. Bickel justified judicial review in terms of the Court's special competence for maintaining a morally principled politics in up-to-date form. Bickel held principles a product of history, however, and he believed that in "evolving" principles the Court spoke for the community's deeper self.

60. See Purcell, "Bickel and the Post-Realist Constitution," 538–39.

61. Dworkin, *Taking Rights Seriously,* 146–47. The following passage refers to this work.

62. Dworkin, *Matter of Principal,* chap. 7; Dworkin, *Law's Empire,* 66–67.

63. This is my assessment of what Moore describes as Dworkin's "'internal realism' about morality." See Moore, "Metaphysics, Epistemology and Legal Theory," 505–6. Dworkin rejects "strict conventionalism" (which claims that legal materials cover only what they cover explicitly or uncontroversially) and embraces "soft conventionalism" (which allows judges to seek what is implicit in conventional material). He asserts that "soft conventionalism is not really a form of conventionalism at all," since it allows for right answers in hard cases, rejects the separation of law and morality, and permits a judge to decide hard cases by "engaging his own controversial moral and political convictions." See Dworkin, *Law's Empire,* chap. 4 generally, and 81–82, 124–28, 134–35. But soft conventionalism is another name for the deep conventionalism of Dworkin's constructive model. Both fail for the same reason: because they must deny that a fully successful tyranny is a tyranny, they cannot affirm the unconditional existence of moral rights against the community and therewith the state.

7. DEFENDING THE CLASSICAL THEORY

1. For an overview, see Moore, "Do We Have an Unwritten Constitution?" 123–37. The following passages refer to this work.

2. 16 Wall. 36 (1873).

3. Walter F. Murphy, "*Slaughter-House, Civil Rights,* and Limits on Constitutional Change," *American Journal of Jurisprudence* 32 (1988): 1.

4. *Wall Street Journal,* Oct. 5, 1987. See Sotirios A. Barber, "The Ninth Amendment: Inkblot or Another Hard Nut to Crack?" *Chicago-Kent Law Review* 64 (1988): 67.

5. Compare Waldron, "Irrelevance of Moral Objectivity," 172–73. Waldron seems to accept this most familiar of all realist arguments against antirealism: "the logical gap

between disagreement and there being no objective fact of the matter." Yet, he says, the fact of moral "disagreement remains a continuing difficulty for realism" as long as realism "fails to establish connections between the idea of truth and the existence of procedures for resolving disagreements." This assertion is puzzling. Aside from his error regarding general method in moral inquiry (discussed in chapter 6), if, as Waldron acknowledges, substantive disagreement cannot prove the nonexistence of moral substance, it is not clear why methodological disagreement should mean no right answer to the question of moral method.

I do not deny that disagreement is a problem, it is simply not the problem that Waldron sees, for the real problem is not a problem that agreement can cure. Agreement is not truth, but (on realist assumptions about human motivations, the mind, and the world) agreement can serve as evidence for truth, especially if that evidence survives a rigorous and honest process of reflection and debate, which is of course a variety of disagreement. Without that process of disagreement you have what Dworkin calls an "unstudied deference to a runic order" whose practice "has the character of taboo" (Dworkin, *Law's Empire*, 47). You have a cognitive blindness, a not-knowing—worse, an ignorance of not-knowing that precludes progress toward knowing, an ignorance that marks the life one realist said was not worth living.

Realists seek truth, not agreement, but in seeking truth they seek agreement willy-nilly, because agreement, properly secured, is evidence of truth. In seeking truth through evidence of truth, realism has no choice but to risk the defeat of its aim. So disagreement is not alone in posing problems for realism; agreement poses problems too. The "realist solution" (I use quotation marks here because, Waldron's canard about realism's craving certainty notwithstanding, realists can be certain only to a point of practical confidence, not logical certainty) is a self-critical and therefore possibly reversible "commitment" to social and academic pluralism. See Sotirios A. Barber, "Normative Theory, the 'New Institutionalism,' and the Future of Public Law," in *Studies in American Political Development,* ed. Karen Orren and Stephen Skowronek (New Haven: Yale University Press, 1989), vol. 3: 67–73.

6. Moore, "Moral Reality," 1117–21.

7. Contrast Perry, *Morality, Politics, and Law,* 35. When Perry pretends to believe that words are mere "memoranda of particulars," he neglects to mention that he has no evidence that a "particular" even exists. He does have evidence of particular kinds of things, like particular dogs and cats, or particular versions of things, like a particular version of due process. But particular dogs and versions of due process are not simple particulars; their identity or being, if you will, seems somehow mixed with the nonparticular kinds or ideas of which they are. Deny the latter real existence and causal force and it seems difficult to explain the way in which all of the world's particulars cluster or can be clustered in an immeasurably smaller number of "memoranda," such that this thing and that thing and countless unseen things are and will be seen and remembered as, in part, one thing, like dog. The same seems true of due process. What can explain our sense that we have different versions of one value? If they are not different versions of one thing, how can we explain their apparent conflict and our apparent ability to distinguish beliefs that are and are not relevant to that conflict?

8. For a fuller elaboration of the argument that such conflicts are best construed as conflicts between parties, not rules, see Barber, *On What the Constitution Means,* 64–68.

9. For an attempt at such a theory, see ibid., chaps. 4-5.

10. Jerome Frank, *Law and the Modern Mind* (Garden City: Doubleday, 1963), 31-32. The following passages refer to this work.

11. Contrast Moore, "Do We Have an Unwritten Constitution?" 119-21. He argues that the quasireligious status of the written Constitution in the public's mind, and the benefits (like national unity) resulting therefrom, are independent reasons for moral realists to accept the authority of the document as axiomatic. For my argument that reaffirming the Constitution's authority depends on a willingness to reject its authority, see Barber, *On What the Constitution Means*, 49-51, 59-61.

12. Barber, *On What the Constitution Means*, 33-37, 105-8.

13. Frank, *Law and the Modern Mind*, xx-xxi (preface to 6th printing).

14. See Brink, *Moral Realism and the Foundations of Ethics*, 31, 125-27.

15. Fish, "Almost Pragmatism," 1451-54, citing Posner, *Problems of Jurisprudence*, 82-83.

16. Fish, "Almost Pragmatism," 1452.

17. Ibid., 1474. This suggestion would constitute the reductio of Fish's skepticism, if he meant it. But he does not seem to, for he repeatedly assumes a God's-eye view and founds his skepticism in what he describes as "the bottom-line fact" of the human condition and the "heterogeneity" of all human perspectives (other than his own?). See Barber, "Stanley Fish and the Future of Pragmatism," 1040-41.

18. Fish ("Almost Pragmatism," 1457-60, 1464-67) criticizes Rorty and Posner for forgetting that pragmatism's antifoundationalism precludes practical "consequences of pragmatism." Fish lapses into the same error by effectively affirming and advocating a practical consequence of pure pragmatism: political silence on the part of pure pragmatists. See Barber, "Stanley Fish and the Future of Pragmatism," 1038-41.

19. The foundation of Fish's skepticism about morality and science seems to be a survival instinct that controls the manner in which evidence is selected, shaped, and ingested both by individuals and institutions (including academic disciplines). This instinct makes us see evidence the way we want to see it in order to perpetuate ourselves as defined in and by conventional norms and expectations. So evidence for Fish is a matter of what counts for our survival as we see it; evidence cannot be evidence of simple, nonconventional truth (see Fish, "Almost Pragmatism," 1466-67, 1469-70). But grounded in illusions or not, our current conventions regarding scholarly integrity would demand the professional demise of any scholar who is widely perceived as incapable of processing evidence in a non-self-aggrandizing way. A survival-minded academic would therefore want his readers to believe he has real evidence for the self-aggrandizing ways of scholars. His report of the self-aggrandizing ways would not itself be self-aggrandizing. Hence the standard scientific tone of Fish's nonpartisan, non-self-aggrandizing account of the partiality and self-aggrandizement that constitute the human condition. Fish's skepticism is thus little more than affectation.

20. See Richard N. Boyd, "How to Be a Moral Realist," in *Essays on Moral Realism*, ed. Geoffrey Sayre-McCord (Ithaca: Cornell University Press, 1988), 183-84, 199-205; Brink, *Moral Realism and the Foundations of Ethics*, 11-12; Moore, "Moral Reality," 1152-53.

21. See Boyd, "How to Be a Moral Realist," 206-9.

22. See Brink, *Moral Realism and the Foundations of Ethics*, 31-36, 122-33; Moore, "Moral Reality," 1106-16, 1149-52.

23. See Brink, *Moral Realism and the Foundations of Ethics,* 156–63, 172–80.

24. Bork, *Tempting of America,* 4–7, 129–30.

25. Dworkin, *Law's Empire,* 65–68.

26. Compare Fish's view that argument can proceed only from beliefs established ultimately through force ("Almost Pragmatism," 1452).

27. Perry, *Morality, Politics, and Law,* 155–56. The following passage refers to this work.

28. Cooke, *Federalist,* 309, 352.

29. See Barber, *On What the Constitution Means,* chap. 2. The following passage refers to this work.

30. See Gordon S. Wood, *The Creation of the American Republic, 1776–1787* (New York: Norton, 1969), 3–10.

31. Cooke, *Federalist,* 3, 6, 51, 309. The following passage refers to this work.

32. Dworkin, *Taking Rights Seriously,* 273–75.

33. Dworkin, *Law's Empire,* 380.

34. Ely, *Democracy and Distrust,* 103.

35. Richards, *Toleration and the Constitution,* 17, 57.

36. Walter F. Murphy, "The Right to Privacy and Legitimate Constitutional Change," in *The Constitutional Bases of Social and Political Change in the United States,* ed. Shlomo Slonim (New York: Praeger, 1990), 221–23. See also Murphy's argument that consent is a necessary but not sufficient condition for legitimacy, in "Consent and Constitutional Change," in *Human Rights: Liber Amicorum for the Hon. Mr. Justice Brian Walsh,* ed. James O'Reilly (Dublin: Round Hall Press, 1992).

37. See Barber, *On What the Constitution Means,* 49–51, 59–61.

38. For a fuller description of this constitutional state of affairs, see ibid., 59–61, 75–76, 126–31, 159–63, 211–13.

39. For a description and defense of such a process, see Moore, "A Natural Law Theory of Interpretation."

40. See Vlastos, "Socratic Elenchus," 35–37.

41. For a comment on Rorty's acknowledged inability to live by his skeptical teachings, see Moore, "Natural Law Theory of Interpretation," 309–11.

42. Moore, "Metaphysics, Epistemology and Legal Theory," 497. The following passages refer to this work.

43. See Dworkin, *Matter of Principle,* 162, 173–74; Dworkin, "Reply," 277–78.

44. Moore, "Metaphysics, Epistemology and Legal Theory," 501. The following passages refer to this work.

45. See Michael Moore, "Precedent, Induction, and Ethical Generalization," in *Precedent in Law,* ed. Laurence Goldstein (Oxford: Oxford University Press, 1986), 197–99, 206–7.

46. Ibid., 206. See also Moore, "Moral Reality," 1106–16.

47. Moore, "Precedent, Induction, and Ethical Generalization," 208. Moore, "Do We Have an Unwritten Constitution?" 134–35.

48. Graham Walker, *Moral Foundations of Constitutional Thought: Current Problems, Augustinian Prospects* (Princeton: Princeton University Press, 1990), 131–33.

49. Fish, "Almost Pragmatism," 1474.

50. Walker, *Moral Foundations of Constitutional Thought,* 131–33. The following passage refers to this work.

51. See Moore, "Do We Have an Unwritten Constitution?" 137-39.

52. See Moore, "Moral Reality," 1106-16, 1149-53; and Brink, *Moral Realism and the Foundations of Ethics,* 11-12, 31-36, 122-33.

53. Walker, *Moral Foundations of Constitutional Thought,* 145. The following passage refers to this work.

54. Moore, "Precedent, Induction, and Ethical Generalization," 207.

55. See Boyd, "How to Be a Moral Realist," 206-9. The following passage refers to this work.

56. Compare and contrast Vlastos, "Socratic Elenchus," 52-57.

57. See Boyd, "How to Be a Moral Realist," 204-5, 207-9, 211-12.

58. Brink, *Moral Realism and the Foundations of Ethics,* 205-7. Another strategy is to claim that the lack of convergence in ethics relative to science is exaggerated or mistaken as a matter of fact. For a discussion, see Moore, "Moral Reality," 1091, n. 69.

59. See Barber, *On What the Constitution Means,* 198-203. The following passage refers to this work.

60. See Posner, *Problems of Jurisprudence,* 47, 73, 83, 95-96; Fish, "Almost Pragmatism," 1449-53.

61. See Barber, *On What the Constitution Means,* 224, n. 23.

INDEX

Agreement (legal-moral): as barrier to moral progress, 265–66 n. 5; as evidence for truth, 265–66 n. 5; as no test for truth, 46–47, 60–61, 204, 265–66 n. 5. *See also* Convergence (of legal-moral opinion); Disagreement (legal-moral)

American Legal Realism: criticism of classical theory of judicial review, 106–7; as precursor to open-ended modernism, 174; skeptical tenets of, as criticized by H. L. A. Hart, 179–80. *See also* Frank, Jerome

Anticonstitutionalism: as by-product of the Constitution, 236; as imputed to New Right theorists, 118, 142–43; of modern thought generally, 114–16

Antifoundationalism. *See* Nonfoundationalism (in epistemology)

Antirationalism (in legal-moral theory): argument for, 218–19, 220, 222–23; as political threat, 221–22; as rationally indefensible, 10, 221; of specific theorists (Berns, Bickel, Bork, Fish, McConnell, Posner), 218, 222

Antirealism (in legal-moral theory): as corrosive of traditional confidence in reason, 217; and force as source of authority, 197 (*see also* Pragmatism); implications of, for community, 192 (*see also* Community); inability of, to interpret political division as political aspiration, 214; political implications of, 197; varieties of, 199. *See also* Conventionalism (in legal-moral theory); Moral skepticism; Waldron, Jeremy

Aspirations. *See* Constitutional aspirations

Authority, popular view of: and decline of public-spiritedness, 113

Baker v. Carr, 5–6

Barron v. Baltimore, 110, 135

Berger, Raoul: approach to constitutional interpretation, 171; conception of original intent, 118, 122–24, 127; criticism of *Brown v. Board of Education,* 127; on limited scope of Fourteenth Amendment, 123; on Warren Court, as tyrannical, 122–24

Berns, Walter: as antirationalist, 218–22; as axiomatic bourgeois liberal, 16, 217; constitutionalism of, compared to John Marshall's, 76–77; constitutionalism of, in relation to moral skepticism, 14–15; on constitutional structures, importance of, 15–16; on the Constitution's ends, 11–14;

271

20, 233–34; and the ends of government, 27–32, 38–39, 60–63, 116, 215–16; as means to justice, 116, 175–76, 235; as open to its own rejection, 60–61, 64–65, 219; proceduralist view of, and substantive rights, 5, 15–16; and toleration, 11–14, 59, 63, 219, 233; whether constitutional ends include the people's moral capacities, 56–57, 88. *See also* Constitutional aspirations; Constitutional ends; Constitutional fidelity

Constitutional amendment: provisions for, and the nation's identity, 124

Constitutional aspirations: conventionalist (Perry's) understanding of, as vacuous, 152–54, 159, 169–70, 215; generally, 60–61, 234–35; and the interpretation of political conflict, 60–61, 213–15. *See also* Constitutional ends; Reasonableness

Constitutional authority: as contingent, 210, 267 n. 11. *See also* Constitutional failure; Constitutional fidelity

Constitutional change: as duty of political leadership, 64; right of the people to effect, 39, 62

Constitutional ends: adequacy of the constitutional document to, 207–8 (*see also* Constitutional failure); and constitutional institutions as means, 28, 56, 216–17; derivation of, 59; priority of, over institutional forms, 28–29, 32, 56–57, 64–65, 116; priority of reasonableness among, 32, 62–63, 65, 217–18; substantive versions of, 11–14, 59, 62–63, 75–76, 88. *See also* Constitutional aspirations

Constitutional failure: as inevitable, 207–8, 215–16, 234–35

Constitutional fidelity: and constitutional authority, 60–61; requirements of, 234–35

Constitutional interpretation: current theories of, 171; ends-oriented approach to, 54–56, 75, 89, 96–98, 224; *The Federalist* on, 33–35, 45–48, 50–51, 54–56, 242 n. 24; judicial monopoly of, 40–42; therapeutic style in, 40. *See also* Constructivist model (of judicial decision)

Constitutional maintenance: checks and balances, role in, 35–37, 44–45, 55–56; and constitutional aspirations, 60–61, 234–35; and judicial power, 111–12; reason versus prejudice, roles in, 22–24, 111; self-criticism, role in, 60–61, 116, 234–35

Constitutional meaning: as inevitably controversial, 45–46; possibility of, 45–48, 203–6, 206–8

Constitutional perfection: impossibility of, 207, 210. *See also* Constitutional failure

Constitutional reaffirmation, 60–61, 65. *See also* Constitutional fidelity

Constitutional state of affairs, 207–8, 219–20

Constitution making: ends-oriented perspective of, 83; paradoxes of, 116

Constructivist model (of judicial decision), 181–82, 188, 199–200; and history as source of rights, 200. *See also* Conventionalism (in legal-moral theory)

Contract clause: John Marshall's expansion of, 76–77

Conventionalism (in legal-moral theory): conception of truth, 153; conceptions of meaning, 106–7, 153; deep versus shallow, 147, 154, 169–70; defined, 199; and force as source of authority and meaning, 67, 165; justification of, as involving moral realist limits on, 249 n. 20; as moral skepticism, 155; and rights as merely conditional, 201. *See also* Community; Nonfoundationalism (in epistemology); Pragmatism (in legal-moral theory)

Convergence (of legal-moral opinion): lack of, as argument for moral antirealism, 233; as object of ambivalence, 233. *See also* Agreement (legal-moral); Disagreement (legal-moral)

Corfield v. Coryell, 90

Crandall v. Nevada, 90

Critical legal studies: as legacy of American Legal Realism, 106; and partisan use of judicial power, 170

Dartmouth College v. Woodward, 77, 78

Disagreement (legal-moral): as a condition for reaffirming the Constitution's authority, 60–61; as essential to legal-moral progress, 184–85; negative implications of, for moral realism, 183–84. *See also* Agreement (legal-moral)

Dworkin, Ronald: as antirationalist, 222; and antirealist metaphysics as irrelevant to political practice, 188, 197, 224; as "conceptualist" (Chemerinsky's term), 171; constitutionalism of, compared to John Marshall's, 77; on the constructivist model of judicial decision, 181–82, 188,